REDBONES OF LOUISIANA

Don C. Marler

Edited by Stacy R. Webb

Transcribed by Farah Norton

Copyright 2021 @ Backintyme Publishing
ALL RIGHTS RESERVED
Backintyme Publishing
1341 Grapevine Rd.
Crofton, Kentucky 42217
redbone@redbonenation.com
www.backintyme.biz
ISBN 978-0-939479-60-3
LOC 2021932945

About the Cover

The Gravehouses or Graveshelters are rapidly disappearing. The Talbert Cemetery, Vernon Parish. Louisiana has the largest collection in the south. We wanted to document their existence before they are all gone. Thanks to Jane McManus, Farah Norton, and April Mullins Mela for their photo contributions and research.

Contents

FOREWARD	ii
INTRODUCTION	v
FROM THE EDITOR	x
THE NAME	1
RACE, RACISM AND SLAVERY	19
WHITE SLAVERY	39
RACIAL MIX	55
GROUPS RESISTING RACISM AND SLAVERY	73
SELECTED LOUISIANA ISOLATED GROUPS	165
REDBONES OF SUMTER COUNTY SOUTH CAROLINA	219
THE LOCATION	253
REDBONE MIGRATIONS TO LOUISIANA	277
NATURE/NURTURE	377
THE REDBONE CULTURE OF VIOLENCE	403
OLD SAYINGS, BELIEFS,	
PRACTICES AND LEGENDS	425
GENETIC STUDIES	489
CONCLUSIONS	530
GLOSSARY	541
ATTACHMENTS	546
BIBLIOGRAPHY	609
INDEX	630

FOREWARD

Don Marler has written a groundbreaking work on a fascinating group of people known collectively as the Redbones. With likely connections to many of the South's early mixed-ethnic populations, the Redbones have almost certainly played a larger role in the westward settlement of this nation than history has heretofore acknowledged. He approaches this subject with a firm hand and takes a broad view of both the importance – and the impact – of these long-ignored settlers.

From their ancestral home in the Carolinas, Marler tracks their passage through Tennessee, Georgia, Alabama, and Mississippi to their present-day locales of Louisiana and Texas. His deft research, both genealogical and historical, creates a supportable mosaic of Redbone history, culture, and oral tradition that underpins his theories on just who the Redbones were, and who they are today.

Marler takes a particularly careful – and necessary – look at those factors that drove the Redbones to both embrace and deny certain heritages, dealing directly with the difficult and emotionally laden issues that surround "race," and what certain racial components, or simply the assumption of those components, meant two centuries ago. The fear of slavery and/or the prejudice focused on those who could not "prove" their "whiteness" was a brutal and overwhelming burden in the 1800s. Redbone attempts to avoid punishment and castigation from their prejudiced neighbors might be seen in today's light as a sort of racism in and of itself (that being, the denial of any non-European admixtures). While a surface argument can certainly be made to demonstrate such attitudes among the early Redbones, to ignore the desperate on-the-ground factors which led to these arguments is to do a great disservice to the ancestral Redbones and, just as detrimentally, to sugarcoat the social environs in which they lived. Don Marler confronts this controversial issue and whether one agrees or disagrees with his premises relating to this subject, his courage in exploring this difficult area allows us to intellectually confront those demons that would otherwise hinder our understanding of Redbone history.

Don Marler's book will likely not be the last word on the Redbones, but it is guaranteed to be a consensus choice as one of, if not the, truly groundbreaking works on their origins, history and culture (along with his earlier book, *The Cherry Winche Country*). In many ways I view this book much as I view my own 1994 volume on the Melungeons, another mixed ethnic population to which my ancestors belonged. Both are books intended to spur other researchers on in our quest to better understand the diversity that is America and, just as importantly, to give some of our nation's long ignored pioneers the respect and honor so long denied them. Don Marler has accomplished these dual goals and I hope that all Redbone descendants, regardless of any possible differences of opinions that they may have with various aspects of his work, will understand both his worthy objective in writing the book and the great contribution he has made to the preservation of their history. As a Melungeon descendant, I am especially pleased with his efforts as, given the more recent timeframe for the migration and assimilation of the Redbones, it can provide a better documented model for how my own Melungeon ancestors might have achieved their survival and eventual assimilation. All Americans with mixed ancestry – which is truly all of us – can learn a great deal from the Redbone story.

I commend Don Marler for a job well done, and I salute all Redbones and Redbone descendants everywhere for contributing to the greatness of our nation.

N. Brent Kennedy, Ph.D.

Author: *The Melungeons: The Resurrection of a Proud People* Mercer University Press, 1994.

From Anatolia to Appalachia: A Turkish-American Dialogue
Mercer University Press (March 1, 2004) March 1, 2004

INTRODUCTION

REDBONE – a term conjuring up as many images as there are people hearing it. The mental images range from the romantic to the fearful. Just who are these mystery people who have fascinated and enchanted us for these past 200 years? Who are these mixed-blood people who have inhabited southwest Louisiana since approximately the time of the Louisiana Purchase in 1803? How and why did they come to the infamous Neutral Zone created in the confusion over boundaries between Spanish Texas and Louisiana? We shall explore these questions.

In the past, the term Redbone has carried a negative connotation, but it is now becoming more a term of positive identification and pride. Information on this group is scarce, often distorted by history that was passed on orally, hiding a past that may have included criminal activities or Black/Indian ancestry. The sparse written information on Redbones is piecemeal, fragmented, scattered and often contradictory.

This book pulls together the relevant information on Redbones. An attempt is made to discover the historic origins of Redbones, describe their culture and their relationship to the dominant society. The origin of the term Redbone will never be known for certain. There are dozens of mixed-blood groups in the United States, and among them the Melungeons, Brass Ankles and Lumbees are, no doubt, related to the Redbones. The ancestral trail of the Melungeons, those isolated mixed-blood people in northeastern Tennessee, is no less obscure than that of the Redbones, who are also known as "mystery people".

Understanding Redbone requires looking at the broader context of the history of race in America. Taking a wide-ranging approach rather than focusing too narrowly on family histories will further enhance understanding. Studies of family histories are needed but are beyond the scope of this book. While written material addressing Redbones specifically is scarce, peripheral material exists in abundance. Some of this material serves as background and is given up front on chapters II through VI. The reader would benefit from reading the Glossary before starting the book.

The book is written for the general reader, and especially for Redbones and other mixed-blood people, but it is hoped that the scholar will benefit from it. Perhaps it will stimulate further research and writing among scholars who have largely neglected the history of this group. This neglect is not entirely the fault of the scholars, however. Redbones have been highly resistant to talking and writing about their past and present. They have survived largely because they have been quick to defend their land, name, heritage and reputation. In this vigorous defense, they have created an additional reputation as a people who react violently against outsiders who try to intrude and are too often violent toward each other. That this quickness to defend may have outlived its usefulness and may have indeed become an impediment in a more tolerant society, is on the periphery of the Redbone group consciousness. Their reluctance to reveal information about their past and present is still active today. This reluctance is compounded by the very success of their forefathers in hiding the past – they simply don't know much about their early history. They continue to hide what they know of their history, and their own "history in the making" will be hidden from their own offspring.

While the Redbone's desire for social acceptance and a higher status in the eyes of white society may have motivated them to be defensive and secretive about their past, the extremity of their effort at secretiveness suggests there was a more compelling reason. That compelling reason is identified and discussed in this book.

A member of the Redbone community, Beverly Jackson, established a Redbone Internet Discussion Group. Another Internet moderator Carolyn Dyess Bales, now assists Beverly in this valuable but thankless service. This group of approximately fifty members has been used as a sounding board for testing certain ideas. One idea discussed at length was the nature-nurture argument as related to the question, "What is the essential element in determining what makes one a Redbone?" Most members responding to this question had difficulty with it. They define their identity as a people who are different from the dominant society, along racial lines as well as in their community-worldview. Many tend to view genetic heritage as the most important aspect in defining who they are, believing that genetics determine their behavior as well as their physical characteristics.

While many Redbones say that they are unconcerned about what is found in their racial history (and this no doubt true for many), when the issue is raised regarding possible Black heritage in certain families the level of negative reaction among members of the Redbone Internet Discussion Group rises sharply. Some families (such as the Goins family) have met this issue and have long ago dealt with it. Nevertheless, the quick and vigorous defense impulse is still alive and well among Redbones. Notwithstanding this hypersensitivity, it is encouraging to see that they are now increasingly willing to speak up and speak out about their heritage and culture and to be recognized as Redbones.

A word of caution is in order. Several lists of names that often arise in Native American, Melungeon, Redbone and other mixed blood groups have been included. While professional genealogists and others frown upon this practice it seems justified here. Some Redbones have asked for a list of Redbone surnames and have participated in developing such a list. It should be clearly understood that: (1) not all people of a particular surname are Redbone, mixed-blood or even related to others of the same name; (2) some of the names mentioned may only be names of allied families. Many of these names are spread throughout the United States and especially in the south.

Much of the literature and language of the past used terms not acceptable today. Sensitivity to feelings surrounding the use of labels and names should not lead to political correctness carried too far. Skirting issues for the sake of such "correctness" compounds the issues by hiding them behind a smokescreen. Terms such as Indian, Native American, mixed-blood, Redbone, Black, Negro, White, are used in this book in a manner consistent with use in historical documents. The author was reared near one of the Redbone communities in central/southwest Louisiana. He was not reared as a Redbone and was unaware of any genetic connections to them, but research revealed such connections. These connections had never been discussed among family members who were normally unusually astute about keeping track of family members past and present.

Don C. Marler

FROM THE EDITOR

It has been an honor and a pleasure to edit Redbones of Louisiana. Don Marler put the Redbones on the map! A forgotten and neglected ethnic group, whose place in the annuals of history were long overdue. We, as Redbones appreciate all the hard work and dogged determination it took to write of our people and their history.

Though new discoveries and findings cease to amaze me, they are massive. The sheer volume of research materials as Don has explained in detail here already but to emphasize his message; the tasks to collect, organize, document, digitize, transcribe, study, and piece together through genealogical pedigree's and publish, nearly overwhelming, even for a Redbone! Sometimes frustrating, I must ask myself often, just how far down that rabbit hole am I willing to go?

It will not due any justice to our people to follow status quo and brisk over the minutia of details. I find myself combing through every borough, trail, turn and switchbacks, to examine every pebble, root, speck, and grain. Only to revisit the same rabbit hole repeatedly in search of a missed or misunderstood clue, a puzzle piece that will help us put back together our most fabulous and well-hidden ancestral history. One thing I have learned in my search is that where you see smoke signals, somewhere there is a campfire with a bunch of Redbones sending those, laughing, and laughing at us for not understanding their meanings!

I am proud of our heritage, all of it, the good, the bad, the ugly, the misunderstood, malign, hidden, buried or the most graphic details. Deep down inside, I am sure all Redbones feel the same, pride in their heritage. It just takes some of us a little longer to 'cut to the chase so to speak than others. I just 'cut and run earlier than most and by the age of twelve, I had found my hearts calling in a genealogy book.

In a lucky chance one hot Texas summer, my mother who was a rambler; not unlike my father's Redbones, had a research trip to Austin, Texas' State Capital building. My older sister and I had each received a genealogy book the year before at Christmas. My sister sort of flipped through her book and tossed it aside. I however was fascinated! I started quizzing my parents, grandparents, uncles, and cousins relentlessly. Learning how to work through a pedigree and studying each generation for details of their lives. I wanted to fill out every spot with an ancestor, it became a driving obsession. In comparison, the addiction level is akin to that of a child with a video game now adays, spending every free moment intensely trying to "beat" the game and solve the mystery.

I was lucky at that time, all my parents, grandparents and several of my great grandparents were still living. But as I quizzed those in the know, they got to certain generations, and the responses varied from… "I don't know" to "they were Indians" to "poor white cotton patch trash" and, "they was some [insert N word] in the wood pile" or, "that son of a bitch!"

It was odd to me how I would get to those certain ancestors and the language became derogatory and dark, with racist terms and flaming slurs used only, in the hushed corners of a room. And so, it appeared all I had learned from my Christmas present, was how to clear a room out quickly with my intrusive genealogy quizzes and questions. It was the power of that shunning, so to say that drove me onto the trail of my Redbone heritage.

I heard; "you'll keep this in the family, right?" and "don't put my name on any list." Later, confrontations came between myself, older members of my family, and contemporary Louisiana descendant Redbones. Neither wanting to be related to the other. As if we could change the colors of our family tree with denial of one another? There were heated discussions, and what I gathered from each side was a need to quiet any talk of a "collective colored tribe of people known as Redbones." All of which were hurtful to me and sincerely my intentions were misunderstood. When the initial DNA results came back in the early 2000's tempers flared, and discussion between the families (Louisiana & Texas) ramped up. The unhappiness they felt in their ancestral heritage, or their DNA results were somehow my doing, as if that could be true? But, as with all Redbones I kept moving forward. It appears things have stabilized and, in the end, even the older generation Redbones are now proud of our heritage.

Some years later, I presented my elders with photos that I had collected from various Louisiana and E. Tx. family functions. Those families, who on both sides, mine, and theirs (E. TX Redbones vs. La. Redbones) rarely if ever recognize one another and were shocked, doubtful, and reluctant to believe we were ever kin. For my family, though not recognizing one another at all, except now through common family member pictures contained in these photo albums. It appeared I had *sparked their memories and jogged their psyche to some long-ago times and topic of their younger days they had sooner forgotten. To see pictures of people they recognized I now heard remarks like… "Oh yes, that's my great aunt, or uncle," or "that's my cousin". And, with tear filled eyes, my grandmother exclaimed, "I've never even seen a picture of any of them" (meaning her grandparents, aunts, uncles, cousins, etc.) then, after she had studied the photos carefully, flipping pages back and forth, setting it aside she left her hand placed on top of it, as if it were a Bible. After she gathered her thoughts for a few minutes, she exclaimed… "I can hardly believe those are my people!" Of course, my heart sunk, and raced a little and my mind searching for a logical reason…I blurted out, "are the pictures labeled incorrectly, do we have the wrong names on some of them?" As she answered me, she pitched her voice high and forcefully, "No! That's not it!" And so, after a few minutes of tensed silence

I asked, "why don't you think those are our people?" She replied in a manner of near bewilderment, "Their too white!" I knew at once I had crossed her at least, over the bridge between what she thought she knew, saw, heard, or was taught about her ancestry was now a paradigm shift! The dichotomy of a modern reality she saw in those photos and that which she believed in her heart was truly contrasted with those photos in black & white. I could still see a struggle in her eyes, but it appeared the blight of her heritage was removed with a few old photos shared in that album.

My father who grew up around Burk (Diboll), Texas, relayed a story to me only in modern years. I will retell it here. He told me the reason he did not remember any of our kin from Louisiana, though they visited often when he was a youngster. He said it was because when they would show up, usually walking and unannounced, he and his little brother Jimmy Neal would run off into the woods nearby and hide, to "watch" their relatives from a distance. His grandparents, "Guide" and "Granny" Missouri Goyens Nash Nash would welcome them in, provide them hospitality, shelter, and food for weeks and months at a time. He said that there in the woods, they would lay out for days while the stranger family would visit. In general, only coming in for food, inclement weather or when their great Aunt Sena Goyens Nash Felder

Morgan Swilley (yes, she was married that many times) a Pentecostal preacher and great Aunt called for revivals she held. Sometimes for days on end these revivals would go on and on, but the children seemed to all enjoy that time. Aunt Sena's reputation known widely was, "she loved everybody, and everybody loved her". Aunt Sena was from around Zwolle [Ybarbo/Ebarb/Choctaw] Louisiana at that time and was in fact her half-sister Missouri's, mother-in-law albeit a "step" relationship. Sena had married Emanuel "Command" as he was called by my family, who was her brother-in law, Guide Nashes' father.

For her revivals she used a small building there in Burke where the airport is now. The building was used for canning tomatoes and during the war was used for making rubber casing for bullets. I asked my Dad why he and his little brother would hide in the woods, were they afraid of them? He responded, "no, it was because they were Black."

Dad spoke of our Indian family who came from Oklahoma. He said they would walk all the way to Burk, TX. just to get something to eat. He spoke of how poorly they dressed and that they had no shoes and most times near starved to death when they arrived. And the stories how his grandfather Guide had contracted TB when he was a young man, about 17 years old. Our family took him to Indian Territory from Texas for healing. Guide said they had put him in a sweat lodge for months and that had they cured him of tuberculosis. He said they performed ceremonies over him, and he danced with his Indian family to sacred drumming.

So, you see, I was lucky my Mother had that trip to Austin. As I had found out earlier that summer through our local library that there were records located in that old historical courthouse about my Redbone family and their early settlements at Austin's Colony. While Mother was busy all week researching in the microfiche department. I would find myself in the most wondrous place I had ever been! Though it was a hot, dust covered room with no air conditioning, and even in those days a great creature comfort in Texas. Climbing the rooms library ladder and moving heavy disorganized books about on tippy toes sometimes, and virtually left alone to my own devises. I am sure now; it was but the first of many Redbone rabbit holes I would need to visit in search of my illusive ancestral heritage, and genealogy.

My immediate family were globe trotters and wanderers before there were globetrotters. My grandfather, Leonard Stringer working in Libya in the late 1940s. Always nomadic, wandering for work my father's family knew dozens of schools throughout Texas, Oklahoma and even Alaska during their growing up years. My family traveled also for work, but we also traveled for leisure in a motor home my parents bought in 1976. We traveled about the country for weeks at a time or just a weekend venture. Our favorite place to camp was at Galveston where we would meet up with our Redbone family. We enjoyed fresh seafood, cooking, and eating together in a camp style and was always the best reunions. Traveling in our motorhome, we visited every landmark on the map. Pit stops here and there to see scenic routes and historical land markers. Dust rolling up the backside of that Jamboree headed down swamp and river roads and trails was a remarkable sight, I am sure.

We took back roads all over Louisiana and now that I reflect, lots of dangerous expeditions into abandoned, dilapidated, and empty plantation homes. Some, only remnants barely standing or on the ground. Once, my father hired a helicopter for a few days to locate remains of old Plantation homes deep in the swamps and bayous even then long forgotten. My parents had the ideas of buying one and restoring it to former glamorous glory. Mother, and my Uncle Bobby Stringer [my father's brother] with their research trips to locate books and local history libraries in efforts to identify locations and histories of any structures Antebellum. Then off we would go on the ground in that Jamboree. My Uncle Bobby and my Mother stopped at every historical marker on the road, we called them "hysterical markers' not in a scoffing manner but just in a funny and rhyming manner. If we were late arriving somewhere, we were expected, we would say, "oh we got caught up at a hysterical marker." The love and passion for history and a nomadic lifestyle is my blood, and now I know, in my genetics.

Though my parents always kept a beautiful home in Sugar Land, Texas my father, grandfather and extended Redbone families all worked in the oil refinement industry, and my father owned an oil company in Argentina. Their work took us to the most remote and exotic locations around the world. When my Father was a newly graduated senior from high school, he bought a car which he had earned the money for by learning the trade of plumbing. He had become the youngest ever licensed master plumber at that time and, perhaps still is in Texas, under the apprenticeship of Hollis Ashworth, the 3rd great grandson of James Ashworth and Keziah Doyle/Dial. The Ashworth's were his neighbors and cousin in Burke, Texas [Stringer Rd.]. My father learned the art and healing practices of herbalism from Hollis's wife, an Indian. She would take the children into the woods and teach them about the native plants, what they could eat and the healing properties and uses of each. He never forgot those skills and our family used many remedies he had learned from her still to this day.

Carl W. Stringer[1] son of Leonard & Robbie L. Nash/Ash Stringer,1996 Sweetwater Co., Wyoming. Father of the editor, TX. Redbone.

Cooking his most famous grilled steaks.

One more fun fact was the legend of Hollis Ashworth. He was by all descriptions of my family a "Negro" and that he was so handsome all the girls and women in the

---

[1] Gedmatch # G428453

neighborhood, married and unmarried would swoon "ever he came around" which apparently caused some rivalry between the females of our E. TX Redbones families who it appears were all smitten with Hollis.

My father used that trade off and on over his life, an unbelievably valuable skill set in the oil refinement industry. In fact, we are direct descendants of Jaccob E. Humble [Stringer side], the first oil company in Texas later bought by Howard E. Hughes [whose family was also intermarried with our Redbone families in Burk, TX. Clyde Tampton Nash married a Hughes's first cousin, Zelma "Zelmer" Hughes], the famous aviator and oil tycoon.

My Dad was ambitious like most Redbones naturally are and he took off for Odessa, Texas the day after he graduated from Diboll HS. He was on a mission to talk to a man he had met some years previous who owned an oil company. The man had promised him a job overseas and all the glory of a high paying position, once he graduated. The man interviewed Dad, but he had suggested my Dad was a little too young and that he should come back when he was older, Well, you do not promise an ambitious Redbone a position, then tell him no, "come back later, your too young!" My father slept in his car in that man's parking lot, greeting him every morning and every evening on his way in and out of work. Persistence pays off, the man hired my Dad and after only a few months working locally in Odessa, he hired Dad for a job in Saudi Arabia. Dad never looked back, he was hooked on travel and seeing the world. My Mom followed with her children in tow, if possible (family status).

I had seen some things in my young years, but nothing caught my attention like this little room that day in Austin, Texas State Capital building. I stepped into my newfound wonderland, full of old tattered with age and marked with character books, ledgers, with their bindings of all sorts and colors, loose brittle and yellowed with age-stained pages, on and written in what was the oldest penmanship and language of course I had ever tried to read. It was an immediate potpourri aroma of that sort of musty smell of old books and buildings; you know the smell?

The books came alive in all my senses, with the characters and the traces of those who held them before, wrote in them, were named in them and the clerks, judges and officials who handled them and who likely loved them as much as I did. Written in those pages was the lives of forgotten people whose life events were tooled in ink with the happiness of a marriage, a birth, a baptismal, or the crushing heartache of a death, loss of a child or just the commonality of disease and depredation, clashes between cultures and people only understood or remembered by those who loved them, now a far-off olden time.

Burk, Angelina Co., Texas Ashworth siblings Left-Right: **Keziah, Hester, Louisa,** and **Joshua Ashworth** (m. Sarah Miracle) TX Redbones. Children of James Ashworth and Sarah Perkins.

It was the disarray and unorganized manner of storing all different sized books and in the diverse and eclectic styles and colors, and book bindings of yesteryears. My senses went in all directions and a flood of where my heart's desire for genealogy and the history of my people took place.

I never heard the word Redbone until I was an adult and had been researching my families for years. Attending a Melungeon Heritage Association meeting at Kingsport, Tn. in the early years of that group's remarkable success. I was accompanied by my Dad's cousin, Aubrey Townsend, and his wife Eleanor, who had introduced me to the Melungeons. How he knew about them is not to my recollection now, genealogically speaking, we could not make the connection between our families then either.

Standing in a crowd of about 100 people outside the venue, waiting for the doors to open. Evelyn Orr said to me after chatting only a few minutes about my ancestry, "Oh you're a Redbone." And the crowd hushed from their idle chatter and with a great sigh! Then, in the near distance I heard, "she's a Redbone' followed shortly by another anonymous person in the now perfectly quiet crowd, "those people like to fight!" From that moment on, I felt like a rock star on a gold platinum album tour. I am a Redbone! Once I realized that, people came forward and the information started flowing, and things just made sense. Why my family was reluctant to remember details, all that shunning and crude memories, at that moment it all became firmly understood by me. I have determined that self-preservation seemed to be our ethical standard, as it came to the racial statuses of our ancestry. I perceive the "culture of violence" Don speaks of here as nothing more than the struggles and determination of a persecuted people.

Dr. Brent Kennedy & Stacy R. Webb at Melungeon Conference, Warren Wilson College, Ashville, NC. 2014.

Turns out I had known Evelyn and her husband John Orr from back in the late 80's when their daughter and son-in-law were living next door to us in Green River, Wyoming. Their son in law and my husband were working together at Texas Gulf Soda Ash mine near Grainger, Wyoming. We could not believe the luck or chance in meeting back up 1000s of miles away while sitting at a beautiful restaurant table overlooking the Holstein River accompanied and surrounded by the greatest Melungeon descendants and researchers our people have ever known. It was meant to be. Evelyn who ended up giving me her massive research materials attended the first

Redbone Heritage Conference along with Dr. Brent Kennedy, Gen Erbon Wise, Wayne Winkler, Dr. Tommy Johnson, and other great early researchers into these ethnic peoples of early American history.

Stacy R. Stringer Webb, Pam Goyens Tatum & Marilyn Baggett Kobliaka. Dowsing Good Hope Cemetery, Beauregard Parish. La.

First Conference of the People Known as Redbones, Alexandria, La. 2002

Dr. Brent Kennedy, Sonya Davis and Wayne Winkler

Evelyn "EV" Orr and Dr. Tommy Johnson

General Erbon Wise, *Sweat Families of The South*
And cousin, Patsy Ball

I still have the genealogical book that I got for a Christmas gift that year, though filled out in some ancestor spaces, still blank for others, scratched through information, liquid paper covered mistakes, scratched notes, and coffee cup stains, junk the kids spilled on it over the years, and a few puppy chews around the corners. But that book has been loved and studied, abandoned sometimes, left on the bookshelf or the trunk of my car. But none the less loved to near pieces, drug through libraries, backwoods cemeteries, and shielded me from a driving freak hailstorm but carried with me like a treasured heirloom all over the country! My sister later gave me her book with not one mark in it. She asked me to give it back when I got it finished…laughing aloud; she is never getting that book back, because I will never be finished!

One thing I never have seen discussed about the Redbones, is that they have their own language, so to speak. Or my Redbone family did. It is a language of hand signs, gestures, body language, a "look" of the eye/s, guttural grunts, whoops, hees, hears and, haws, whistles, and such. Some you could tell were learned from working with livestock and training horses and human interactions associated with livestock husbandry, others seem military or through tracking, hunting, guiding. And the understanding of their meanings without knowing just how you learned them. No one ever told me what they mean, I just knew their meanings without verbal description. I guess my kids were the ones who pointed it out to me. As my children grew, I also had passed these gestures and language onto them. Even their friends became familiar with those. Especially one. A particular whistle, I learned to make when it was time to "head'em up and move 'em out" or come immediately to a prearranged or understood location, or to message another that, I've found it, whatever we were "looking" for. My kids could be in a mall or crowd and hear my whistle, they knew it was time to finish their business and meet me from wherever they were.

It never dawned on us until a friend commented with a question, "where did you learn those?" I had to laugh because I had never thought about it, and I could not answer that question. I had to think about how I learned those and their meanings. However, they must be meaningful as I had unknowingly or unwarily passed them onto my children also. I use those also with my animals, horses, and dogs, they all get the meaning also with training.

I asked my father how he knew those commands and language, and who taught them to him? My mother still could not understand even after being married to my Dad for 45 years, but then again, she was not a Redbone! My Dad thought about it for a long while, but he still could not answer how he learned them either. I guess it was like a second language to the Redbone families of East Texas? I have not noticed it or asked the Louisiana Redbones if they also have any cultural language passed down? After speaking with an anthropologist, Dr. Charles Bright of Nacogdoches, Texas who worked with the Redbones at Kisatchie Hills and had repaired Wm Goyens of Nacogdoches Republic of TX. headstone twice over his life. He suggested this to be a hybridized cattle culture language based in a Mobilian sort of trader language.

Another cultural practice passed down to me is dowsing,[2] from my father, and Grandfathers and Mothers before him. I am especially keen to work over Redbone and all types of cemeteries or burial locations, for unmarked and lost graves. I have documented the following cemeteries: Fields Cemetery, Trinity Co., TX., Nash Cemetery, No. Zulch, Madison Co., Tx. Half Moon Prairie, Nacogdoches Co., TX. Glass Window Cemetery, Vernon Parish, La. Drakes Crossing, Vernon Parish, La. and Bearhead Redbone community, Good Hope Cemetery in Beauregard Parish, La.

---

[2] Dowsing is a type of divination employed in attempts to locate ground water, buried metals or ores, gemstones, oil, gravesites, malign 'earth vibrations' and many other objects and materials without the use of a scientific apparatus.

Don speaks briefly about dowsing here. I do not presume to defend this ancient practice or explain how it works. My goal is just to pass on the knowledge; that Redbones used dowsing work for a variety of reasons; locate water, lost items, buried and or concealed artifacts.

April Mullins Mela, Scott Withrow and **Stacy R. Webb** (editor). Melungeon Heritage Gathering, 2010.

Don's books were self-published so, distributions from the trunks of our car were our only option. None of his manuscripts had ever been digitized and so, all work was from the ground up to reassemble the book. Pictures and images were lost in later years. Scott Withrow helped search to find originals, but to no luck either. Farah Norton transcribed the book into digital format and revisited Pine Grove Talbert Cemetery, Vernon Parish, La. to replace lost photos of grave houses. April Mullins Mela also contributed gravehouse photos and research. We could not have gotten the book up to date without each of their great contributions.

Editor dowsing, Half Moon Prairie, Nacogdoches, Tx. Burial location at an original Spanish and Shawnee burial grounds at William Goyens, of Nacogdoches homestead and he and his wife's burial location. His markers and the cemetery were destroyed by later landowners.

Redbones of Louisiana presented here in its original form, no text was removed. If we disagreed with something or had further knowledge since this publication, we simply put a line through those remarks, so that the reader could determine for themselves what has changed or deemed outdated materials.

One warning in passing concerning the content language presented here. Don, and I have used real terms, remarks, and original sentiment. Sometimes those thought of as racists and or callous but that are presented in their true historical light here not to offend but that we present an accurate historical context of the people known as Redbone, their history, experiences, and truth.

We did add a good portion of new materials, however there are still neglected Redbone settlements and deep pockets of communities we have not included. We discuss much of these and other details in the Redbone Heritage Foundation publishing, *The Redbone Chronicles* written between 2007-2012. As in this publishing, those have become unavailable and are being republished one at a time. Now available through Amazon Kindle, and Barnes and Nobles as they are completed.

I have presented a chapter on genetic studies of DNA results and surname cases where applicable. I have updated current information from the original publishing, but Don's work remains valid and relative to this day. I hope you enjoy the title and all the recently discovered details about these fascinating people. But without the help and support of the Redbone communities and extended family, neither Don, nor I could never have completed this work.

To the *Goins Book* (forthcoming title) Family, we must thank all those contributing authors who met up in remote "haunted" locations, cemeteries, and museums, and who provided pictures, stories, lore and untold personal time from their families, financing trips, DNA test kits, interviewing people and pulling together facts and details paramount to a successful publishing. Their eagerness to help in every capacity, and their personal encouragements meant that I could forge on in my journey here.

To *the North Florida Indians*, Steven Pony Hill, Scott Hodalee Sewell whose writings, and work with their community ARCITO group hosted the Redbones in their conferences. And, who shared genealogical information, DNA results that lead us to some of the history and mystery surrounding Redbone connections to other marginalized remnant ethnic groups; Poarch Creek[3] Indians, Dominicker, Brass Ankles, Catawba, Cheraw, Creek, and other related tribal family. And their work on *The Late Migrations of Redbones from Holmes County, Florida*. And their informational Blogtalk radio interviews about our Native American familial ties. And for introducing us to other descendants. I thank you, sincerely for all you do!

---

[3] The Poarch Band of Creek Indians is the only federally recognized tribe of Native Americans in Alabama. Speaking the Muscogee language, they were formerly known as the Creek Nation East of the Mississippi. They are located mostly in Escambia County.

In remembrance of and appreciation and love to Dr. Brent Kennedy (deceased) and his beautiful wife Robyn, who paved the way for the Melungeons, Redbones and all mixed-ethnic peoples of America. And, for my father, Carl "Pod" Stringer (deceased), who could pack a bag to go faster than I and whose encouragement and pride in my efforts is the crowning glory for me. To our Redbone Chief, Chickasaw Gary "Mishiho" Gabehart (deceased), who had forgotten more than I will ever know about our people! To Aubrey & Eleanor Townsend (both deceased) for taking me to every graveyard, home place and historical location searching for our Redbone ancestry. And, for introducing me to the Melungeons all those years ago. You guys were the best, my research road buddies, confidants and mission soldiers. To Oscar Talmedge Goins (deceased) for telling us everything he knew, supporting our efforts and for being a great sport as our DNA model. And James Ray Johnson (deceased) author of *Drake Family Cousins* who shared, attended countless conferences, and worked tirelessly on Redbone genealogy projects. He and Don Marler were exceptionally good friends. We could not have accomplished this publishing without each of your help and support.

Special thanks to Lorene Varner Brown, Marilyn Baggett Kobliaka, Donna Webb Blaisdell, Pam Goyens Tatum, Twila

Chaney and Cheryl Tilley Perkins. And, with special thanks to my granddaughter, Lina Abukuppeh who made numerous "vacation" trips to Melungeon gatherings, Newman's Ridge (Vardy Valley), Rose Hill Cemetery, Meridian Mississippi, court houses, cemeteries, and historical destinations all over the country. Dr. Frank & Mary Lee Sweet, Scott Withrow, the Melungeon Heritage Association without each of you, this could never have been possible. And, of course to Don Marler, who without his dedication to the Redbones and their history, I would not be writing to you today.

An incredibly special note of appreciation must go to Farah Norton for all her transcription work, input, and field work. A fellow Redbone, and lifelong family friend to Don and Sybil Marler, her found passions for our Redbone history and ancestry is a real joy to our people. April Mullins Mela, a Melungeon cousin to all of us, for her work on the origins of grave houses and contributions to Redbones of Louisiana.

I have presented materials here that are republished either in condensed form or in whole from, *The Redbone Chronicles*, presentations and maps from research and intensive studies of the Natchez Trace and, the Mississippi Territory (Cherokee Old Settlers) as well as Upper Louisiana which included modern states Missouri, Arkansas, Montana with concentration on the French Fur Trade up and down the Mississippi through Canada, and Kaskaskia where some Redbones settled, as well of course, lower Louisiana studies.

I have traced extensively the westward migrations of modern-day Missouri & Arkansas Cherokee from Tennessee and North Georgia who removed to "passed the Rockies", Wyoming, Oregon, Canada, and the Dakotas among the local Basque sheepherder culture, Wind River Tribes; Eastern Shoshone Chief Joseph's Nez Perce, Sioux (Pine Ridge). All in search of our illusive and complex ethnic ancestry, known as Redbone.

I reference research gathered from: The Library of Congress and the Congressional Papers, the Natchez Trace Collection at Briscoe Center for American History, University of Texas at Austin. Jacob's Collection, Sam Houston Regional Library at Liberty, Texas. Primary source documents from the Territorial collections at The University of Mississippi Library at Hattiesburg, Mississippi the State and National Archives, Jackson Mississippi and republished materials, sources, and citations from my chapter in the title *Carolina Genesis, Beyond the Color Line, They Were Other,* as well as *The Journey, 2019* and *The Journey*, A Genetic Genealogy Handbook, Guide with case studies. Redbone, Melungeon and *Twenty and Odd* by K.I. Knight concerning the first Slave Ship (Portuguese) to Jamestown. I have also referenced citational work and timelines from a forthcoming book based on my presentation, GTT…*Redbones Gone to Texas!* All titles from Backintyme Publishing are available at Amazon, Kindle, Nook and Barnes & Nobles. As well we are making the Don Marler & Dogwood Press collections available at Amazon.

The most fascinating new facts come from the Redbone DNA studies. The relevance of which is to establish the earliest Redbone settlers to Louisiana, explore their origins, ethnic, religious, and cultural admixtures and their migration paths through genealogical research and DNA results. But, most importantly to the Redbones of Louisiana are the strides made concerning our genealogical relationship between the Redbones, and other marginalized ethnic groups of American history. In an effort not to become too long winded or complicate with the results of DNA analysis. We have attempted to state only the results, and the meanings of such in lay terms. I have made little attempted to educate the reader on the topics presented.

We (MEHRA) have Y, Mt and autosomal study groups and a platform developed through Family Tree DNA for

Redbones and Seminole Scouts that migrated to the Santa Rosa Mountains, Mexico and back to Forts Concho and Fort Clark, Bracketville, Texas. We have developed a handbook and study guide designed to help endogamous tribal families to rebuild our genealogical trees one chromosome at a time. If you are interested in DNA study groups online, please contact MEHRAssociation platforms on social media. Though I will inform the leisurely reader that we are strictly Redbone or Melungeon descended, and proof of your descent will be examined and compared to other members in acceptance of participations to the DNA studies. We believe it is important to concentrate our efforts on the living descendants in that regard.

In closing, I must thank all the MEHRAssociation members who made research reconnaissance, verified source citational works, supplied details of their DNA results and who work tirelessly at times of mind-bending DNA information, exhaustive searches, documenting lineages and genealogy to our families known as Redbones but not necessarily their own families. All which takes great commitment to our heritage, dedication to the truth and a great love of our history, thank you, Me Familia~

It is with honor that I have update, edited, and add new research to the groundbreaking title of its time by Don C. Marler & Dogwood Press, *Redbones of Louisiana*. I am sure he would [BIG GRIN] this one! I hope you enjoy all the new work done to reproduce this treasured Redbone book. And that you will join us in the next few years, as more of Don's Books are scheduled for republish.

Stacy R. Webb

I'm A Redbone
A song
Words and Music by Bearhead Redbone, Hershel Frazier

When Jean Laffite left Barbateria Island, they fled for their lives,
From Florida to Galveston Island, many took Indian wives
From the mixture of many nationalities, a new race was born,
With high cheek bones and an olive complexion, we're called Redbones
Yes, I'm a Redbone, a Melungeon if you please
My ancestors were the Natchez, Choctaw, and the Cherokee
Yes, I'm a Redbone, I'm proud I'm one
All of us Redbones are real native sons
Black, white, red and yellow, a real potpourri
Doctors, Lawyers, Heads of State, many in the ministry
We've always answered our country's call to defend our great land
And many have died on the battlefield with a weapon in their hand
Yes, I'm a Redbone, a Melungeon if you please
My ancestors were the Caddo, Seminole, and the Creek
Yes, I'm a Redbone, I'm proud I'm one
All of us Redbones are real native sons

Some may look down their nose at a people so proud
Their bright shiny dress stands out in any crowd
With a trace of blood in their own veins, they scoff and poke fun
But nine times out of ten, their son or their daughter will marry one.
Yes, I'm a Redbone, a Melungeon if you please
My ancestors were Alabama Coushatta, Atakapass-nee
Yes, I'm a Redbone, I'm proud I'm one
All of us Redbones are real native sons
Yes, I'm a Redbone, a Melungeon if you please
My ancestors were Karankawan, Tomoka'(n), Apalachee
Yes, I'm a Redbone, I'm proud that I'm one
All of us Redbones are real native sons
Yeah and some of us were hog thieves, moon-shiners, women-chasers, hotheads, draft-dodgers
Why, they'd qualify to be President!!

Left to right, Stacy R. Webb, Lorene Varner Brown, background Mishiho (Gary Gabehart Chickasaw Redbone), foreground Oscar Talmadge Goins, Carl "Pod" Stringer, Marilyn Baggett Kobliaka, James Ray Johnson, and Lyle Goins, not pictured, Donna Webb Blaisdell. Our haunted historical B&B, Tol Barrett House, Nacogdoches, Texas.

Scientists found that there are exactly as many skin pigment colors to the various races of this world as there are different colors of soil [dirt]. Stacy R. Webb

The Most Famous Picture of Redbones, we could not have published this book without sharing a copy.

Left to Right: **Josh Perkins**, unknown
Elmer Willis, unknown
Solomon Doyle, 1888-1936, son of Isaiah Ashworth & Catherine Doyle. He married Bertha Ashworth, 1893-? Daughter of Isaiah T. & Lavinia Ware Ashworth.
Mae Ashworth Willis, sister of Nora Ashworth.
Nora Ashworth Griffin 1897-1938 daughter of Ezra & Ella A. Nelson Ashworth she married unknown her name is listed as Traughber on her death certificate.
Shelby Ashworth 1886-1960 son of Abner & Emily Dyson Ashworth, married Rosetta Burgess.

THE NAME

No one knows where the term Redbone originated. Names such as Redbone can arise from many sources and for a variety of reasons such as what a group wore or ate, how they behaved, looked, or talked, what their beliefs or customs were, their origins, or because of the mispronunciation of their name. Strange or unusual names are assigned to people for a variety of reasons, including those of a derogatory or hostile nature. These names might be self-assigned for the same reasons.

Examples abound. The term "Jayhawker" may have been given to the Kansas marauding group because they were fierce like a hawk and thieving like a Blue Jay. The term "coonass" was assigned to south Louisiana French trappers who wore a cap made of coon skin with the tail still attached. This same group was called "cajun" as a corruption of Acadia or Acadian, the land from which they came. "Snake Handlers" is the term applied to those religious people who test their faith by handling snakes in their church services. White men who once drove to Harlem to pick up black lovers would stay in their cars and "honk" the car horn until the lover heard and came out, earning them the appellation "honkys." Red Man was first applied to the Beothuk Indians of Newfoundland because of their habit of painting their bodies and possessions with red ocher.⁴ During the Radical Reconstruction period (late 1860s to mid-1870s) in South Carolina, a group in opposition dyed their shirts red, killed some Blacks, and paraded in their red shirts. Their red shirts became a symbol of defiance that they wore when the occasion demanded; they became known as The Red Shirts.⁵

Some terms have lost their original meaning. Poor southern white farmers are called "Rednecks" because the sunburned neck is evidence that they have to do their own work. It is a snobbish and derogatory term based on economic and social status. Nevertheless, according to University of Kentucky researcher Darlene Wilson:

> "...the earliest mention of the term "Redneck" is found in the mid-19th century to describe anti-slavery people in the mountains of Virginia, Tennessee, Kentucky, and North Carolina who called themselves "Sons of Rahab"...and who marked their houses and cabins as "safe houses" with red cords or strips of "quilt pieces usually red" and who wore red...so they would know one another. There are Civil War reports of the Confederates trying to subject..."rednecks" to a court-martial for continuing to wear their red bandanas tied around their necks (when they had

---

4 Bruce Grant, *Concise Encyclopedia of the American Indian* (New York: Random House, 1994), p.264.

5 Isabel Vandervelde, Aiken County: The Only South Carolina County Founded During Reconstruction (Spartanburg, 1999), p.196.

The Name

> *been ordered to remove them) and for suspicion of aiding the escape of both runaway slaves and Confederate deserters....*[6]

The term "Redbone" is reported to have come about as a comparison to the red bones of the squirrel. It may have been a description of disinterred human bones that were buried in clay or iron ore. Reverend Greene Strother, writing on the heritage of Reverend Joseph Willis, cites a letter from J.E. Strother as follows:

> When I was a small boy, I heard a little story from Mother that I think gives the origin of the term. Just before the Westport fight, when the strife was arising between some of the people on Tenmile and the people in Vernon Parish, a Frenchman by the name of Louis Lacaze possibly started it. He said, 'A fox squirrel has red bones' and ventured the guess, 'That these dark-skinned people round here have red bones too.' If I remember correctly, Mother thought this was where the term started.[7]

In Louisiana, the Westport fight occurred in 1881. This is, perhaps, a little late to have been the time of the origin of the name. Shugg, writing of Natchitoches, Louisiana in the

---

6 Darlene Wilson, email, 9-17-97.
7 Greene W. Strother, *About Joseph Willis* (New Orleans: Baptist Bible Institute, 1934), (Unpublished Thesis, Baptist Bible Institute, 1934), p.23.

1850s, said that its notoriously mixed populations contained "red-bones."[8]

The term may have been, as suggested by Kniffen *et al*, a corruption of the West Indies term, Reddy Ebo, pronounced Reddy Bone, meaning mixture of races.[9] It may have derived from Redman or Redskin as applied to Native Americans with emphasis on red as in "red to the bone." Author Brewton Berry related that "there was a wide superstition that the bones of an Indian have a reddish hue."[10] One ninety-three year old man told historian Edward Price, that as a young man living in the Cherry Winche country in southwest Louisiana in the years following the Civil War, he heard a man say of another: "If we could see his bones, they would be as red as any chief's in the nation." This old gentleman said that if people knew this story, it might ease some of the bitterness caused by using the name.[11] Could this man have been suggesting that the name "Redbone" was to Native Americans synonymous with the use of "Blue Blood" among

---

8 Shugg, Roger W., *Origins of Class Struggle in Louisiana* (Baton Rouge: LSU Press, 1939), p.43.
9 Fred B. Kniffen, Hiram F. Gregory, and George A. Stokes, *The Historic Indian Tribes of Louisiana*, (Baton Rouge: LSU Press, 1987), p.92.
10 Brewton Berry, *Almost White: A Study of Certain Racial Hybrids in the Eastern United States* (New York: Macmillan, 1963), p. 39.
11 Edward T. Price, Jr., *Mixed-Blood Populations of Eastern United States as to Origins, Localization's, and Persistence*, (PhD. Dissertation, University of California, 1937), p.127.

The Name

whites? Professor Pamela Munro said that, to her, his statement meant simply that he was as Indian as any chief. She is unaware of Native Americans using the term Redbone (foni homma in Choctaw) in any special sense or to refer to an ethnic group. They did, however, use the term homma (red) to refer to Indian ethnicity.[12]

In the late 1990s, a search of the internet for the term Redbone revealed only a few results. Most were related to the musician Leon Redbone, the Redbone Barbecue Restaurant chain and Redbone coonhounds. In late 2002, a check of the same source produced almost 700 results.

Originally any red coonhound of unknown ancestry, but proven ability, was called a Redbone hound. Later, serious breeders developed the breed based upon stock owned by Dr. George F. L. Birdsong of Georgia. He obtained the pack of Dr. Thomas Henry in the 1840s, and the breed he developed from these were the second coonhounds to be registered by the United Kennel Club. They were registered in 1902.[13] The reference to the color and unknown ancestry suggests that the name given these dogs may have been a carryover from the

---

12 Pamela Munro email to author 9/11/2002. She is Professor of Linguistics at UCLA.
13 From the Home Page of the United Kennel Club.

people who shared these characteristics and carried the name, but no definite documentation was found.

Further internet references, in addition to the above stated ones, include: Martha Redbone (singer), Redbone Press, Redbone Graphics, Redbone Kelly (guitar player and blues singer), Rob "Redbone" Martin (maker of fishing lures), Redbone Alley Restaurant, Redbone Creations (maker of log furniture), Redbone Art Gallery, Redbone Hair Stylist, Redbone North American Indian Band, Redbone Knives and Daggers, Redbone Journal, Redbone Dancers, Redbone Pornography and Redbone Fishing Tournament.

There are places named Redbone such as: Redbone, Mississippi, Redbone Road (in Mississippi), Redbone Methodist Church (in Mississippi), Redbone Street (in Fayetteville, North Carolina), Redbone, Georgia and Redbone Crossroads, Georgia.

An internet search for the surname, Redbone, reveals none of the celebrities claiming the name as their birth name. One suspects that for them it is an assumed name – a stage name; none responded to queries. There were three legitimate Redbone surnames found on the internet. Two were contacted by phone, and Ms. Jennifer Redbone, a full-blood

The Name

Apache, said that the Apache word for Redbone is Psellee. Some of her family use that name.[14] The one person who was not contacted was her cousin. It is recognized that having Redbone as a surname does not make one a Redbone any more than the name White makes one white, but Redbone is an unusual surname, and its use is curious.

Professor Geoffrey Kimball relates that the Koasati/Coushatta name for Redbone is Nipihomma. When he asked his informant for an example of its use in a sentence, he was given – Nipihomma tayyik stipislapalammi – meaning, "Redbone women are very sexy."[15] In many black communities, light-skinned people, especially young ladies, are sometimes referred to as Redbones.

In Southwest Louisiana, especially in the Westport area, Redbones were historically called Ten Milers and in the Pitkin area they were often called Six Milers. They were referred to as Ten Milers or Six Milers because these were neutral, non-offensive, and safer terms. These terms were based on where they lived. Six Mile and Ten Mile Creeks are approximately six and ten miles from Hineston, Louisiana, and legend has it that they were given these names based on

---

14 Telephone conversation with Jennifer Redbone on 8/27/2002.
15 Email to the author from professor, Geoffrey Kimball, 7/24/2002.

their location relative to this, the oldest and largest settlement in the area at that time. However, there are creeks by these names in southeastern states and those names could have been brought to southwest Louisiana by early settlers. There is also a Ten Mile, Mississippi.

Dr. Brent Kennedy, author of *Melungeons: Resurrection of a Proud People*, says the term used by Turks for Redbone is "Redi-böne," pronounced "Reddy-bohrn." It means "lost fool." [16] Kennedy believes Melungeons have a large component of Turkish heritage and that Melungeons and Redbones are related.

It is widely believed, and evidence supports, that many Redbones migrated to Louisiana from South Carolina. Although they lived in several parts of the state, the best-known group lived near Sumter in a community known as Ramsey. There they had a friend and advocate, McDonald Furman, who sought information about them. He wrote many letters and short newspaper articles supporting them and calling attention to their interesting history. (More on Furman will be related later in this book.) He talked to Redbones who lived near the family plantation, visited their church and took statements from them about their history. His papers are

---

16 Email to the author from Dr. Brent Kennedy, 10/21/2002.

The Name

located in the South Carolinian Library in Columbia, South Carolina. A careful review of his many letters and articles is revealing regarding the name Redbone.

Furman advocated use of the term Redbone. He used the following phrase or a variation of it with almost numbing regularity,

"There is a peculiar, isolated people found scattered about in South Carolina whose proper racial name is "Redbone," a people who as a race were never slaves and are mixed with Indian."

In discussion with the oldest member of the Ramsey community, James E. Smiling, and another prominent community member, Nelson Chavis, he learned that at about the time the Civil War began they were called "Pioneers" and after the war they were called "Old Issue," "Old Issue Freedmen" or "Free Colored." (See the Glossary for a discussion of Old Issue.) The Redbones resented the term "Old Issue." In the words of Mr. Smiling: *I can't tell where the name 'Old Issue' started from – never heard it until since the war, we don't accept the name...we take it as a slur.*[17]

---

17 *The Register*, May 9, 1898—From the Furman Collection at The South Caroliniana Library in Columbia, South Carolina.

In all of the Furman papers there is not one incidence in which any person objected to his strong advocacy of the use of the term Redbone. Perhaps it was seen as an improvement over the other terms used. Since he was a friend, it is inconceivable that he would have advocated that name over their objections. It is evident however from his writing that he did not create the term Redbone, nor did he know its origin. He sought information on the meaning and origin of this term as well as the term "Old Issue" as we do today.

Furman wrote to the Treasurer of Calcasieu Parish, Louisiana, Mr. A. Rigmaiden, making inquiry about the origin of the name Redbone. Mr. Rigmaiden's letter in reply follows. Spelling, etc. are as written without correction or alteration.

The Name

TREASURER'S OFFICE

A. RIGMAIDEN

Lake Charles, LA. May 6, 1893
Mr. McDonald Furman
Ramsey, S.C.

Dear Sir

In reply to yours of April 22nd I will state that I am unable to tell you how the Name Red bone originated for the People who are Called Redbones, but I think, the Negroes were the first to give them that Name, as they (the Negroes) has no use or love for them & they do not like the Negroes any better. I suppose you know the kind of People who are called red bones, they are Neither white nor black & as well as I can find out, the oldest ones came from S.C. many years ago. There are a great many of them in this Parish & in Rapides & Vernon Parishes & Some in other Parishes in this State & a good many in Texas too, Some of these people are as good citizens as any body & Some are rascally & treacherous but you will find that among any People, but I think these are the most treacherous when they take a dislike to any one I will give you the names of Some of the principal & oldest families that I know of they are – Ashworth – Goins – Perkins – Drake – Hoozer – Sweat – Buxton – Doil or Dial – Johnson – Esclavant – these people keepe pretty well together & Marry

amongs themselves mostly, but occassionally a white man or woman marries among them but if they do it is generally a low class of white people – It is a very unpleasent to live about these people, for this reason, they are not looked on as being – Negroes-Indians nor white People & as this is a white Peoples country, they (the white people) don't put themselves on equality, socially, with any other people except white People. Although Some of these People are perfect gentlemen & lades & well educated, I think they get along exceedingly well & Peaceably, Considering all of these draw backs. I have given you as near the facts as I am able trusting it will give you the desired information.
Yours Truly
A Rigmaiden[18]

Mr. Rigmaiden's idea that Negroes originated the name as a derogatory appellation is not in harmony with their habit of calling attractive young women Redbones. No evidence has been found to support it.

Ethnologist, W. H. Gilbert stated, without documenting his assertion, that the name "Red Bone" derived from the French

---

18 From the Furman Collection at The South Caroliniana Library in Columbia, South Carolina.

The Name

term Os Rouge (Red Bone) that had been applied to persons who were part Indian.[19]

It is regrettable that Gilbert did not document his source for the statement that the French applied the term, Os Rouge, to people who were part Indian. One is inclined to discard this as a possible origin as the French influence *vis a vis* the Louisiana Redbones was and is minimal – Gilbert's statement to the contrary notwithstanding. However, given that Redbones rejected the term, we must remember that the influence of the French would have been on the non-Redbone population. The earliest Redbones to enter the state/territory came by way of French south Louisiana. The French could easily have attached this name to these early Redbone settlers, and it might have been adopted by the non-French, Whites and Blacks.

Author, Brewton Berry in discussing the origin of names derived from family names, says a group was called Bones – "an impudent corruption of the family name Boone."[20] Mr. Berry did not make a connection between this name and Redbone or Red Bone. A family of Boones who were Indian

---

19 William Harlan Gilbert, Jr., "Memorandum Concerning the Characteristics of the Larger Mixed-Blood Racial Islands of the Eastern United States," *Social Forces*, May 1946, p.445.
20 Berry, op. cit., pp.34-35.

could easily have been called Red Boones which was then corrupted to Red Bones. No evidence was found that this was the case, however.

~~Furthermore, no evidence was found that the term Redbone was used in South Carolina or anywhere in the southeast before their entry into Louisiana.~~ [21] Given the negative reaction the Redbones of Louisiana and Texas had to their ascribed name, it is remarkable that their South Carolina relatives apparently did not have the same negative reaction. Furman espoused the name and advocated its use in support of his Redbone friends. Today the South Carolina Redbones have adopted an attitude toward the name that is more negative than it was in Furman's time.

The Melungeons in the southeast, on the other hand, who are no doubt related to the Redbones, rejected the name Melungeon until modern times. Now, some Louisiana Redbones wish to adopt the name Melungeon or Louisiana Melungeon. Changing the name from Redbone to Melungeon would confuse the identity that has been building for more than 200 years. It would reflect a rejection and unwillingness to deal with any negative aspects of the self-identity associated with the name Redbone.

[21] Update p. 16

The Name

Perhaps the reaction to an ascribed name is more important than the origin of the name or the motivation for ascribing it. There is a positive relationship between the level of self-confidence of the target of this name-calling and the strength of the negative reaction to it. The name and its impact are enhanced by the negative reaction. Name-calling gets a response, and the response reinforces its use. White men seldom respond to "Honky" choosing rather to ignore it. The result is that the name is used less now than in the past and it never had much of an impact. Could the lack of response have something to do with its ineffectiveness and decline? The south Louisiana French learned to turn the two terms, "Coonass" and "Cajun," into positive cultural icons. The Melungeons have done the same thing with the name Melungeon. Less than fifty years ago the term Melungeon was a negative epithet; today, wannabes are lining up to claim kinship with members of this once maligned group. There is evidence that "Redbones" are turning around the negative image evoked by the name and are beginning to feel pride in it.

The search is not over, but today no one know when, where and by whom the name "Redbone," or as it sometimes used, "Red Bone," started. No one seems to know why the term was originally objectionable. Today many Redbones are beginning to take pride in the name. That acceptance, positive attitude and pride can only work to their advantage.

The Name "RED BONE"
Talbot County. (Georgia)

An early community was located at the site of the present YPSILANTI, Georgia. Ypsilanti was named for the noted Greek revolutionary leader Demetrios Ypsilanti who fought the Turks to free his people.[22] The community "Red Bone" was taken from an old Indian chief, Red Bone, that died here ca. 1690. All that remains of the location is a crossroads called "Red Bone Crossroads" a short distance from the original village. The location name Red Bone was changed to Ypsilanti in 1895.[23] Its location is between Macon and Columbus, and south of Atlanta. Situated on the trade path to Savannah and Charleston. The families who first settled the area are Smedly family, early settlers known as, The Society of Friends who settled among the Native Indians at Talbot Co., Maryland, Northern Necks of Virginia. This Smedely (Smiley) removed from the New Kent, originally York County, Virginia to the Ypsilanti area of now, Talbot County,

---

[22] Placenames of Georgia, John H. Goff University of Georgia Press, Dec 1, 2007; p444
[23] Red Bone none name changed to Ypsilanti - Krakow, Georgia Place-Names, p.189

The Name

Georgia, in the late 1600's.[24] The Talbot's migrated to the area and operated a tavern and settlement which included the: Voohries (married into the Ben Ishmael Tribe, aka Grasshopper Gypsies), Whitehead, Ramsey, Mitchell, Gibson, Powell, Mosley, Hardy, Reece, Cox, McNichols (Nikles), Williams, Evans, Moore, Green, Thompson, Thomas Charry (Cherry), Talbots and others.[25] The original settlers to Talbot as follows: George Tilley, William Evans, Marcus Andrews, Asa Alexander, William Little, S. Creighton, William Gunn, Amos Stewart, H. Ellington, B. Jones, G. Kent, A. B. Stephens, W. Anderson, R. King, N. Chapman, A. Graham, and S. Harris.[26] [27]

Talbot County was created by an act of the Georgia legislature in 1827. The county was formerly a part of Muscogee County. It is located thirty miles northeast of Columbus and sixty miles west of Macon in west central Georgia. The Flint River forms the northeastern boundary,

---

[24] There Was a Land: A History of Talbot County, GA. And Its People; Jordan, Robert H. 1971 November: Columbus Office Supply Co.
[25] Cope, Compiled by Gilbert, 1840-1928, Samuel Lightfoot 1732-1894. 1901. Genealogy of the Smedley Family From George and Sarah Smedley: Settlers in Chester County, Penna. On Line. Prod. Internet Library of the American Library of Congress. Lancaster: Wickersham Printing Company.
http://www.archive.org/stream/genealogyofsmedl00cope/genealogyofsmedl00cope_djvu.txt.
[26] Talbot County, Georgia History, White,
[27] Krakow, Kenneth K. (1975). Georgia Place-Names: Their History and Origins (PDF). Macon, GA: Winship Press. p. 219.

and Talbotton is the seat of the 393-square-mile county. Both the town and the county are named for Captain Matthew Talbot, who served as Georgia's governor for a short time in 1819. Collinsworth Institute and Talbotton Female Academy (later LeVert College), one of the first schools for females in Georgia, were located in Talbotton.

In 1836 the last of the Creek Indians were forcibly removed from the area.

Notable People from Talbot County, John W. Bower, signatory to the Texas Declaration of Independence, member of the House of Representatives of the Republic of Texas, and Chief justice of Refugio County, Texas; born in Talbotton.

RACE, RACISM AND SLAVERY

Racism is an age-old, worldwide, pernicious, contagious disease that infects its victim and its carrier. It is popular today to lay racism at the feet of Americans and especially those of colonial times. While it is true that the colonists institutionalized slavery and solidified racism as perhaps no other group has, it should be remembered that the seeds of that racism were planted, tilled and brought to maturity by Europeans. Racism was brought to the new world by Spaniards, Portuguese, Dutch, French and English – to name the principals. Western racism was matched, and in certain ways exceeded, by eastern racism that still exists in virulent form. The Japanese are champions of the eastern brand, but they also have no corner on that issue. Presenting racism as an ageless, global phenomenon makes it no less painful, fallacious, or destructive, but it does put it into perspective. The purpose here is to attempt to deal with reality and not to assign blame or to castigate. *Humans are all more alike than they are different, therefore, given the right time, circumstances, and environment any people are capable of enslaving another.*

Americans made slavery a race-based institution as opposed to other slavery systems, such as those that made slaves of captives of war. To make the system work, a definition of race and slavery was necessary. The American definition was atrocious in itself. What made the definition so unique was that it was presented against a backdrop of freedom and equality of man, embedded in a Christian context. Never mind that the centerpiece of the Christian belief is God's creation of mankind. This act is depicted in the Biblical story as the creation of one couple – not of several different races. No satisfactory explanation of how we, from this one couple, came to be people of differing characteristics, has been presented by the religious world. Without question, the scientific world has made harmful mistakes in developing its racial theories, but it keeps accumulating evidence and refining its theories with a view to reaching a solution to questions of differences among people. One cannot discuss concepts of race, and especially the history of such concepts, without experiencing an overwhelming sense of the uselessness and utter depravity involved in racial labeling and categorizations, whether they are based on religion or science.

One has no choice but to discuss, and make reference to, these labels and concepts as they are now a pervasive part of our lives, affecting our peace, well-being and interpersonal relationships. The pain Redbones experienced because of such labels is only a small fraction of the pain felt from such practices worldwide through the ages. That pain is reflected in the care that the ancestors of present-day Redbones and similar groups took to hide perceived unacceptable racial components from their children. Though racism, the disease, still exists today, it has lessened in intensity. Being a racist now is unfashionable, and to publicly display racial attitudes or behavior is socially disapproved. This development presents a challenge to Redbones. Shall they rid themselves of their own racism and take advantage of the lessened antagonism toward them? This is not an idle question. If they decide in the affirmative, their identity as a people set apart may eventually be lost. Amalgamation with the dominant society threatens their group identity. To the extent that personal identity is bound to group identity, the personal identity is threatened.

Any discussion of race should proceed with the understanding that racial categories are artificial, and that currently such divisions are not considered scientifically valid. (This issue will be discussed in more detail later). Race, in essence, is an artificial division of humans based upon constantly shifting criteria such as skin color, hair texture, facial features, head shape, social and economic status, geography, lines of descent, family names, blood (genetics), laws of free/slave status, depending on time, circumstances, and who is defining the categories.

The first known attempt to categorize humans and all over living things was made in 1735 by Swedish botanist Carl Linnaeus. This led to increased efforts by scientists to define and redefine Homo Sapiens into separate racial groups.

One of the more functional definitions of race is one proposed by Alice Brues. Race is "a division of a species which differs from other divisions by the frequency with which hereditary traits appear among its members."[28] It should be noted that her operative phrase is the "frequency with which hereditary traits appear." Paul R. Spickard makes clear what this statement means in his comment that:

> *On the average, the White and Black populations are distinct from each other in skin color. But a very large number of individuals who are classified as White have darker skin color than some people classified as Black, and vice versa. The so-called races are not biological categories at all; rather, they are primarily social divisions that rely only partly on physical*

---

28 A. Brues, *People and Races* (New York: McMillan, 1977) p.1.

> *markers such as skin color to identify group membership.*[29]

The "One-Drop Rule" (one drop of Black blood makes one a Black) introduced early on by many state legislative bodies, was good evidence that race was a social/legal issue and not one of genetics. The rule could have, of course, been reversed – one drop of White blood makes one a White. If one drop of Native American blood made one Native American, the number of Native Americans in America would be staggering. As was most often the case, predominance of genetics was not the defining issue; economics and social class were salient. Race was also an issue of descent – not to be confused with the predominance of genetics. Under the One-Drop Rule, a person with all White progenitors, except one, was to be classified as Black. If there was ever a Black or part-Black in their line, then they were defined as Black. And there was no need for objective proof of the race of the Black relative – it was sufficient that he/she should have been socially considered Black by his/her peers. If blood was to be used to determine race, was it logical and reasonable that one drop rather than the predominant blood should determine one's race? Adoption of the One-Drop Rule was, no doubt,

---

[29] Paul R. Spikard, "The Illogic of Racial Categories" in Maria P.P. Root, editor, *Racially Mixed People in America* (Newbury Park: Sage Publications, 1992), p.17.

the most pernicious, desperate and illogical act taken by the slavery/racist establishment.

The tragedy of the One-Drop Rule is that it is still accepted. But the more fundamental tragedy is that the concept of race is still accepted. As Rainier Spencer, a mixed-blood scholar, has dramatically pointed out, acceptance of the various mixed-blood categories perpetrates the myth of race. Describing his awakening to the issue, he said:

> *"...initially, it was just a feeling that logically it made no sense to categorize myself as black or half-black when I was half white as well. And if some rule said I couldn't be white, then surely I couldn't be black either. It seemed to me strange and inconsistent that racially mixed people could be black or mixed but not White. What was the secret?"*[30]

Does it not seem strange and tragic that Thomas Jefferson, third president of the United States, and one of the most revered moral and political leaders; a man who penned the "all men are created equal" phrase, should own slaves? Is it not strange and tragic that this man who presented himself as a man of the people should have made the choice that his own children, born of his slave companion, were half-black,

---

30 William S. Penn, *As We Are Now* (Berkeley: University of California Press, 1997), p.134.

condemning them to a life of slavery? Why were they not defined as half-white and therefore free?

Geneticist King says "there are no objective boundaries to set off one subspecies from another…[and] Genetic variability within populations is greater than the variability between them"[31] This means that the genetic differences between members of the Black population, for example, are greater than the differences between the Black and White populations.

Racial categories (labels) were necessary in early American so the dominant group could know whom to subjugate. Consequently, as the need for slave labor and the opportunity to enslave increased, the categories were manipulated – that is, broadened. Therefore, for example, at one time Indians, Blacks and mixed-bloods were known by those labels and at other times all were known as Black – making their enslavement easier. Mixed-blood people were known by a confusing array of labels: Mulatto, (Mulato), Metis, (Mestes), Mestizo, Mustee, Indian, Negro, Black, Hybrids, Mixed-Bloods, Free Persons of Color, Creoles, etc. To make things worse, these labels were applied in different ways at

---

31 King, J.C., *The Biology of Race* (Berkeley: University of California Press, 1981), pp.157-8.

different times and places by the English, French, Spanish, Portuguese, American and Dutch with extremely confusing results.

Author Lawrence Tenzer has argued that a major cause of the Civil War was the threat felt by some in the north of the growing trend in the south of enslaving Whites. He showed that persons who had one Black ancestor many generations back and who had no Black physical features were held in slavery. Some of these persons escaped to the non-slaveholding states and joined free white society. By law, slaveholders could come into these communities, apprehend Whites without due process, and take them to slaveholding states as slaves.[32] If this practice, backed as it was by the legal system, frightened White and mixed-blood northerners, it must have been terrifying to Redbones and other mixed-blood groups living in the slave-holding states. Enslavement of Whites who were not of mixed blood will be discussed elsewhere in this book.

Efforts to trace family histories today are complicated and confused by this plethora of labels, laws and changing definitions, all of which are shrouded in the fog of historical distance. Nowhere is this confusion more evident than in the

---

32 Lawrence R. Tenzer, *The Forgotten Cause of the Civil War* (Manahawkin: Scholar's Publishing House, 1997).

changing criteria of the U. S. Census. The confusion is reflected in the following data:

Census 1790 – The instruction to the enumerator was to place all free persons in two categories: white and all other free persons except Indians not taxed.[33]

Census 1800, 1810, 1820 and 1830 – used Free Persons of Color for most non-whites including Indians.[34]

Census 1840, 1850 and 1860 – were so fraudulent that they served as pro-slavery propaganda. Their use in studying anything to do with mixed-blood people must be done with extreme care.

Census 1870 – The term mulatto was included and defined "to include quadroons, octoroons, and all persons having any respectable trace of African blood...."[35]

Census 1890 – In 1890, a Black was a person with ¾ "black blood" and others with any Black blood were counted as mulattos.

---

33 Jack D. Forbes, Africans and Native Americans: The Language of Race and the Evolution of Red-Black Peoples (Urbana: University of Illinois Press, 1993), p.199.
34 Ibid.
35 *Ibid.*, p. 203.

Census 1910 – Black included all "full-blooded Negroes" and mulatto included all persons having some portion of Negro blood. In later censuses persons of Indian/African mix tended to be included in the Negro group, thereby increasing the size of that group.

Census 1930 – Census takers were instructed to count as Indians those of mixed White and Indian ancestry, except where the percentage of Indian blood was very small, in which case they should be counted as White. But the Indian and African mix was to be counted as Negro unless the Indian blood predominated.

Census 1940 – The 1940 instructions required that an African/Indian mix be counted as Negro unless the Indian ancestry very definitely predominated, and he was universally accepted in his community as Indian.[36]

In more recent censuses, mixed-blood people are often miscounted because they could only be counted in one category. If they checked two categories, they were counted in the first one checked. Since the categories were in order – White, Black and Indian – they were counted as Black if they checked that they were Black and Indian, and as White if they

36 *Ibid.*

checked White and Indian. Thus, any Indian who also checked Black or White was not counted as an Indian.

Census 1980 – The 1980 census had an expanded list that included: White, Black, Hispanic, Japanese, Chinese, Filipino, Korean, Vietnamese, American Indian, Asian Indian, Hawaiian, Guamanian, Samoan, Eskimo, Aleut, and others. The term mulatto is no longer used in the U.S. Census and most have been classified in the Negro category. In Brazil, there are ten gradations between black and white.[37]

Classifying the mulatto as Negro is at least consistent with the One Drop Rule. One Drop puts them in the Negro category eliminating the need for a mulatto category. There is no intermediate category – one is either Black or White. The 1980 census enumerated about seven million Americans with some degree of Indian ancestry – which is likely a gross underestimate.[38]

Census 2000 – The 2000 Census contained 132 race groups, 78 of which were American Indian including Alaskans. There were 39 divisions for Hispanic or Latin groups.

---

37 Spikard *op. cit.*, p. 18.
38 Terry P. Wilson, "Blood Quantum: Native American Mixed Bloods" in Maria P.P. Root, editor, *Racially Mixed People in America* (Newbury Park: Sage Publications, 1992), p. 116.

Census data must be used with care since that which is included reflects not only current thinking regarding race, but also economic and political action and political pressures. Many people who could easily be classified as Indian, White, Asian, etc. are often classified as Black. Black groups oppose any changes as the larger numbers reflecting more Blacks often benefit them.

George Will, ultraconservative political commentator, who may be described as the 21st century's greatest 19th century thinker, denounced the One Drop Rule – a creation of 19th century conservatives. His position is surprising until one realizes that the One Drop Rule now qualifies more people for protection of minorities under such programs as the Affirmative Action program. Since One Drop makes them Black, they fall under the purview of the various programs designed for protection of Blacks.

Forbes related that tax rolls before 1783 in Virginia are missing but:

> *From 1783 to the early 1800s no race is given for free persons – all are classified (for tax purposes) as 'white-tithable.' From 1809 to1812, 'free negro' is placed after the names of some free persons but mixed-bloods are still treated as white. Beginning in*

> *1813 however, the word 'mulatto' appears beside mixed people's names, and 'free negro' for others. Persons who can be identified as Chickahominy Indians or as ancestors of the present-day Chickahominy are uniformly classified as mulattoes...In other countries Indians are classified as above but also in several cases as 'F.N.' (free negro). It is very rare to see a person classified as 'Indian' in pre-Civil War Virginia records....[39]*

As late as 1857, American Indians who were part African were listed in Virginia as mulattoes.[40] The term mulatto often referred to a hybrid and, sometimes, specifically to a mule. Author Jack D. Forbes reminds us that in Roman times, the term Hybrida (hybrid) referred to the product of a domestic sow and a wild boar. Over time, the term was applied to the child of a domestic person and a stranger, or to a free person and a slave.[41] The term "mulatto" was first used by the Spaniards in the Americas in 1530. In Spain in the 1500s, it was a catch-all phrase used to refer to all slaves regardless of color.[42] In Virginia in 1705, a person of mixed European and Native American heritage was labeled a mulatto.[43] Forbes states, "it is very likely that from the beginning the English used the term mulatto to refer to a wide range of brown

---

39 Forbes, *op.cit.* p. 119.
40 *Ibid.,* p.196.
41 *Ibid.,* p.100.
42 Ibid., p. 159.
43 Ibid., p.193.

mixed-bloods, especially since precise ancestry of most such persons could not be known."[44]

At various times the term mulatto was used in more specific ways. It was sometimes used to mean a Black-White mixture and sometimes Indian-White or Indian-Black. In South Carolina in 1831, the court commented that it was unfair to label anyone who had any Negro blood a mulatto "…but where there is a distinct and visible admixture of negro (sic) blood the person is to be denominated a mulatto, or a person of color."[45] In the Spanish colonies, the term "mestizo" appeared in 1553.[46]

Stock breeders have long known that crossbreeding cattle and other livestock produced a phenomenon known as "hybrid vigor." Moreover, it was recognized that when Native Americans mixed with Blacks or Whites, the offspring acquired a degree of immunity from diseases not ordinarily available to them. Despite this knowledge, a contrary theory advanced by Dr. Josiah Clark Nott, a well-known physician of Mobile, Alabama, was widely accepted in both the north and south. This theory asserted that Blacks and Whites were

---

44 *Ibid.,* p. 194.
45 *State v. Davis, State v. Hanna* 2 Bailey 558, Dec. 1831. As used in Forbes, op. cit., p. 197.
46 Forbes, *op.cit.*, p. 129.

of different species and therefore, any offspring resulting from their mating would be hybrids, as were the offspring of a horse and donkey mating being a mule (mule is from the foundation word mulatto) – an animal incapable of reproduction. The mule was a remarkably healthy animal, prone to longevity and prodigious strength, but conversely the human "so-called hybrid" was said to be weak, sickly, and short lived. Since it was obvious that mixed-blood people were reproducing, it was asserted that their reproductive ability would fade to extinction in four or five generations. Other physicians and educated people adopted this theory and the uneducated masses seldom questioned it.[47]

The first black slaves imported into North America were brought to present-day South Carolina Pee Dee River in 1526. Lucas Vasquez de Allyon brought 100 slaves from Haiti. Disease and hostile Indians forced him to return, leaving the slaves with the Indians.[48]

Since, in South Carolina, Native American slaves were taxed at a lower rate than Africans, legislation was passed that stated: "And for preventing all doubts and scruples that may

---

47 Lawrence R. Tenzer, *The Forgotten Cause of the Civil War* (Manahawkin: Scholar's Publishing House, 1997).
48 Doug Sivad "African Seminoles" in Ron Sakolsky, and James Koehnline, *Gone to Croatan: Origins of North American Dropout Culture* (New York: Autonomedia, 1993), p. 265.

arise what ought to be rated on mustees, mulattoes, etc., all such slaves as are not *entirely* Indian shall be accounted as negroe."[49] [Emphasis mine]. This legislation, designed to increase the number of slaves for whom taxes were highest, classified those who were part Indian as Negroes making this an economic and politically motivated classification and robbing the Indians of their identity.

Until recently, the history of the extent of Indian slavery in the southeastern United States has been somewhat neglected. Especially neglected is the account of the exportation of Native Americans as slaves to South America and islands to the south. South Carolina planters/slave traders were at the forefront of this trade.

Prior to the 18th century, Cherokees practiced a form of slavery different from the system introduced to them by the Europeans. In the Cherokee slavery system, a person captured in war was often made a slave. The slave was not expected to make an economic contribution since the Cherokee placed little or no value on material possessions. In September 1708, South Carolina Governor, Nathaniel Johnson, reported that there were 1400 Indian slaves in the

---

49 Forbes op.cit., p. 196 quoting Peter H. Wood, *Black Majority: Negroes in Colonial South Carolina* (New York: Knopf, 1974), p. 99ff.

state.[50] But this number was to change in the early 1700s, as the Cherokees were induced to capture Indians for trade to South Carolina planters who sold them to New York, New England, and the West Indies. Some were sold locally.[51]

The purchase of Indian slaves by South Carolina planters caused the Cherokee to increase intertribal wars in order to get slaves to trade. Indians, Cherokees especially, were hired to hunt runaway slaves (Black and Indian) and fight rebellious Indians. The European/American brand of slavery was introduced to Indians as a way to divide and conquer them. It was a way to prevent them from uniting with each other and with Blacks against their White oppressors.

INDIAN SLAVES were being sold abroad by the English before the Revolutionary War. According to Forbes:

> *From 1670 onwards the English of South Carolina engaged regularly in the American slave trade, sending natives in the tens of thousands to the West Indies and other markets. In 1674 a group was sent to Jamaica.*[52]

---

50 Almon Wheeler Laubey, *Indian Slavery in Colonial Times Within the Present Limits of the United States* (Williamstown: Corner House Publications, 1913), p. 106.
51 Theda, Perdue, Slavery and the Evolution of Cherokee Society, 1540-1866 (Knoxville: University of Tennessee Press, 1979), p. 28.
52 Forbes, *op.cit.*, p. 56.

In 1693, a Cherokee delegation at Charleston requested the return of their relatives who had been taken to Jamaica. Many of those going to Jamaica were from Florida and some were Choctaws from the Mississippi area.[53] South Carolina was not the only state engaged in international Indian slave trade – Virginia, North Carolina and other states sold Native American slaves in the West Indies and Bermuda. Some were also sent to Spain and the Mediterranean during and after King Philip's War.[54]

The French in Louisiana, while pretending to protect the Indians from British slave raiders, bought and sold Indian slaves and exported some to the French West Indies.[55] "Bienville forged an alliance with the Choctaw to help protect them against slave raiders from South Carolina and their Indian allies."[56]

Cree Indians, though they were not slaves, were taken to Scotland.

---

53 *Ibid.*, p. 56.
54 *Ibid.*, pp. 55-56
55 Gwendolyn Midlo-Hall, Africans in Colonial Louisiana: The Development of Afro-Creole Culture in the Eighteenth Century. (Baton Rouge: LSU Press, 1992), p.97.
56 *Ibid.*, 14. Jean-Baptiste Le Moyne de Bienville was an explorer and governor of Louisiana in the early 1700s. He joined his brother, Iberville, there in 1699. Bienville's tenure was beset with problems including various Indian Wars. He explored the lower Mississippi River and assisted in settling New Orleans.

Race, Racism and Slavery

> *Many of the most prominent men...in the North of Scotland...are of Indian descent. Most of these persons are of Cree blood. For many years the Scotch have been active traders...and scores of them have brought back with them their Cree wives. Even the Cree men intermarried with Scotch lassies....*"[57]

BLACK SLAVES were introduced by the Spaniards into Mexico in 1553 mainly as servants. By 1650, Mexico had an African-Indian population of 10,000. Some of these people were part white.[58] After slavery was abolished there in 1828, 3000 Africans from the United States went to Mexico. In 1849, 800 Seminoles led by Wildcat and John Horse, seeking to avoid the threat of slavery, went to Mexico.[59] By the middle of the 18th century part-African people were the second largest component of the Mexican population – second only to the Native American population. By 1900, the mestizos were the largest group in Mexico. It is now estimated that 85 to 90 percent of the population is mixed blood.[60]

---

57 Forbes, *op. cit.*, p. 57. "Scotch Indians in Scotland" *Quarterly Journal of the Society of American Indians.* (Vol.2 1915), p.231.
58 William Loren Katz, *Black Indians: A Hidden Heritage* (Antheneum: Macmillan Publishing Co., 1986), p. 29.
59 *Ibid.*, p. 71.
60 Carlos A. Fernández "La Raza and the Melting Pot: A Comparative Look at Multiplicity" in Maria P.P. Root, editor, *Racially Mixed People in America* (Newbury Park: Sage Publications, 1992), pp. 128-29.

Comanche Indian Family ca. 1900 Back row L to R Tatatty Comanche with her niece, Wifeper or Frances Wright Comanche African American, and Tatatty's husband, Tatenequer Comanche.

WHITE SLAVERY

White slavery has been a part of the human condition as long as there has been recorded history. Biblical heroes experienced, practiced, and approved it, while Greeks and Romans built empires on white slavery. Until American colonial times, most enslaved people were white. Black slavery, or rather slavery based on color, is a relatively recent phenomenon.

This discussion of white slavery in America is not intended to distract in any way from the horrors of black slavery. What it does do is point out that slavery in America began as basically a class-based system and not one based on notions of racial superiority.

Colonial America had white slaves from the time the Mayflower arrived, but it was so successful with black slavery, that slavery became equated in the public mind with Blacks. In the mind of the planter class in the American south, slavery was seen as a natural and necessary condition quite apart from race; consequently, poor whites were candidates for slavery. In the 1830s, the rhetoric about white slavery began to heat up again and in the decade before the war, white slavery was an open issue. Influential White spokespersons and large influential southern newspapers began a bold effort to assure that "capital should own labor and not hire it."

White enslavement in America is one of the most submerged topics of American/British history. After centuries of ignoring the subject, and of outright Orwellian obfuscation, this sordid history is beginning to be exposed by contemporary historians.[61] It may be too late to sensitize the public consciousness to a sordid past that it wishes to forget and has now forgotten. The memory that more than half of the original White colonists came to the New World not by choice, but in chains, is painful indeed. As Elaine Kendall, writing in the *Los Angeles Times* in 1985, said, "...we continue to gloss over it...we'd prefer to forget the whole sorry chapter...."[62]

It was in the interest of slaveholders to soften the practice of enslavement of Whites in its public perception and giving it a softer name did this. Thus, "in the North American colonies

---

61 Michael A. Hoffman, *They Were White and They Were Slaves* (Coeur d'Alene: Independent History & Research Co., 1991). Lawrence R. Tenzer, *The Forgotten Cause of the Civil War: A New Look at the Slavery Issue* (Manahawken: Scholars Publishing, 1997). Much of the material in this chapter is drawn from these two books. They are highly recommended for anyone wishing to study this issue further.
62 Elaine Kendall, *Los Angeles Times*, September 1, 1985.

White Slavery

in the 17th and 18th centuries, and subsequently in the United States, servant was the usual designation for slave." [63] Indentured servant was, in the strict sense of the term, those who voluntarily bound themselves for a service for a number of years in payment of a debt. Not all, perhaps not a majority, of the colonists came voluntarily or for a specified number of years, nor for payment of debt.

Upon arrival in America, white slaves were "put up for sale by the ships' captains or merchants...Families were often separated under these circumstances when wives and offspring were auctioned off to the highest bidder."[64]

White slaves were "rated as inventories and disposed of by will and by deed along with the rest of the property. They were bought, sold, bartered, gambled away, mortgaged, weighed on scales like farm animals and taxed as property."[65]

According to historian Oscar Handlin, white servants in America "could be bartered for a profit, sold to the highest bidder...and otherwise transferred like movable goods or chattels."[66] Some white slaves were owned by Negroes and

---

63 Compact edition of the *Oxford English Dictionary*.
64 Foster R. Dulles, *Labor in America, A History*, p. 7.
65 Hoffman, *op. cit.*, p. 53.
66 Oscar and Mary F. Handlin, "Origins of the Southern Labor System," *William and Mary Quarterly*, April, 1950, p. 202.

Indians. Virginia passed a law in 1670 prohibiting such ownership.[67]

Cromwell, in February 1656, ordered his soldiers to find 1200 women for enslavement and deportation to the colonies, and in March that year ordered 2000 more. In the same year, his Council of State ordered all of Scotland's homeless poor transported to Jamaica for enslavement.[68] Tens of thousands of Whites were enslaved in Barbados, the majority of whom died in slavery. Furthermore, "Hundreds of thousands of Whites in colonial America were owned outright by their masters and died in slavery. They...were auctioned on the block and examined like livestock exactly like Black slaves...."[69] Ten thousand Whites were kidnapped from England in the year 1670 alone.[70]

The enslavement of Whites extended throughout the American colonies and:

> *White slave labor was a crucial factor in the economic development of the colonies. Gradually it*

---

[67] Statutes of the Virginia Assembly, Vol. 2, 1860, pp. 280-281.
[68] Eric Williams, *From Columbus to Castro: The History of the Caribbean, 1492-1969*, 1970, p.101 as referenced by Hoffman.
[69] Hoffman, *op. cit.*, p. 51.
[70] Edward Channing, *History of the United States*, p. 369.

White Slavery

> *developed into a fixed system every bit as rigid and codified as negro (sic) slavery was to become. In fact, ... Black slaves were governed, organized and controlled by the structures and organization that were first used to enslave and control Whites.*[71]

Black slaves were "late-comers fitted into a system already developed."[72]

In the 17th century, "White slaves were cheaper to acquire than Negroes and therefore were often mistreated to a greater extent."[73] Having paid more for the Black slave, "the planters treated the Black better than they did their 'Christian' white servant. Even the Negroes recognized this and did not hesitate to show their contempt for those white men who, they could see, were worse off than themselves...."[74] Thus, proving again the truth of the statement that we are all more alike as human beings than we are different.

In the United States, white children who were illegitimate or destitute were involuntarily indentured (enslaved or bound

---

71 Hoffman, *op. cit.*, p. 47.
72 Philips, Ulrich B. *Life and Labor in the Old South*, pp. 25-26.
73 Hoffman, *op. cit.*, p. 50.
74 Carl and Roberta Bridenbaugh, No Peace Beyond the Line: The English in the Caribbean, 1624-1690, p. 118.

out) for thirty years.[75] Child labor in England was worse than slavery, and the children fared little better in the colonies. Since the "master" had little or no investment in the children, he simply worked them to death or subjected them to conditions that injured or maimed. Often, they were forced to go to the streets to beg food after long hours of work.

Suddenly in the 19th century, the good citizens of England became concerned with the conditions of black slavery in American while continuing to ignore the pitiful conditions of the poor Whites in their country who were no better off.[76] Poor people were considered trash or refuse in England and

---

[75] The abuses of child labor continued in the United States until the 20th century. It is ironic justice that perhaps the most successful relief program in the history of mankind was instituted in America during the Great Depression of the 1930s by a man who had never experienced the whiplash of hunger, President Franklin Roosevelt, and administered by Aubrey Williams, a man who had. At six years of age, Williams was employed in an Alabama munitions factory screwing nose cones onto torpedoes. (Harry Hopkins, Fortune Magazine July, 1935, p. 64). As administrator of the New Deal's Works Progress Administration (WPA), Williams frustrated the efforts of local powerful politicians to siphon off relief funds that were intended for the poor. The WPA was one of the most graft free large programs ever administered by the federal government. It was perhaps an aberration.

[76] In America there is an inverse relationship between the generosity of religious, political and other charitable givers and the distance the recipient lives from the giver. That is, we are enthusiastic about giving to Blacks in Africa, for example, but reluctant to give aid to the Black child who is sick and hungry at home. The closer to home the recipient lives the less we wish to assist; it is, Marler's Law. British citizens were anxious to focus attention on those laboring under hardship in America, but oblivious to those so laboring on their streets. The same sentiment prevails today.

this attitude prevailed in the colonies. It served as the basis for the disdain southern planters and other elitists held for poor farmers, and for the disparaging attitude held toward rural people today. The resistance that the southern planters exercised to restrict and withhold publicly funded education from those who could not afford to send their offspring to private schools was part of an effort to keep poor Whites in a servile condition. The planters also resisted the Homestead Act that gave government-owned land to freemen so they could scratch out a living, independent of the large planters.

By the 1830s, the 1808 law prohibiting importation of foreign slaves was having the effect of reducing the supply of labor while the demand for it was increasing. The price of slaves was rising. The planter elite began looking for new sources or ways to renew old sources of cheap or slave labor. The definition of who could be enslaved again reverted to a focus on social class. Poor White laborers could with increasing frequency become enslaved and, furthermore, the stealing of children for enslavement increased.[77]

Twenty years later, the 1850 compromise was passed. It included a new fugitive slave law under which a slave owner or his representative could go into any state and apprehend

---

77 Tenzer, *op. cit.*, p. 76.

an alleged runaway slave. Anyone who hindered this effort in any way was subject to a one thousand dollar fine, a huge amount in that day. So, if one saw his wife or child being apprehended, he could not intervene. Once apprehended, the subject could not speak on his own behalf, nor could he have legal counsel. If he/she was not simply "spirited away," he was taken before a commissioner who had the authority to act immediately to issue a certificate to free the captive or immediately enslave him/her without due process of law. The commissioner was paid $5.00 to set the captive free or $10.00 to enslave him/her. It was kidnapping protected by law.[78]

A March 1844 issue of *Herald of Freedom* quoted Chancellor William Harper of South Carolina as saying, "It is as much in the order of nature that men should enslave each other, as that animals should prey upon each other." This was followed by an editorial comment that:

> *In the above abominable sentiment…no allusion is made to color as constituting a barrier to the encroachments of tyranny. In fact, that distinction, if it ever did exist is fast fading away…. They have (southerners) become so accustomed to the spectacle of white slaves that they cannot contemplate northern*

[78] *Ibid.*, p. 84.

> *operatives (the farmers and mechanics of the free states) in any other light than as the legitimate property of the capitalist, to be bought, and worked, and flogged, and sold, at the will and pleasure of the master.*[79]

Publication of *Sociology for the South, or the Failure of Free Society*, by George Fitzhugh in 1854 was a turning point. Fitzhugh perhaps was not typical of the south, but he made his views clear; they were touted by major newspapers in the south and not repudiated by southern planters or politicians. He believed that free society was a failure and that "Universal slavery, black or white, was right and necessary."[80] His ideas were enunciated further by South Carolina Senator, James Henry Hammond, who called the working class the mudsills of society. And he believed that poor Whites in the north fared worse than slaves in the south.[1]

In the same vein, the *Richmond Examiner* argued that:

> *Slavery is the natural and normal condition of the labouring man, whether WHITE or black. The great evil of Northern free society is, that it is burdened*

---
79 *Ibid.*, pp. 112-113.
80 *Ibid.*, p. 113.

> with a servile class of MECHANICS and LABOURERS, unfit for self-government, yet clothed with the attributes and powers of citizens. Master and slave is a relation in society as necessary as that of parent and child; and the Northern States will yet have to introduce it. Their theory of free government is a delusion.[2]

Closer to the home of Redbones, Louisiana Senator, Solomon W. Downs, was quoted by *The Day Book* as follows:

> I call upon the opponents of slavery to prove that the WHITE LABOURERS of the North are as happy, as contented, or as comfortable as the slaves of the South. In the South the slaves do not suffer one-tenth of the evils endured by the white labourers of the North. Poverty is unknown to the Southern slave, for as soon as the master of slaves becomes too poor to provide for them, he SELLS them to others who can take care of them. This, sir, is one of the excellencies of the system of slavery, and this the superior condition of the Southern slave over the Northern WHITE labourer.[3]

The One-Drop Rule seems to have been an effort to continue white slavery by broadening the definition to include those considered socially equal with Blacks without regard to genetics. As the color line began to rapidly disappear, the basis for enslavement broadened to include those who were essentially White – albeit poor White.

Rebecca, Charley & Rosa
Slave Children from New Orleans

Redbones, knowing they were of mixed-heritage and usually poor, no doubt felt great anxiety about the future of their freedom. Claiming Indian heritage was little better than claiming Black heritage, and in some areas and eras, the claim was indistinguishable from it. Besides, Redbones could not, in most cases, prove Indian heritage. They had long ago forgotten any Indian language and did not practice Indian customs or government. They did not maintain a tribal identity and usually did not even know from what tribe they descended. Ignorance of their history endangered their freedom.

Once could argue that the threat of slavery discussed in this chapter and elsewhere is still with us in the control of labor by the institutional power structure – albeit in modern clothing. There is no effective denial of this. The issue has escalated from the raw power of the planter elite and his efforts to enslave, or keep ignorant, the poor White, Black, and mixed-blood worker, to more sophisticated political and industrial efforts to keep poor workers at a subsistence wage level. It is reflected in the effort to keep unemployment at an "optimal" level – meaning, one supposes, at a level where the supply of labor exceeds the demand for it, assuring that it will remain cheap. The battleground has shifted to a level where large corporations now use labor and discard it when it is no longer needed or when it becomes too expensive. There is little real loyalty to the worker and the worker has responded by taking a stance of loyalty only to himself or herself, discarding long-term loyalty to corporations. This means that in order to compete, the worker must have education and training for a broad range of employment options so he or she can go where the opportunities are. The worker must have skills that are in demand so he/she can sell them to the highest bidder.

The dangers for those in isolated communities, such as the Redbone community, are obvious. As the world moves to a more mobile, technical, and integrated society that demands and rewards a higher level of knowledge and skill, members of isolated communities will generally get rewards much less frequently and at lower levels than will others. This happens precisely because the isolation assures that members are not sufficiently in touch with the developments outside the isolated community. Furthermore, it is estimated that seventy percent of people being terminated from jobs (for reasons other than large lay-off) are terminated, not for lack of skills, but for reasons related to poor interpersonal relationships – they are hypersensitive to criticism, are too quick to take offense and too quickly get into confrontations that are disruptive.

It is recognized here that isolation is a matter of degree and that no group is totally isolated. The world is incredibly competitive and remaining isolated is perhaps a statement that the community refuses to engage in that competition or that it will limit the competition. Who is to say that this is not a wise choice? However, in a world that continues to see work as the major measure of human worth, while the need for human work diminishes, the frustration of all will increase and those in isolated communities all the more so.

Texana Bell Perkins Duty, Annie, Wm. Harvey, Wm. Warren Duty, Annie Stein Duty Singleton. She was the daughter of Absalom & Anestine (Annie Stein) Hetty Goyens Clan. Her father Absalom Perkins pictured elsewhere here. Courtesy Wm Duty.

M Adeline Ashworth Simmons with Daughter **Lutisha Simmons Ashworth**. Courtesy Marilyn Baggett Kobliaka

REPUBLICAN BULLETIN, No. 9.

THE ISSUE.

WHITE SLAVERY.

THE EXTENSION OF SLAVERY IS THE QUESTION NOT ONLY OVER **FREE SOIL**, BUT OVER **FREE MEN**. DO YOU DOUBT IT? READ THE WORDS OF THE HIGHEST AUTHORITIES IN THE SOUTH.

The *Richmond (Va.) Enquirer*, the oldest Democratic paper in the Old Dominion, a most able supporter of Buchanan for the Presidency, and of the Cincinnati Platform, speaks thus on this question. We take its own forcible words.

"Until recently, the defence of Slavery has labored under great difficulties, because its apologists, (for they were mere apologists,) took half way ground. They confined the defence of slavery to mere *negro slavery*; thereby giving up the slavery *principle*, admitting *other* forms of slavery to be *wrong*.

that SLAVERY IS RIGHT, NATURAL, AND NECESSARY, AND DOES NOT DEPEND UPON DIFFERENCE OF COMPLEXION. THE LAWS OF THE SLAVE STATES JUSTIFY THE HOLDING OF WHITE MEN IN BONDAGE."

Another leading press of the Democratic party, and a worthy organ of Mr. Buchanan, published in South Carolina, sustains the views we have quoted from the Enquirer. It uses this plain, straightforward language on the subject:—

"*Slavery is the natural and normal condition of the laboring man, whether white or black.* The great evil of Northern *free* society is, that it is burthened with a SERVILE CLASS OF MECHANICS AND LABORERS, UNFIT FOR SELF-GOVERNMENT, and yet clothed with the attributes and powers of citizens. Master and slave is a relation in society as necessary as that of parent and child; and the Northern States will yet have to introduce it. Their *theory of a free government* is a delusion."

But there is still broader ground on the subject of society, taken by the *Richmond Enquirer*. It says, in a recent number:—

"Repeatedly have we asked the North, 'Has not the experiment of universal liberty FAILED? Are not the evils of FREE SOCIETY INSUFFERABLE? And do not most thinking men among you propose to subvert and reconstruct it?' Still no answer. This gloomy silence is another conclusive proof, added to many other conclusive evidences we have furnished, THAT FREE SOCIETY, IN THE LONG RUN, IS AN IMPRACTICABLE FORM OF SOCIETY."

Another paper, published in Virginia, the *South Side Democrat*, a journal distinguished for its faithful support of Mr. Buchanan, says:

that "SLAVERY IS RIGHT, NATURAL AND NECESSARY, AND DOES NOT DEPEND UPON DIFFERENCES OF COMPLEXION. THE LAWS OF THE SLAVE STATUES JUSTIFY THE HOLDING OF WHITE MEN IN BONDAGE."

Texas Redbone **Lorene Varner Brown**

James Nash/Ash born ca 1813 died June 1850, married Mary Polly Perkins (pictured elsewhere here). May have died after the Raw Hide Fight, Vernon Parish, La. He is listed in the 1850 census mortality schedule, Rapides Parish as "killed by knife." He was the son of Thomas Nash/Ash "Ashnoya/Ashyoka" and (1) Emily Slater. His descendants: Emily Nash/Ash Allen Arthur, Emanuel "Command" and Burrell Nash /Ash applied Cherokee Nation, 1896. Cherokee "by blood" through "Thomas Nash/Ash "Ashnoya or Ashyoka" a "Full blood Cherokee" and by mother, Mary Polly Perkins Nash/Ash "by blood."

---

[1] *Ibid.*, p. 114.
[2] *Ibid.*, p. 126.
[3] *Ibid.*, p. 129.

RACIAL MIX

The extent of racial mixture in early America has been grossly understated. Times and circumstances were such that racial/sexual mixing was necessary. Early on, race was not as great a deterrent to marriage or sexual relationships inside or outside of marriage as it was later. There was an imbalance in the ratio of men to women in both Black and White Societies. Women, both slave and free, were available to White, Indian, and Black men. White women of low status (principally indentured servants who were, in most cases, actually slaves) often married or had children by Indians or Blacks. Paul Heinegg in his monumental study of Free African Americans of the Carolinas and Virginia, documented the sexual involvement that led to mixed-blood offspring. Blacks, Whites, and Indians, both slave and free, associated with each other and "married openly in a manner that would later be condemned by custom and prohibited by law…Everywhere whites, blacks and Indians united in both long-term and casual sexual relations." [81] Heinegg

---

81 Paul Heinegg, Free African Americans of North Carolina, Virginia, and South Carolina: From the Colonial Period to About 1820 (Baltimore: Publishing Co. 2001), 4th Edition. Heinegg's work is not accepted without reservations; for example, his lack of recognition of the indiscriminate use made of terms that were often applied to mixed-bloods, Negroes and Indians interchangeably. Nevertheless, it is a most

maintained that relationships between slave owners and their female servants and slaves accounts for perhaps only one percent of the free children of color in the 436 families he studied. The majority of the families of free African Americans studied, who were from Virginia or the Carolinas, came from relations between white women (slave and free) and black men (slave and free). This resulted eventually in legal proscriptions against interracial unions. Children of such unions were declared illegitimate and could be bound out (enslaved) for as much as thirty-one years. Miscegenation laws passed after the Civil War were not repealed until 1967.

Heinegg's documentation of the contribution of white women to the growth of the free persons of color (or mulatto) population reinforced other accounts. Reformists such as Ida B. Wells-Barnett,[82] W.E.B. Du Bois, Frederick Douglas, and many others wrote early about such liaisons. More recently,

---

valuable work for anyone interested in the history of families of people of mixed heritage who had any connection to Virginia or the Carolinas. His work is full of material pertinent to families of Redbones and should be consulted by all who want to know more about their history. He studied 436 families; they include many names that are of interest to Redbones.
An increasing number of more recent works add to the history of the white woman's contribution to the mixed-blood population. See for example Martha Hodes, *White Women, Black Men: Illicit Sex in the 19th-Century South*. This carefully crafted work is drawn upon heavily in this chapter.
82 Patricia A. Schechter, *Ida B. Wells-Barnett an American, 1880-1930* (Chapel Hill: University of North Carolina Press, 2001)

Racial Mix

Martha Hodes has elucidated the issue of sex between white women and black men in a series of case examples. Her treatment of the history of sexual liaisons between white women and black men reveals that not all of the white women involved were indentured servants or lower-class single whites. She found that attitudes about the race of the offspring were secondary to their free/slave status and the economic consequence of that status. The principle of patrilineal descent (descent from the father, as in English law) broke down in Colonial America perhaps due to the economic implications of offspring born to white mothers and black fathers. Colonial inheritance laws were written to follow the principle of *partus sequiter ventrem* (progeny follows the womb); thus, if the mother was a slave (indentured servant), the child followed as slave.[83] If the mother was free, but without means of supporting herself and the child, she and her child would have been bound out as indentured.

Without question, societal attitudes toward Black/White sexual liaisons and legal marriage was much more tolerant prior to the nineteenth century. Violence toward black men for sexual liaisons with white women, though not unknown,

---

83 Hodes, Martha, *White Women, Black Men: Illicit Sex in the 19th-Century South* (New Haven, Yale University Press 1997), pp. 29-30.

was nowhere near what it became after the Civil War. White women were often more severely criticized for these liaisons than were the black men with whom they were involved. The motivations for this tolerance were complex. Status was of more concern than race and initially slavery was not established as a race-based institution. The distinction between indenture and outright slavery constituted a fine line – the definition of which could shift. Whites as well as Blacks could be enslaved, ensuring a low status for both regardless of race.

The main motivation of the English slave masters was to make money as fast and easily as possible. They perceived that slavery was the main engine for accomplishing this purpose. It followed, therefore, that it made no economic sense to kill or maim a valuable male slave for cohabiting with a female slave (white or black) especially when any offspring from such activity could add to his stock of slaves. Making an issue of the liaisons between Whites and Blacks (slave or free) only tended to call attention to a part of the slave system they had rather not contemplate or advertise. Such liaisons eventually were seen as a threat to slavery precisely because it brought Whites and mixed-bloods into the system. The case of Nell Butler, white female indentured servant, illustrates the consequences of this Black/White-

Racial Mix

Slave/Free issue. As a result of her 1681 marriage to a black slave in Maryland, her children were enslaved. In the 1760s, some of her grandchildren petitioned the court for their freedom from slavery on the grounds that their grandmother was a free white woman.[84] The wedding of Nell and the slave, performed by a Catholic priest, was attended by some of the most powerful people in the community, but the children born later were enslaved from birth. Nell had been warned against marrying the slave – not because of race mixture issues but because of the issue of slavery.

Many of the cases of white women and their liaisons with black men recounted by Hodes are of well-to-do married women or daughters of well-to-do families. These cases ended up in court (often divorce court), providing records of the proceedings. Offspring of these free women were not automatically enslaved, as was the case with children of indentured servants (white slave women) or white women who could not support their "base born" child, which meant that more people of mixed-blood were introduced into the free population. This increased mixed-blood population complicated the growing popularity of the definition of slavery as a race-based institution.

[84] Ibid.

White women who were engaged in sexual relations with black men were often criticized and taunted in the local community, but the men with whom they were involved were mostly unmolested, and even, in many cases, unnamed. Such affairs were treated as local drama and seldom as a regional matter and almost never as a partisan political issue. After the Civil War, this changed dramatically. Displaced southern politicians sought to control Blacks through legal and illegal violence, and sexual contact between white women and black men became an issue of white female purity against black male depravity. Lynching of black men for "rape" of white women became common place and the Ku Klux Klan existed in all southern states as promoters of violence aimed at intimidation. Following the war, the issue of relations between white women and black men was so sensitive that the American Freedmen's Inquiry Commission kept the testimony it had heard secret from Congress and the public. The material they possessed was made even more sensitive because it could not be written off as relating primarily to the province of poor white women.[85]

The reluctance to discuss the role of white women in the sexual crossing of racial lines continues today for perhaps

---

[85] *Ibid.*, p. 146.

different reasons. Today the reasons are less economic, and status related, and more related to the idealistic notions of female purity (especially white female purity) and misguided notions of race purity itself.

Blame for the existence of mixed-blood people has been laid almost exclusively at the feet of white male slave masters who exploited the female slaves they owned. That they did exploit them and produce a mixed-blood progeny from them is without question. Their acts were more visible partly because these men were so dominant and powerful, they could do openly what females had to do in relative secrecy. That white females could, and did, seduce and coerce black men into sexual liaisons spoke to their power and influence, as well as to societal toleration of such acts. Their behavior spoke also of their unmet emotional and sexual needs and perhaps of their desire to retaliate against a system that was oppressive to them. No doubt many such women were abused by their husbands and sought solace in companionship of lovers – some of whom were slaves. The Civil War drew away most of the white men, leaving the women with the male slaves. The myths surrounded this issue are beginning to break down.

The list of names of women involved in the cases documented by Hodes is given below because some are names recognized as relevant to Redbones. No attempt has been made to study the history of these particular names or to connect them to the present time or to a particular people. The information is furnished for those who may wish to pursue further studies and to illustrate that sexual/racial missing was more extensive than has been presented in the immediate past. Follow-up on the history of some of these names will be difficult due to the descent being from maternal lines – the father being unknown. This presentation also points out the evolving history of such interrelationships from the social, legal, and economic perspective.

Elizabeth Burgess Sweat wife of L.C. Sweat, Sr. born 1813-1861. Daughter of John Burgess (Polk Co., Coushatta Reservation Pakana Muscogee) & Unknown Nash/Ash daughter of Thomas Nash/Ash 1. Emily Slater, or 2. Anna Goings.

Racial Mix

Millie "Emily" (Groves) Bass

1806-1860 Daughter of James, Sr. & Mary Polly Nash/Ash Groves she married James Bass.

Elizabeth Groves Bass Hunt 1842-1911 the daughter of James Groves, Jr. & Nancy Perkins (daughter of Joseph & Sarah Perkins (daughter of Nancy Perkins) Calhoun she married 1. Gilbert Bass, 2. James H. Hunt.

Example of Heinegg's "free African American"

Talitha Nations Banks Stringer, 1770-after 1850 she married William Banks in 1802 in Old 96 District, South Carolina. She is also cross referenced by the Carolina Costal Indians as a Mingo Indian, born SC to Coweta, Ga. to Alabama. In 1836 at forced removals, she ran away to rejoin Texas relatives. Dorothy Stringer, and Talitha also known as "Free Dolls of Hancock's Creek" Ga. (Oconee River).[86] With a migration to Florida somewhere in there, likely Alabama which was West British Florida. She lived to be very elderly and cohabitated with her son in law, Zacharia Stringer born 1799-after 1866 an early Republic of Texas Settler both buried in Angelina Co, TX. unmarked grave near Burk/Diboll area. Daughter Lovinia Banks Stringer is buried near Groveton at Apple Springs, Trinity Co., Tx. where her husband, Cornelius "Neil" Stringer (son of Zachariah) was killed coming back from Louisiana in a freight wagon; and a black man hung for his murder at the courthouse square. It is also the location of some Tx. Redbone riots and courthouse take over and stand offs, and burnings to be discussed in *GTT...Redbones Gone To Texas!*

[86] http://www.freeafricanamericans.com/Stringer-Talbot.htm

Racial Mix

Mary Polly Perkins Nash/Ash, 1820-after 1870 Alexandria Rapides Parish, La. Wife of James "killed by knife wound" 1850 also pictured elsewhere here. Daughter of Nancy Perkins, Walnut Grove settlement, Vernon Parish, La. "Raw Hide Fight" location and that of Glass Window Cemetery where Nancy Perkins is buried. No known husband or father for Mary, it is rumored her children were fathered by a Perkins perhaps even an "Old Jock" and that she herself was also a Perkins.[87] In the Nash/Ash 1896 Cherokee aps. Mary is named as "daughter of Nancy Perkins" and sworn affidavits that she was also Indian "by blood." Sister of Hannah Perkins Nash/Ash buried Nash/Ash cemetery, No Zulch, Madison Co., TX and thought to be newly found headstone next to husband Benjamin Nash/Ash pictured elsewhere here. Her MtDNA discussed here, Nancy Perkins.

---

[87] Cheryl Tilly Perkins, descendant historian of the Walnut Grove Settlement & lifelong caretaker of the Glass Window Cemetery.

Redbones of Louisiana

Nancy Perkins 1780-1869 Headstone at Glass Window Cemetery, Vernon Parish, Louisiana. Nancy's MtDNA was traced to a T2 haplo assignment which is a Near East origins. This MtDNA has exact matches throughout England, Ireland, Germany, and France with an exact oldest known match location at the border region of Georgia, Armenia & Turkey. Testing lineage surnames are Goins-Burgess-Nash/Ash-Perkins-Perkins. She was the mother of Sarah Perkins Calhoun, Nathan Perkins, Elizabeth Perkins Calhoun, Mary "Polly" Perkins Nash/Ash (pictured here), Hannah Perkins Nash/Ash (headstone pictured here), Reason Perkins (m. Martha A. Ashworth), Emanuel & Robert Perkins no details on either of these sons.

Exact MtDNA origin match to Nancy Perkins.

Racial Mix

Nancy Perkins Groves, 1820-1902 daughter of Joseph & Sarah Calhoun Perkins, gr granddaughter of Nancy Perkins, she married James Groves, Jr. they are buried at Glass Window Cemetery, location of the famous Rawhide Fight.

White Women and Black Men
Compiled from Hode's case examples.

Legend:

chn = child or children (not all were known)
bm = black male (includes slaves and free persons of color and may include Indians and mixed blood persons)
wm = white male
fpc = free persons of color

Number of white women in the study included in this list is 98, all of whom had some sexual involvement with black men.
Number of white women married to black men = 14
Number of white women married to white men and having sexual relations with black men = 49 (exactly 50%)

Number of white women known to have had at least one mixed blood child = 31 Children were not always relevant to the legal case and thus may not have been mentioned in the legal documents.

Name:

Abercrombe, Ida – liaison with Peter Stamps, bm
Anderson, Lucy – liaison with Joseph Nunez – perhaps married to him – chn
Anderson, Penny – liaison with Griffin Stewart, bm
Atkinson, Julie married Aaron Green, bm
Bailey, Linda – liaison with unnamed, bm
Baker, Amy – liaison with Louis, slave
Barber, Jane – liaison with Caleb Watts, bm
Barden, Ann married to wm – liaison with unnamed bm, chn
Baylis, Rebecca married to wm – liaison with Wilford Mortimer, fpc
Beck, Catherine married to wm – liaison with family slave, chn
Bourne, Dorothea married to wm – liaison with Edmond, slave
Brewer, Maggie married to wm – liaison with Manley McCauley, bm
Bridget married Joseph Guy, bm, chn
Brinal, Catherine – liaison with Carter, slave
Britt, Catharine – liaison with Delks Moses, bm
Butler, Eleanor (Nell) married Charles, bm, chn
Butt, Lydia married to Benjamin Butt – liaison with Robin, slave
Cain, Mrs. Thomas – liaison with unnamed bm
Chestnut, Susan – liaison with Joel Fore, bm

Racial Mix

Clark, Sarah – liaison with unnamed bm
Cole, Pleasant – liaison with unnamed bm
Cook, Elizabeth married to wm – liaison with unnamed bm, chn
Corder, Elvira – liaison with unnamed bm
Cowan, Sarah married to wm – liaison with unnamed bm
Crabtree, Betsey – liaison with Harry Wall, bm
Culpepper, Caroline married to wm – liaison with unnamed bm
Davis, Mary married to (Mingo) Domingo, bm, chn
Dever, Elizabeth married to wm – liaison with unnamed bm, chn
Dunn, Mary – liaison with Warrick, slave
Fouch, Elizabeth married to wm – liaison with James Watt, fpc
Furlow, Mollie – liaison with Ben Leslie, bm
Gappins, Mary – liaison with unnamed bm, chn
Getts, Dolly (single daughter of slave owner) – liaison with bm
Grady, Thomason cohabitated with James Hog (aka James Grady)
Green, Rosanna – liaison with Gabriel, slave
Gresham, Sarah married to wm – liaison with unnamed bm, chn
Hall, Carrie married Sandy Hall bm
Hall, Sarah married to wm – liaison with unnamed bm, chn
Hancock, Tabitha married to wm – liaison with unnamed bm, chn
Hansford, Maria married to Girard Hansford fpc, chn
Harris, Mary liaison with Sampson, bm
Hide, Mrs. married to wm – liaison with unnamed bm

Hoffler, Deborah married to wm – liaison with John Lowance, fpc
Horton, Mrs. – liaison with unnamed bm
Howard, Elizabeth married to wm – liaison with Aldridge Evans, bm
Howard, Mrs. James – liaison with her slave Henry
Hugly, Caroline – liaison with slave, chn
Johnson, Hannah married to wm – liaison with bm, chn
Johnson, Peggy married to wm – liaison with unnamed bm
Jones, Peggy married to wm – liaison with unnamed bm
Kelly, Martha married to wm – liaison unnamed bm
Lane, Polly – liaison with "Slave Jim" chn
Leonard, Matilda – liaison with N. J. Steward, bm
Litsey, Betsey married Robert Hoover, bm
Logan, Mrs. Joh married to wm – liaison with slave, chn
Lucas, Candace – liaison with Wesley-Dean's Pete, slave
Mack, Delia – liaison with unname bm
Marshall, Mrs. – liaison with unnamed bm
Meadows, Mary – liaison with George, a slave
Middleton, Mrs. – liaison with unnamed bm
Midgett, Nancy – liaison with unnamed bm
Morris, Elizabeth married Dabney Pettus – liaison with unnamed bm
Mosby, Betsy married to wm – liaison with unnamed bm, chn
Newton, Nancy married to wm – liaison with unnamed bm
Oliver, Mary married to wm – liaison with unnamed bm
Owen, Nancy married to wm – liaison with unnamed bm
Parker (Miller) Jane married to wm – liaison with unnamed slaves, chn
Pearl, Elizabeth married Daniel Pearl, bm
Peck, Mary married bm, chn
Peters, Mary married a slave and thereby became a slave

Racial Mix

Plum, Mary Jane – liaison with unnamed bm, chn
Plummer, Miss – liaison with unnamed bm
Pruden, Louisa married to wm – liaison with unnamed bm, chn
Rawls, Rachel married to wm – liaison with unnamed bm, chn
Reid, Mrs. married to wm – liaison with unnamed bm
Roberts, Elizabeth married to wm – liaison with Jefferson a slave, chn
Rose, Henrietta married to wm – liaison with unnamed slave, chn
Rucker, Elizabeth – liaison with unnamed bm, chn
Sands, Sarah – liaison with Jerry, slave
Smith, Sarah – liaison with unnamed bm, had son Jonathan Glover
Scott, Louisa – liaison with Jesse Brady, mulatto man
Scroggins, Lucretia married to wm – liaison with unnamed bm
Shorter, Elizabeth married to Little Robin bm, chn
Sikes, Elizabeth – liaison with unnamed bm
Skinner, Mary married to wm – liaison with unnamed slave, chn
Smith, Mrs. James – liaison with Redding Evans, bm
Suttles, Elizabeth married Alfred Hooper, fpc
Tatham, Tabitha married to wm – liaison with unnamed bm, chn
Thompson, Zilpha married William Watters, bm
Tombereau, Peggy married to wm – liaison with Roland Colanche, mulatto, chn
Twitchell, Cora – liaison with Paul Davis, bm, child
Wallis, Nancy – liaison with Juba, slave
Walters, Elizabeth married to wm – liaison with unnamed bm

Watkins, Katherine married to wm – liaison with Dirke, bm and Mulatto Jack
Whittington, Lucy married to wm – liaison with unnamed bm
Williamson, Mary – liaison with William, bm
White, Mrs. James – liaison with Richard Neale, bm[88]

A Mixed-Race Marriage

A rare photograph. James William Evans and his wife, Mary Eliza Hoggard, a free African American from North Carolina, along with their three children. They were married in 1844 and moved to Missouri to raise their family.

88 Ibid.

GROUPS RESISTING RACISM AND SLAVERY

Redbones began coming into Louisiana around 1800, fully sixty-five years before the end of the Civil War. Some arriving even earlier, about 1770 according to land claims and the map presented here, River Mississippi, 1770. While few, if any, of them were of slave background, the shifting definition of who could be enslaved and the growing rigidity of the enforcement of the One-Drop Rule must have caused them much anxiety. As a result, there is little wonder that they sought a remote land that they could defend. Redbones were part of a sizeable group of people who had the strength and spirit to oppose slavery for themselves, though some Redbones were slave owners. Owning slaves and displaying a rejecting attitude toward Blacks was perhaps a way to assure the dominant society that they were separate and distinct from Blacks, and therefore not a candidate for slavery. The violence that often attached to Redbones may also have been a statement that they were unsuited for slavery, assuring that no attempt would be made to enslave them.

The resistance model developed by maroons (discussed below) and other groups was available to Redbones and may have influenced their choices of location, lifestyle, method of self-defense and their attitude toward the dominant society. This is supposition, of course, but the similarities in philosophy, attitudes and behavior between Redbones and other isolated groups are striking. More will be said later about the Redbone motivation for migrating out of the southeast. Discussed below are some groups that developed their own modes of survival and likely have influenced Redbones in developing theirs.

The term maroon comes from the Spanish "cimarrón," first used to refer to feral cattle, then to American Indians who fled to escape the brutality of the Spanish, and then primarily to slaves who fled slavery. It may be applied to an individual, but it is more often used to refer to a group or community. The best-known maroon group in the United States is the Black Seminoles. It is estimated that there were hundreds of maroon communities in North America. Maroon communities were well under development before the American Revolutionary War. It is ironic that the Whites who rebelled against their British masters were called heroes and patriots while Blacks who rebelled against their owners/masters were called renegades, outlaws, maroons, desperadoes, assassins, banditti and worse. They both sought freedom.

Groups Resisting Racism and Slavery

Black slaves are often portrayed as having been passive in their servitude. The truth is that the distance from their homeland and the severity of the well-organized slave system in the Americas demanded that they submit in the interest of survival. Nevertheless, a significant number did not submit – some that resisted survived and some did not. The existence of maroon societies was an embarrassment to the slavery system. Memory of the extent of the rebellion against slavery was suppressed and eventually passed from the consciousness of white America and, unfortunately, from that of Black and mixed-blood Americans. In the last quarter century, this resistance history has resurfaced in the story of the maroon societies. This emerging story is one not of renegades, outlaws and desperadoes, but of heroes fighting for their freedom with the resources and methods available to them. Their struggle for freedom should be no less a source of pride to their descendants, as the struggle of those who fought in the American Revolutionary War is to theirs.

Many maroons along the Gulf coast joined pirates and privateers, sailing, and fighting with them. Richard Price states, "…for three centuries, beginning in the early 1500s, maroons fought alongside pirates in their naval battles, guided them in their raids on major cities and participated with them in widespread, illicit international trade."[89] Pirates adopted the verb "to maroon" to describe the abandonment of an unwanted person in a remote spot.

Maroons required or sought inaccessible remote areas such as swamps for their settlements. Usually, their desire was to settle in an area that was defensible – not to rove the countryside as nomads. They were excellent guerilla fighters specializing in the ambush.[90] Maroons settled in the Dismal Swamp, between Virginia and North Carolina, and in the swamps of Georgia, South Carolina, Florida, Alabama, Mississippi, Louisiana, and other southern states. On November 12, 1841, *The Liberator* reported that a group of runaway slaves in Terrebonne Parish, Louisiana was attacking Whites, and in 1846, the same paper reported a gang of six runaway slaves was cornered in St. Landry Parish, Louisiana. An organized camp of Whites and Blacks was discovered in Talladega County, Alabama in 1860.[91]

Gwendolyn Hall reported that the earliest slaves in Louisiana were Indian, and that Indians and Blacks ran away together

---

89 Richard. Price, *Maroon Societies: Rebel Slave Communities in the Americas* (Baltimore: The John Hopkins University Press, 1996), p.14.
90 *Ibid.*, p.7.
91 Laura White, *Journal of Southern History* (I, 1935, p.47). As reported by Richard Price in *Maroon Societies*.

Groups Resisting Racism and Slavery

to live in Indian (Choctaw and other tribes) villages. The maroons of Louisiana were seldom caught because of the cover provided by the thick swamps. An abundance of food along the coast and in the swamps allowed them to subsist. Two of the largest maroon communities in south Louisiana were: des Natanapallé (Indian and Black) and Bas du Fleuve. "By the time the American Revolution was drawing to a close, the maroons of Louisiana had asserted their control over a strategically vital part of the territory – Bas du Fleuve, the area between the mouth of the Mississippi River and New Orleans."[92]

Jean Laffite, 1780-1832 a Jewish Outcast family from Bordeaux Region of France[93].

It has been suggested that the privateer, Jean Laffite, had Redbones in his crews.

---

92 Gwendolyn Midlo-Hall, Africans in Colonial Louisiana: The Development of Afro-Creole Culture in the Eighteenth Century (Baton Rouge: LSU Press, 1992), p.205.

[93] Lafitte was "unique" according to Edward Glick of the Jerusalem Post: He was a Sephardi Jew, as was his first wife, who was born in the Danish Virgin Islands. In his prime, Lafitte ran not just one pirate sloop

Redbones of Louisiana

The Laffites (Jean and Pierre) were in southwest Louisiana and southeast Texas from approximately 1802-1820 – and a motley crew of many nationalities manned their ships. Jean Laffite may have been sympathetic to maroons or anyone whom he considered at a disadvantage to the power structure. At the Battle of New Orleans,[94] he no doubt met many people who later settled in the Neutral Zone and it is likely he traded with them. He traded slaves he found on captured ships, along with cloth, jewelry, wine, spices and other goods for supplies needed by his crews up and down both the Calcasieu and Sabine Rivers, where Redbones were settling. James Groves, who some consider a Redbone (he was an Indian), was at the Battle of New Orleans and later operated a trading post at Walnut Hill, Louisiana. Recent family sentiment was James Groves, Sr. was listed in the free person of color and somewhat literate according to documents surfaced in recent years which he crafted for himself and other Redbones. His trading post was on a trade route in the Neutral Zone. It is

---

but a whole fleet of them simultaneously. By EDWARD BERNARD GLICK   JULY 13, 2006.

[94] Just two weeks after the signing of the Treaty of Ghent, U.S. General Andrew Jackson achieves the greatest American victory of the War of 1812 at the Battle of New Orleans. The Battle of New Orleans was fought on January 8, 1815 between the British Army under Major General Sir Edward Pakenham and the United States Army under Brevet Major General Andrew Jackson, roughly 5 miles southeast of the French Quarter of New Orleans, in the current suburb of Chalmette, Louisiana.

quite likely that he and Laffite were acquainted. When Laffite was forced by the Americans to leave Galveston in 1820 (Galveston was not then American territory), many of his crew stayed in the Neutral Zone and in east Texas. However, no direct evidence has been found linking any known Redbone to the Laffite's or to members of their crew. But, then again, considering the business arrangements he conducted, it is not hard to imagine all was done in the light of secrecy.

UPDATE

Baratarian Redbones

In recent years, significant facts that correspond with oral traditions that Laffite's men, the Baratarians were Redbones. A few of those facts are business connections between Spanish land grants into the Neutral Zone Contraband Courts. Which we elaborate later here. A strong relationship between Lafitte, and cattle baron James Taylor White "LaBlanc," a Redbone progenitor and his colony at Campeche, Galveston. Aaron Charry (Cherry), head Baratarian and Chief of the Coushatta's. and owned land up the Trinity River at Old El Orquisac, aka Ironwood, aka Sam Houston's Grand Cane Plantation built for consort Talihana Rogers (Ark/Mo Cherokee) and Nancy Johnson Goyens,

Redbones of Louisiana

Isaiah Sion Fields (Fields Settlement, No Man's Land) at Liberty, Liberty Co., Texas. His ties into the Alabama Coushatta's at Polk Co., TX Burgess Settlement (Red River Pakana Muscogee). Aaron Charry was also related to the Louisiana Doyle/Dial/Dyal and Buxton lines as well as the Goyens, at Liberty and Polk counties, Texas. All which are shared in portions here and in, *The Redbone Chronicles*, and forthcoming book titled *GTT...Redbones Gone to Texas!*

Aaron Charry or **Cherry**. Lafitte's Baratarian Headman. Born in 1778 in Pennsylvania, or Ohio and died 1856 at Romayor, Liberty Co., TX. He is buried at the Plantation Ranch Cemetery. He married Eleanor Spencer (1781-1850). He is enumerated in the Mexican census 1826. He removed to Louisiana in 1813. He and many male generations from him all served as Chief's or Headmen of the Alabama Coushatta, Liberty, Harden and Polk counties, TX. His children were **Sara Jane Cherry** 1805-1880 she married Dempsey Iles and is buried DeRidder, Beauregard Parish, La. **John Cherry** 1808 in Ohio and died 1891 in Tarkington Prairie, Liberty Co., TX., he married 1. Matilda Bridges 1812-1850, 2. Francis K. Holt 1828-1891, 3. Roxalyn Buxton Merritt 1814-1898. **Aaron Cherry, Jr.** he was born 1811 in Louisiana and died 1880 at Burleson Co., TX. He married Laura Holt. Jean Laffite often sailed ships up the Trinity River to Aaron Cherry's ranch.

Groups Resisting Racism and Slavery

BLACK SEMINOLES constituted perhaps the most powerful maroon community in the United States.[95] In the early 1700s, South Carolina governor, James Moore, along with some Creek Indians, invaded the Florida territory carrying off most of the native Apalachees who were then resettled or sold to the West Indies as slaves. The desolation continued until most of the natives were destroyed or removed, being replaced by lower Creeks who left their Alabama and Georgia homes due to pressures there. These newcomers, referred to as Seminoles, owned black slaves whom they treated with kindness and humanity. They afforded runaway slaves some protection from their former white masters.

These blacks, who came to be known as Black Seminoles, lived in separate villages next to the Seminole Indians and had their own government. They developed their own separate culture, containing elements of African, White, and Indian cultures. They paid tribute to the Seminole Indians, usually through giving them a portion of their crops. Black Seminoles were valuable to Seminole Indians as their interpreters and fierce fighters – they were fighting for their own highly valued freedom. Black Seminoles only numbered

---

95 Price says that the group in the Dismal Swamp was the largest with 2000 members.

a few hundred warriors at any one time, but combined with the more numerous Indians, they fought one of the costliest wars the United States had experienced to that time. Known as the Second Seminole Way – it lasted from 1835 to 1842. It was their War of Independence.[96]

Intermarriage and interbreeding between the Seminoles and black slaves was a natural result of their peaceful association, though there is no evidence that this occurred to a large extent. Cuban fishermen lived in Florida where they fished and dried their catch. Many of these men lived with local women and some had legal marriages to them. It was estimated that at any one point in time, there were from 50 to 100 mixed-blood children from these unions.[97] No estimate has been made of the number of mixed-blood children who were born to Spaniards, Cubans and Indian women in the more than 300 years before they left Florida. Marriage and interbreeding with Cuban fishermen continued until the Cubans left Florida in the 1800s.

---

96 Trace Etienne -Gray, "Black Seminole Indians," in *The New Handbook of Texas* (Austin: The Texas State Historical Association, 1996), Vol. 1, p. 571.
97 James W. Coventon, *The Seminoles of Florida* (Gainsville: University of Florida Press, 1993), p.27.

Groups Resisting Racism and Slavery

In the mid-1800s, many Black Seminoles migrated to Mexico where slavery had been abolished. After the Civil War, many returned to the United States and served the U.S. Army as scouts and Indian fighters in the western territories. They were known there as the Buffalo Soldiers. (See Attachment A for a list of Black Seminole surnames).

A Group of Buffalo Soldiers

UPDATE
Seminole's and Redbone YDNA Connections

Redbone male lineage YDNA have made a positive match between Seminole Resistance Leader, William Billy Powell, Jr. better known as Oceola.[98] And that of several of our progenitor forefathers. These male lineages will be closely followed in the forthcoming, *Goins Book I & II*. You will read throughout the updates that we mention "exact" YDNA matches, regardless of surname. The following male lineages

---

[98] I do not use an s in the spelling of his name, as this is a more modern adaption.

are 100% YDNA matches for one another, in a little more simplistic terms, they all come from the exact same male progenitor on the YDNA line (father to son).

"Goyens Clan", Sweat, Powell, Warwick, Perkins and Williams [99]

Oldest Genetic YDNA is Thomas J. Goyens line, born ca. 1820 in Louisiana and died in Nacogdoches, TX. his father (Unknown) was born in North Carolina and his mother (Unknown) was born in Tennessee. All males below fall under his male line of genetics.

1. **Thomas Goyens**, born abt. 1774 in South Carolina died 1825 St. Landry, Lafayette Parish, Louisiana. Married probably unknown and Nancy Johnson who was probably married previously also.
2. **Leonard Covington Sweat,** Rawhide Fight, Jayhawker (Gideon, Ephraim, Robert) born 1812 in Alabama m. E. Burgess, he was ambushed and killed around Jasper, Jasper Co., TX. by the Nash/Ash & Keefer families. [100] (s/o Gideon Gadi x L. Letty Johnson, s/o Ephraim x Olive Perkins, speculated s/o Robert x Margaret Cornish Sweat).
3. **Berry Hamilton Williams**, Married Martha Gibbes or Sweat, she could have been married to a Sweat first and male offspring went by Williams? Bullock Co.,

---

[99] We use the term "clan" to separate YDNA matched male lineages with the same surname. Spellings are based on those most used by that family.
[100] Legends of L.C. Sweat, as told by Cheryl Tilley Perkins.

Groups Resisting Racism and Slavery

Georgia. Texas progenitor Old Thomas Williams married Pus Brooks arrived from Chief Bowles Cherokee, Ark. Camp, Louisiana Progenitor "Choctaw Bill" Williams married Penelope Richardson.

4. **Allen J. Perkins** born in Georgia, died Louisiana. Mentioned here, in the Ten-Miler voting affidavits as son of "Old Jo" Perkins.
5. **William Billy Powell, Jr.** "Oceola" (mother was Anne Polly Moniac Coppinger, daughter of Don Jose Maria Coppinger (Cuban Spaniard) and Nancy Ann McQueen daughter of James (Ireland) and Catherine Redstick Fraser McQueen (Tallassee, Georgia/Alabama). Oceola was not the son of William Billy Powell, Sr., with whom his mother briefly was a mate. Raised by his grandparents, his great uncle Peter Talmuches McQueen, a Tulsa Indian and war chief of the Red Sticks, born 1780 would influence Oceola's resistance movement and the great Seminole Wars.

This YDNA match led us onto the Seminole's in a biological way. It is of note also that Oceola spoke Gullah Geechee[101],

---

[101] The Gullah language, typically referred to as "Geechee" in Georgia, is technically known as an English-based creole language, created when peoples from diverse backgrounds find themselves thrown together and must communicate. Through research it has also been found that there is in particular, a strong connection between the Gullah language and the Krio language spoken in Sierra Leone. This is the native language of the Krios, the descendants of freed slaves, but it is also their national language, the most commonly spoken language in Sierra Leone today. The word, "Gullah" is thought to be derived from "Angola", as many slaves originated from that part of Africa, or "Gola" a tribe on the Sierra Leone-Liberia border.

a language only known among the Maroon community along the Carolina Coast. The group comprised of runaway slaves who were mohammedan. [102] And relevant that thar this YDNA are direct male descendants of the ancient pharaonic male line of King Ramses III.

MEHRAssociation has started a YDNA study at Family Tree DNA for those men who were buried at their cemetery in Bracketville, Texas. Here is a list of their names.

Buried Seminole Soldiers [Seminole Scouts, in general were buried outside of the fort where they resided. Seminole Scouts were not regular military and served in no capacity as soldiers. There are no formal records on those men who served as Indian Scouts at Fort Concho, or Fort Clark] at Fort Clark, Brackettville, TX. and subsequently reinterred at the National Cemetery in San Antonio, Texas. As follows:

13 **Priest, J.A.** Chief Musician, 25, U.S., Inf., Aug. 8, 1870, 13 Note: Removal to SHNC "I.A." Isaac A. Priest "white", Chief of Musician, White, 24 Inf, Ulcerated Bowels, yes (originated in line of duty), Fort Clark, Texas, See Report Donald Jackson, AAS (remarks). **Reinterred as "Priest, I.A.":** Ft. Sam Houston National Cemetery
14 **Johnson, Miles** Musician, I, 4/25, U.S., Inf., Nov. 15, 1870, 14 (Gun-Shot Wound)
15 **Erums, Primus**, Musician, F, 25, U.S., Inf., Janr'y 19, 1871, 15

---

[102] Mohammedan is a term for a follower of Muhammad, the Islamic prophet. It is used as both a noun and an adjective, meaning belonging or relating to, either Muhammad or the religion, doctrines, institutions, and practices that he established

Groups Resisting Racism and Slavery

16 **Bennet, Thomas** Private B, Private, D, 25, U.S., Inf., Feb. 3, 1871,

17 **Sheppard, Horace**, Musc. Band, D, 25, U.S., Inf., Mrch 4, 1871 (Gun-Shot Wound)

18 **Turner, John L.**, Pvt., D, 25, U.S., Inf., Sept 16, 1871 (Gun-Shot Wound)

19 **Wright, William**, Pvt., E, 25, U.S., Inf., Nov. 5, 1871

20 **Thomas, Henry**, Pvt., A, 25, U.S, Inf., Dec. 5/15, 1871

21 **Smith, John**, Pvt, E, 25, U.S., Inf., Jan'y, 10 (4), 1872

22 **Johnson, Alexander**, Musician, A, 25, U.S., Inf., Mrch, 7, 1872

23 **Blake, Cyrus**, discharged Soldier, C, 25, U.S. Inf., Mrch 22, 1872

24 **Hagger, William**, Pvt, G, 9, Inf., Cav, April, 18, 1872

25 **Duffield, Thomas**, Pvt, A, 25, U.S., Inf, April, 27, 1872

26 **Brown, Red**, Corpl, B, 25, U.S., Inf., May, 3, 1872

27 **Celestine, Joseph**, Pvt D, 25, U.S., Inf., May, 15, 1872

28 **Lee, Samuel**, Pvt., E, 25, U.S., Inf., Cav, June, 7, 1872 (Gun-Shot Wound)

29 **Steele, Richard**, Pvt., C, 25, U.S., Cav, Nov, 19, 1872

30 **Alphonse, Peter**, 1st Srgt., A, 25, U.S., Cav, Dec, 1, 1872 (Gun-Shot Wound)

31 **Gilmore, Michael,** Pvt., C, 10, U.S., Inf., Dec, 18, 1872

32 **Harris, John,** Pvt., E, 9, U.S., Cav, Mch., 12, 1873 (Suicide)

33 **Leigh, John**. Corpl., H, 10, U.S., Inf, Dec., 1, 1873

34 **Vincent, T.R.**, 1st Lieut., A, 9, U.S., Cav., April, 20, 1872 (Killed by Indians)

35 **Corrigan, Peter**, Pvt., D, 4, U.S., Cav., April, 20, 1872 (Gun-Shot Wound)

36 **Wheeler, Wm**, Corpl., C, 4, U.S., Cav., May, 23, 1873

37 **Baker, Wm. D.,** Pvt, D, 4, U.S., Cav, Sept, 4, 1873

Redbones of Louisiana

38 **White, Edward,** Pvt., D, 4, U.S., Cav., Oct, 3, 1873
39 **Hickey, John,** Pvt., K, 10, U.S., Inf., Oct, 10, 1873
40 **Holbrook, Samuel**, Pvt, I., 4, Cav, Nov., 6, 1873
41 **Mullhall, John**, Pvt., F, 4, U.S., Cav., Jan'y, 2, 1874 (Gun-Shot Wound)
42 **Myers, Frederick**, Sergt., A, 4, U.S., Cav, Jan'y, 2, 1874
43 **Fisher, Thomas**, Corpl, K, 4, U.S., Cav., Jan'y, 4, 1874
44 **Hudson, Charles L.**, 1st Lieut., I, 4, U.S., Cav., Jan'y, 5, 1874 (Gun-Shot Wound)
45 **Brown, Thomas,** Pvt., K, 10, U.S., Inf., July, 12, 1874
46 **O'Neil, Thomas**, Private, B, 4, U.S., Cav, Oct, 4. 1874 (Gun-Shot Wound)
47 **Owens, Charles**, Private, B, 4, U.S., Cav, Nov., 8, 1874 (Suddenly from alcohol)
48 **Hurlbert, Sheldon**, Private, H, 10, U.S., Cav, Nov, 22, 1874
49 **Lynch, Dominic, Jr.**, 1st. Luint., B, 4, U.S., Cav, Feb., 21, 1875 (Deliri *illegible)
50 **Cogdel, Robert**, Recrui't., -, -, 4, Cav, April 23, 1875
51 **Smith, George B.**, Recrui't., -, -, 4, Cav, April 15, 1875
52 **Young, William C.**, Recrui't, -, 9, U.S., Cav, May, 3, 1875

Original Leger Renumbered at Number 53 Peacock, John, "omitted" Next Numbering

53-54 **Peacock, John,** Pvt., H, 10, U.S., Inf, May 12, 1875, Omitted on report, 54 (Gun-Shot Wound)
54 55 **White, Marshall**, Corporal, A, 9, Inf, Cav, Dec, 25, 1875
55-56 **O'Hern, John**, Private C/G?, 10, U.S., Inf, Nov., 18, 1876

Groups Resisting Racism and Slavery

56-57 **Gergon, Henry**, Private, K, 10, U.S., Cav, Dec, 10, 1876

57-58 **Goins, Thomas**, Private, B, 10, U.S., Cav, Feb, 13, 1877, (Inflammation of lungs)

58-59 **Taylor, Louis**, Private, B, 10, U.S., Cav, June, 16, 1877

59-60 **Hall, Francis**, Pvt., F, 8, U.S., Cav, June, 16, 1877,

60-61 **Smith, Henry**, Pvt, M, 10, U.S., Inf., Aug, 11, 1877

61-62 **Lyons, Henry**, Pvt, A, 24, U.S., Inf., Aug, 14, 1877

62-63 **Fleming, Joseph**, Pvt., D, 24, U.S., Inf, Sept., 16, 1877

63-64 **McGarrell, John**, Pvt., K, 8, U.S., Cav, Feb., 14, 1878

64-65 **Connell, William**, Pvt, G, 10, U.S., Inf, Feb., 14, 1878

65-66 **Copp, Wm. A.**, Pvt., F, 8, U.S., Cav, Feb 24, 1878

66-67 **Leonard, John,** Pvt., M, 4, U.S., Cav, -, -, - (Murder)

67-68 **Monahan, Michael,** Farrier, M, 4, U.S., Cav, Mrch, 27, 1878 (Inebriation)

68-69 **Johnson, Hugh**, Pvt., A, 8, U.S., Cav, Mrch, 28, 1878

69-70 **Lee, Joseph**, Pvt, K, 10, U.S., Inf, Mrch, 28, 1878 (Gun-Shot Wound)

70-71 **Mitchell, Wm. H.**, Pvt, A, 8, U.S., Cav, Aprl, 18, 1878

71-72 **Fallon, Michael**, Pvt, H, 10, U.S., Inf, Aprl, 28, 1878 (Gun-Shot Wound)

72-73 **Wall, Thomas**, Trumpeter, B, 8, U.S., Cav, May, 2, 1878

73-74 **Rufsell (Russell), Herbert**, Pvt, H, 20, U.S., Inf, May, 8, 1878

74-75 **Graham, W.J.**, Pvt, F, 2, U.S., Cal, June, 14, 1878,

75-76 **Jacoby, John**, Pvt. F, 10, U.S., Inf, July 5, 1878

76-77 **Benne, John** C., Pvt, E, 4, U.S., Cav, Aug 4, 1878

77-78 **Weaver, Charles**, Pvt, E, 4, U.S., Cav, Aug, 17, 1878

78-79 **Mackin, Robert**, Pvt, F, 20, U.S., Inf, Aug, 18, 1878

Fort Clark Cemetery Original 1940 with headstones still standing. Courtesy, Mr. Russell Nowell, Bracketville, Texas Original Internments at Post Cemetery, Fort Clark, Texas. No Located at National Archives, "Thomas Goins" Plus 11 burials below, not found on re-internment list, perhaps they are on the "continued page" but those have been lost or misplaced at the National Military Archives Level. It might be these records also burned in a fire at St. Louis, Missouri destroying thousands of military personnel files?

The Following Burials Are Not Listed in the Re-internment/Renumbered List Taken 1883. These are taken from the original ledger.

79 **Smith, John W**., Pvt., E, 20, U.S., Cav., Sept. 10, 1878

80 **Ulrich, Jacob L**., Trumpeter, A, 8, U.S., Cav. Sept. 14, 1878

81 **Kuykendoll, Joseph B**, Private, K, 4, U.S., Cav, Sept. 16, 1878

82 **Boyle, James,** Private, K, 8, U.S., Cav., Sept., 18, 1878

83 **Burroughs, Geo. E.**, Private, E, 20, U.S., Inf, Oct., 5, 1878

84 **Luchell, Louis**, Private, F, 10, U.S., Inf, Oct, 13, 1878

85 **Burke, John**, Private, G, 10, U.S., Inf, Nov, 17, 1878

86 **Hickey, Michael**, Private, L, 4, U.S., Cav, Nov, 17, 1878

87 **Elsaser, Wm. H.**, Private, F, 10, U.S., Inf, Nov, 18, 1878

88 **Mull, Franklin M.**, Private, L, 8, U.S., Cav, Jar'y, 8, 1879

89 **Bafse (Bass) Chas. A.H.**, Private, G, 10, U.S., Inf., -, -, - Continued page 387 (We are searching for the continued pages at National Archives)

Page 76-77 **Thomas (E.) Goins**, Private B, 10 Calv, Ft. Clark, Texas, Cause of Death: Inflammation of lungs, originated in the line of duty: No, Remarks: P. Middleton, A.S.U.S.A. Located, National Archives, through search records term; "Thomas Goins" Page 76-77 **Thomas Goins**, Private B, 10 Calv, Ft. Clark, Texas, Inflammation of lungs, No, P. Middleton, A.S.U.S.A. Died Column, **Thomas E. Gowens**, Pvt. B, Feb 13, 1877, Ft. Clark, Tex., Of Consumption in Post Hospital In The ALTERATIONS, since last return, among the Enlisted Men Column, 1876 #15 **Thomas E. Going**, **Henry Goyen** "supply"

1870 Fort Clark Census

Priest, Ermus, Bennett, Sheppard. Turner, Wright, Thomas, Smith, Johnson, Smith, Blake, Hagger, Duffield, Brown, Celestine, Steele, Lee, Alphonse, Gilmore, Harris, Leigh, Vincent, Corrigan, Wheeler, Baker, White, Hickey, Holbrok,

Mullhall, Myers, Fisher, Hudson, Brown, O'Neil, Owens, Hurlbert, Lynch, Cogdel, Smith, Young, Peacock, White, O'Hern, Gergon, Goins/Gowen/Goyens, Taylor, Hall, Smith, Lyons, Fleming, McGarrell, Connell, Copp, Leonard, Monohan, Johnson, Lee, Mitchell, Fallon, Wall, Russell, Graham, Jacoby, Benne/Bean, Weaver, Mackin, Ulrich, Kuykendoll, Boyle, Burroughs/Burris, Luchell, Burke, Hickey, Elsaser, Mull, Bass.

There are many other resistance groups not considered maroon communities of which the following are examples.

THE BEN ISHMAEL TRIBE had a charismatic leader, Ben Ishmael, who organized the tribe between 1785 and 1790 in Bourbon (then Noble) County Kentucky. He gathered the tribe from Tennessee, the Carolinas, Kentucky, Virginia, and Maryland. Hugo P. Leaming, writing about the tribe, says,

> *That the Ishmaelites were fugitives is shown by their double removal, first from the Southeast to frontier Kentucky, then on to the unexplored Old Northwest; and by their ethnic composition, the three subject peoples of the South's slavery society: Chattel slaves or "free blacks, remnants of destroyed Native*

Groups Resisting Racism and Slavery

American Nations, and European indentured servants or their landless, despised children.[103]

This nomadic community numbering about 10,000 migrated from the south to Ohio and Indiana in the early part of the nineteenth century.[104] The tribe settled around present-day Cincinnati and Indianapolis. From their home bases, they went on long treks covering several states in a kind of nomadic existence. Renouncing regular work as defined by the dominant culture, they existed as hunters, thieves, and scavengers. Though they were mostly illiterate, one member, Robert Chism (slave name of Ben Ishmael), wrote two books. James Fenimore Cooper wrote about the Ishmaelites in *The Prairie,* and "Little Orphan Annie" was modeled after an Ishmaelite. In 1907, Indiana passed a compulsory sterilization law aimed at the Ishmaelites based on their refusal to engage in wage labor and their alternative activities, some of which were outside the law. This effort at sterilization was led by Rev. Oscar C. McCulloch of the Congregational Church in Indianapolis. His work was used worldwide in the eugenics movement and even influenced

---

103 Hugo P., Leaming "The Ben Ishmael Tribe: A Fugitive 'Nation' of the Old Northwest" in *Gone to Croatan: Origins of North American Dropout Culture*, Eds. Ron Sakolsky, and James Koehnline (New York: Autonomedia, 1993), p. 20.
104 *Ibid.*, p.19.

the Nazi eugenics efforts and those of six other nations as well.[105]

Ishmaelites were a mixture of white slaves, Native Americans, and Blacks. They perhaps represented remnants of African Islam; the influence of which in Appalachia has received too little attention.

Regarding the Ben Ishmael Tribe were more aligned with the Grasshopper Gypsy (Chicago) and Native American than any others. They intermingled with the Pawnee and Kickapoo tribes and setup a nomadic lifestyle. Their leaders, Ben and Jennie Ishmael were known as fine artisans and musicians. They taught polygamy, a nomadic existence, and racial mixing. Genetically, it does not appear that Anglo-Americans mixed with the Grasshopper Gypsy, the cause likely was tribal endogamy.[106]

---

[105] *Ibid.*, p. 45. Dr. W. A. Plecker, Registrar for the state of Virginia in the 1940s, was influenced by the Indiana work and he, too, influenced the Nazi efforts. He is thoroughly hated by Melungeions as a racist but was revered by many white Virginians in his time. He carried on a campaign to identify all persons of mixed-blood and label them as Negro. As part of the campaign, Plecker wrote letters to officials of Tennessee inquiring about the heritage of the Melungeons.
See also, Daniel J. Kevles, *In the Name of Eugenics: Genetics and the Uses of Human Heredity*, (New York: Alfred A. Knopf, 1985), pp. 74-75. (See Attachment D for a sample of Plecker's letters.)
[106] the custom of marrying only within the limits of a local community, clan, or tribe.

Groups Resisting Racism and Slavery

Much like the Redbones, for many generations, we have not married outside of our tribal families. These practices carry on until present era. Though recent DNA autosomal (cousins) results would confirm some ancestral ties with the Ben Ishmael Grasshopper Gypsies, it is unknown at this writing just how they are in line with Redbone genealogy. In 1850 there was a huge genealogical chart completed by the Eugenics movement, but the connection/generational matches c1650's. Not much is known of Ben Ishmael and no records exist on who his parents were, or that of his wife "Jennie" described as a "half-bred Indian". Some Ishmaels' from Kentucky and Indiana settled in Newton and Nacogdoches, Texas however the lack of documented genealogy and the fact they are still a wandering people it has been difficult to trace. More research is needed.

CHRISTIAN PRIBER, an educated German, arrived in the New World in the 1730s with a goal of establishing a utopian society among the Indians of Georgia and South Carolina. He

BIOLOGY the fusion of reproductive cells from related individuals; inbreeding; self-pollination.

wanted to establish a town among the Cherokees that would be a city of refuge for all criminals, debtors, slaves, Creeks, Cherokees, French, English and all colors and complexions so long as they subscribed to the principles he enunciated. There would be, in his city, complete equality between the sexes and complete sexual freedom. He lived with the Cherokees and adopted their lifestyle and culture. The Cherokees embraced him and his philosophy, but he was imprisoned for his advocacy of these plans and died in prison before he could implement his program.[107]

THE FREE STATE OF JONES was a Civil War aberration. During the Civil War, Jones County, Mississippi seceded from the Union and the Confederacy, declaring itself the Free State of Jones. Leadership for the secession was provided largely by mixed-blood people from South Carolina, whose ancestors had a history of the resistance to authority in North Carolina during the American Revolution.[108] The principal character in the conflict was Newton Knight, who was assisted by a slave woman, Rachal. The conflict between the Knight Clan and the Confederates

---

107 Verner W. Crane, "A Lost Utopia of the First American Frontier," in *The Sewanee Review Quarterly*, Jan-Mar, 1919), pp. 48-61.
108 Victoria E. Bynum, *The Free State of Jones: Mississippi's Longest Civil War* (Chapel Hill: University of North Carolina Press, 2001), p.11ff.

Groups Resisting Racism and Slavery

was long and brutal, lasting several years after the end of the war. After the war, Knight, a white man, lived with Rachal and had children by her and perhaps one of her daughters. He defied the miscegenation laws and customs of the state by encouraging his children, by his white wife, to marry children of Rachal, who were fathered by someone other than himself. In so doing, he and his family contributed to the interracial mixture of an already heavily mixed community.

Newton Knight

Following the war, the racial identity of many of Knight's family was changed many times, primarily based on whether they married persons considered by the dominant society as Black or White. Knight, himself, was finally deprived of his

White status in the 1900 census.[109] Some of the names associated with the Jones County secession, many of which are considered Redbone names, were:

Jones, Welborn, Welch, Colins, Sumeral, Bynum, Valentine, Knight (Nite), Wesley, Whitehead, Mauldin, Sims, Dykes, Griffin, Rainey, Gibson, Summerlin, Lee, Courtney, Delancy, Dixon, Benson, Rayford, Necaise, Andrews, Laird, Holifield, Coats, Turner, Eulin, Herrington, Owens, Sullivan, Gunter, Powell, Huff, Craft, Chain, Gibbons, Blackledge, Coleman, Wheeler, Ates, Parker, Walters, Reddoch, McGee, Gilbert and Yawn.

THE LOWERY BAND galvanized the Lumbee Indians. During the Civil War and in the years immediately following it, the Lowery Band, led by Henry Berry Lowery (Lowrie, Lowry), put up resistance to the repressive social order that would have made a Redbone proud. Indeed, some Redbones today likely have their roots in this Robeson County, North Carolina group. They are known today as Lumbee Indians.

---

109 *Ibid.*, pp.158-159. Several books give accounts of the Free State. *Echo of the Black Horn* by Ethel Knight is largely a defense of the Confederate cause and is thus quite subjective. *The Free State of Jones: Mississippi's Longest Civil War*, by Victoria Bynum, is more objective and served as a major source in the above account.

Groups Resisting Racism and Slavery

About one quarter of the Indians east of the Mississippi River live in North Carolina along the Lumbee River.[110] In the 1960 census, one-third of the inhabitants of Robeson County were Indians.[111] In the early 1700s, the region was occupied by several Indian tribes. As Evans recounts in *To Die Game*, the Siouan-speaking tribes to the south and west were pressed by the Cherokee to the west and the Spanish from the south. To the north and east, the Iroquoian tribes, including the Tuscarora, were in a squeeze play, as were the Algonquin-speaking tribes of which one may have absorbed the "Lost Colonists" from Roanoke Island. "As a result, by the beginning of the eighteenth century, some half-dozen small Siouan peoples had converged around the upper Pee Dee, into which the Lumbee River empties."[112]

---

110 Brewton, Berry, *Almost White: A Study of Certain Racial Hybrids in the Eastern United States* (New York: Macmillan, 1963), p. 14.
111 W. McKee Evans, *To Die Game* (Nashville: Parthenon Press, 1971), p. 20. Including the Catawba, Eno, Keyauwee, Occaneechi, Saponi, and Tutelo as used by Evans quoting Swanton, in *Probable Identity of the Croatans*, p. 3.
112 *Ibid.*, p. 23.

Redbones of Louisiana

Henry Berry Lowery 1845-unknown, he married Rhoda Lowery. Lumbee Indian who led a resistance in North Carolina during and after the American Civil War. He is sometimes viewed as a Robin Hood type figure and a pioneer in the struggle for civil rights.

The Tuscaroras were defeated in 1713 and most moved away, but some settled in the Pee Dee region and the Lowry Clan traces back to them.[113] But Dial, in *The Only Land I Know,* questions the extent of the Tuscaroras hereditary influence on Indians of the Pee Dee region.[114] About this same time, Scots began moving into the domain of Indians of the Pee Dee. The Indians had been speaking English so long they had lost their original language, and the Gaelic-speaking Scots spoke no

---

113 *Ibid.*, p. 24.
114 Adoph L. Dial, *The Only Land I Know: A History of the Lumbee Indians* (San Francisco: The Indian Historian Press, 1975), p. 22.

Groups Resisting Racism and Slavery

English. Many of the Scots were indentured servants called "Buckskins" because they dressed like Indians.[115]

In 1835, North Carolina ratified a new constitution which took away most of the rights of free black citizens, including the right to bear arms. Since the Indians had given up their language and tribal organization, they could not prove they were Indian. They were a mixture of Indian, White and Black. The new constitution included the wording "free persons of mixed blood" and while it was not originally intended for Indians, it was gradually applied to them. The Confederate government conscripted many of the Indians on the Pee Dee and heaped hardships on them in building forts, enraging them in the process. The four sons of Allen Lowry and their kinsmen led by son, Henry Berry, went to the swamps to avoid the Confederate Home Guard.[116] During the Civil War and into the reconstruction years, they excelled as guerilla fighters.

During reconstruction:

> *"...it appeared that nothing could stop the winners from putting the Lumbee River Indians into the same half-free 'place' in which they generally succeeded in putting the blacks. But this effort failed. It appears to*

---

115 Evans, *op. cit.*, p. 30.
116 *Ibid.*, p. 36.

have failed, furthermore, to a great extent because of the bold deeds of the Lowrys, which filled the Lumbee Indians with a new pride....[117]

The following statement relative to the Lumbee, by the author of *To Die Game,* may explain why Redbones were so protective and reactive.

"If, during the past two hundred years, the brown-skinned people in this region have acquired a reputation for reacting fiercely to any affront to their dignity, for challenging a slight that others might allow to pass, perhaps it is because they have come to realize that long ago retreat ceased to be a practical possibility."[118]

They simply had had enough. (A list of names associated with the Lumbee is included as Attachment B).

THE MOWA CHOCTAWS, a group of mixed-blood people formerly known as Alabama Cajans or "Cajan Indians," live north of Mobile Alabama. The term Cajan, also sometimes referred to as "Cajun," was from the beginning a misnomer and was considered a derogatory name. It has now been replaced by MOWA Choctaw which is an

---

117 *Ibid.*, p. 259.
118 *Ibid.*, p. 25.

Groups Resisting Racism and Slavery

amalgamation of Mobile and Washington after the Alabama counties in which they principally reside.[119]

Ms. Laura F. Murphy left a description of what they were like when she taught in their rural schools in the late 1920s and early 30s. In 1950, author Edward T. Price, wrote of them, revealing that their economic and social conditions had not changed much in the interim.[120] From the description left by these two observers, one can see many similarities between this group and the Redbones of the 1930s and 50s. Both the MOWA and the Redbones have made great progress since 1950.

Ancestors of the MOWA were in the area north of Mobile as early as 1791, but most moved into the area in the late 1800s.[121] The tradition among MOWA ancestors was that they were a mixture of Choctaw, Cherokee, Apache, French, English, German and Russian. They denied Negro blood ties, however, later this too was added to the mix through a freed

---

119 The MOWA Choctaws have achieved state recognition but no recognition by the federal government. In Louisiana, two groups have received state, but not federal recognition: the Ebarb Choctaw at Ebarb, and the Clifton Choctaw west of Alexandria.
120 Edward T. Price, Jr., Mixed-Blood Populations of Eastern United States as to Origins, Localizations, and Persistence. (Ph.D. Dissertation, University of California, 1937).
121 Laura Frances Murphy, *The Cajans of Mobile County, Alabama* (Thesis, Searitt College, June, 1935), p. 9.

slave named Reed.[122] Murphy states though, that "Within the last half of the century there has been practically no other new blood added to the racial mixture...."[123] In the 1930s, the MOWA lived principally in three communities: Chastang, Shady Grove and the largest, the Byrd settlement. Today there are other communities, such as Reed's Chapel, McIntosh, Tibbie, Mt. Vernon, Calvertt and others. The Byrd settlement is comprised of about four hundred fifty square miles. The founder was Lem Byrd, aka Captain Red Byrd.

The MOWA considered Blacks inferior to them, and this belief was reciprocated by Blacks who considered them a mongrel race.[124] In the 1930s, the school board in Mobile instructed teachers to send a "Cajan" home if he tried to enroll. One member of the board referred to them as "those black birds." However, "teachers were unable to recognize a Cajan as such by sight and many families who lived in town continued to send their children to white schools...[so] in 1933, a blacklist was prepared, and a copy sent to the principals of white schools in Mobile County."[125] Many of these children had one white parent.

---

122 *Ibid.*, p. 12.
123 *Ibid.*, p. 13.
124 *Ibid.*, p. 21.
125 *Ibid.*, p. 23.

Groups Resisting Racism and Slavery

Most MOWA Choctaws in the 1930s were illiterate. They lived on small farms and worked in the timber industry, hunted, fished and were involved in the making and distribution of homemade alcoholic beverages. They were so isolated from the rest of the world that they considered those who went to prison as well informed, interesting persons and viewed them with pride.[126] A high percentage of the men in the community had been to prison for bootlegging, theft or murder. Homicide among the MOWA people was usually related to old family feuds.[127]

Marriage was almost always to a relative, but the group tried to keep it no closer than fourth cousin. An instance of a white teacher marrying a "Cajan" was disapproved by both the Whites and Indians. The community would no longer accept her as teacher.[128]

Murphy described the MOWA as friendly, superstitious, poor and uneducated. In the 1930s, they had not embraced organized religion but did have religious beliefs. Most weddings were performed by local officials rather than by clergy in churches. The predominant denominations were

---

126 *Ibid.*, p. 27.
127 *Ibid.*, p. 43.
128 *Ibid.*, p. 32.

Catholic, Baptist, Methodist Episcopal and Nazarene. The lifestyle in the 1930s was more oriented toward that of Native Americans than to that of Blacks or Whites. Some men had more than one wife.

Recent information on the MOWA Choctaw shows that they have made great strides in the last forty years by focusing on education for young people. The Civil Rights Movement and laws resulting from it gave them the impetus needed to push for better schools. Furthermore, the state of Alabama recognized the MOWA as a tribe in 1979 and it was incorporated with officers and official offices. In what has become a generic tradition among Twentieth Century tribal communities, their first Pow Wow was held in 1980.[129] Through federal assistance, they now have family housing and a community center. Their reservation has a multipurpose tribal complex with a clinic, recreational facilities, offices, etc.

Repeated petitions to the Bureau of Indian Affairs for official federal recognition as a tribe have been unsuccessful, despite the fact that they have been an organized Indian group from

---

[129] Jacqueline A. Matte, *They Say the Wind is Red* (Montgomery: New South Books, 2002), pp. 150-51. This is an excellent resource book for those interested in the MOWA Choctaws.

the beginning. They were there when Indians were cheated at Dancing Rabbit Creek and when most Indians were forced to go to Oklahoma, yet other Indian groups actively opposed their petition for recognition, not wanting to share the federal pie:

> *In 1991 Sen. Shelby introduced for the third time a bill that would provide federal recognition for the MOWA Choctaw. The Poarch Band of Creeks, Alabama's only federally recognized Indian tribe, opposed the legislation and went so far as to hire historians to refute the MOWA petition, although their chief had encouraged "Indian brotherhood" in 1981 when the Poarch Creeks were seeking federal recognition and needed MOWA support. The Philadelphia, Mississippi, Band of Choctaw who also opposed the legislation hired an anthropologist to refute the MOWA petition.*[130]

The intertribal backstabbing proves once again one of the tenants of this book – *that all people are more alike than they are different*. It is obvious from the writings of Jacqueline Matte, and from the persistent efforts of the MOWA, that they are survivors. They will persist in efforts to get federal recognition, but they will survive whether they get such recognition or not. They are survivors, persisting against

---

130 *Ibid.*, p. 157.

great odds, including Andrew Jackson's past reign of terror and continued exploitation.

Surnames among the group are given below as an item of interest and to provide possible leads for future research:

Allen, Bodiford, Brashears, Bretina, Bru, Bruner, Byrd, Campbell, Chastang, Christian, Colbert, Cole, Covington, Douglas, Eaton, Everett, Fisher, Fotenay, Frazier, Gaines, Gibson, Hollinger, Holm, Hopkins, Howell, Johnson, Johnston, Jordon, Lane, Laurendine, (Londine, Rondine), Loftin, Lofton, Logan, McWane, Miller, Moniac, Murphy, Newbern, Orso, Pargade, Parnell, Patrick, Reed, Rivers, Ryan, Sanderson, Seals, Shepard, Smith, Snow, Starland, Stevenson, Sullivan, Taylor, Timms, Weatherford, Weaver, Webb, White, Wiggin, Wilkerson, Williams, Wind.[131]

THE BIG BLACK BAND OF CHOCTAW, this mixed-blood Indian group were enumerated on the Big Black Lake and River, Choctaw Agency. [Mississippi Territory][132] by

---

131 These names were gleaned from:
Laura Frances Murphy, "Mobile County Cajans," in *Alabama Historical Quarterly*, Vol. 1 No. 1, pp.76-86, 1930.
Laura Frances Murphy, *The Cajans of Mobile County, Alabama* Thesis, Searitt College, June, 1935
Edward T. Price. *Mixed-Blood Populations of the Eastern United States as to Origins, Locations, and Persistence.* (Ph.D. Dissertation: University of California, 1950), p. 50ff.
Jacqueline A. Matte, *They Say the Wind is Red* (Montgomery: New South Books, 2002).
[132] *Choctaw and Chickasaw Early Census Records*, Compiled by Betty Wiltshire, Pioneer Publishing Co., Carrollton, Ms.

Groups Resisting Racism and Slavery

the United States Military in preparations for Indian removals and again in preparation of forced removals. This band of Choctaw resisted every effort to be removed from their homelands. Though some of them had settled into Calcasieu area, and are the founders of the Bearhead Redbones, they notoriously traveled back and forth, as was their nomadic lifestyles. At forced removals, more than 80 families left Mississippi, but only a handful of women, children and the Crowder's seem to have made it to the muster roll at Fort Coffee. Gibson Goings Clan who left with his wife, and children, was not mustard, as well James Goings (1) Clan and Thomas, perhaps Thomas D. Goyens Clan were missing and presumed dead. They are buried in mass at a gravesite near Mayhew Mission, Boggy Mountain Depot, Choctaw Agency.

The Big Black Band, who were forced and late arrivers to the nation were assigned rationings from the already established Choctaw. The Choctaw, rationed themselves, were incensed to share or split their portions of food, clothing, medicine, and bedding. They were assigned truly little, some was rotten food and contaminated bedding, no medicines to speak of and were living a harsh existence on what they had been rationed already. An Indian revolt ensued against the Mixed-blood Big Black Band and many were massacred and or ran away.

A muster was taken a day later, at Fort Coffee where Sukky, wife of Gibson Goings Clan was enumerated head of household and three men and one woman, no children. And, Eli Crowder, husband of Martha Patsy Goings (1) Clan Crowder family. The Crowder's remained in Choctaw Reservation lands in Oklahoma and became important political tribal figures. They visited and their children later intermarried with Gibson Goings lines in Texas. There is more on these families ties and relationships to the Jeremiah and his wife Sarophina Drake Goings (1) Clan, who settled in the San Antonio, Texas area in the forthcoming title, *The Goins Book I* chapter by Gary "Mishiho" Gabehart.

Somehow, a great portion of these men and or boys (Redbones of Louisiana, Mississippi, Oklahoma & Texas) ended up in the western United States Territories in the Wind River region of Wyoming. First settling Fort Bridger, Wyoming along the Green River until the sweet grasses ran out. [133] These men were known as "Squaw Men" and "Mountain Men" popular Hollywood term or moniker, the previous though now considered offensive was what they were called in their times. Some remnants of these mixed-blood men not only mixed with the Native tribal woman, but

---

[133] Fort Bridger is located in Sweetwater County, Wyoming and is about 15 miles NW of Green River.

Groups Resisting Racism and Slavery

also a great portion are remembered among the Basque Sheepherder culture which thrived in the western states. We find their YDNA among; Chief Joseph's Nez Perce Indians at Coleville, Oregon, Reservation: Sizemore & Nickens. Eastern Shoshone and Arapaho we find Nash/Ash and Williams, among the Pine Ridge Sioux we find Nelson and Goings Clan, to date. These men were very colorful characters. They had many wives concurrently, each competing to provide their women and families with the best of everything, furs, horses, weapons, beads, gold, food, and to stock their camps and homes with a haberdashery of trade good inventories and gifts of all kinds etc. Though they were a reckless breed of men, the women were pretty much free to choose, or there are no real tales of "women being kidnapped or carried away." John Y. Nelson, a professed "Squaw Man" and driver of the Deadwood Stagecoach in the Bill Cody Wild West Show; returned two Native wives to their tribal families; one he returned was a Shoshone, and the other one ran away, a Crow Indian. One left her two young sons with him, but he stated, "she was too mean spirited," or something similar. The other, he charged with melancholy.

However, life was not so peachy for these women, though likely easier than most in those times. They processed hides and made clothing and outfitted materials for lodging, moved camps and followed seasonal migrations hunting, trade and trapping paths. They were hardly industrious and in general had multiple husbands themselves. They all worked together, and from what I understand from documented descendant stories [134], an incredibly happy lifestyle though rugged and perilous living at times. Many of these men's legacies[135] still live onto this day, like Jim Bridger and John Y. Nelson, who was called by Bill Cody as "the best liar he ever knew." John wrote a book about his life, though who knows what the truth was, or not?[136] We did locate his male descendants in Arkansas. There are no confirmations between Jim Bridger, and the Redbone Bridger male lineage YDNA but it would be interesting to compare.

---

[134] Snodgrass, Mary Ellen (2015). Settlers of the American West: The Lives of 231 Notable Pioneers. Jefferson, NC: McFarland & Company, Inc.
[135] Humfreville, James Lee (1897). Twenty Years Among Our Savage Indians: A Record of Personal Experiences, Observations, and Adventures Among the Indians of the Wild West. Hartford: Hartford Publishing Company.
[136] Fifty Years On The Trail: The True Story of John Y. Nelson, Frontiersman, Scout, and Guide Paperback – March 16, 2011 by John Y Nelson (Author), Harrington O'Reilly (Author)

Groups Resisting Racism and Slavery

Valentine Garfield Nelson 1836-1918 & **Nancy Varner Nelson** 1839-1915 buried at Good Hope Cemetery, Beauregard Parish, Louisiana.

John Y Nelson "Squaw Man" & **Jennie Lone Wolf** Family daughter to John's left Julia Nelson married Frank C. Goings descendant of Gibson Goings and Sukky/Sokey Big Black Band of Choctaw. Present day Pine Ridge Sioux. Jennie Lone Wolf according to census records was listed as head of her own household & John his own household.

Some were performers in the Bill Cody Wild West Show. They toured the world as Sioux Indian Interpreters and Showmen. Gibson Goings Clan [m. Suk/key, or Sookie] descendants enumerated on the Big Black River, 1832. George Nelson, born in Virginia, a descendant of the Melungeon Nelson/Goins [YDNA] are modern Pine Ridge Sioux Nation, South Dakota. We will follow more closely the history of these men and track their YDNA around the country and into Canada in the upcoming title *Goings Book I & II*. A fascinating tale no doubt but here is the early history of these families.

John Y Nelson's other wife and children Ogallala Sioux.

Groups Resisting Racism and Slavery

The Big Black Band of Choctaw was a sad story. But one example of the harsh realities of survival for some of our families.

The following census records are extracted from the compilation records compiled by Betty Wiltshire, Choctaw and Chickasaw Early Census Records, Armstrong Roll, 1831. I have only listed those living along the Big Black here.

Old Choctaw Agency

E side Big Black on Bul-look-cha-sha Creek 1831
Charles Durant, James Gipson

Wolf Creek, West side Big Black 1831
Garnet E. Nelson, George Nelson, Isaac Nelson, Eaton Nelson, Blount Nelson, Solomon Nelson, (east side) Robert Cole, (west side) Coleman Cole, Simon Fraser, (west side) Jefferson Sexton, Davie Sexton, (south side) Wallace, Charles Bacon, (@Shaum-tok-ha-la Village) Susan Carns, John Pikins (Perkins), William Black, George Presley, Samuel McGowen (Goyens Clan), Mousa McKinney widow, Robert McKinney, (@Oak chi ah Kecah-tah-le-yah Creek) Gibson Gowen, William Taylor, James Choat, Charles Durant, Billy Duel, (@Bul-look-chah-sha Creek, E. side BB[137])Eli Crowden (Crowder), Jack Crowden (Crowder), Amos Wilson, Lua Wilson, (@Bul-look-chah-sha Creek, E.

---

[137] Big Black

side BB) Thomas Ward, Mrs Ward, James Cobb, (@Long Creek E., side BB) Edon Ward, Adam, Pierre Durant, Leroy Griggs, James Gibson, John Cooper, Benjamin Bacon, Issac Baptin, Isaac Baptin/Basstin, John R Lynch

W. Big Black

North to South on Kecah-tah-le-yah Creek 1832

Gipson Gowen 4 members,
Williams Taylor 6 members, 1 mo16, 4 mfu10. He is probably the same Wm Taylor that married a daughter of the Choctaw headman Jeremiah Carney who later filed a law suit in Superior Court Mississippi Territory against him for the return of his land.

In hast of the arrival of the White American government, Carney signed over his land to his son-in-law Wm Taylor, who shortly then removed to Texas. When Mississippi became a U.S. Territory, Jeremiah realized that the White laws prevented Indians from owning land. He put his holdings into the name of his son-in-law Wm Taylor. The attorney for Jeremiah said that he did not speak English, and at appointments appeared at his office with a large group of Indian headmen and interpreters who also paid him well for his time. He also paid for the education of Samuel Gibson who married his sister, and who settled the slave trade and Port Gibson, Mississippi. Though Jeremiah pursued his son in law, Wm Taylor and his daughter into Texas through the court system to recover his land; Carney died before the land was restored to him. Eventually, the land was awarded to Carney's wife, and then subsequently taken back by the

Groups Resisting Racism and Slavery

courts, as female and Indians were forbidden land ownership at all.

Old Chickasaw Nation

1839 census Chickasaw Nation Census

John Gains, Nancy Guinn, Charles Gibson, Cooper, John Lewis, Mrs. Pettigrew, Jim Porter, Rutha James, Harry Fraiser, Rachel Davis, Eliza Collins, Gilbert Collins, William Key, Levi Thomas, Wy o Key, James McCoy, Edmund Pickins, Samuel Moore, Joel Kemp, Dyer, Rufus Lowry.

Eli N. and Patsy Goings (1) Clan Crowder's family are also enumerated on Bul-look-chah-sha Creek, E. side of Big Black. Their family members totaled nine, with two males over sixteen, four males and females under ten years old, one slave. Their closest neighbors included: Jack Crowder, Amos Wilson, Thomas, Mrs., and Edon Ward. [138]

An affidavit, which was subsequently given during the court case of Robert Goins vs. Choctaw Nation, by witnesses who knew the Jeremiah (Phillip[1]) Goings (1) Clan lines intimately, includes the story of James, "Gip" and Phillip Goins, as follows.

---

[138] Choctaw and Chickasaw Early Census Records, Compiled by Betty Wiltshire. pg. 44.

**The Affidavit of Patsy Hall
Indian Territory.**

Southern Judicial District} Before me, C.G. Kean, a Notary Public within and for the Southern District of District of the Indian Territory personally appeared Mrs. Patsy Hall, who, after being by me duly sworn deposed and says:

That affiant was born in the state of Mississippi, at Little River, in the year 1835; that affiant is a daughter of Tom Martin and Mary Martin; that her mother's maiden name was Mary Fry and that her said mother was a full-blooded Choctaw Indian; that the name of affiants mothers father was Bill Fry. Affiant further states that when she was a small child that she came that she came with her said parents from the state of Mississippi to a place on Kiamishi river, in the Choctaw Nation Indian Territory, about 8 miles south of Doaksville (a trading point established after affiants family reached said point) that her said parents settled at said point on the Kiamishi river, and remained there until affiant was quite a large girl when she and her parents removed from the place on Kiamishi to Mayhew Mission, near Boggy Creek in the Choctaw Nation, where we lived about two years when affiants mother, whilst on a visit to her sister on Kiamishi river died.

At the time of death of affiant's father, as above stated, he left surviving him five children, viz: Louise, Beckie, Isabella, Clarissa, and this affiant, Patsy. Affiant states that amount the number who accompanied her father and family from Mississippi to the Kiamishi river was a man named *Gip Goins* and *wife [Sukey]*, and a man named *James Goins* were halfblooded Choctaw Indians and were always recognized as members of the tribe of Choctaw Indians: That said James and Gip Goins died and were buried near Mayhew in the Choctaw Nation. Affiant further states that her brother and all her sisters-affiants' brothers and sisters are now dead. Affiant states that she lived on the Kimishi river until she married Perry Hall, when she and her husband moved to the Chickasaw Nation.

Affiant further states that while she and her family were living near Mayhew that Jerry or **Jeremiah Goins**, came from Texas to visit **James** and **Gip Goins** ; That she affiant was personally well acquainted with Robert Goins, who now lives near Owl in the Choctaw Nation and knows that the said Robert Goins is the legitimate son of said Jeremiah Goins and knows that the sad Robert Goins is a one fourth Choctaw Indian by blood.

Witness

                Chas. Winter.   Signed Her X Patsy Hall

Subscribed and sworn to before me this the 10th day of August, 1896 and I further certify that I am acquainted with the said Patsy Hall and saw her sign the foregoing statement. In testimony whereof witness my hand and seal of of-fice, at Wynnewood, Ind. Ter. This the 10th day of August 1896.

        (Signed)   Cyrus G. Kean.
   (Seal) Notary Public Southern
   Judicial District of the Indian Territory.

The Muster Roll Taken after forced removal and Indian uprising (massacre).

I certify on honor that the foregoing is a correct roll of the party which was landed at Fort Coffee this morning and for which the contractors for removing Choctaws are entitled to compensation as per contract with the War Department.

William Wilson
Issuing Commissary
June 10th, 1847.

No	Names of heads of Family	Men	Women	Children	Total
1	Eli W. Crowder	1	1	6	8
2	Charles Bench	1	1	2	4
3	Henry C. D. Massy	2	11	52	8
4	William Jones	1	1	14	1
5	Ah hook lachr	2	1	2	4
6	Jackson	11	1	2	3
7	James McCans wife	1	2	1	1
8	An to na	4	1	1	5
9	Pipa la ho ka	1	1		4
10	Chuffa tubbee	12	1	2	6
11	Nuk ah na cha	1	2	1	6
12	Emah a chi tubbee	2	1	5	3
13	Ah loh ma tubbee	1	1	3	2
14	Hannah	1	1		4
15	Co mon tah ho nah	1	1	2	4
16	Poh sha to nubbee	1	1		7
17	Emath la chubbee	1	11	2	6
18	Kann pa tubbee		1		2
19	Ish to ma nubbee	1	1	1	4
20	Loh ma chubbee		1		2
21	Bottish	3	1	43	1
22	Tik e tin tubbee	1			4
23	Sukky	3	1		1
24	John Hardaway	1	6		2
25	Lucy McEwen	1			1
26	Mak a too na	35	32		1
27	Ho bah ta cha				3
28	Pah lun tubbee				3
29	Hartwell Hardaway				9
	Simpson Colbert				1

120

| 30 | Mary | Sims | | | 1 |
| 31 | Total | | | | 110 |

THE MELUNGEONS are perhaps the closest mixed blood group, both culturally and genetically to the Redbones. Their origins are, like that of the Redbones, shrouded in mystery. The two groups are similar in lifestyle and certain customs; both claim to be descended from Portuguese and Indians and there is considerable overlap of surnames. The name "Melungeon" was as odious to them as "Redbone" was to the South Carolina and Louisiana people to whom the name was applied. In recent times, the term Melungeon has been largely stripped of its negative meaning and it is now used with pride.

The origin of the term Melungeon is unknown, but this obscurity, as usual, leads to speculation. A common theory is that it came from the French *mélange*, meaning mixture. Another is that it derived from the Green *melan* meaning dark, or from *melungo*, Afro-Portuguese, meaning shipmate or companion.

One of the most logical explanations was given by French Dr. Celestin Pierre Cambiaire:

The word "Melungeon" is evidently a slight transformation of the French word, "Melangeon"...The French came into Tennessee a long time before the English...Some trappers or traders must have given the name of Melangeons to the descendants of a few white men and Indians, who originated the strange race of people now lost among descendants of the first American pioneers. As Melangeons from the French word, melanger, means mixed-breed, and as these people have English surnames, and speak old-time English, they certainly have English ancestry. [139]

The history of Melungeons is intertwined with that of Redbones. They, too, settled in the southeastern United States, shared the same general time frame and shared many surnames and customs. They were, as were Redbones, isolated from the dominant society. Like Redbones, they also claimed descent from the "Portygee" (Portuguese), their skin color was copper or dark, and their eyes dark and sometimes gray or blue.

---

139 Celestin Pierre Cambiarie, Ph. D., *Western Virginia Mountain Ballads, The Last Stand of American Pioneer Civilization* (London: The Mitre Press, 1935), pp. 4-6, as given in Bible's *Melungeons: Yesterday and Today*, pp. 11-12. Bible's summary of the origin of the name Melungeon is one of the best found.

Groups Resisting Racism and Slavery

The group first identified as Melungeons were a few mixed-blood families located on Newman's Ridge in what is now Hancock County, in extreme northeast Tennessee. The earliest known use of the term discovered by author Jack Goins was in the 1813 minutes of the Stony Creek Church.[140] Goins traced these early families from Virginia to Newman's Ridge. He commented:

"Trailing Charles Gibson helps to establish and properly identify the migration of the Melungeons, which began in the 1720s for the John Bunch and Gilbert Gibson children, Paul Bunch and Gideon Gibson families, and the 1730s for the Thomas Collins, Thomas Gibson and several other families."[141]

Author Pat Elder concluded after thirty years of study, that only two families made up the core Melungeon families – Collins and Gibson.[142] Others disagree with her conclusion.

---

140 Jack Goins, *Melungeons: And Other Pioneer Families*, NP, 2000, p. 9.
141 *Ibid.*, P. 86.
142 Pat Spurlock Elder, *Melungeons: Examining an Appalachian Legend* (Blountville: Continuity Press, 1999), p. 201ff.

A Melungeon Family

The interest that has been building for the last few years toward an understanding of who the Melungeons are, peaked in 1994 when Brent and Robyn Kennedy published *The Melungeons: The Resurrection of a Proud People*. The Kennedys built on work by Ball, Bible and others, but they also broke new ground.[143] Publication of this work generated interest, both positive and negative. Brent Kennedy received threats against his life, criticism from some of his peers and praise from a host of admirers. The Kennedy book suffers from some inaccuracies and lack of documentation (See DeMarce), but its main purpose was to create interest and further research on Melungeons, and it did. *The National*

---

143 N. Brent. Kennedy, and Robyn Kennedy, Vaughn, *The Melungeons: The Resurrection of a Proud People* (Macon: Mercer University Press, 1994, Revised 1997).

Groups Resisting Racism and Slavery

Genealogical Society Quarterly joined the debate by publication of a review of the Kennedy book by Virginia E. DeMarce.[144] The review was overly critical of Brent Kennedy personally and of his book. While many of her criticisms were justified, some were not, and feelings ran high when the NGSQ refused to run the Kennedy response, and even higher when it published a statement that Kennedy had failed to make a response.

In *The Melungeons: The Resurrection of a Proud People*, Kennedy recognized that Melungeons were the product of white Europeans, Blacks and Indians, but he went further, trying especially to identify their earlier "offshore" roots. Further, he sought to broaden the definition of who is a Melungeon to include a large portion of the "mixed blood" population. DeMarce, on the other hand, took an opposite approach. She focused on the more recent history involving a few families of mixed blood, rejecting Kennedy's attempt to tie Melungeons to Turks, Berbers, Portuguese, Moors, Jews, and Iberians.[145]

---

144 Virginia Easley DeMarce, "Review Essay: The Melungeons" in *National Genealogical Society Quarterly*, Vol. 84, No. 2, June 1996, pp. 134-149.
145 In 1982, two petroglyphs in West Virginia came to the attention of archaeologist Robert L. Pyle. He contacted Ida Jan Gallagher and Berry, an expert in epigraphy who studied the site and the ancient messages

Author Pat S. Elder, in her book *Melungeons: Examining An Appalachian Legend*, agreed with the DeMarce approach, asserting that only those who are descended from the original group on Newman's Ridge and the surrounding territory were Melungeons. Perhaps a reflection of the level of feeling generated by the DeMarce/Kennedy dispute is that Elder ignored the Kennedy book. *The Melungeons: The Resurrection of a Proud People* is not even in the bibliography included in her book, nor are the books by Ball and Bible upon which Kennedy relied.[146]

---

found there. Fell, who apparently did not visit the site, interpreted the writings to contain messages in ancient Irish languages as well as Iberian. He believed the writings dated to sometime between 600-800 AD. Fell, now deceased, was a controversial figure who challenged the historical and archaeological establishment position that only Native Americans predated Columbus' discovery of America. Mira presents a view that Portuguese influence should not be easily written off. He presents the Celtics as barbarian tribes who spoke the ancient Irish language and who settled the Iberian Peninsula (Spain and Portugal). See also:
Barry Fell, "Christian Messages in Old Irish Script Deciphered from Rock Carvings in West Virginia", *Wonderful West Virginia* (Charleston: State of West Virginia Department of Natural Resources, March 1983).
Robert L. Pyle "A Message from the Past" in *Wonderful West Virginia* (Charleston: State of West Virginia Department of Natural Resources, March 1983).
Ida Jane Gallagher "Light Dawns on West Virginia History" in *Wonderful West Virginia* (Charleston: State of West Virginia Department of Natural Resources, March 1983).
Mira, Manuel, *The Forgotten Portuguese: The Melungeons and Other Groups* (Franklin: Portuguese American Historical Research Foundation, 1998), p. 127.
146 Anyone wishing to explore their possible Melungeon ancestry should read the Kennedy/Elder books, both of which accomplish their

Groups Resisting Racism and Slavery

Evelyn McKinley Orr joined the discussion writing for the Gowen Foundation. She said:

Scholars and researchers willing to look past the narrow scope of the nationalities known to have been in the colonies, joined with Dr. Kennedy to take a wider look for unanswered questions. What was happening in the World that could have brought dark skinned peoples from the Middle East, Mediterranean, Southern Europe to the colonies by accident or design?[147]

The upshot of the controversy between Kennedy and his supporters and DeMarce and her supporters is that research on a broader base has emerged and continues to emerge, the strife and ill feelings notwithstanding.

Space does not allow a thorough presentation of all the theories of the origin of the Melungeons, but some are identified, and others discussed briefly below.

The first and most often-stated claim of Melungeons is the one they have heard passed on through their oral traditions –

---

goals and have something valuable to contribute. They should also read the books by Jack Goins, Jim Calahan, Jean Bible, Mattie Ruth Johnson and Bonnie Ball and the articles by Virginia DeMarce – all referenced in the Bibliography.

147 Evelyn McKinley Orr, "The Origin of Name Melungeon – Wider World Views", in *Gowen Research Foundation Electronic Newsletter*, September 2000, Vol. 3 No. 9, p. 2.

they were "Portygee" – Portuguese. Manual Mira in *The Forgotten Portuguese*, explored the role of the Portuguese in the early settlement of North America. That they were a world class sea power and had an exploring will is without doubt. Mira reminds us once again of their policy of secrecy with regard to their explorations. The Portuguese were, perhaps, the best navigators in the world in the 15th century. They made twenty private explorations to the west between 1419 and 1433 but little is known about what they found. Passing secrets of voyages to the Spanish or others was punishable by death.[148] Thus, we are deprived of much of the hard evidence needed to establish a descent of the Melungeons and Redbones from the Portuguese. A careful reading of *The Forgotten Portuguese* suggests that the Redbones and Melungeons may not have been just trying to deny Black heritage, as many Portuguese were an amalgamation that included Africans. Eloy Gallegos stated it clearly: "Just as the United States is often referred to as the "melting pot" of North American, so was the Iberian Peninsula [Spain and Portugal] the melting pot of Europe...."[149]

---

148 Mira, *op. cit.*, pp. 142-43.
149 Eloy Gallegos, The Spanish Pioneers in United States History: The Melungeons (Knoxville: Villagra Press, 1997), p.71.

Groups Resisting Racism and Slavery

Many theories have been proposed around the claims that there were pre-Columbian European or Euro-Asian visitors to the New World including Phoenicians, Carthaginians, Celts, Welsh, Basques, Turks, Jews, Africans, Moors and others. There are other theories related to the Lost Colony of Roanoke (Croatans), Prince Madoc and his Welsh settlers (the supposed progenitors of the blue-eyed Indians), the Santa Elena expeditions of Juan Pardo, the incursion of Scots into the southeast and Gypsies from Europe.[150] Aware of such divergent theories, the Melungeon's created, in 1997, a nonprofit organization the purpose of which is:

"...to document and preserve the heritage and cultural legacy of mixed-ancestry peoples in or associated with the southern Appalachians. While our focus will be on those of Melungeon heritage, we will not restrict ourselves to honoring only this group. We firmly believe in the dignity of all such mixed ancestry groups of southern Appalachia and commit to preserving this rich heritage of racial harmony and diversity that years of legalized racism is almost annihilated from our history and memory."[151]

---

150 James G. Leyburn, *The Scotch-Irish: A Social History* (Chapel Hill: University of North Carolina Presss, 1962), pp. 327ff.
151 Taken from the Melungeon website Home Page at http://melungeon.org

The goals of the association are to:

1. Set up a "clearinghouse" of Melungeon-related information and an archive of such materials,
2. Facilitate future Melungeon gatherings and events,
3. Make research and information about the Melungeon's and other similar groups available to the general public,
4. Become a central exchange registry for mixed-ancestry groups in the southern Appalachians whereby an exchange of relevant information and documents can occur.[152]

The latest development in the Melungeon research effort is a DNA study conducted through the University of Virginia at Wise, Virginia by Dr. Kevin Jones. He presented his findings at the fourth annual meeting of the Melungeon Heritage Association at Kingsport, Tennessee on June 21, 2002. Jones reported the results of one hundred maternal DNA samples collected from persons of known Melungeon ancestry and twenty samples from the male lineage. The results show that Melungeons are a self-defining population. They are not a narrowly defined group genetically. The twenty samples

152 Ibid.

Groups Resisting Racism and Slavery

from the male lineage reveal a widely diverse range – wider than for all of the hundreds of samples taken in England. The maternal samples reveal three groups as follows:

- African (including African Americans), 5 percent
- Native Americans, 5 percent
- Eurasian, 85 percent.

Of the 85 percent, 5 percent are a combination of sequences found frequently in Turks and Siddis from India. Dr. Jones concluded that one can make of the results what one wishes to, however, there is no DNA sequence that says you are a Melungeon. The Eurasians are from "just about every place that is not Asia or the Americas," certainly not just northern Europe. Also included in the definition of Eurasia, are Middle Eastern and Mediterranean countries. Kennedy, Orr, and others have been saying for some time that Melungeon heritage included these countries. Was that what the old tradition that "we are Portygee" was trying to tell us?[153] The DNA study does not answer specific genealogical questions related to individual families. (See Attachment C for a list of Melungeon related surnames).

---

153 From notes taken while attending the presentation of Osborne, J. H. "Researcher: Melungeons "Self Defining", *Kingsport Times – News* June 21, 2002.

Melungeons have identified several physical characteristics that are believed to aid in identification. It should be noted however that none of these items is exclusive to Melungeons. There might be a tendency for Melungeons to have these characteristics more frequently than other groups, but this has not been documented. A study of the relationship of these characteristics to ethnic groups including Melungeons, Native Americans and Redbones would be interesting.

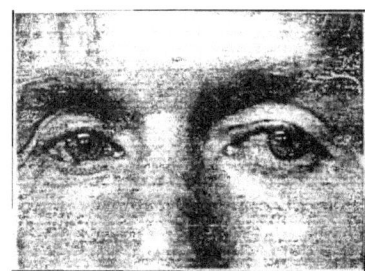

Asian Eyefold

HAPPY YOUNG MELUNGEONS.

Groups Resisting Racism and Slavery

Six fingers or Six Toes. The phenomenon of children born with six fingers or six toes is thought by Kennedy and others to be more frequent among Melungeons than other groups in America. Anecdotal evidence suggests that it may indeed be true for Melungeons and Redbones, but no study has been done that substantiates it. The phenomenon has ancient and intriguing roots. The Bible records an early reference.

And there was again war at Gath, where there was a man of great stature, who had six fingers on each hand and six toes on each foot, twenty-four in number; and he also was descended from the giants.[154]

Fragments of a six-toed human interred about 9000 years ago have been excavated near Jericho. And clay statues with six toes have been excavated from the same site.[155] Evidence of people with these extra digits is found in Egypt, Africa, the Pyrenees Mountains and in North America. Gloria Farley has recorded petroglyphs (recordings on rocks) in Colorado, Utah, New Mexico and Oklahoma that depict people with the extra digit.[156] Ms. Farley also records an account by Ted

---

154 *The Holy Bible*, Revised Standard Version, 1 Chronicles 20:6
155 *The Oklahoma United Methodist Contact*, Vol. 130, Number 32, January 13, 1984, as quoted by Farley in, *In Plain Sight*, p. 323.
Richard D. Barnett "Polydactlism in the Ancient World", *Biblical Archaeology Review*, Vol. 16 Number 3, May-June 1990, pp. 46-51.
156 Gloria Farley, *In Plain Sight: Old World Records in Ancient America* (Columbus: ISAC Press, 1994), pp. 323-327.

Barker, a WWII soldier who, while searching for a downed plane in 1945 in the Pyrenees Mountains (the land of the Basques), found himself in an isolated village inhabited entirely by people with six fingers, six toes or both. Barker learned that in ancient times in Europe, people with extra digits were believed to be witches, devil possessed or to have special powers. From time to time, they were brought to the valley that had limited ingress and egress and were not allowed to leave. They called themselves the "Mal Venue" and the valley was known as Valley of the Mal Venue. By necessity, there was much inbreeding among the inhabitants, so most offspring had extra digits. Those who were born with no extra digits were allowed to leave, and most did so.[157] Mooney commented on a six-toed figure of a human foot carved into rock found at Track Rock Gap, Georgia.[158]

Asian Shovel Teeth. There is a ridge behind the first four teeth, both upper and lower, on persons who have shovel teeth. By placing the fingernail at the gum line and moving it up or down, one can make a slight clicking sound. The back of the teeth curve outward. This trait is present in many

---

157 *Ibid.*, p. 330.
158 James Mooney, *History, Myths and Sacred Formulas of the Cherokees* (Asheville: Historical Images, 1992), p. 419.

persons with Asian or Native American heritage, while others have straight teeth.

Anatolian Bump or Asian Cranial Ridge. The Anatolian Bump is a protrusion about the size of a marble sliced in half, located on the back of the head at the centerline just above where the head joins the vertebrae. Similarly, the *Central Asian Cranial Ridge* is an enlarged ridge across the back of the head that crosses where the head joins the neck. (If the Anatolian Bump is not present, the ridge might be if the individual has Anatolian heritage.) It is argued that only people whose ancestors lived in the Anatolian region of Turkey or Central Asia have the ridge or bump. No study has been found that documents this claim.

Asian Eyefold (Epicanthic eyefold). At the inner or outer corners of the eye, the upper lid attaches lower than the lower lid causing the upper lid to overhang the lower one. This creates a sleepy-eyed look. Some Native Americans have the Asian eyefold, and consequently some that are Native American mixed have it also.

Mongolian Spots. These are "birthmark" like spots that appear on babies and usually disappear in a few months or years. They might occur in any group but more frequently in certain populations such as Asian, Native American and Black babies.

Cherokee Streak. This is a gray spot or patch appearing in the hair, usually in the front, near the forehead, at an early age. This phenomenon occurs more frequently in females than in males.

Melungeons have also identified certain diseases that are common among them. It should be noted, however, that as with the physical characteristics discussed above, none of these items are exclusive to Melungeons. There could be a tendency for them to have these diseases more frequently than other groups, but this has not been documented in anything approaching a scientific study. Physical characteristics and diseases are of interest and may serve as a clue for further study and research.

DISEASES and conditions common to Melungeons are: Sarcoidosis, Bechet's Syndrome, Macado-Joseph's Disease, Lactose Intolerance, Thalassemia, Familial Mediterranean Fever, Reiter's Syndrome and Ulcerative Colitis.[159] A study of the relationship between the various ethnic groups and

---

159 Taken from Nancy Sparks Morrison at the Melungeon website Home Page at http://melungeon.org

these diseases might be helpful in diagnosis, prevention and treatment.

W.A. PLECKER, M.D., the state of Virginia's first Registrar of Vital Statistics, waged a mean-spirited bureaucratic paper war against mixed-blood populations in that state in the mid-1900s, in which he took particular aim at Melungeons. He was invited to speak to, or present papers to professional and governmental groups as early as the 1920s. In recent times, Melungeon researcher, Ms. S. J. Arthur, found letters he wrote in his official capacity as Registrar. These letters show some of the prejudice that mixed-blood people experienced in the United States in the 20th century. (A sampling of these letters and the text of one of his public speeches are included in Attachment D.)

BRASS ANKLES have much in common with Redbones, though there are cultural differences. Enrique Gildemeister included the Brass Ankles in a 1977 study he did of mixed-blood groups in South Carolina. He reported that there were three groups of Brass Ankles living near each other in the vicinity of Charleston, South Carolina, and there were other such groups throughout the state. He found that they lived apart from the larger society in small family groups and were not organized into groups with a formal structure. They are

White, Indian and Black mixed. Brass Ankles, in his study, tended to be associated with people in their own group who were of a similar shade, to the exclusion of those who were darker. They were being absorbed into the larger society through marriage.[160] Gildemeister found that white society was aware of this absorption phenomenon but was reluctant to discuss it openly. There had been so much mixing that it was difficult to determine who was and wasn't of mixed blood. In his opinion, this reluctance to confront the mixing issue constituted a compromise, or suspension, of the One-Drop Rule, which is implicitly still in vogue.

Author Brewton Berry discussed the possible origins of the name Brass Ankle, which is, like the names Melungeon and Redbones, a mystery name. One popular explanation of how they got the name is that they wore pants that were above the ankle, exposing a tan or brass-colored ankle. Another is that they descended from a boatload of white slaves that had been brought into the area and were restrained by brass chains attached to their ankles. Another version is that they wore

---

160 Enrique Eugene, Gildemeister, *Local Complexities of Race in the Rural South: Racially Mixed People in South Carolina*, (Thesis: State University of New York, June 1977), pp. 41-42.

Groups Resisting Racism and Slavery

brass anklets as a mark of their caste.[161] Yet, another version is that they were metal workers working with brass.

Some common surnames among the Brass Ankles are: Boone (could be some truth to the term "Red Boones" for (Redbones), Braveboy, Bunch, Chavis, Criel, Driggers, Goins, Goings, Harmon, Jackson, Russell, Sammons, Scott, Shavis, (Chavis), Sweat, Swett, Williams.[162] Thus, it is evident that the thread of common names between mixed-blood groups continues into the group known as Brass Ankles, creating possible links to Redbones.

THE TURKS of South Carolina are said to be related to the Redbones. Wes D. White, Jr., writing a report for the Smithsonian Institution in 1975, has provided a short history of these people. Turks live near Sumter, South Carolina.[163]

The White report refers to a petition submitted by Abel

---

161 Brewton Berry, *Almost White: A Study of Certain Racial Hybrids in the Eastern United States* (New York: Macmillan, 1963), pp. 38-39.
162 Kennedy, *op. cit.*, p. 172.
163 Wes D. White, Jr., *A History of the Turks Who Live in Sumter County, South Carolina, From 1805-1972* (Written for the Smithsonian Institution, Washington, D. C., 1975. Located in the Sumter County Genealogical Society Library, Sumter, South Carolina). This is from a draft copy of the manuscript.

Conder and Mahemut in Arabick (sic) to the authorities in 1753. The petition is as follows:

May it please your Excellency

Your most humble petitioners Abel Conder and Mahemut are of a place called Sally [Sali – a city in Morocco] born subjects to the state, who have long had the honor & happiness of being at amity with the Crown of Great Britain, beg leave to prostrate ourselves before your Excellency in the most submissive manner, and acquaint your Excellency that about 15 years ago we together with about 50 of our countrymen, being soldiers, were commanded to patrol in the neighborhood of a place called Maguson, belonging to the King of Portugal, to act hostilities against them, being at war with them.

And it was our unhappy fate to lose a battle and be taken prisoner of war by the Portuguize, who led us captives into Magason where we remained about three months, when Captain Henry Daubrig came amongst us and enquired if we were willing to serve him 5 years in Carolina on condition of his purchasing or obtaining our freedom from the Portuguize.

And the petitioners were the only two that accepted his offer, and accordingly came with him into this captivity; where instead of 5 years we have served him and Mr. Daniel Larouche 15 years, serving in all things as though we were real slaves, and treated no other than the negroes are.

Groups Resisting Racism and Slavery

We have often humbly demanded our liberty but cannot attain it. And instead of any prospect of liberty, we understand that we are very shortly to be sold at Public Sale with Mr. Larouche's negroes. We must submissively fall down and prostrate ourselves before your Excellency, pray for your most gracious protection, and with the utmost humility submit ourselves and our most miserable circumstances to your Excellency's most sublime goodness. And may the Almighty God guide your Excellency, is the fervent prayer of your lowest servants.

Abel Conder & Mahamt[164]

Those Carolinians known as "Sundry Free Moors" filed another petition to the House of Representatives in 1790s. A report of it follows:

A petition was presented to the House from sundry free moors, (subjects of the Emperor of Morocco, and residents of this state) praying that in case they should commit any fault amenable to be brought to justice, that they (as subjects to a Prince in alliance with the United States) be tried under the same laws as the citizens of this state, and would not be liable to be tried...under the negro (sic) acts....[165]

---

164 *Council Journal,* No. 21, pages 298-299, (March 3rd, 1753), S.C. Archives. As referenced in White's account. Spelling and punctuations are as found.
165 *House of Representatives Journals 1789-1790,* Part Two, pages 92-93, 107, S.C. Archives. January 20th, 1790. As presented in White, p. 1.

The petition was referred to a committee and the House agreed with the committee report that they should not be tried as slaves.

Thus, it was established that citizens of Morocco were in South Carolina and that their status as free citizens were denied or in jeopardy. White believed that present-day Turks descended from the two who petitioned the Crown in 1753. This group can be traced back to Joseph Benenhaley (Joseph Benegeli or Ben "Ali" – anglicized to Benenhaley) who married Elizabeth Miller around 1800. The couple show up on the 1810 census. White originally believed that Joseph was from Turkey but later concluded that he was likely a son or grandson of one of the 1753 petitioners. In the 1820 census, they were listed as White. In 1810, there were seven people in the Benenhaley family and, by 1972, there were 500 people in the community.[166] They have two churches, Long Branch Baptist and Spring Bank Baptist. The Long Branch church split, forming a second Baptist church, Spring Bank Baptist. As former Sumter Mayor and local avocational historian, W. A. McElveen, Jr. said of this split, "You can't get more American than that." Most Turks are Democrats, Baptist and small farmers or work at Shaw Air Force Base.

166 White, *op. cit.*, pp. 2-4.

Groups Resisting Racism and Slavery

Shaw AFB is made up partly of land purchased from the Turks. They live on Hwy 441 near Stateburg and Dalzell, South Carolina, near Shaw Air Force Base.

In 1969, Calvin Trillin writing about the Turks in *The New Yorker Magazine*, stated that:

Before the Second World War, Turks married almost exclusively within their community...a rural people with their own church and school...Their neighbors knew them as poor people who were usually law-abiding and who loved to hunt and fish and who distrusted outsiders.[167]

An unsigned newspaper article in *The State,* dated March 18, 1928, praised the Turks as a law-abiding group. The children were described as eager and capable of learning, coming from homes where cleanliness and good morals prevailed, and:

They are not aggressive and seem to accept their lot in life with truly Eastern fatalism...[but] the most conspicuous characteristic of all, however, is their utter lack of spontaneous joy. They wear, one and all, the air of patient and unquestioning acceptance of life as they find it.[168]

---

167 Calvin Trillin, "U.S. Journal: Sumter County, S.C. – Turks" *The New Yorker Magazine*, March 8, 1969, pp. 104-105.
168 White, *op. cit.*, pp. 42-43.

The State article continues:

"...*The oldest living member of the tribe, Mary Ann Benenhaley Oxendine, 86, daughter of Joseph Benenhaley 2nd, and granddaughter of the first Joseph, has blue eyes, dark skin and straight white hair. She says her grandmother, wife of the first Joseph, was a white woman named Miller, and her own mother was a Scott...She married a man named Oxendine, her first cousin, whose mother was also a Scott. Oxendine's father, she says, came from North Carolina.*"

The writer of the above article would likely have been surprised when in the 1950s, they sued for admittance to white schools. Their aggressiveness and persistence paid off when they won the battle and were admitted to white schools.[169]

Trillin, in the article referenced above, related that Muhuttin Guven, Turkish member of Parliament, on a State Department tour in 1963, stopped by Sumter to pay a visit to the South Carolina Turks. He reportedly had a fine time and thought the Turks were Maltese while his interpreter believed they were from North America, which was part of the Ottoman Empire.[170]

---

169 *Ibid.*, pp. 47-48.
170 *Ibid.*, p. 53.

Groups Resisting Racism and Slavery

On a recent visit to this community, it was noted that the cemetery at Long Branch Baptist Church is well-kept – a practice that seems to be in keeping with the cemeteries of many other mixed-blood peoples, the poor condition of the Redbone Cemetery in Sumter notwithstanding.[171]

Some of the names associated with the Turks are Benenhaley (with its various spellings), Oxendine, Wray, Buckner, Scott and Hood.

Family and relatives of **Noah and Rosa Benenhaley**

---

171 Thanks to former Mayor, W. A. McElveen, Jr. for his invaluable assistance in locating the community and providing information and background on the Redbones and Turks whom he considers a real asset to the Sumter community. Scott Withrow assisted in every way he could in gathering and discussing the information found.

descendants of Joseph Benenhaley.

A Typical Turk
Photo Brewton Berry

THE SMILING INDIANS arose out of the struggles of the North Carolina Lumbee for an independent identity. Smiling Indians were those rejected by the Lumbee. Among the Redbones of Sumter County, South Carolina, was a family of Indians with the surname Smiling, and another of Goins. Three Goins brothers from Sumter County initiated legal actions that resulted in the creation of the group known as the Smiling Indians. (For more on the Smiling and Goins families, see Chapter 7 of this book). The brothers who were born and reared in Sumter County, moved to Robeson County, North Carolina, in 1907 and attempted to enroll their children in the Indian Normal School where their sister had

Groups Resisting Racism and Slavery

attended. This sister, Fannie Chavis, was a teacher in the Indian graded school in the county. When the brother's children were denied admittance, the Goins brothers went to court and won.

In order to win the case, the Goins took it to the Supreme Court. An excerpt from the testimony of W. W. Goins, one of the three brothers, gives historical information on the family.

> *I am a brother of W. D. Goins. Was born and raised in Sumter County, S. C. My mother is there. I have been living in Robeson County, N. C. for the past eight years. I have one child of school age...Dr. Furman traced up our origin and found out that we – our parents went from North Carolina, some of the older ones, and there were a lot of names, Oxendine, Hunt, Chavis and Goins. Names of the families in the Indian colonies down there were Smilings, Chavis, Goins, the Oxendines are dead. Old Bill Chavis was my great-grandfather went from this [Robeson] county. Tom and Bill Chavis came from Robeson and old man Goins came from Cumberland County. My wife's name was Pauline Epps. Her father was Edward Epps and her mother was Adeline Epps. Her mother was supposed to be half white and half Indian (sic).*[172]

172 Gerald M. Sider, Lumbee Indian Histories: Race,

The response of the school board to the loss of the case was to build a separate school for the Smilings. With this development, they became an identified and separate group living a rather isolated existence. By 1960, with the disappearance of their special school, the Smiling Indians were no longer seen as a distinct people.[173]

Sider, commenting on the origins of the Smiling Indians, related that:

> *While Smiling origins lie deep in the colonial period, in the same firestorms and cauldrons that gave birth to the Lumbee...as distinct peoples, their social emergence as a distinct people in the Robeson County [North Carolina] started with a school admission case in 1915.*[174]

BLACK DUTCH is another mystery word. Many Redbones and Melungeons have often heard that they were related to the Black Dutch. There is much that is perplexing about this elusive term. The origins of the term Black Dutch, also known as Pennsylvania Dutch, are not precisely known, but that uncertainty had only fueled the development of theories.

Ethnicity, and Indian Identity in the Southern United States (Cambridge: Cambridge University Press, 1993), p.
173 *Ibid.*, pp. 76-77.
174 Most of the information above on the Smiling Indians came from the account by Sider.

Groups Resisting Racism and Slavery

The speculation on origins ranges from simple to complex. Some of the theories follow.

1. In the 16th century, the Dutch revolted against the Spanish monarch. Spain could not field enough of its own soldiers to defend its interests, so it impressed Portuguese men who fought their battles with the Dutch. Holland lost many men in the battles, and the dominating Spanish and Portuguese soldiers mixed with Dutch women, creating a group of dark-skinned children, the Black Dutch. This popular theory is supported by some and denied by others.
2. Many Germans settled in Pennsylvania. The German word for German is Deutsche, pronounced almost the same as Dutch. Over time, the real identity of the immigrant Germans was lost because the name was corrupted from Deutsche to Dutch. These Germans were small, dark-skinned and dark-eyed people. It has been asserted that they may have come to Pennsylvania from the Black Forest area of Germany.
3. Ian Hancock, in *The Pariah Syndrome*, relates that Germany, wishing to rid its territories of Gypsies as far back as the early 15th century, dumped them in their small colony in Pennsylvania. Most were brought to the German colony as indentured servants

without passports; this meant they had no legal means of returning to Europe.[175] These Gypsies were a dark-skinned people, Deutsche speakers from Germany.

4. Black Dutch were Sephardic Jews from Spain who, fleeing the Spanish Inquisition, married Dutch Protestants to avoid persecution.

5. The Black Dutch were remnants of the lost tribes of Israel.

6. Ozarks folklorist, Gordon McCann, is quoted as speculating that "Black Dutch" might be a derogatory expression labeling German Union troops in the Civil War.[176] McCann, in a telephone interview, said he had no real evidence for this speculation and did not remember making the statement. The German troops who came into the south as part of the Union Army were disliked even by the other Union troops according to McCann.[177]

7. A final theory is that Native Americans and mixed-blood people claimed they were Black Dutch in order to gain acceptance by the dominant white society.

---

175 Ian Hancock, *The Pariah Syndrome* (Partin WebJournal edition, 1999).
176 Los Angeles Times, 1998 as quoted in *Ancestry Home Town Daily* " A Daily   Dose of Genealogy" April 2, 1998.
177 Telephone Interview with Gordon McCann, Aug. 1, 2002.

Groups Resisting Racism and Slavery

They sometimes used the term Black German or Black Irish for the same reasons.[178]

BLACK IRISH is still another mystery term sometimes confused with Black Dutch. "Black Irish" refers to people of Irish descent who have dark hair, and sometimes dark complexion and dark eyes, as opposed to those who have blond or red hair and blue eyes. In America, the very poorest Irish were sometimes known as "Shanty Irish," presumably because they lived in houses known as shanties. Used infrequently in Ireland, these terms may have been started in America.

The Black Irish and Black Dutch are not the same, despite similarities between them. There are overlapping claims of origins between the two groups, but differences exist as well. The major overlapping claims are that the Black Irish, as did the Black Dutch, got their dark color from Spanish invaders or shipwrecked Spanish sailors, or that it was from a mixture acquired during an invasion from the Roman Empire. Laney, in *My Family Traditions: The Sons of Joseph and the Diaspora*, suggests that they may be descended from Manasseh, son of biblical Joseph. He said that in Gaelic, the

---

178 Background material for the Black Dutch included Internet articles by Arlee Gowan, Linda Griggs and Mike Nassau.

Sons of Joseph were called "Dubslaines," meaning the "dark-haired ones of Slaney."[179]

In the 17th century, Irish had poured into the islands of the West Indies by the tens of thousands. Cromwell's wholesale deportation created an even greater flood of Irish men and women seeking refuge from oppression. Montserrat, an island of the West Indies (though not containing the larger number of Irish on Barbados), had a majority of Irish. Most were indentured servants (white slaves) and remained poor. A group of Irishmen on St. Kitts sought protection from abuse in a request to the Portuguese King. Though they sought permission to go to Brazil, they were allowed to move to Montserrat instead.[180] There, these Irish mixed genetically with Africans and are known as "Black Irish."

UPDATE:

Black Dutch could be a combination of old-world Berber through tribes of the Northern Necks of Virginia and Old Swedes of Fort Christiana, Delaware.

---

[179] Melvin J. Laney, "My Family Traditions: The Sons of Joseph and the Diaspora" http://www.ubalt.edu/kulan/laney.html, p. 2.
[180] Brian McGinn, "How Irish is Montserrat" http://www.iol.ie/~irishrts/Montserrat.html, p. 2.

Groups Resisting Racism and Slavery

Genetically, we have discovered that a great majority of the Redbones return with an Old Swedes, Finish and or Scandinavian MtDNA haplo assignment origin. It appears we trace these lines through to the Wilmington Delaware area where they first settled on these shores in 1638 at Fort Christina. We believe they were the first to marry among us and that they in fact included the Talbot's known as "the Brethren" and whose mitochondrial DNA is widely spread out among the Moor's of Delaware (Mitsawokett Indians), the Delaware, and Lenape (Cherokee) Indians who all trace a great portion of their matched mitochondrial DNA to these women. These MtDNA also follow the lines of the "Gooltowners/Goole Town Range" Wilmington, New Castle Delaware settlement lineages, the Moors and "Guineas" of Virginia. Along with most of Fort Christiana families were an anabaptist faith and called themselves, "the Brethren". It appears, they were in fact some of the earliest to remove from the area of Bohemia River, once known as Oppoquimimi River, whose drainage is the Chesapeake Bay. This group removed to the area of Redbone Crossroads, Ypsilanti, Georgia where we find the first use of the term "Red Bone". It appears that most, if not all Scandinavian's of North Europe carry a Berber mitochondrial DNA.[181]

---

[181] Achilli A, Rengo C, Battaglia V, et al. Saami and Berbers--an

Little distinctions can be made however between, a "Berber" mitochondrial and that of a "Moorish" one.[182] Both very closely related to the Saami peoples of North Russia and Scandinavia, but their origins are North African. However, the Spaniards also carry much of this same MtDNA which was interjected into their gene pool through the Moorish Conquest of the Iberian Peninsula.[183] The prehistoric populations of Morocco, who were ancestral to Berbers, were related to the wider group of Paleo-Mediterranean peoples. The Afroasiatic family probably originated during the Mesolithic period, perhaps in the context of the Capsian culture.[184][185] DNA analysis has found commonalities between Berber Moroccan populations and those of the Sami people of Scandinavia showing a link dating from around 9,000 years ago.[186]

---

unexpected mitochondrial DNA link. *Am J Hum Genet*. 2005;76(5):883-886. doi:10.1086/430073

[182] "Reduced Genetic Structure for Iberian Peninsula: implications for population demography. (2004)" (PDF). Archived from the original (PDF) on 2008-04-06. Retrieved 2011-08-01.

[183] Capelli C, Onofri V, Brisighelli F, et al. Moors and Saracens in Europe: estimating the medieval North African male legacy in southern Europe. Eur J Hum Genet. 2009;17(6):848-852. doi:10.1038/ejhg.2008.258

[184] Abdallah Laroui, The History of the Maghrib (Paris 1970; Princeton 1977) at 17, 60 (re S.W.Asians, referencing the earlier work of Gsell).

[185] Camps, Gabriel (1996), Les Berbères, Edisud, pp. 11–14, 65

[186] Achilli, A.; Rengo, C.; Battaglia, V.; Pala, M.; Olivieri, A.; Fornarino, S.; Magri, C.; Scozzari, R.; Babudri, N. (2005). "Saami and Berbers—An Unexpected Mitochondrial DNA Link". The American

Groups Resisting Racism and Slavery

The Moor's of Delaware male YDNA is also among the Nanticoke Indians. The Nanticoke having a living legend and inclusion of their Moorish ancestry among their tribal culture and memory.[187] I include that the Nash/Ash male YDNA lineage is an early mix of the Nanticoke and Delaware Moors. As well as the Harmon[188] surname line. I believe they derived their surname from among those who settled at Fort Christiana, the Ash/e/Ashes family.

I also include these surnames who returned Old Swedes, Scandinavian (Berber) MtDNA: Mary "Polly" Black Perkins, b. 1739 Essex Co., Mass and died Carter Co., Tn. who may have been a Bradford, or married to one previously? She married Joshua "Old Jock" Perkins of Carter Co., Roan Mountain, Tenn., her mother was an Ober born 1710 but no other information above her. This type MtDNA traces through dozens of Redbones and Melungeon's and include Doyle/Dyal/Dial, Buxton, Ashworth (Elizabeth Hill), Hill,

---

Journal of Human Genetics. 76 (5): 883–886. doi:10.1086/430073. PMC 1199377. PMID 15791543.

[187] These legends stated that Spanish or Moorish pirates, in the later eighteenth century, were shipwrecked off the Delaware coast in the Delaware Bay or near the Indian River Inlet. The shipwrecked men were taken in by the Nanticoke Indians and came to marry Indian women, thus beginning the mixed stock of Delaware Moors.

[188] Fisher, George P. (George Purnell), 1817-1899. The so-called "Moors" of Delaware. By Hon. George P. Fisher. [n.p., n.d.] https://lccn.loc.gov/tmp92006657 6 l. 21 cm. F142.S9 F5

Mixon, Sherill, Byrd, Epsom/n, Strothers, Willis, Bradford, Perkins, Evans, Howard, Boone [189] (Red Boones?) Whit/ted/head, Howell, Coward.

Example Black Dutch, Pennsylvania Dutch etc. monikers. **Arrieta Conrad/Coonrad/rod or Conart**. Great grandparents were born in Germany/Prussia and who immigrated to the American colonies. Great grandmother of the editor, not on my Redbone side. An example of Berber/Saami MtDNA and so called "Black Dutch" she was Black Stockings religion, who also follow an anabaptist faith.

---

[189] Please see MtDNA study of Doyle/Dial and Buxton YDNA and MtDNA study in, *The Journey*: Genetic Genealogy Handbook and Case Studies by Stacy R. Webb, Backintyme, 2020.

Groups Resisting Racism and Slavery

THE MOORS are also a relatively unknown group in America. The term "moor" likely derived from the Greek word "Mauros," meaning dark. The term remains ambiguous; it was applied 2000 years ago by Romans to Africans but has evolved over the years to include Berbers, Arabs and, more generally, Muslims. Although the term is usually thought of as referring to Blacks, some Moors are White. An unknown number of slaves brought to North America were Muslim – "Moors." As the term was used, they were not a specific race of people, but a mixture of nationalities and ethnic groups usually of the Muslim faith. Dominant in Spain from approximately 700 to 1492, their reign was more enlightened than that of the balance of Europe.

Some Moors in Mauritania are still, in the 21st century, held in chattel slavery – having Arab masters. They are now exploited by Muslim Africa, much as the Black slaves and Native Americans were by Christian America 150 years ago.

Among the Delaware Moors, the following surnames are prevalent: Carney, Carver, Coker, Dean, Durham, Hansley, Hughes, Moore, Morgan, Mosley, Munce, Reed, Ridgeway,

Sammon and Sweeney.[190] Author, Scott Withrow, believes that the Redbone families known as Moore, who married into the Ashworth family, derived from the Moors.

Update

Ashworth YDNA

The Ashworth male YDNA is of an Armenian, or Anatolian Turk (Tajiks) origin haplo assignment with a Eurasian origin migration which tends to lean towards a Turkish mainstream lineage.[191] These two populations are very similarly related, with only minor European, ancient Near East, Mongolian, or Greek variations.192 The only other family who returned with the same haplo origin assignment, is the Carriere surname lineage, who considered themselves French.[193] This lineage however appeared not to match other Carriere's in their study group. The Morisco[194] are genetically like, or

---

[190] Bonnie Ball, The Melungeons: Their Origin and Kin, 8th edition, 1984, p. 60.
[191] Genetic evidence for an origin of the Armenians from Bronze Age mixing of multiple populations Marc Haber1, Massimo Mezzavilla1,2, Yali Xue1, David Comas3, Paolo Gasparini2, Pierre Zalloua4, Chris Tyler-Smith
[192] Haber, M., Mezzavilla, M., Xue, Y. et al. Genetic evidence for an origin of the Armenians from Bronze Age mixing of multiple populations. Eur J Hum Genet 24, 931–936 (2016). https://doi.org/10.1038/ejhg.2015.206
[193] https://www.familytreedna.com/groups/carriere/about/goals
[194] a Moor in Spain, especially one who had accepted Christian baptism

similar to both ethnic groups.[195] Carrier's appeared to be a French migration rather than a Byzantine or Ottoman migrations. The Nash/Ash male YDNA is most similar to the Moors of Delaware, a North African origin.

GYPSIES or Romani were mentioned by Bonnie Ball in the context of her discussion of Melungeons. She believed they had a possible connection to Redbones.[196] They hadsurnames in common with Redbones and they shared common physical characteristics. Their ability to live in a dominant society while retaining their own identity was like that of Redbones. In Louisiana, the two groups shared common ground. Hineston, Louisiana is near two of the major Redbone communities – Westport and Pitkin, Louisiana. Until the 1950s, Gypsies came to Hineston and these surrounding communities every year. They engaged in horse-trading, metal work – such as repairing the wood stoves used in these farming communities – and "fortune telling." Today, they are much more numerous, successful, and integrated than ever.

---

[195] Moriscos were former Muslims and their descendants whom the Roman Catholic church and the Spanish Crown obliged, under threat of death, to convert to Christianity or self-exile after Spain outlawed the open practice of Islam by its sizeable Muslim population in the early 16th century.

[196] Ibid., pp.21-22. These names do note appear in later editions of this book.

For an account of their adaptation and life in Texas, see the Skip Hollandsworth account in the Texas Monthly.[197]

Only one person of Redbone heritage was found in Louisiana who had married a Gypsy.[198] He was a man whose surname was Droddy. Droddy and his wife settled in the Redbone community rather than wander as Gypsies. Gypsies were in most of the countries from which Melungeons are said to have derived, and England and France exported them to Louisiana and South Carolina, the two states most heavily populated with Redbones.

Update

Gibson/Gypson Gypsy

There are a family of Redbones living around Starks, La. who still speak the Gypsy language. This lineage is Gibson's, but they are descendants of an Indian uprising, we believe in Polk County, Texas and were raised by relatives in Louisiana. It is hard to get a good grasp on their genealogy because vital details are not remembered. However, it would appear they

---

[197] Skip Hollandsworth, "The Curse of Romeo and Juliet," *Texas Monthly*, Vol. 25, No. 6, 1997, pp. 82-112.
[198] Don C. Marler, "The Louisiana Redbones", paper presented at First Union, a meeting of Melungeons at the University of Virginia at Wise, Virginia, 1997 and is available on the internet at http://dogwoodpress.myriad.net.

are somehow related to the Varner, Goyens, Buxton lineages who removed to Texas.

No direct connections were found to Melungeons or Redbones, but since Romani are masters at adapting, hiding their past and disguising in the present, it may be possible that some were Gypsies in Redbone or Melungeon clothing. On the other hand, it is difficult to disguise DNA. The evidence thus far is that a small percentage of Melungeons has DNA traceable to Gypies of India; ~~the relationship to Redbones has not been tested~~. Interest in a connection between Romani (Gypsies) and Redbones is renewed by the findings of the Melungeon DNA study referenced earlier. This study revealed that about five percent of the participants had DNA characteristic of Siddis from India.

Update

Please see chapter, "Genetic studies" where we discuss several mainline families, Melungeon, Cherokee, Lumbee and Redbone who returned with an anomalous and "specific" to Gypsies MtDNA haplo assignment. And, where I also share connections to a set of DNA markers, also specific to the Kalderash Gypsy.

Redbones of Louisiana

The Romani left India about the year 1000 and made their way across Europe and most of Africa. The name Gypsy, a corruption of Egyptian, was given them by the British, but over the years, they have referred to themselves as Rom or Romani.

The Rom people have been persecuted wherever they lived. In the 15th century, Germany exported them to Pennsylvania and during WWII, executed hundreds of thousands of them on racial grounds. England exported them to the West Indies in the 15th and 16th centuries and also to North America. The Dutch, French, Portuguese, and Spaniards also exported them to America.

Some of the Romani names in America, listed below, are consistent with those of the Redbones.

The names offered are: Bailee, Blackwell, Boswell, Campbell, Collins, Cooley, Cooper, Evans, Gibson, Gipson, Goins, Hall, Hancock, Harrison, Jeffery, Lee, Locks, Lovell, Mitchell, Mullins, Pierce, Short, Smith, Stanley, Trent, Warsing, Watson, West, Woods and Young.[199]

---

199 Bart McDowell, *Gypsies: Wanderers of the World* (Washington, D.C., National Geographic Society, 1970). Some of these names were furnished by Romani descendant and researcher, Jerry Warsing.

Groups Resisting Racism and Slavery

REDLEGS were another 17th century group in the West Indies, principally on the island of Barbados. The group was made up of political prisoners and indentured servants (white slaves) from England and Ireland. Men, women, and children were "shanghaied" or "barbadoed" and forced to come to the islands. Author Edward T. Price, who wrote about the Redlegs of South Carolina, originally thought that since many Barbadians came to South Carolina, the two were related, but he found no evidence of such a relationship. The Barbadian Redlegs were a fair-skinned people who suffered from the intense exposure to the sun while working in the sun-drenched islands. They likely got the name Redlegs from the discoloration caused by such exposure.[200] This issue needs further exploration. Many persons coming to America from Barbados have names common among Melungeons and Redbones. (See Attachment E for a list of names of persons migrating from Barbados to America)

---

200 Edward T. Price, Jr. Mixed-Blood Populations of Eastern United States as to Origins, Localizations, and Persistence, (PhD. Dissertation, University of California, 1937).

Redbones of Louisiana

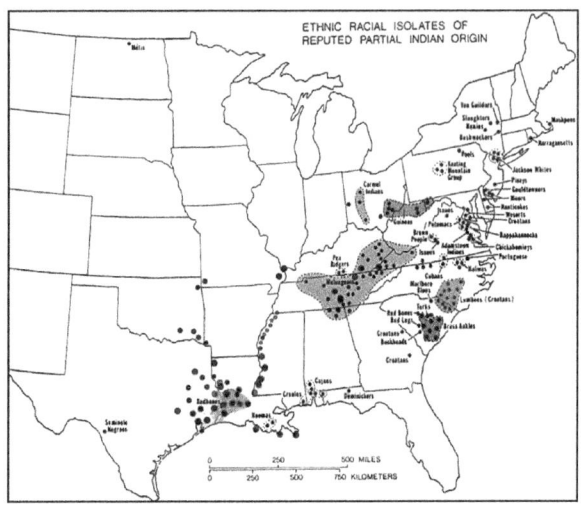

Ethnic Racial Isolates of Reputed Indian Ancestry

North to South

Van Guilders	Potomacs	Red Legs
Slaughters	Guineas	Brass Ankles
Moonies	Caramel	Croatans
Bushwakers	Indians	Buckheads
Mashpees (coast)	Rappahannock	Croatans
Narragansetts (coat)Jackson	Chiclahomiays	Dominickers
Whites	Portuguese	Cajuns
Pools	Mahstown Indians	(MOWA)
Keating Mountain Group	Brown People	Creoles
	Issues	Huomas
	Haliwas	Redbones
Pisays	Cubans	Seminole
Gouldtowners	Pea Ridgers	Negroes
Moors	Melungeons	(Mexico)
Nanticokes	Marlboro	Metis(Canadian Border)
Wesorts	Blues	
Croatans	Lumbee	
Issues	Turks	
	Redbones	

SELECTED LOUISIANA ISOLATED GROUPS

Certain groups in Louisiana have been identified falsely as Redbone groups. The following brief sketches should be of assistance in sorting out which communities are and are not Redbone.

THE CLIFTON CHOCTAW Community located on Hwy 28, west of Alexandria, Louisiana was settled in the mid-1800s by people who are a mixture of Caucasian, Native American and African American. Community members have been involved in trying to attain official Indian status and have therefore created a position of Tribal Chief. Members of this community maintain a tribal office after decades of neglecting this function. Clifton Choctaw have been recognized as a tribe by the state, but not by the federal government. Traditionally timber workers and operators of small farms, they are socially and physically isolated from the dominant society. One student of this group claims that some members came to Louisiana from North Carolina and are descended from Lumbee Indians, but this claim has not

Redbones of Louisiana

been documented.[201] Clifton Choctaws claim no kinship to Redbones nor do Redbones claim kinship with them.[202] The groups do have some similar physical and social characteristics. The Clifton Choctaws, however, are more isolated than Redbones and have resisted assimilation into the dominant society more strenuously.

Common family names among the Clifton Choctaw are Baptiste, Burgender, Cantu, Clifton, Foster, Henderson, Neal, Shackleford, Smith, Thomas, Tyler, White and Wright.

Two illustrious historical names from this community are King Brandy and Amos Blue-Eye. King Brandy was a flamboyant drummer (salesman) and Amos Blue-Eye was a musician who eventually moved to Oklahoma.

THE EBARB COMMUNITY is located near Zwolle, Louisiana. The Ebarb Choctaw-Apache group is a state recognized tribe that has lived in Sabine Parish since the 1700s. It takes its name from Antonio Gil Y'Barbo – Ebarb being an English corruption of Y'Barbo. The tribe maintains

---

201 Interview with Dr. Donald W. Hatley, Director The Louisiana Folk Center, Northwestern State University, Natchitoches, Louisiana, March 4, 1997.
202 Don C. Marler, *Historic Hineston*, (Hemphill, Tx: Dogwood Press, 2002, Second Edition), p. 112ff.

Selected Louisiana Isolated Groups

a tribal office in Zwolle and a Pow Wow ground at Ebarb, both located in Sabine Parish. Members of this community are of Choctaw, Lipan Apache and Spanish heritage. Spaniards brought Apaches into Louisiana as slaves in the eighteenth century. Perhaps it became evident to the Spaniards that they could keep an Apache prisoner but could not easily make him a slave. The Apaches caused so much trouble for their captors, they were finally freed. Author Webster Talma Crawford stated that Redbones are related to these Apaches. Crawford believed that as the Apaches were freed, they went south and married into the Redbone group. He wrote that it was the Apache who provided the "noxious blood" to the Redbones. While there may have been a mixing of these two groups, Crawford's timing was somewhat off as the Apaches had already been released when the Redbones arrived.[203]

Common family names among the Ebarb group are Basco, Bison, Ebarb, Ezernack, Garcia, Garcie, Leone, Malmay, Manshack, Martinez, Meshell, Moore, Mora, Paddie,

---

203 Don C. Marler, "The Louisiana Redbones", paper presented at First Union, a meeting of Melungeons at the University of Virginia at Wise, VA., 1997 and available on the internet at
http://dogwoodpress.myriad.net/
See also a full account of Crawford's views in Don C. Marler and Jane McManus, *The Cherry Winche Country*.

Pantalion, Parrie, Procell, Remedies, Rivers, Santos and Sepulvado.

Antonio Gil Y'Barbo

CANE RIVER CREOLES are located near Natchitoches (Nak-a tosh), Louisiana. They are named for the Cane River that runs from near its former parent, Red River, south to the Isle Brevelle area and winds its way back to the Red River.

Selected Louisiana Isolated Groups

The beginnings of the group known as the Cane River Creoles involved a slave woman, Marie Thérèse, whose African name was "Coincoin."

Marie Thérèse – "Coincoin"

Legend has it that she gained manumission (freedom) from her master's family (Sieur Louis Juachereau de St. Denis) and bought the freedom of her daughter and grandson. She had numerous children by a Frenchman, Claude Thomas Pierre Metoyer. After receiving a land grant, she built the Yucca Plantation, now known as the famous Melrose Plantation. From this beginning, her family served as a nucleus for the group known today as the Cane River Creoles. They were then known as *gens de couleur libre* (free gentlemen of color), and they constituted a third caste – a distinct ethnic group that was afforded a status intermediate between Blacks and Caucasians.[204]

THE UNITED HOUMA INDIAN TRIBE or SABINES embraced French, Whites and Blacks, and from this amalgamation came the "Sabines." Occasionally, one hears Redbones referred to as Sabines. Perhaps the confusion is because so many Redbones live in the Sabine River area. The Sabines, however, live along the Gulf Coast in Terrebonne and Lafourche Parishes, and are historically French speaking

---

[204] Gary B. Mills in *The Forgotten People: Cane River's Creoles of Color* said that some Cane River area slaves ran away and joined the redbones (sic), which he described as a marauding group of mixed bloods. Whatever else they may have been, Redbones were not marauders. They generally stayed in their settlements and protected their property. Mills does make it clear that Cane River Creoles are not Redbones. *The Forgotten People* is an excellent source for information on Cane River's Creoles of Color but is lacking on Redbones.
William Harlan Gilbert, "Memorandum Concerning the Characteristics of the Larger Mixed-Blood Racial Islands of the Eastern United States", *Social Forces*, May 1946, pp. 445-446.
Gilbert said erroneously that "Cane River Mulattoes", "Houmas" and "Sabines" are all Redbones.

Selected Louisiana Isolated Groups

fishermen and trappers. This Native American tribe is state recognized.[205] Another possible reason for confusing them with Redbones is the belief among some that anyone with a mixture of White, Black and Native American is a Redbone.

United Houma Indian Children

Author W. H. Gilbert, on the other hand, said that "Cane River Mulattoes," "Houmas" and "Sabines" are all Redbones who were so named as "Os Rouge" (Red Bone) by the French to designate those persons who were partly Indian. He gives no documentation for this origin of the name. Gilbert's work, published by the Library of Congress, is so highly inaccurate

---

205 Vernon J. Parenton and Roland J. Pellegrin "The Sabines: A Study of Racial Hybrids in a Louisiana Coastal Parish", *Social Forces,* 29 (195), pp. 148-154.

that it is not considered as a reliable source. Much of the error of his work is due to his tendency to lump too many diverse groups together. This grouping of Cane River Creoles, whom he calls Mulattoes, Sabines and Houmas, with Redbones and calling all of them Redbones is a prime example. His work is frequently cited, however, without question.

THE ALABAMA COUSHATTA came into Louisiana in the late 1760s as two separate groups. They settled in north Louisiana along the Red River in the Opelousas District and on Bayou Boeuf. Some of them moved to the Sabine River near present day Merryville, and eventually to Tyler County and Polk County, Texas. There, they combined as the Alabama-Coushatta Tribe. Throughout their known history, they were related tribes with few differences. They came together in the Big Thicket of east Texas in the 1780s. Some of the Alabama-Coushatta names in the group now located in Texas are: Abbey, Battise, Bullock, Boatman, Colabe, John, Johnson, Polite, Rodriguez, Scott, Sylestine and Williams.[206]

---

[206] Jonathan B. Hook The Alabama-Coushatta Indians. (College Station: Texas A&M University, 1997). This tribe is tightly closed, refusing to give even a list of common surnames without approval of the Tribal Council. It has rigid definitions of who can be admitted as a tribal member.

This is an extremely closed group with rigid requirements for membership. The tribal office could not release a list of surnames without approval of the tribal council. The above list is therefore not official.

Afro-Romani Inquisitional Exiles in Louisiana

The Pariah Syndrome
VII. Treatment Elsewhere in Europe:
Spain, Portugal and France

In 1568, Pope Pius V attempted to drive all Gypsies from the domain of the Roman Catholic Church; similar expulsion orders were already in effect in individual countries, resulting in an ongoing shuffling back and forth of Gypsy populations between them. With the maritime expansion, and the establishment of a colonial plantation economy, however, a way was finally found to clear Gypsies out of western Europe more efficiently. The Spanish were the first Europeans to convey Gypsies to the Americas, although a reference dated February 11th, 1581, indicates that the earliest made their way there on their own. Referring to Charcas Province in Peru (corresponding to part of present-day Bolivia), it tells of Gypsies who had "passed secretly to some parts of our Indies [and ...] who go about with their native dress and language...among the Indians, whom they dupe easily, on account of their simplicity" ("pasado a algunas partes de las Nuestras Yndias xitanos ... que andan en su traxe y lengua ... entre los yndios, a los quales por su simplicad engañan con facilidad"). (Colección, 1872:138-139). Ironically, this early document asked that those Gypsies be rounded up and returned to Spain, although that country had begun ordering their expulsion as early as 1499. Before that, it had briefly considered attempting their assimilation into the Spanish population, possibly because a labor force was needed to replace the expelled Moors and Jews (Alfaro, 1982).

Evidence that Gypsies could be made the property, for perpetuity, of Spanish citizens in the sixteenth century is found in a document published in Valladolid in 1538:

Gypsies are not to move about these kingdoms, and those that may be there, are to leave them, or take trades, or live with their overlords under penalty of a hundred lashes for the first time, and for the second time that their ears be cut off, and that they be chained for sixty days, and that for the third time that they remain captive forever to them who take them. Decree of their Highnesses given in the year 1499, and Law No.104 in the Decrees; confirmed and ordered to be observed in the court which was celebrated in Toledo in the year 1525, Law No.58, in spite of any clause which may have been given to the contrary (de Celso, 1538).

Selected Louisiana Isolated Groups

Moraes (1886), Coelho (1892) and more recently Couto (1973) and Locatelli (1981) have all documented the shipment of Gypsies out of Portugal. In the 17th and 18th centuries, Ciganos were being sent to work in the Portuguese colonies in South America, Africa, and India. One can only imagine how the latter individuals must have reacted upon finding themselves in the land of their ancestors. Boxer briefly mentions the victimization of entire communities of Gypsies, against whom King John V seems to have conceived an obsessive hatred, for no reason that I can discover. These unfortunates of all ages, and both sexes were shipped off in successive levies to Brazil and Angola, without any specific charge being brought against them, in a (largely futile) attempt to banish the Romany race from Portugal altogether (1969:314).

It was in this particular respect that the trans-Atlantic shipment of the Africans differed from that of Gypsies: the former were transported for economic reasons; the latter, for reasons of hate. A decree which came into effect in August 1685, redirected the shipments from the African settlements at Cabinda, Quicombo and Mossamedes to Maranhão, a vast colony to the north of Brazil. In 1718, the Brazilian city of Bahia became the central offloading point for Gypsies from Portugal. The governor was ordered at that time to make it illegal for Gypsies to speak Romani or to teach it to their children, in order that it should quickly become extinct:

Foram degrados os ciganos do reino para a praça da cidade da Bahia, ordinando-se ao governador que ponha cobro a cuidado na prohibição do uso da sua lingua e giria, não permitindo que se ensine a seus filhos, a fim de obter-se a sua extincção (Moraes, 1886:24).

Expulsion orders in France go back to 1427 but were applied only sporadically at that early date. By 1560, Gypsies were being ordered to leave that country at once, or be committed to the galleys, a practice which was also in effect in Spain at that time. In 1682, Louis XIV ordered bailiffs throughout France to arrest, and cause to be arrested, all those who are called Bohemians or Egyptians ... to secure the men to the convicts' chain to be led to our galleys and to serve there in perpetuity, [and as for the women, they were to be] flogged and banished out of the kingdom; all this without any other form of trial (de Fréminville, 1775:305).

Gypsies were probably reaching North America within two or three decades after this order was effected; Jones, writing of these transportees from France, says that ..

Selected Louisiana Isolated Groups

There is a colony of 'Gypsies' on Biloxi Bay in Louisiana [now in Mississippi] who were brought over and colonized by the French at a very early period of the first settlement of the state [i.e., ca.1700]. They are French 'Gypsies' and speak the French language, they call themselves 'Egyptians' or 'Gypsies' (1834:189).

Olmsted provides a further interesting account of Gypsies in French North America, in the form of a conversation with a local planter while he was visiting Louisiana:

> I afterwards spent the night at the house of a white planter, who told me that, when he was a boy, he had lived at Alexandria. It was then under the Spanish rule, and 'the people they was all sorts. They was French and Spanish, and Egyptian and Indian, and Mulattoes and Niggers'. 'Egyptians?'. 'Yes, there was some of the real old Egyptians there then'. 'Where did they come from?. 'From some of the Northern islands'. 'What language did they speak?. 'Well, they had a language of their own, which some of 'em used among themselves, Egyptian, I suppose it was, but they could talk in French and Spanish too'. 'What color were they?. 'They was black, but not very black. Oh! they was citizens, as good as any. They passed for white folks'. 'Did they keep close by themselves, or did they intermarry with white folks?. 'They married mulattoes mostly, I believe. There was heaps of Mulattoes in Alexandria then-free niggers-their fathers was French and Spanish men, and their

mothers right black niggers. Good many of them had Egyptian blood in 'em too ...' The Egyptians were probably Spanish Gypsies; though I have never heard of any of them being in America in any other way (1861:638).

The population Olmsted refers to were probably from France rather than Spain as he suggests and related to the earlier transportees mentioned by Jones. Spanish shipments to Louisiana, their solución americana, part of a proclamation issued in 1749, is discussed by Alfaro (1982:318,329). Roma had already been transported out of Spain with Columbus on his third voyage in 1498 (Wilford, 1984:C1,3; Lyon, 1986:604), and were similarly expelled during the time of the Inquisition (Ortega, 1985). A mixed Afro-Romani community lives near Atchefalaya in St. Martin Parish, some seventy-five miles south-east of Alexandria, though it shuns social intercourse with the surrounding black, white and American Indian populations, as well as with the Vlax and Romanichal Gypsies who live in the state.

A further account from the same region from about 1780 of another mixed Romani population, though here with the local Indians, is found in Milfort (1802:39):

Selected Louisiana Isolated Groups

> On leaving Mobile, I went to Paskagola. The inhabitants of this village are very lazy; but, since they have little ambition, they are happy, and lead a completely tranquil life. They are for the most part Gypsy men who married Indian women; there are a few French Creole men among them. They are all carpenters and build schooners with which they engage in coasting trade in Mobile Bay, at New Orleans, and at Pantsakole.

Cuban anthropologist Dr. Beatrice Morales-Cozier of Georgia State University in Atlanta is working with another mixed African-Romani community which lives in the interior of her own country. On July 30th, 1749, King Ferdinand VI ordered the wholesale redada or arrest of all Roma throughout Spain, to "extinguish once and for all" this population which had "infected (his domains) for so many years." Many where imprisoned; others were sent by sea to La Coruña on English and Swedish vessels "with the loss of many people" (Alfaro, 1993:103).

On November 22nd, 1802, the Prefect of the department of Basses Pyrenees, M. de Castellane, issued an order calling for measures to be taken "to purge the country of Gypsies"; subsequently, ... on the night of December 6th, the date set by the Prefect, all of the Gypsies throughout the Basque Country were rounded up, as though in a net, and were taken via various depots to ships which put them off on the coast of Africa. "This vigorous measure which, on being put into effect, brought all the approval which humanity and justice could muster," said a writer of the time, and "was a veritable kindness to the Department" (Michel, 1857:136).

In an unsigned article which appeared in the first issue of the Journal of the Gypsy Lore Society (1888:54), it was suggested that the Lowbey people of the Senegambia may be the descendants of these transportees; they are said never to marry out of their community, are reputed to have come from somewhere far away, and to be cursed to keep on the move for stealing. They make a living from carving wooden utensils for sale, and in an earlier article in the Archaeological Review (Hartland, 1888:15), they are referred to as "the Gypsies of the Gambia." Michel's report does not give the destination of the French ships, but it seems unlikely that they would have traveled as far south along the African coast as the Gambia before disembarking their human cargo. There is a town on the Senegambian coast, however called Ziguinchor (pronounced "ziganshor") whose name, it has been suggested, may derive from Tzigane. Lespinasse (1863:42) had earlier suggested that those vessels may not in fact have left European waters but might instead have been waylaid off the French coast by a British naval blockade and returned to shore.

French court order dated 1612 ordering all Gypsies out of France.

Center, **King Emil Mitchell**, right nephew **Slatcho "Mike Wilson" Mitchell**, 1897-1942, left son name unknown or unsure. Royal Kalderash markers.

Gypsy Mitchell/Marks Clan
A DNA Match

New Orleans, Old Mobile Bay, Biloxi Mississippi Territory Emil Mitchell born ca 1857 in Rio De Janeiro, Brazil, died at Albertville, at Alabama 's Sand Mountain, near Attala, Ala., on Oct. 16, 1942. at age 85. The Meridian Newspaper says he came to New Orleans when he was 5 (ca 1862) with his parents. A Meridian, MS, Newspaper states that Emil obtained his citizenship in 1884, perhaps in Cleveland, Ohio. The Meridian, MS, newspaper accounts state that the headquarters of Emil Mitchell had been Washington, D. C. at the time of his death.

Emil Mitchell first married Callie "Kelly", born about 1868, Kelly was the mother of 15 children, she died Jan. 31, 1915, at the age of forty-seven. Her death occurred while the tribe was camped Coatopa, Ala., and her body was brought to the Horace C. Smith Undertaking Co. in Meridian. The decision to bury her here brought about the formation of this Gypsies Southern burial ground. The other Northern burial ground is at Chicago, Illinois.

Queen Kelly struggled to deliver her 15th child. The labor had been long and intensive, the bleeding unrelenting, and the queen's death was imminent. King Emil Mitchell searched the faces of the gathered crowd. He offered a $10,000 reward to anyone who could save her. It wasn't meant to be, and his Queen soon passed away. An estimated 20,000 Roma Gypsies arrived in Meridian for the funeral service. The horse-drawn hearse traveled west on Seventh Street, followed by carriages of her female family and tribe members. Although it was a cold February day, as Romany tradition required, all the men were on foot and bare headed as they trudged toward Rose Hill Cemetery.

A description of the scene at the undertaking company, appeared in the Feb. 7, 1915 issue of the Meridian Dispatch. "At one side of the parlors, with candelabra at the head and foot, stands the magnificent silver-trimmed metallic casket. Hermetically sealed within, in all the barbaric splendor of a medieval Queen lies Mrs. Callie [Kelly] Mitchell. Queen of the Gypsies of America. The swarthy face, with its high cheek bones, is typical of the Romany tribes, and the head, the upper portion of which is covered with bright silken drapery pinned at the back with pins, rests upon a cushion of filmy silk and satin. The hair is braided Gypsy fashion, and the dark tresses shine. "The body was attired in a Royal robe of Gypsy Green and other bright colors, contrasting vividly with the somber hues usual under such circumstances. Two necklaces are around the neck, one of shells, an heirloom which was descended through generations. "The lower portion of the body is draped with 'Sacred linen' treasured by the Gypsy bands for the use only when death overtakes one of their number. When the children arrive, each will put a memento of some kind in the casket and it will devolve upon the youngest child to place her mother's earrings in the ear." In order that the journey of the Queen might be without discomfort, the coffin was equipped with comb, brush, and other toilet accessories, as well as a supply of working clothes, "for use on the other side of the Styx".

It was estimated that more than 20,000 people viewed the body of the dead Gypsy Queen after it was brought to Meridian. Members of the Mitchell tribe, one of the largest in the country, came here from all parts of the United States to pay tribute. a newsreel made of their camp at Bonita was exhibited throughout the country. The funeral services took place on Feb. 12 and were held from St. Paul's Episcopal Church with the rector, The Rev. H. W. Wells, officiating. More than 5,000 persons were at the cemetery to witness the last rites. "It was a large and imposing funeral procession that wended its way from the undertaking establishment to the Episcopal Church," the Dispatch reported. "The college band headed the procession, followed by the male members of the gypsy band on foot and bare headed, with Chief Mitchell, members of his immediate family, and the women and children in carriages. The hearse, with the remains of the Gypsy Queen, headed the carriage procession. The attendance at the church was large....so large that it was impossible for all the people to gain entrance. The services were those of the Episcopal Church and were in no way added to by the Gypsies...."

Succeeds to the Throne. At the death of Queen Kelly, Flora Mitchell, sister of King Emil, succeeded to the throne. Nothing more was heard of the Mitchell Gypsy tribe for several years, and then word came of the death of Flora in Yazoo City on Jan. 8, 1930, at the age of 70. Her body was brought to Meridian for funeral services and burial on Jan. 11. Father [now the Rt. Rev. Monsignor] John J. Burns of St. Patrick's Catholic church officiated at the services, which were delayed from morning until evening, awaiting the arrival of the tribe high in Gypsy councils. A story of the event published in The Meridian star said," As the Gypsies carried the casket from the chapel and down to the level of the pavement, the procession, headed by the casket and followed by King Mitchell and the balance of the Gypsy band, proceeded through a line of curious onlookers standing behind a band which played Chopin's funeral march. As the Gypsies reached the street, the band swung into line and, still playing the funeral march, proceeded down 7th Street to where the hearse was waiting." At the cemetery, the ceremonies were as simple as at the funeral home…No talking took place, even among themselves, and the silence of the Gypsies.

King Emil Dies. Death came to king Emil Mitchell, who was 85, near Attala, Ala., Oct. 16, 1942. "The King died under a tent Friday at Albertville, high upon Alabama's Sand Mountain," the Meridian Star reported on Oct. 20.1942. "He died the way he wanted to——under a tent. He came into the world under a tent at Rio De Janeiro, Brazil." The King's nephew, Slatcho "Mike Wilson" Mitchell, 45-year-old leader of a Mississippi tribe, died in Houston, Miss., the following day, and both bodies were brought to Meridian for burial. Double funeral services were conducted at the Webb Home by Father Burns. Emil's body was placed by the side of his wife, Kelly, and the nephew was buried just a few feet away. tribesmen supervised the ancient burial ceremony which included sprinkling of fruit juice so that the dead would have something to drink "on the other side". Gypsy burial rites are likened to the ancient Greek and Egyptian services. When a member of royalty dies, their belongings are entombed with the body.

Selected Louisiana Isolated Groups

In accordance with custom, several changes of clothing were also placed in each casket. Contending that it would fetch them "bad luck", the women gypsies would neither pose for photographs nor tell a fortune "at any price" before the funeral services.

Closed with Concrete. After the services, the graves were closed with layers of concrete, reinforced by steel bars. During the years, grave robbers have sought unsuccessfully to dig up the caskets. Because of the war, the American gypsies did not put on as big a funeral for their beloved King as they had for Queen Kelly. M. H. Frank, who once made his home in Meridian, was chosen acting King following Emil's death. The headquarters of Emil Mitchell had been Washington, D. C. but branches of the Romany's which acknowledged his rule made headquarters in Chicago, Cleveland. St. Louis, Kansas City, Cincinnati, and other large cities. Members of the tribe were mixed as to nationality and included Hungarians, Syrians, Brazilian and natives of nearly every country in Southern Europe. Mitchell with his roaming parents, had landed in New Orleans when he was five years old and lived there off and on. In 1884, the year he obtained his American Citizenship, he became King of the Gypsies at a great color-drenched ceremony in Cleveland, Ohio.

Emil & Callie's descendants at the time of his death included nine sons, five daughters and more than 100 grandchildren and great-grandchildren. His second wife, Queen Lapa Mitchell, remained in Atlanta, Ga. as she was too ill to attend the services. Several of the King's children were scattered around the globe.

Gypsies prefer a nomadic life and live under the laws and customs of their ancestors. To this day there are no actual records of their wanderings and no fixed century from which they sprang. However, records of them existed as early 1348 in Serbia (now Yugoslavia). There is not up to date census of the number of Gypsies in the world today. Russia has about 1,000,000 Gypsies, Bulgaria, Romania, and Hungary each claim between 200,000 to 250,000, while Yugoslavia has 116,000, Turkey and Greece 200,000 each and Czechoslovakia and Poland about 150,000 each. During World War ll close to 500,000 Gypsies were exterminated by the Germans, adding to a long history of repression's against Gypsies. There is no statistical count of Gypsies, or those who identify as Gypsies in America.

It is of note that at Rose Hill Cemetery within the Gypsy burial plots are a family of **Gibsons**: Sam Gibson, 1849-1906, Sarah Ann Gibson, 1850-1931, Tomas Gibson, 1864-

1918, Mary E. Fontan Gibson, 1883-1959, Margaret Wells Gibson, 1896-1959 which appears to be the latest burial of Gibson's there. Also, of note Anna Virginia **Mitchell** buried with her parents., Benjamin J. & Nancy **Dial** Mitchell. Nancy Dial was the daughter of David M. Dial, Newberry County, South Carolina and died Sumter County, Alabama. Some **Burwell's** are also laid to rest near the Mitchell family plot. The Gypsy Mitchell clans have ties to Stockton, Florida, and Tulsa Oklahoma where they also serve as headmen of their tribes. No attempt was made to locate the families or their genealogy at this writing.

Diana Sharkey Mitchell, 1918-1960

Gypsy funeral processional, March 25, 1924
Rose Hill Cemetery, Meridian, Ms. [207]

Queen Callie Marks Mitchell, grave offerings, Rose Hill Cemetery.
Royal Kalderash Gypsy Queen

Photos contributed by editor, Stacy R. Webb, 2007

[207] Library of Congress Prints and Photographs DivisionWashington, D.C. 20540 npcc 10838 //hdl.loc.gov/loc.pnp/npcc.10838

TEN -MILE REDBONES In an article from the Alexandria American, 29th Aug 1857. All transcriptions are as they appeared in their original form.

DEMONCRATIC NOMINEE FOR TRESURER NEGRO SUFFERAGE.

The charge against Mr. R. A. Hunter, Democratic candidate for State Treasurer, of complicity with free negro suffrage in the parish of Rapides, is one well worth the serious attention and investigation of every man who has a voice in the selection of that officer. It is not an implied charge, inferred from circumstances and occurrences that admit of doubt or contradiction, but it is made openly, broadly, and directly, with names, places, dates, facts, and every particular necessary to make out a complete case, sworn and subscribed to by numerous witnesses of the highest respectability. The charge rests upon three distinct and simple propositions, viz: Are the people of the Ten-Mile precinct of the African race? Do they vote? Does Mr. Hunter abet and aid them in the exercise of that function? It is only necessary to establish the affirmative of these propositions to convict that individual of the offence charged, to convict him of the grossest outrage upon society and upon the elective franchise that ever was perpetrated by a soulless demagogue in grasping for office. Have these propositions been established in the affirmative?

We answer yes, established so clearly that no amount of sophistry and mere denial will avail against them, as we will proceed to show.

But first let us briefly glance at the facts of the origin and present condition of this free negro colony, as we have obtained them from several prominent citizens of Rapides parish. Many years ago, a large number of negroes and mulattoes, having been set free in North Carolina, were transported, by parties interested in the matter, to the parish of St. Landry, in this State. Becoming exceedingly troublesome to the people of that region, they were expelled from their settlement in the vicinity of the place now called Chicotville, and a portion of them "squatted" upon lands in Calcasieu parish, and the remainder in what is now known as the Ten-Mile precinct in the parish of Rapides. There they now are, living together in large families and squads in the midst of a thinly settled country, and forming a regular colony, distinct in everything from the white population of the parish. So thoroughly have they become related by intermarriage, that a list of sixty or seventy of their voters exhibits only about a dozen different names. They are represented by the white people who live in that region (the western part of the parish) as exhibiting the worst traits of the human character, seldom relieved by its better attributes.

Vindictive, revengeful, treacherous, cowardly, and cruel, their deeds of secret malice and open outrage have made them a terror to the few white inhabitants scattered through the "piny woods" country round about them.

And this state of things exists not only in Rapides, but in Calcasieu, not more than a year having elapsed since their bloody deeds in the latter parish compelled the white people to seek protection in the formation of a sort of vigilance committee. Why they are not brought to justice and punished for their numerous violations of law, and especially in Rapides for voting, is a question easily answered. They live in a wilderness, sixty miles from the parish seat, and the persons who suffer most from this colony of black and yellow thieves and desperadoes are poor white men, to whom the satisfaction of appealing to the law would be no recompense for the further wrongs certain to be inflicted upon them in consequence.

Regarding their exercise of the elective function, while nearly everybody in the parish of Rapides, without distinction of party, concedes it to be scandal and outrageously wrong, few seem willing to put themselves to trouble and expense to bring the matter again before a court of law, since it requires nothing but the false ruling of a judge or the empaneling of a political jury to acquit a person of any shade of color on the charge of illegal voting. Beside-, a strong party influence is exerted in their favor, and who deserve and receive the contempt of the community in which they live. And make of going among them previous to every election and encouraging them to rally to the polls. And now to the proof that these people are colored, that they vote, and that label. is their chief aider and abettor in that shameful violation of the law.

In the Red River American of the 21st of Aug. Appears an affidavit made in due form before a justice of the peace by Mr. James Johnson, a citizen of Rapides parish. Mr. Johnson testifies that he has known the families (giving many of their names) now living in the Ten-Mile precinct for more than fifty-nine years, and a portion of the affidavit of this respectable old land contains the whole matter in a nutshell, so far as their status is concerned. He says:
"nothing extenuate [sic], nor aught set down in malice."

We feel it to be our duty as faithful journalists, to make good on the charges that have been adduced through our columns, as to the complicity of Col. R. A. Hunter in the free negro suffrage in this parish. As what we have to say emanates from the threshold of Col. H., we called upon, by a strict sense of

Selected Louisiana Isolated Groups

justice, to "nothing extenuate [sic], nor aught set down in malice."

We have charged that there are a large number of *free negroes* inhabiting a section of this parish known as "Ten-Mile Creek;" that an election precinct is there established for the benefit of free negroes by the Locofoco[208] party. And we have further charged that the candidate for State Treasurer of the so-called Democratic party, aids and abets these people in the exercise of the elective franchise; that he had descended still further in degradation; he has gone voluntary to the polls armed these free negroes, and with them erected defenses to repel any resistance that might present itself against the lawless outrage.

---

[208] a member of a radical group of New York Democrats organized in 1835 in opposition to the regular party organization: DEMOCRAT Locofoco burned brightest in 19th-cenutry America, where it designated a new type of self-igniting match or cigar capable of being lit by friction on a hard surface. The word is believed to combine the adjective locomotive (which was commonly taken to mean "self-propelled," though loco actually means "place," not "self," in Latin) and the Italian word for "fire," fuoco. The political meaning of Locofoco is a story in itself. In 1835, a group of radical Democrats brought locofoco matches to one of their meetings after hearing that their adversaries were plotting to disrupt the meeting by putting out the gas lights. The room did indeed go black but was soon relit, thus earning the group its name. First Known Use of Locofoco 1835.

Col Hunter admitted in his speech at Richmond, Madison parish, that "these people, who live in the prolific hills of Ten-Mile, have African blood in their veins, and had never voted until 1838." But we propose, notwithstanding, to produce from an ample stock such evidences of that fact as will place the matter beyond all cavil, or the possibility of a doubt for all time to come.

To show the status of these Ten-Mile people, we offer in evidence the affidavits of some of the oldest and most respectable inhabitants of Rapides. No men are better known in the section of country where they live, and there are none in whose veracity greater reliance would be placed. They are all persons of truth an honesty:

The State of Louisiana-Parish of Rapides.
Personally, appeared before me., the undersigned. Justice of the Peace in and for the State in and for the State and parish aforesaid, JAMES JOHNSON, aged ninety-four years, a citizen of the State and parish aforesaid, that being duly sworn according to the law, says that he had been a resident of the State of Louisiana for something near fifty-nine years. I have known the PERKINS, SWEATS, JOHNSONS, RAYS, DYALS or DOYLES, GIBSONS and WILLISES, the most of whom now live on Ten Mile creek, or near the

Ten Mile precinct, in the parish of Rapides, ever since I first came to the State. Old Joseph Willis, the Baptist preacher, was the first of that tribe of people that I knew; he was a mulatto. And was born a slave in North Carolina, and it was reported that a few years previous to the first of my acquaintance with him that he sold his mother. He was considered a free man of color, and, in fact, I called him a negro. He was not allowed to vote. All the Willises now living near Ten Mile precinct are descendants of the said Joseph Willis., The PERKINS, SWEATS, JOHNSONS, RAYS, DYALS or DOYALS, and GIBSONS, are all more or less connected with the said Joseph Willis and were all considered free men of color or mulattoes; none of them were allowed to vote or send their children to the public schools, nor to muster.

I was very astonished to hear that some few of them were allowed first to vote in the parish of Rapides; I think in the year 1841.

James X Johnson

Sworn to and subscribed before me, this 26th day of August. A.D. 1857.   WM. RANDOLPH, J.P.

Parish of Rapides—State of Louisiana.

For me, William Randolph, justice of the peace, being duly commissioned, appeared this day Michael Paul, who made oath that he was born and raised in the parish and state aforesaid. That he is over 56 years old; that he has been a voter ever since his majority, and that from his birth to the present time has lived in the parish and state aforesaid. They said Paul further states that, for the first 35 years he has resided within 6 miles of what he called the Calcasieu precinct, which is his usual place of voting and that during the period of 35 years he has frequently acted as a commissioner of elections for said precinct, and that he has always with the other commissioners acting with him, refused to take the votes of the free Nick rose, most of whom now vote at the Ten-Mile precinct. And said Paul further states, that the voters of these free negros were not received generally until the precinct of Ten-Mile was established , where they now vote the Democratic ticket without let or hindrance, to the number of 40 or upwards, and that he has always considered the permitting of these free Nick rose to vote, a great outrage upon the rights and privileges of the free white citizens, an that by thus equalizing them with the white population they would become turbulent an insolent.

Michael Paul, Sr.

sworn to and subscribed before me this 27th day of August A period D., 1857   William Randolph, J. P.

Selected Louisiana Isolated Groups

State of Louisiana Parish of Rapides

The undersigned has been inhabited of the said parish of Rapides 55 years, and during the last seven years has lived on Calcasieu within 15 miles of "Ten-Mile," alias "Stanley's precinct". In quotation my occupation has been that of a merchant, which brought me in frequent contact with the people of Ten-Mile Creek, and I can state that there are upwards of 40 votes given at the said precinct who are considered mulatto or free men of color, and that they vote the Democratic ticket. I have frequently heard John Dyal or Doyle call himself mixed blood. He is the father of five voters at the said precinct.

Joseph T. Hatch.

Sworn to and subscribed before me, this 26 day of August A period D. 1857. William Randolph, J. P.

The state of Louisiana Parish of Rapides

personally, appeared before the undersigned authority, Mrs Rebecca Ritchie, who, being sworn in do form of law, says that in the year 1804, they arrived in the parish of Saint Landry a number of families, who were known as the Carolina mulattos never regarded in any light than free people of color, and never claimed to be white. Among that number was Isaac Perkins, is descended the Isaac Perkins, Sr., Willis Perkins, Sr., and Louis Perkins, who are his sons;

Robert A. Perkins and Isaac Perkins Jr., are the sons of Willis Perkins; Daniel Perkins and Willis Perkins are the sons of Lewis Perkins. The Dyal's, on Mr. Boyce's list, came from an ancestry of the name. John Doyle, and his son Solomon Dyal, W. Dyal and Jackson Dyal, and their cousin Henderson Dial, are so marked that no one can hesitate in declaring them negroes Ruben Reyes mother is a Sweat, the sister of Johnson Sweat, of undoubted origin, whilst Washington Ray and Adam Ray are Rubin Ray's sons. Gibson Johnson, Burrell Johnson, Carroll Johnson, Calvin Johnson and Obadiah Johnson, are the descendants of Gibson Johnson, a genuine mulatto. Ezekiel Gibson, a very good old darkie but I cannot recollect the mother of him. Thomas Goins, she is not able to identify; knows there was a family of that name, who came over with the others, and who were mulattos; Edgington [Aggerton] Willis and Joseph Willis, Sr., are sons of old Joe Willis, the preacher who was always regarded as a mulatto. Rumor having made him notorious by the sale of his mother, the sale she had heard reported and does not give the facts of her personal knowledge. William Willis is the son of Edington [Aggerton]Willis, and Joseph Willis and Charles Willis are the sons of Joseph Willis. The Jew Miracles William and Joseph had a Johnson for grandmother; Jacob Gunter is a descendant of the of a family of the Sweat; Old Johnson Sweat is his great uncle and he is a mulatto. Aaron

Selected Louisiana Isolated Groups

Drake's grandmother was a genuine negro. Alexander Buxton is crossed with the Drake. William Slaughters grandmother and Gunter's grandmother is the same woman.

John and James are the sons of Hannah Perkins, who is of African descent; Hawkins Martin, she is told, is a grandson of old Joe Willis. None of the old stock ever exercised the rights of white men in Saint Landry. They were not permitted even to muster and were never received as associates by decent people. There was but one opinion among the respectable inhabitants, and that was they were free people of color.

Rebecca Richey

sworn to, and subscribe before me this the 23rd day Of June January, A period D. 1856, at COILLE, Louisiana

WC James , J. P.

Mr. John Richey, being sworn, says that he heard the affidavit by of Mrs. R. Richey read, and concurs in every word, except he does not recollect the time of the arrival of the old mulatto families in Saint Landry, it being before his time.

John Ritchie

sworn to and subscribed before me at COTILE, Louisiana this 23rd day of January, A period D., 1856.

W. C. James , J. P.

State of Louisiana Parish of Rapides

personally appeared before me, the undersigned justice of the peace, in in for the state and parish aforesaid, Simon C. Nichols and James Hicks, citizens of this Parish of Rapides and state of Louisiana who, being duly sworn according to law say that they were commissioners of election for Calcasieu precinct in the year 1855, and at that election held at said precinct, Ephraim Sweat, Robert Perkins and Alexander Buxton were there and wanted to vote , and, we believe, would have voted the American ticket but we were not willing to receive their votes, because we believe them mixed with African blood. In fact Buxton and Sweat offered their votes, but would not swear they were right, freeborn citizens. We Furthermore swear that we believe that there is upwards of 40 voters who vote at Ten-Mile precinct who are also mixed with the African blood. We Furthermore declared that we are members of the American party.

S. C. Nichols, James Hicks

sworn to and subscribed before me this 26 day of August A. D., 1857

This evidence is clear and unquestionable. It establishes beyond all doubt, that q" these people, who live in the prolific Hills of Ten-Mile, have African blood in their veins," and that they do vote the Democratic ticket.

Selected Louisiana Isolated Groups

We will now prove, by evidence equally reliable and incontestable, that Colonel Hunter did, on the 5th day of November last, at the presidential election of the free Kansas Buchanan, assemble an arm the free negroes up Ten-Mile, and fortified them so at the polls, the night before the election, that it would have required a large force of well-armed men to have gained access to the ballot box:

The State of Louisiana Parish of Rapides.
Before the ender sun authority personally appeared Edmond Johnson , a citizen of the state and parish above mentioned, who, being duly sworn according to law, affirmed that, on the 4th day of N8 D, 1850 6, in company with other citizens of the aforesaid state and parish accompany the challenging committee of the American party to Stanley's, alias Ten-Mile precinct, in the parish of Rapides and state up Louisiana, for the purpose of protecting the said committee in their rights having heard that the free negroes of the said precinct were determined that their votes should not be challenged, and then they were determined to vote regardless of all law.
I did, then and there, at the said precinct and on the day and date above written, see Robert a period Hunter, armed with a double-barreled shotgun and a revolver, he might have had more arms rallying the free's around him, all armed with double barreled shotguns and rifles for the purpose as I

believe to force in their ballots regardless of all consequences. I do Furthermore affirm that I heard Robert a period Hunter say to the free knee grows, that, let them come on and we will make them smoke, meaning that challenging committee, and those who were in company with the said committee. I do Furthermore from then I believe that all the names on the list called races list, are mixed with African blood in fact some of them are so black, that, offered for sale, the purchaser would not ask if they were free. I Furthermore believe that they said Robert a Hunter has attended the said precinct at every election held at it for the last three years, and I do know that said Robert A period Hunter gave a fall at one of their houses near the said Stanley's or Ten-Mile precinct, for the benefit or pleasure of the said free negroes, and danced with them, and met with them on equality.

Edmond Johnson

sworn to and subscribed before me, this 26th day of August, A period D. 1857. William Randolph, J. P.

The state of Louisiana Parish of Rapides
personally appeared before me the undersigned justice of the peace in an for the parish of Rapids and state of Louisiana , Levi Boyd and William Boyd citizens of the state and parish of four said, who being duly sworn according to law, say that

they accompanied the American challenging committee to the precinct called Ten-Mile, in the afor said state and parish, for the purpose of assisting the said committee in their rights, in November, 1856, having heard that the mulatto's upset breezing were determined that their votes should not be challenged, and were going to vote regardless of all law. When we arrived within a short distance of the said precinct, we saw that there were armed and barricaded, and lead on by Colonel Robert A. Hunter. I, Levi Boyd, swear that I saw the said Hunter at the said precinct, at the election for president of the United States, in November last, armed, and, I believe, leading on the mulattos of the said precinct, all armed, for the purpose of voting them, regardless of the law.

We further believe that there is upwards of 40 votes polled at the said Ten-Mile precinct, that are given by persons of mixed African blood, in vote the Democratic ticket.

Levi Boyd William Boyd sworn to and subscribed before me, this 26 day of August 1857. The parties made their mark.

       William Randolph J. P.

Clerk's office, District Court, Parish of Rapides I hereby certify that R. Legras, William C. James, and William. Rudolph, esquires, are justices of the peace in and for the Parish of Rapides, do commissioned and qualified.

In witness whereof I have hereunto set my hand an affixed the seal of said cord, at it at Alexandria, the 28th day of August, A.D. 1857.					M. R. Arial, clerk

Alexandria, Louisiana, August 28th, 1857

Mr. editor Colin as requested; I give you an account of what transpired at the Ten-Mile precinct at the last presidential election. I was on a visit to Mr. James Hicks, and on the day previous to the election was informed that a committee of the American party would, on the next day, go to the Ten-Mile precinct for the purpose of challenging the votes of the free negroes who had previously been in the habit of voting there. Having seen a good many of these persons and being convinced by their color and general appearance that they were of African origin, I felt some curiosity to know how the matter would terminate, and I therefore went with this committee. Having been raised in a slave state and looking upon them as an inferior race to the white and knowing them to be possessed of no political rights whatever, you may imagine my surprise when on arriving at the place of voting I found these negroes armed and fortified and headed by an encouraged by white men holding high official and social positions in the country.

Before this committee arrived at the place of voting, they halted and held a constitution as to the mood of proceeding. They determined to go peaceably and quietly to the polls, to challenge each and every who should offer his boat, and to take every precaution to avoid a collision with the negroes arose. When we arrived at the place, we halted at the distance of about 100 yards from the stand; for then we saw them getting into the stables an behind the houses and fences, and making every demonstration indicating that the party would be fired on if they rode any nearer the house. At this, Mr. J. C. Wise, the Sheriff who was at the house, was sent for, and came out. Mr. Hunter was also sent for but did not make his appearance. Mr. Wise told the party that it was the determination of the negroes at the house to fire on them if they attempted to approach the poles; said he, if you will lay aside all your arms, I'll guarantee you may go safely to the house and not be molested. A very pretty proposition, to be sure! The very idea of a white man laying down his arms to a sable son of Africa, is revolting to the sense of everyman caring within his breasts the spirit of a free man. The party of course declined to accept the hospitality of the negroes on any such disgraceful terms. Upon finding that we would not be allowed to go to the house without running the risk of being most ingloriously shot by these negroes, we deemed it advisable, taking the number of negroes into consideration, to depart in peace.

I make this communication to you, not as a member of the American party, but as a Democrat, honestly opposed to all illegal voting and to all persons upholding encouraging the free in the exercise of the elective franchise.
Very respectfully John a Myers

Comments upon the character of this testimony would be idle. The witnesses are citizens of the parish they are all well-known and are engaged in the various pursuits of life all able and ready at all times to defend their integrity and honor.
It is well to say, in this connection, that it is a custom with Colonel Hunter to deal in brave denials, and to meet such charges as are here made, with the "lie" As this matter is now placed in a specific intangible form, he can, if he chooses, adopt A mode of vindication which would appear more consistent with an assumed dignity and an unaffected courage.

Their certificates here presented show conclusively that Colonel Hunter has banded his fate to free suffrage. He is so linked with them, that with them he must sink or swim. Like Macbeth, he is so steeped in crime it is easier for him to go on then to turn back. In all state elections every white man's vote is affected by the free vote of Ten-Mile, and it is the constitutional voters of the state to decide in this election whether or not they will sanction the damning outrage upon their rights and privileges whether they're willing that free nigro's shall become the arbiters of the elections in Louisiana. Colonel Hunter, in vindicating the rights of these free negroes to vote, says that their voting began in 1838, and that the Whig Party first voted them this he asserted not only in his Richmond speech but elsewhere, by this mode of argument he begs the question, for he admits the important fact that the right to vote was non in the people of Ten-Mile but was assumed by them, and he fixes the time when the assumption began. No one denies that they are natives of this country; Being natives, if they were white, the right of suffrage would naturally follow, and the time to exercise which shall begin, is fixed by the constitution to say that it is proper for these free negroes now to vote because this or that party commenced it, is worse than a fool's argument it is the argument of rogues 4, by a parody of reasoning any other crime, it matters not how monstrous, could be justified.

Party access is under a state of high political excitement may be excused; it may find appellation in the passions of the hour, but to attempt a deliberate defense of it when the excitement that produced it has passed away, is but adding insult to injury.

George Washington & Missouri "Missouria" Josephine Pelt Nash/Ash. Son of Benjamin, Jr. and Almirinda Johnson Nash/Ash. Born 1867 Vernon Parish, La. Died Leesville, Vernon Parish, La

Columbus Williamson son of Henry M. and Elverna Ashworth Williamson, grandson of Drury and E. Ann Nelson Ashworth, great grandson of Moses Ashworth and Anna Bunch, great-great grandson of Drury Bunch and Rhoda Mosley Bunch.

Robbie Looney Nash/Ash Stringer daughter of Guide & Missouri L. Goyens Nash. The Looney family name passed down through the Goyens lineage for Chief John Looney, TN.-Ark Cherokee. **Leonard Stringer** son of Doc Willis & Corene R. Stephens Stringer Y-DNA to R1b1a origins Iran/Iraq. Direct descendant of Pocahontas, Jamestown. Also listed in Paul Heinegg's Free African American and descendant of Mingo Stringer (Cooper/Banks/Nations). Robbie & two of her sisters (Audy "Bill & Maxine) married Leonard & two of his brothers (Brink & Deward Stringer). It is said these Stringer Boys (5 of them) would have starved to death after their mother died during the great depression, had it not been for Guide & Granny Nash/Ash or, Robbie's parents. Louisiana to E. TX Redbones, and Grandparents of editor.

Photos

Author, historian, and Redbone Researcher **James Ray Johnson** (deceased), *Drake Cousins*.

Drake Family Photo, No. Zulch, Madison Co., TX.

Tom Nash in full headdress along the Shoshone River, Wind River Indian at Fort Washakie, Wyoming.[209] YDNA matched lineage with New York & TX. births, to Cheyenne Wyoming and up to Tuscarora, Ontario Canada First Nations, and with the Lakota Sioux Nation. [210] YDNA matched also to the HILL surname, New York.

[209] Library of Congress, Images of Indians of North America LC-USZC4-4168 On-Line Finding Aids
https://www.loc.gov/rr/print/coll/232_naov.html
[210] Pharaoh Nash in the Ontario, Canada Census Index, 1871

Photos

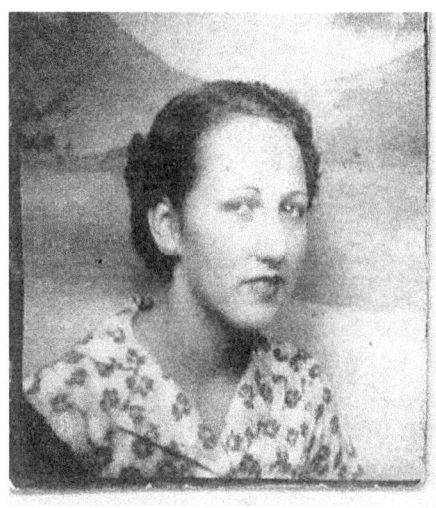

Robbie Looney Nash/Ash Stringer MtDNA through Samford, Lee, Weaver, Kyzer/Snyder, Tuberville, surnames to Orangeburg, South Carolina to Arkansas, Missouri & Louisiana to Shelby Co., TX. Haplo assignment X2b-T226C to Fars, Iran (Persia). This female lineage has exact matches all over the world including surnames in the US Evans, Hill, Robinson, Clark, Dickerson, Griffin, Tioga Co., Pa.

Absalom Perkins 1833-1886 son of Nathan & Sarah C. Drake Perkins, grandson of Nancy Perkins. He died in Clarksville, Red River Co., TX. He married 1. Anestine Hetty Goyens Clan, 2. Elizabeth Goodman 1847-1874. His daughter Texana Bell Perkins Duty pictured elsewhere here with her children. Courtesy Wm Duty.

Dr. Brent Kennedy's Nash lineage (his mother was a Nash) Waycliff Hendricks and wife Louisa E. Hall Nash, Scott Co., Va. Waycliff was born in 1840 in Scott Co., Va. And died 1897 in Wise, Wise Co., Virginia. He was the son of William Henry "Billy" Nash III and Margaret Ramey. Louisa E. born 1844 in Russell Co., Va. And died 1915 in Wise, Va. She was the daughter of John A. (s/o Isham & Mary J. Mullins Hall) and Mary "Polly" Roberson (d/o Wm & Hannah Hutchinson Roberson) Hall. Mary J. Mullins Hall was the daughter of John W. and Mariah Reed Mullins, North Carolina. Mariah was the daughter of **George Reed**[211] & Sarah Reed.

Floyd Ashworth Nash son of above couple. Born 1882 and died 1923, he married Margaret "Belle" Bennett. She was the daughter of Spencer B. and Dicey H. Mullins Bennett. All of Wise Co., Virginia. Dicey H. Bennett was the daughter of Wm Bacon Bill & Sarah Rose Bennett.

---

[211] REED YDNA to PERKINS, BLAIR, CORNELIUS male lineages further mentioned here in Genetic Studies, Perkins YDNA study case.

Photos

Archibald "Archie" & Elizabeth Ann Ashworth Clark's daughters at their home. Archie born 1856 in Calcasieu Parish and died 1941 in Clark Settlement, Beauregard Parish, Louisiana. He was the son of John Harvey & Rachel Drake. Elizabeth Ann Ashworth born 1862 in Singer, Beauregard Parish and died 1951 at Clark Settlement, Beauregard Parish, Louisiana. She was the daughter of Andrew Jackson & Annie Missouri Burgess Ashworth.

Andrew Jackson Ashworth was born 1830 at Bayou Choupique, Calcasieu Parish and died 1897 in Singer, Beauregard Parish, Louisiana. He was the son of Moses & Anna Bunch Ashworth. He married Annie Missouri Burgess born 1825 in Alabama and died 1874 at Singer, Beauregard Parish, La.

Redbones of Louisiana

Chief John Looney
Chief of the Cherokee Nation Arkansas; Listed Cherokee Reservations in 1818 on the Creekpath, Alabama. He was a nephew of Chief Black Fox "Enoli." He volunteered for service as Capt. under Andrew Jackson and negotiated the conflicts with rival Eastern Cherokee against the Creek Indians in Dec. 1813. He was wounded at Talladega and pensioned in 1842. He died while representing the Cherokee delegate to Washington DC and is buried at the Congressional Cemetery, Washington, DC. Chief Looney was the son of "Mother of Looney" who was the daughter of Chief Black Fox (1). He married before 1816, (1) Susan (Unkn) who was born ca.1790; they had 2 children: Eleanor born ca. 1816 married Chief Stand Watie, and a daughter Rachel, 1818-1867 she married John Nave. He later married in 1824 to Betsy Webber, daughter of Willliam Webber and Sarah Unknown, they had the following children: Eliza Abigal 1824-1867 she married Daniel Rattling Gourd; and Nancy Looney born ca. 1828, she married Christopher C. Sage.

Above Mattie Looney, granddaughter of Chief John Looney.

Left My Great Grandmother Missouri L. Goyens Nash Nash (passed down the Looney name & had a brother named John Looney Goyens). Daughter of Wm Collins & A. L. Samford Latham Goyens. I think there is a familial connection.

Photos

REDBONES OF SUMTER COUNTY SOUTH CAROLINA

There are several groups of mixed-blood people in the Carolinas with which the Louisiana Redbones are often said to be related or associated. One of these groups, and the one about which we have the most information, was located near Sumter, South Carolina. Located on Highway 15 South (Old Stone Road) near Ramsey, South Carolina, approximately 15 miles from Sumter, is Bethesda Baptist Church dating back to 1850. The church and cemetery are located in the community where the Redbones resided just prior to the Civil War. The old "Redbone Church" is now occupied by Blacks. It is near the site of the Furman plantation known as Cornhill. McDonald Furman, as a young man, became interested in the Redbones, Catawbas and Melungeons, but especially the Redbones.

McDonald Furman (1864-1904) is buried at the nearby Bethel Baptist Church Cemetery along with other members of this prominent family after whom Furman University, Greenville, South Carolina, is named. The McDonald Furman home is still standing though it has been remodeled.

Furman's father was a physician, and his office building is still standing.

Exercising his interest in Redbones, Furman communicated with a variety of people regarding their history, including James Mooney and officials in Louisiana where Redbones from the Carolinas had settled. He read widely about them and other local minority groups, becoming perhaps the most knowledgeable person in the state about Redbones and Catawba Indians. He wrote short articles for various newspapers, the collection of which is at The South Carolinian Library in Columbia, South Carolina.

Furman grew up during the years of Radical Reconstruction, which were grim years for South Carolina. In this atmosphere that did so much damage to Black and White relationships, in what may be termed a hardening of his attitudes, Furman was considered an eccentric individual. He advocated for Redbones, education for minorities, a sympathetic attitude toward Blacks and suffrage and equal pay for equal work for women.[212]

---

212 E. L. Inabinett, *McDonald Furman: As Seen Through His Papers*, Presented to the Sumter County Historical Society, 2 Oct. 1954.

Furman searched for the origins of Sumter County Redbones and the name Redbone. From his letters, it is apparent that he did not coin the term, but he advocated its use at every opportunity, perhaps as an alternative to terms considered derogatory by Sumter County Redbones with whom he was friends.

Below are samples of his newspaper articles and letters he received. The usage, spelling and punctuation is as given without notation.

"The Privateer Redbones"

Mr. McDonald Furman Makes a Study of this Isolated and Unique People

Twenty years ago, during my childhood days, I became interested in that isolated people of this township, whose correct racial name is Redbone. For the last ten years, I have been making a study of them, and although I have already written a good deal about them for the papers, yet there remains much to tell, and as the proprietor of the Watchman and Southron has kindly given me space, I will now write more about them.

Redbones of Louisiana

These people are known as "free negroes", also "old issues", but, as I said above, their correct name is Redbone. I will try to give the reader a clear meaning, according to my understanding, of this word, also its use, which is this: the word "Redbone" is and should be used, to designate those mixed breed people who as a race were never slaves, although they may have negro blood, and who have, or are supposed to have, Indian blood. If my understanding of the name "Redbone" is correct and this mixed breeded, isolated people in Privateer Township can't be classed as Redbones, then what are they? As a people, they are a combination of the white, the negro and the Indian races.

From the best accounts, there are at present between 70 and 80 of these people in this township; they are Chavises, Gibbeses, Goines, Smilings and some others. This enumeration does not include some of this stock in the township who appear to have become weaned off from the main body. Of the four families mentioned above, I have never discovered that any of them, as families, are descendants of slave negroes. With probably less than half a dozen exceptions, all of these 70 redbones are descended from Tom Gibbes, the Revolutionary character of whom I spoke in these columns a while back. Whether all of these have Indian blood, I can't positively say, though my opinion is that they have. Over half of them are descended from Jerry and Edie Goins, the latter was a mixed breed Indian woman who appears to have been a well known fortune teller in her day. Her name is probably familiar to many of my older readers, and from what I have learned of her, she must have been quite an interesting character. I may mention here that of these people (I mean those who are identified with the main body), less than half a dozen have married other than among their race. It would be hard (if it could be done at all) to estimate the racial percent, of white, negro and Indian blood among these people, which varies in different individuals.

As interesting character is Wade Goins, who is considerably mixed with Indian and is descended from Jerry and Edie Goins. He is as straight as an arrow, his skin is decidedly copper colored and his face, I think, looks more like that of an Indian or white man that a negro. He is now an old man, aged 70 or 72, and is one of the deacons of Bethesda Church. During a portion of the war, he ran on a government train.

Tom Gibbes, who may be called the spiritual head of these Redbones, is another descendent of Jerry and Edie Goins, and has the same amount of Indian blood as Wade Goins has. Gibbes is the pastor of Bethesda and is about 60 years of age. A gentleman of this township informs me that for years he has been renting land to Gibbes without taking the scratch of a pen.

The oldest of these people is J.E. Smiling, who over 50 years ago married Matilda Goins, sister of Wade Goins. During reconstruction times in South Carolina, Smiling was a somewhat prominent figure in county politics. At a future time I may give a more extended notice of this remarkable old man, who is a person of considerable intelligence.

As a race I have found the Redbones polite. An intelligent late freedman was speaking to me about them and I remarked that they were more polite than the white people or the late freedmen, and the late freedman replied, "yes sir, they is."

The following statement will give the reader an idea as to the quiet character of these people. During the time that Mr. W.A. Nettles has filled the position of trial justice and magistrate (about 9 ½ years) only one criminal case has been brought before him against any of the Redbones, and they were acquitted by a jury of white men... They are certainly an isolated people...they are, if anything, more apart to themselves than are the Hebrews of our state....[213]

213 McDonald Furman, "The Privateer Redbones", *The Watchman and Southron*, May 27, 1896. Located in the Furman Collection in the South

Redbones of Sumter County South Carolina

"The Redbones"
An interesting people who live in South Carolina
To the Editor of The News & Courier

There is an interesting people living in this State whose right name is "Redbones." When, where or how this peculiar name (which is not confined to our State) came into use, I do not know; nor have I ever seen a definition of it. My own definition of the name, as I understand its use in South Carolina, is this:

Redbone – a name applied to those mixed breed people who were never slaves & who have Indian blood in their veins.

The "Redbones" of South Carolina are an interesting people for study, but I do not intend to attempt a sketch of them here; my object is to call attention to their unique name. Perhaps my definition is not altogether correct & some of your other readers may be able to give a better definition. I would also be glad to see articles from your readers about the "Redbone" people themselves.[214]

Caroliniana Library. All of the Furman letters reproduced here are by permission of The South Caroliniana Library located in Columbus, South Carolina.
214 McDonald Furman "The Redbones" Original longhand copy in the South Carolinian Library.

Redbones of Louisiana

"Old Issue v Redbones"

Information asked regarding this isolated people in South Carolina.
To the Editor of The State.

The odd sounding name of "old issue" is applied to that isolated, mixed breed people, whose proper racial name is "redbone", & who are found scattered about in South Carolina – a people, who as a race, were never slaves. Any information which your readers can give me either through your columns or by letter, in regard to these people will be much appreciated. I can't say to what extent the name "old issue" is applied to them, though it seems to be largely used. I should say, from what I can learn, that people of this race (for these people may properly be classed as a different race from the whites & late freedmen) are found in the following & perhaps some other counties – Marlborough, Marion, Chesterfield, Sumter, Clarendon, Williamsburg, Berkely, Richland, Orangeburg, Colleton, Hampton & Aiken.

Beyond these people in my immediate township, I have little practical knowledge of them as a race – those in my township come chiefly of families named: Chavis, Gibbs, Goins & Smiling. They have a Baptist Church the pastor of which is

Redbones of Sumter County South Carolina

Tom Gibbs, who is of this race & is largely mixed with Indian. ~~In Buk~~ *In Berkley there is (or was) a Baptist Church of this same kind of people, which if I mistake not, was called the Indian Church. I learned a few years ago that there were two Baptist Churches of them in Marlborough.*[215]

"Old Issue"
Information Sought About a Unique Name and Race
To the Editor of the Register:

Can any of your readers give me any information in regard to the origin of that unique name "Old Issue" which is applied to that peculiar, isolated people who are found scattered about in South Carolina, and whose proper racial name is "Redbone" – a people, who as a race, were never slaves and were mixed with Indian.

James Smiling, the patriarch of a branch of these people found in Privateer Township and a Republican ex-member of the Legislature, told me this two years ago:

---

215 McDonald Furman, "Old Issues v Redbones" A letter to the editor of *The State* in longhand. It is item #46 in the Furman Collection in the South Caroliniana Library. The letter was published in *The State* on July 16, 1896.

"I can't tell where the name 'Old Issue' started from – never heard it until since the war, we don't accept the name. The first way in which I heard the name 'Old Issue' is through the late freedman, and we take it as a slur."

Nelson Chavis, another member of this race in this township, told me this last March:

"I can't remember hearing anything about the name 'Old Issue' until since the war. I don't think the name is becoming. We used to be called pioneers at the time we used to clean the muster grounds. I thought the name 'Old Issue' was only here with us. I thought the name was some kind of slang and I thought maybe we were called so as the late freedmen might be new issues."

The Hampton correspondent of the News and Courier, in June 1884, writing about one of these people in that county named Candey Mims, spoke of him as "one of a rather peculiar race of people who live in the river section of this county, locally known as 'Old Issue'. They are a mixed race, and have never been slaves. They are supposed to be descendants of Indians and negroes, but nothing is definitely known of their origin."

Redbones of Sumter County South Carolina

Some years ago a gentleman of Aiken County, writing to me about people of this sort found in that county, stated that they were classed as 'Old Issue' freedmen.

I don't mean to say that all people of this kind are called "Old Issue", but as will be seen, the name is found over a considerable area. These people in Privateer Township are mixed with the white, the negro, and the Indian races, and are classed as colored.[216]

Senator Wade Hampton tells about a race of people in South Carolina called Redbones. Says he,

> *"Their origin is unknown." They resemble in appearance the gypsies, but in complexion they are red. They have accumulated considerable property and are industrious and peaceable. They live in small settlements at the foot of the mountains and associate with non but their own people. They are a proud and high-spirited people. Caste is very strong among them. They enjoy life, visit the watering places and mountain resorts, but eat by themselves and keep by themselves. When the war broke out several of them*

---

216 McDonald Furman, "Old Issue" *The Register* May 9, 1898. Located in the Furman Collection in the South Caroliniana Library.

enlisted in Hampton Legion, and when the legion reached Virginia there was a great outcry among the Virginians and the troops from other States against enlisting negroes. They did not resemble the African in the least, except in the cases where Africans had amalgamated with Indians. This intermixture, which is common in the Carolinas, produced marvelous results. It takes the kink out of the hair of the African, straightens his features and improves him in every way except temper. These Afro Indo people are devils when aroused and as slaves were hard to manage. In the first Bull Run battle they proved how well they could fight and all prejudices against them disappeared."

Red Springs, NC
    Mr. McDonald Furman   **Oct. 12. 1889**

Dear Sir.

Your favor of recent date to hand. I was much pleased on reading the slips sent me.

The exodus of the Croatans English Colonists from Roanoke Island after the departure of Gov. White took place under the leadership of a Croatan Chief whose name was Ey-an-oe (or something like that), as appears from ancient maps discovered recently in Europe. The route as laid down on the maps which bear date of 1608 and 1610, was across Croatan Sound and up the Roanoke River to an Indian Village – thence Southward around Pamlico Sound to a Croatan settlement on the Neuse River. From this settlement began the second exodus of the Indians and Whites or half breeds to a place on the Cohavies in what is now Sampson County and on the Lombee (Lumber) river and Pee Dee. The time of the second exodus is uncertain perhaps as late as 1650. The early immigrants to Eastern Carolina according to tradition, intermarried with the Croatans and of this fact is to be ascribed the frequency of German English and Irish and French names among these people today.

I think the name Oxendine was originally Ocksenstein, a German name. The families of that name show many German peculiarities. The name Dial or Dile was I think an Irish name, Goins was O'Guin (not D'Guin) Leary was O'Leary & so on. The name among them of Blanx or Blanc is French. The early Huguenot emigrants of that name came from the Department of the Moselle and those of the family who changed the <u>Blanc</u> to <u>White</u> its English synonym, was designated as the "Moselle" Whites and the name is now changed to *Musslewhite* and is confined to the White people. The French name of Bressi is now Braey and *Turbeville* is now *Troublefield*. The Braeys and Troublefields live on the border of North Carolina & South Carolina and have intermarried with the Coratons or "Melange".

Henry Berry Lowrie takes his Christian name from *Henry Berry* one of the lost Colonists of Roanoke as you will see by reference to the list in the pamphlet. Many of the Lowrie's settled in Robeson – others went to the French Broad in Western N.C. and those in Robeson claim that David *Lowrie* Swain Ex-Gov. and *James Lowrie* Robinson late Lt. Gov of this state were of this stock. The tribe once stretched from Cape Fear to Pee Dee and the Redbones of your section are a part of the tribe as are the "Melungeons" of East Tennessee. The French immigrants called the half breeds Melangè or Mixed and the term evidently has been changed to Melungeons".

The wife of Henry Berry Lowrie was Rhoda Strong, (not Oxendine) Her brother Andrew Strong and Boss Strong belonged to the outlaws. His band of outlaws was organized by a Naval Officer who escaped from Florence prison and took refuge among these people. The Confederate Soldiers on their return from war shot old Allan Lowrie The father of

Henry Berry Lowrie, as stolen goods were found in his possession. This made bad blood – After peace Henry Berry Lowrie was for a time a fireman on The Carolina Central Railway till he was outlawed for some crime. Then came the reorganization of the outlaws. There was one white man – Zack McLaughlin two negroes, Applewhite and "Shoemaker John" and 5 of the Croatans viz. Henry Berry, Stephen and Tom Lowrie. There was an addition to the gang in the person of Henderson Oxendine who was hung.

The report of the Correspondent of the Macon Telegraph that Lowrie is still living is false. There is not a bit of truth in it. He was killed at the house of Tom Lowrie. His widow soon after married again and is living in this county.

The tradition here as to the name Braboy is that it was originally "Brave Boy" and was given by a man named "Bonnul" to one of the tribe. Bonnul was evidently Colonel Barnwell who came to our own state with troops from S. C. during the war with the Tuscaroras.

The history of the people has interested one in the days past, but of late I have had my attention directed almost entirely to other matters. The History of Education in N. C. I have read – <u>Chavis</u> I think was of Indian stock. He was naturalized which has led some to think he was from the West Indies. He was disfranchised in 1835 and in the Carolinas of that year *his naturalization papers it is said were exhibited. to the convention of that year. We have a Normal School for education of Croatan Teachers in this County, conducted by Prof. Bauder of Va. We have also a ~~separate~~ school fund for the Public Croatan Schools separate and apart from other races. Separate School districts and Separate Sch. Committeemen. etc.*

What effect education will have on the race is a problem yet to be solved.

I am writing you at a high rate of speed but I hope you can read these lines and understand my meaning. I will be pleased to hear from you at any time.

With My highest regards
I am yours truly
Hamilton McMillon[217]

---

217 Letter in longhand to McDonald Furman from Hamilton McMillon dated Aug. 8, 1889 – located in the Furman Collection in the South Caroliniana Library.

Redbones of Sumter County South Carolina

Bennettsville
May 17, 1893

Mr. McDonald Furman

My Dear Sir

Yours of 13th inst is before me and in reply let me say that I not only appreciate your laudable desire to rescue the traditions of an obscure race, sometimes wronged, from oblivion, but to call the public mind to a number of important facts of our brief history, both secular and religious, which in the eager haste of this fast age, our people are liable to forget. Your brief, but important, communication to the public press calling attention to things of this sort have always interested one reader at least. You will permit me to thank you very sincerely, that you, young man, as you are, have respect to the days, and the men of "auld lang syne" and can find interest and worth, if not beauty and charms amid the bygone years. And I trust that if the response of your contemporaries is not always as generous as your fond wishes may desire, that still your inquiries may bring to light facts and principles, that shall gratify and profit your own mind, and help your generation, and those who shall come after.

The question now upon your mind, of which you write me is not unworthy your research. And I wish that I were able to give you more information than I can. Of course, the people of "mixed breed," that we have among us in Marlborough are not known as "Redbones," and not until recently have they been called "Croatans," a name which some of them are now adopting. For generations, they have claimed to have been of "Portuguese" extraction, while commonly the white people have thought them mulattos. Since the "Revolutionary War" the Quicks and a few other names connected with them, have enjoyed the respect of white people; and all the privileges of citizenship were accorded them in consideration of "distinguished services," they rendered to the cause of independence. And the consequence has been that their complexion, their circumstances, and general character has wonderfully improved, until now they are scarcely recognized as having "mixed blood" in their veins. You can see how on account of the special favor shown this family, other men of "mixed breed" would naturally claim and seek alliances with them: and so, it came to pass in the years "before the war between the states," that questions would sometimes arise as to the citizenship of parties making the claim as only free whites were so accounted and many a long controversy arose in the courts over such "points in law." Judge Hudsen, was an attorney in a case of this sort, and made a very thorough investigation of the question of descent and has told me more than once that he was satisfied that "several of the larger families of this color, were free from Negro blood." He says that "they have a well authenticated claim that they sprang from a parentage that came from the south of Europe, Spain or Portugal, and that with this European blood was probably some Moorish, but no evidence of Negro." Other families claim affinity with the American Indian and there can be little doubt but that their claim is just, as they have the natural characteristic marks of that aboriginal people clearly developed. While everybody believes, that some who claim to be Indian, or Moor, are unquestionably mixed with Negro.

You ask me if we have "any Chavis" in Marlborough? They are here, and have been for two or three generations, and are among the best known people we have after the Quicks. And it is very likely that they have intermarried. Why, Sir, if you were here to accompany me to one of my appointments next Sunday and take a seat in the "a... corner," [might be Arian! Or amen] just about the hour for the service to commence, looking through the window blinds, you might see a "covered buggy with two horses (or mules) drive up, and presently a young man about "six foot three" would enter the door, lift his beaver, and with slow and courtly tread walk down the aisle," straight as an arrow, raven locks, prominent raised cheeks, complexion brownish red," and take a seat about mid way the house, and if you were not looking for "Redbones," you might ask, "what fine looking well behaved man is that," well that is "Lewis Chavis." He has a valuable farm, a "good bank account," his mother owns a fine place, and valuable mortgages, and he has a younger brother just as good looking, only not quite so tall. And has some cousins that are enterprising valuable citizens. But there are others of the name, not so well to do, and not so well received in social circles. These better ones however when they open their lips, betray their origins as they tell you of the "housens" and "chillens," etc.

And then we have a large family of Locklears, another of Jacob Turners, in making a society and class of their own, who do not seem to aspire to anything higher. Poor pitiable creatures, they scorn to associate with Negroes, cannot with the better class of whites, and yet many of them are good people, industrious, honest, humble citizens. Of course you will find vicious, envious, worthless fellows among them, but no more than may a "pale face" or "black skin." They have two Baptist churches in Marlborough, one of them located near the little town of Clio, where they have a large congregation, and well behaved. And the existence of the church, and a comfortable framed building to worship in, makes them a fixture in the community, and an advantage in the way of farm laborers. The other is in the upper part of the county and is not doing so well, I judge mainly for lack of a sensible pastor. The young man who does most of their preaching, being a noisy, ignorant sort of fellow, and yet sharp enough to keep his place among them. This latter church is known, in doctrine and practice, as badly mixed as the blood of its members. Feet washing, free will, immersionists. And yet the leading people of the community, who are mostly Methodists, enjoy having the church among them because it moralizes and improves the character, as well as settles and fixes laborers on their farms.

Now I have filled up my space, and fear that with it all I have not met your wishes, as I certainly desired to do. If however from what I have written you shall suppose that I may yet help you in the way of information you will not hesitate to command me. With the kindest regards to your excellent father and profound veneration for your honored name through three generations, I am yours with great respect.
J.A.W. Thomas[218]

---

218 Handwritten letter to McDonald Furman from J.A.W. Thomas dated May 17, 1893. This letter to Furman is found on the Internet in several sources and in the Furman Collection at the South Carolinian Library.

Certificate

This is to certify that Preston Mishoe belongs to that peculiar mixed breed whose proper name is "Redbone" – a people who as a race were not slaves. I am acquainted with Preston & know his people in this (Privateer) township well – have studied their history & written a good deal about them for the newspapers. I can say for these "Redbones" people of Privateer Township that they are quiet, peaceable & polite. McDonald Furman.[219]

Since these Sumter County Redbones are vital to the story of the Redbones generally, and so little is known of them, the list of Bethesda Church membership and a list of those buried in the cemetery are given in their entirety. It is likely that there are many unmarked graves in the cemetery. The cemetery is not overgrown, but there is evidence of beginning neglect. A tract of timberland adjoins it and within a few weeks of this visit (October 2002) a bulldozer had plowed the outside row of headstones into scattered rubble. Had this happened to a cemetery in the Louisiana Redbone country, not a single tree owned by the landowner next to the cemetery would escape being burned. This wanton destruction of a whole section of cemetery markers deserves some response.

---

219 McDonald Furman, "Certificate" Correspondent *Charleston News & Courier & Columbia State*, March 3, 1902. Handwritten copy in The South Caroliniana Library – Furman Collection.

Redbones of Sumter County South Carolina

The cemetery and church membership records are as follows. The punctuation is as given in the document.[220]

Cemetery List

Abin, Abigail
Born_____
Died Aug. 3, 1886
Aged about 76 years

Andrew,_____
Born Apr. 3 1893
Died Sep. 15 1943

Brown, Frankie Lee
Born Apr. 29 1946
Died Dec. 31 1983

Busby, Joyce Sweat
Born May 30 1957
Died Dec. 21 1994

Chavis, Infant
Born May 7 1916
Died May 8 1916
D/O A J & CM Chavis

Chavis, Infant
Born_____
Died Nov 1 1914
D/O A J & CM Chavis

Chavis, Infant
Born May 30 1917
Died May 30 1917
D/O A J & CM Chavis

Chavis, Jackson
Born 1831
Died 1908

Chavis, Nelson
Born Oct. 14 1835
Died Oct 15 1909

Conyers, Latonyas
Born Aug 30 1983
Died Aug 27 1990

Davis, Annie

Davis, Marcus

---

[220] Emily E. Vaughn, *Index of Black Churches and Cemeteries, Sumter County; Headstones and Inscriptions*, New York. Copy in the Sumter County Genealogical Society Museum Library.
W/O = wife of; S/O = son of; D/O = daughter of.

Born Feb 20 1900 Born Feb 8 1890
Died Jun 30 1979 Died Mar 19 1969

Davis Marion Epps, Roosevelt
Born Aug 15 1922 Born Jan 1905
Died Jun 19 1961 Died Mar 24 1905
S/O Lucius & Novell Epps
Epps, Thomas Gibbs, Edie
Born_____ Born Mar 15 1918
Died Aug 4 1919 Died Oct 10 1918
S/O Lucius & Novell Epps D/O Appell & Luveda Gibbs

Goban, Rev. L.G. Goines, Baby Boy
Born 1883 Born _____
Died 1958 Died Jan 11 1977

Goins, Hughie Goins, Levicy
Born May 1900 Born_____
Died 1909 Died Oct 27 1887
S/O James and Lucia 92 years

Goins, Lonee Goins, Nelson N.
Born 1912 Born_____
Died 1990 Died_____

Goins, Sal Goins, Tom
Born 1834 Born 1860
Died 1921 Died 1931

Gowings, Infant Williams Gowings
Born Aug 26 1892 Riley's Letha S.
Died Sep 27 1892 Born Mar 21 1912
 Died Sep 4 1987

Redbones of Sumter County South Carolina

Holliday, Ames
Born Oct 1 1915
Died Jul 3 1988

Jones, James Smiling
Born_____
Died Oct 19 1992

Johnson, Matthew B.
Born 1915
Died 1983

Jordon, Julia
Born Sep 16 1914
Died Sep 30 1983

Murray, Elena
Born Feb 15 1908
Died Nov 27 1989

Oxendine, Harrison
Born June 18 19--
Died Oct 1 1994

Queen, Daisey Ramsey
Born Oct 1 1901
Died Sept 30 1968

Ramsey, Arthur K.
Born Dec 23 1909
Died Jun 22 1965

Ramsey, Betty L.
Born Apr 15 1945
Died May 21 1974

Ramsey, Solomon
Born Jul 28 1885
Died Feb 6 1963

Riley, Betty Joan
Born Apr 21 1945
Died_____

Riley, Harvey Jr.
Born Dec 1 1939
Died Feb 9 1990

Riley, Harvey Sr.
Born Aug 1 1912
Died Sept 4 1987

Riley, Lepher
Born 1912
Died 1949

Smiling, Anthony
Born_____
Died Sept 21 1985

Smiling, Fannie
Born_____
Died Jul 8 1914

Smiling, G. G.

Smiling, George Lee

Born Dec 1878
Died Feb 28 1920

Smiling, Georgia
Born Nov 16 1893
Died Dec 29 1946?

Smiling, H.
Born 1906
Died 1950

Smiling, Infant
Born May 11 1902
Died May 23 1902

Smiling, Jack
Born 1897
Died 1931

Smiling, Leler
Born 1908
Died 1984
Smiling, Mattie
Born Jun 30 1901
Died Mar 13 1918

Smiling, Nancy A.
Born Jun 21 1880
Died Nov 18 1913

Smiling, Ruth L.

Born Jul 15 1947
Died Oct 31 1990

Smiling, Gilbert
Born Aug 3 1913
Died Jun 6 1975

Smiling, Harry Sr.
Born 1929
Died 1984

Smiling, Infant
Born May 7 1910
Died Jul 1 1910
S/O JH & RL

Smiling, Laura
Born Feb 6 1891
Died Jul 5 1918
W/O J.H.

Smiling, Mary Ann
Born 1975
Died Jun 9 1940
Smiling, Mitch
Born_____
Died Jun 29 1989

Smiling, Pauline
Born Apr 22 1880
Died Apr 21 1900

Smiling, Ruth N.

Redbones of Sumter County South Carolina

Born 1884
Died 1910

Born_____
Died Mar 11 1988

Smiling, Sarah
Born 1895
Died 1965

Smiling, Whitefield
Born_____
Died_____

Smyth, Caroline
Born_____
Died 1978

Smyth, Edith
Born 1894
Died 1973

Smyth, Marcus R.
Born 1989
Died 1990

Stukes, Bessie
Born Aug 12 1916
Died Mar 23 1931

Spann, Henrietta Brown
Born_____
Died Sep 26 1992

Stukes, Crystal
Born Dec 1902
Died Dec 1902

Stukes, Crystal
Born _____
Died Jul 12 1984

Stukes, Rev. Jr
Born_____
Died Aug 1966

Stukes Martha
Born_____
Died Nov 25 1923
Age 42 years

Sweat, Alice
Born 1893
Died 1931

Stukes, Willie
Born 1888
Died 1960

Sweat, Ardaller
Born 1857
Died 1950

Sweat, Allan
Born 1885

Sweat, Ellen
Born 1896

Died 1967

Sweat, Eliza
Born 1895
Died Oct 24 1980

Sweat, James
Born 1888
Died 1930

Sweat, Shead
Born Nov 27 1904
Died Feb 22 1982

Sweat, Wesley
Born 1919
Died 1985

Sweat, West Allan
Born ____
Died 1970

Thompson, Bloomer
Bernice
Born 1906
Died 1977

Thompson, L. D.
Born 1919
Died 1991

Thompson, Washington

Died 1947

Sweat, Levi
Born 1935
Died 1984

Sweat, Spencer
Born 1900
Died 1911

Sweat, West
Born 1862
Died 1901

Thompson, Bessie
Born 1918
Died 1989

Thompson, John
Born 1906
Died 1978

Thompson, Thomas
Born 1938
Died 1989

Tindal, Rev. E. P.
Born 1884
Died 1941

Weathers, Rev. Thomas

Redbones of Sumter County South Carolina

Born 1832
Died 1902

Born Jun 20 1886
Died Mar 30 1063

Weathers, Hallie T.
Born Feb 17 1886
Died Mar 24 1984

Wright, Glen L.
Born Mar 12 1913
Died Aug 2 1972

Wells, Hilda Mae
Born Dec 12 1912
Died Jun 6 1989

Wright, Glen Jr.
Born Feb 23 1954
Died Jun 20 1992

Officers & Members of
Bethesda Baptist Church

April 14, 1986

Pastor T.C. Gibbs
Deacons:
Nelson Chavis
John Gibbs
Wade Gibbs
Clerk:
Nelson Chavis

Members of Bethesda:

Members in Sumter County

Elijah Chavis
Jackson Chavis

Elizabeth Smiling
Ellis Chavis

Redbones of Louisiana

Shack Smiling
Albert Chavis
J.S. Smiling
Moultre Smiling
Joseph Thompson
Charley Pack
Horace Stokes
Benjamin Smiling
Ervin Chavis
Frank Smiling
Marey Smiling
Calvin Chavis
Rintha Chavis
Marey Gibbs
Rebecca Jacobs
Emma Goins
Harriet Gibbs
Lucy Gibbs

Josephine "
Louisa Smiling
Durntte? Thompson

Members in Clarendon
Henry Smiling
Colwell Smiling
Joe Smiling
Harriet Smiling
Essey Smiling
Salley Smiling
Ida Smiling
Aner Smiling
Poline Smiling
Wesley Sweat
Ed Pack
Andeline Sweat

Members in Orangeburg:

Members in Williamsburg:
Edward Epps & Wife Adeline
Fred Gibbs & Wife Viciy

Members in Georgia:
Daniel Goins
Reubin Goins
Martha Goins
J (P?) essey Oxidine
Clarence Smalls

Redbones of Sumter County South Carolina

Joc Thompson
Catherine Chavis
Fedix Chavis[221]

As related above some Sumter County Redbones migrated to (perhaps returned to) North Carolina in the early part of the 20th Century; others remained in the area. A cursory check of the Sumter phone book in the year 2002 revealed that many Redbone related names such as Goins, Goings, Goine, Ramsey, Smiley, Smiling, Chavis, Ray, Riley, Epps and Thompson are still living in the area. Bethesda Baptist Church has evolved from a Redbone to a Black church.

According to one informant, the Redbones initially did not allow persons with a dark brown skin or darker to belong to this church. However, over time they began marrying progressively darker mates and eventually, as a result of this practice, the church became a Black church. Redbone names are still represented in the Bethesda Church. Today, there is a Redbone church in Sumter known as the Goodwill Shepherd Church.[222]

---

221 The handwritten copy was made by Maud B. Chavis – a teacher. She was not listed as a member of the church. McDonald Furman certified that the list was a list of the church membership. Located in the South Caroliniana Library – Furman Collection.

222 This information was provided by Tarsha Clark, Sumter, South

Louisiana Redbones **Mamie Perkins** 1893-1942 daughter of Joshua "Josh" & Mary E. Perkins Perkins and **Lexie S. Hobo Ashworth** 1892-1974 son of Amos Ashworth & Mary Heard Ashworth Simmons.

Carolina. Much of the information in this chapter was provided by Dorothy Reynolds, Sumter County Genealogical Society, W.A. "Bubba" McElveen, Jr., former Mayor of Sumter and Tarsha Clark of Sumter.

Photos

Juanita Smiling Great niece of James E. Smiling. Here she models her hand made Indian costume, won during religious ceremonies.

Martha Mae Goins Smiling Mother of Juanita and sister to James E. Smiling. On the right is her sister, **Louella Goins Bullard**

Redbones of Louisiana

McDonald Furman Home and Dr. Furman's Office
By Scott Withrow [both removed for quality reasons]

Bethesda Baptist Church
Near Sumter, South Carolina

THE LOCATION

FOLLOWING the purchase of the vast Louisiana Territory from France in late 1803, the U.S. Congress divided it into two sections designated (1) Territory of Louisiana – above the 33rd latitude and (2) Territory of Orleans – below the 33rd latitude. Later, in 1804, the Territory of Orleans was divided into twelve counties (they were not then called parishes), namely: Opelousas, Acadia, Attakapas, Concordia, German Coast, Iberville, Lafourche, Natchitoches, Ouchita, Pointe Coupee and Rapides. In 1805, St. Landry County was formed, and in 1840, Calcasieu Parish was created out of St. Landry. Beauregard Parish was formed out of Calcasieu Parish in 1912. Vernon Parish was created out of Sabine, Natchitoches and Rapides Parish in 1871.

The Neutral Zone 1806-1821

Early Redbones were located principally throughout what is now known as the former Neutral Zone, which extended from the Sabine River on the west, to the Calcasieu River to the east, and from the Gulf of Mexico to the 32nd parallel in the north. Their presence was greatest in the southwestern and western part of Rapides Parish and in Natchitoches, Sabine,

Vernon, Beauregard, Allen and Calcasieu Parishes. They lived mostly in small rural communities and isolated areas.

Although Redbones were dispersed throughout central and southwest Louisiana and east Texas, the heaviest concentrations in Louisiana were in Pitkin, Westport, Starks, DeQuincy, Elizabeth, Merryville, Fields, Longville, Bearhead, DeRidder, Sugartown, Oakdale, Leesville, Rosepine, Forest Hill, Glenmora, Walnut Hill, New Hope and Hineston. In Texas, they lived just west of the Sabine River from the Gulf to the northeast Texas in small rural areas such as Newton and Burkeville. Today, descendants of these early Redbones still dominate these and surrounding areas, but many have dispersed all over the world.

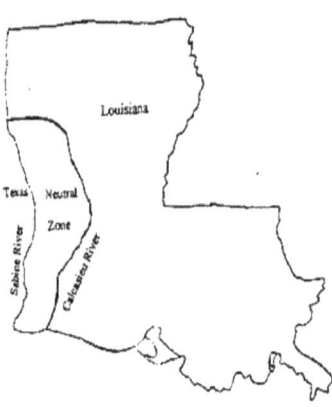

The Location

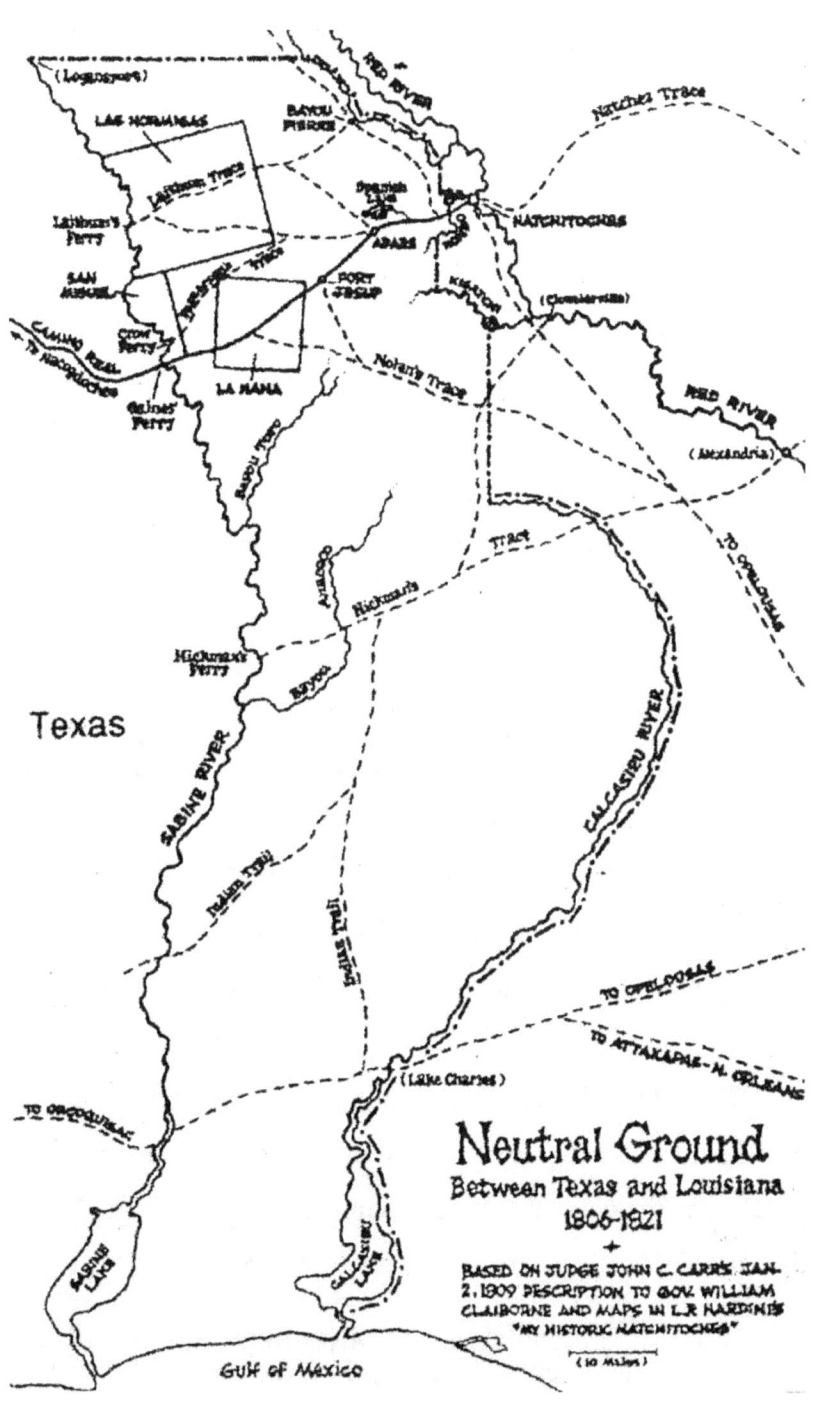

Groups, such as the Redbones that lived on the margin of the dominant society, often sought borderlands between states or countries. The Neutral Zone was perfect for them; it was wild, sparsely settled and largely not policed. In the early 1800s, this territory bordered Spanish/Mexican Texas allowing its Redbone inhabitants to move across the border either way if the need arose. It might have become necessary to cross the border because of difficulty with the law, family or community fights or feuds, and changes in the legal definition of race, and free or slave status. Mexico gained ownership of Texas in 1821 and abolished slavery in 1828. The phenomenon of settling near the border therefore gave them more options and served as a safety valve. Researcher, Scott Withrow, has termed this practice and inclination "border psychology."[223]

The following are brief descriptions of some of the communities that were home to early Redbone settlers.

HINESTON is located just east of the Calcasieu River and therefore outside the official Neutral Zone; but it is the oldest town in the general area and some Redbones lived and traded

---

223 Scott, Withrow "Red Bones: The Appalachian Connection" (Paper presented at the Fourth Union, Kingsport, Tennessee, June 22, 2002), p. 10.

The Location

there. This community, located in Rapides Parish, almost certainly existed from around the time the Neutral Zone treaty was signed (1806), and indeed may have been created partly to serve that area.[224] A myriad of families with the names common among Redbones were early settlers there. The often-mentioned Redbone surnames Perkins, Johnson, James, Mullins and Bass were common there. The concentration, nevertheless, was not as great as in some of the following communities.

WESTPORT is located near Cherry Winche Creek and Ten Mile Creek in Rapides Parish and in the former Neutral Zone. It is near the towns of Union Hill, Elizabeth and Pitkin. This community is the site of an infamous fight between Redbones and other settlers in 1881, known as The Westport Fight. More about the fight will be given later. The founding date of this community is unknown. Occupy #1 Baptist Church, located at Westport, was established in 1832, by Rev. Joseph Willis. The strange sounding name of this church was taken from the New Testament, where Jesus instructed his followers to "Occupy Till I Come."

---

[224] Don C. Marler, *Historic Hineston*, Second edition (Hemphill, Texas: Dogwood Press, 2001).

Some prominent names of early settlers in this community are: Maricle, Day, Johnson, Perkins, Ray, Watson, Doyle (Dial, Doyal, Dyal), Davis, Moore, Hamilton, Hatch and Musgrove. [225] Many of the Redbones in this area were referred to as Ten Milers. This term is still used by some today as a neutral name that is safer and less likely to offend than is the term Redbone. It was derived from the nearby Ten Mile Creek.

PITKIN is located in Vernon Parish, cut out of Rapides Parish in 1871, located approximately 19 miles from Hineston. Pitkin is near Six Mile Creek and some Redbones who lived there were known in earlier times as Six Milers. The term "Six Milers" was like Ten Milers, also considered a neutral and safer term than Redbone. The term was used frequently until the 1950s; it is seldom used now. Six Mile Creek is so named, it has been said, because its beginning is located approximately six miles from Hineston.

Some settlers in Pitkin were: Arnold, Bass, Beeson, Bond, Brack, Buxton, Cain, Chisholm, Clark, Cole, Davis, Day, Doyle, Farris, Glass, Gray, Green, Hall, Harland, Harper, Haymon, Hill, Howard, Howell, Jackson, Jean, Jeter,

---

225 Don C. Marler and Jane McManus, editors, *The Cherry Winche Country* (Hemphill, Texas: Dogwood Press, 1993).

The Location

Johnson, Jones, LaCaze, Laird, Lambright, Legg, Lewis, Maddox, Mancil, Martin, Mathis, McDonald, Miller, Moore, Morrison, Mullins, Neal, Nye, Parker, Perkins, Reed, Reid, Smith, Stalsby, Strother, Sweat, Thompson, Townley, Weatherford, Welch, Weldon, West, Willis, Wilson and Wise.

SUGARTOWN was first surveyed in 1807 and settlers began moving into the area in about 1816. It is located in the northeast corner of Beauregard Parish. Some family names of settlers in Sugartown were: Andrews, Baggett, Bailey, Boggs, Escobas, Caraway, Cockran, Cole, Gill, Johnson, Jones, Holoway, Isles, Kemp, Lyons, McDonald, McFatter, Moore, Sanders, Seamon, Simmons, Smith, Spears, Stracener, Watson, Welborn, Welch, Weldon and Young.[226]

STARKS is located in the former Neutral Zone in Calcasieu Parish about six miles east of the Sabine River. There is no evidence that there was anyone other than Native Americans living there during the time the territory was officially part of the Neutral Zone.

---

226 Luther Sandel, *The Free State of Sabine and Western Louisiana* (Many: Jet Publications, 1982), p. 53.
Don McFatter, "History of Sugartown," Paper presented to members of the Beauregard Museum on June 16, 1996.

The exact date the town of Starks, Louisiana was founded is unknown, and there is some disagreement over the supposed dates. The confusion is exacerbated by the fact that there were several small communities in the immediate area and the names changed. In those days, communities often grew up with a name given it by the person who applied to operate a post office. The applicant named the "town" if it had no name, and if a post office closed and later opened, the name was often changed. The town could have been a store and nothing more. Thus, Gillis, writing in 1993, said that the community of Starks was known as early as 1852 as Pine Hill, Louisiana and had a post office by that name. It was located four miles north of the present-day post office at Starks. The name Starks was given in honor of Bill Starks, son-in-law of the owner of the Lutcher-Moore Lumber Company, out of Orange, Texas.[227]

Student of local history, James A. Johnson presented the issue differently; he could find no proof of a date for the beginning of Starks. He cites Ransom Clark as saying he came down a road through where Starks is today in 1895, and there were no houses, only pine timber there at the time. But

---

227 Charles F. Gillis, "Early Starks History and the Logging Camps", *No Man's Land* (Starks: Starks Historical Society, Publishers, Vol. 1 No. 1, March 1993). Pp. 25-27

The Location

by 1900, Charles Batchelor moved to Starks to work for Faxon's store.[228] Therefore, according to this version, a store was built there between 1895 and 1900.

Curtis Jacobs wrote that the following people moved into other Beauregard Parish communities: In 1813 John Hoosier moved into the Bearhead community and Moses Bass moved to the same community in 1837; both moved from Mississippi. Aaron and John Drake came into the area to be near their Ashworth relatives.[229]

James A. Johnson identified the earliest Beauregard Parish settlers as: Matthew Poole, Sr., John H. Clark, Sr., Solomon Doyle, Jr., William Doyle, Dr. L. N. Mims, Andrew J. Johnson, John Hoosier, Aaron Bass, Moses Bass, James Wisby, Samuel A. Fairchild, John Drake, Jr., James W. Drake, William Fountain, Jonathan Malachi Fountain, Benjamin Foster and John Pinder. These families came, according to Johnson, between 1864 and 1868. And following them were Hyatt, Mazilly, Ashworth, Buxton and others.[230]

---

[228] James A. Johnson, "Starks," in *No Man's Land* (Starks: Starks Historical Society, Publishers, Vol. 1 No. 1, March, 1993), p. 19.
[229] Curtis Jacobs, "The Early History of the Starks Area," No Man's Land (Starks: Starks Historical Society, Publishers, Vol. 1 No. 1, March 1993), p. 30.
[230] Johnson, op. cit., p. 17.

The families of Emile Mazilly, Andrew J. Johnson, William Johnson, and William M. Phillips came down the military road between 1870-1880. The Military Road, established during the Civil War, opened up the area for new settlers.[231]

TEN MILE, Glenmora east of PITKIN and west of Westport (fight) in Rapides Parish. Is a community of Redbones whose history Occupy#1 Cemetery and Occupy#2 Cemeteries on the Creek Road. Reverend Father Joseph Willis along with Redbone family are buried in these two cemeteries. See also details of the "Negro Suffrage" articles and affidavits, on the illegal voting charges against the Ten Mile Redbones.

THE KISATCHIE HILLS south of Natchitoches, Louisiana is the home of several small communities: Simpson, Mora, Gorum, Flatwoods, Provencal and others. While these communities have traditionally not been identified as heavily populated by Redbones, there are many people with the proper heritage, culture and name of Redbones living there. Redbone influence in this area has likely been underestimated.

---

231 Jacobs, *op. cit.*, P. 30.

The Location

One native of the area with the surname Basco wrote:

> *"I have a rich cultural background. My ancestors came to the New World by way of Canada. They came to Louisiana with Iberville and Bienville and they settled at Gorum, a unique culture of Basque (from the Pyrenees Mountains) people. Because they spoke an antique, rich Basque type of language they didn't get along with the rest of the hill-country people."*[232]

It has been suggested that Redbones and Melungeons are related to the Basque. While there are certain similarities such as physical appearance, certain common occupations and blood type, no documented evidence has been found that these Kisatchie Hills people, Redbones or Melungeons, are related to the Basque.

Some of the settlers in the area before 1820 were Spanish and they received Spanish land grants. Settlers in the area before 1820 were Cole, Beasley, Bludwurth, Smith, Morrell, Grappe, Grubb, Nash, Warrick, Withers, Madden, Yarbarough, Wrinkles, Montgomery and Adley.[233] These early settlers lived in the Neutral Zone while it was officially the Neutral Zone; that is, ownership was still in dispute. In

---

232 Mabell R. Kadlecek and Marion C. Bullard, *Louisiana's Kisatchie Hills: History Tradition and Folklore*.
Alexandria: 1994., p. 490.
233 *Ibid.*, p. 28.

the years following the settlement of the dispute between Spain and the United States over who owned the Neutral Ground, many more people came into the area.

Of those who came later, some names of interest to this study are: [234] Adams, Basco, Basquez, Bishop, Black, Bolin, Bolton, Boswell, Brown, Burns, Bynog, Canady, Cedars, Chelette, Clark, Cooley, Corley, Cox, Dees, Dodd, Dove, Dowden, Edwards, Gandy, Goins, Goodman, Groves, Hagan, Hardiman, Holt, Hunt, Johnson, Jones, Kerry, Key, Kile, Laird, Lee, Martin, Massey, Matthews, McAlpin, McDaniel, McQueen, Monk, Moore, Morris, Norsworthy, Ott, Owen, Parker, Phillips, Porter, Powell, Rachal, Ray, Roberts, Russell, Sparks, Sweat, Taylor, Thomas, Tucker, Vascoco, Vesquez, Wade, Weeks, Weldon, White, Wiley, Williams, Wilson and Wray.

Some of these families claim a Redbone or mixed-blood status while others deny it. These names are given for those who may wish to explore their ancestry further. No doubt Redbones were scattered throughout Neutral Ground.

---

234 Mabel R. Kadlecek and Marion C. Bullard, op. cit., and Sharon Sholars Brown, *Four Generations of the Marino Basquez Family*, Jonesboro, LA. 1983.

The Location

WALNUT HILL, located in Vernon Parish between Hineston and Leesville, was once a thriving community, with a horse racetrack, stagecoach station and store. It was in this area that the Rawhide fight occurred in 1850 or 51. In this fight, several people were killed over a school that had just been built and deliberately burned. Those killed are buried in the nearby Glass Window Cemetery. The names of people known to have been involved in this fight were: Lacaze, Sweat, Fairchild, Weeks, Groves, Jenkins, Harrison, Hawkins, Hardcastle and Simon.[235] [Goins] Other early settlers in this community were: Burton, Bryant, Johnson, Garland, Tippitt, Cragers, Boswell, Richey, Bolton, Bass, Turner and Crumpler. There were other families in nearby Simpson including the families Bennett, Parker, Jackson, Temple, and Williamson.[236]

MERRYVILLE is located in Beauregard Parish near the Sabine River. Nearby is an old campground where the Alabama-Coushatta Indians once camped. This community grew up during the years when the virgin timber was being harvested. Redbones participated fully in the timber harvest

---

235 Don C. Marler, and Jane McManus, editors, *The Cherry Winche Country* (Hemphill, Texas: Dogwood Press, 1993).
Luther Sandel, *The Free State of Sabine and Western Louisiana* (Many: Jet Publications, 1982), p. 100.
236 Ibid., p. 102.

Redbones of Louisiana

across southwest Louisiana. Today, many families with common Redbone surnames are living in Merryville.

THE BEARHEAD COMMUNITY was the scene of a fight that has been lost to history. In August 1891, in this community, located in what is now Beauregard Parish – approximately 20-25 miles northwest of Lake Charles, there occurred a fight between Redbones and Whites. Six people were killed. Among those involved were common family names such as Ashworth, Perkins, Dial, Dyson, Ward, Murcle, Morris, Baggett, Kellen, Fulton, Elliot, King, La Comb, Mouton, Marco, Dupries, Willis and Swan. (See the chapter entitled "Redbone Culture of Violence" for the account of this fight).

VERNON PARISH was created out of Rapides, Natchitoches and Sabine Parishes in 1871. Local author, Sandel lists several families that lived in what is now Vernon Parish before February 22, 1819:

> *Wm. C. Alexander, John Allen, Asa Beckcum, John Bennett, Rezin Bowie (who designed the Bowie knife made famous by his brother the Hero of the Alamo, Jim Bowie), James Bridges, Drury Bunch, John Bush, Thomas Butler, Alexander Calhoun, Aaron Cherry, Samuel Davenport, Isaac Foster, John Freeland,*

The Location

James Gibson, James Going, John Gordon, John Graham, Nancy R. Hays, John Henderson, Asa Hickman, Thomas Hicks, Vincent Jackson, Gibson Johnson, Joshua Johnson, Azor Mathis, Frederick McMullen, Robert McDonald, Benjamin Morris, Thomas Nash, Michael Neal, Jourdan Perkins, William Pinchback, Joseph Robinson, James Self, Shadrick Stanly, Terrill, Archibald Thompson, James Walker, Absolom Winfree, Benjamin Winfree, Jacob Winfree, Phillip Winfree, Allis Woods.[237]

BEAUREGARD PARISH was created by act of the Louisiana legislature in 1912. Author, Sandel asserted that Martin Le Bleu was the first settler in what is now Beauregard Parish, arriving there in 1770. He was followed by Louis Reon, Henry Moss, Jacob Ryan, Pierre Vincent, and Thomas Rigmaiden.[238]

Once these early settlers arrived, they began adapting to an amazing array of events and challenges. Over the past two hundred years, the environment of the Redbones has been

---

[237] *Ibid.*, p. 108. Sandel notes that he got his information from American State Papers wherein was recorded individuals were making claims on land grants. These claims were made by people trying to prove they lived in the area before the settlement between Spain and the United States in 1819 and therefore may be subject to error. There were also some that likely did not make a claim; for example, Sandel also notes that James Groves and Lucius Hawkins and others were living in the area in 1810, but their names do not show in these papers.
[238] *Ibid.*, p. 53.

disturbed by economic, political, social, and technological events effecting change.

These events often brought Redbones and the dominant society together, providing opportunities for exposure to each other through sponsorship by government or large companies.

The first major event was the official transfer of the Neutral Zone from Spain to Louisiana; the second was the Civil War. While some Redbones served in the Confederate Army, others did not. Redbones had settled in the former Neutral Zone early in the 19th century, and by the time of the Civil War, it was still a place of relative lawlessness and sparse settlement. Those persons, both Redbones and non-Redbones, not wanting to participate in the war effort used the Neutral Zone as a place to hide out. At least three persons thought by some to be Redbones were active officers in the effort to capture and kill "conscientious objectors" known as "Jayhawkers." Captains David Paul, William Ivey, and Robert W. Martin were all residents of the area and were assigned the duty of prosecuting their uncooperative

The Location

neighbors. Robert W. Martin was the great grandfather of comedian Steve Martin.[239]

Beginning in the 1880s, with the introduction of large steam powered sawmills financed by northern financiers, the huge timber resources of east Texas and southwest Louisiana provided another opportunity for mixing of Redbones and members of the dominant society, as well as with Mexicans and Blacks brought in by the timber companies. Crews of black men usually did the work of the naval stores industry that preceded the actual cutting of the timber. Often, the "turpentine camps," logging camps and sawmills were all located in one community. This togetherness brought its share of violent incidents, but also brought men together daily over an extended period of time, allowing opportunity for them to develop positive acquaintances. Redbones were known as good timber workers, and they owned land in the area. Their residence in the area gave them an unequaled opportunity to participate in the benefits of the logging

---

239 Don C. Marler, "Louisiana Redbones" – a paper presented in 1997, and Arthur W. Bergeron, Jr. "Dennis Haynes and His Thrilling Narrative of the Sufferings of...the Martyrs of Liberty of Western Louisiana", *Louisiana History* Vol. XXXVIII, No. 1 1997, pp. 29-42. These jayhawkers are not to be confused with the "Kansas Jayhawkers." The term is likely a combination of Jay as in the Blue Jay, a thief, and the warlike hawk.

activity, and they exercised that opportunity. They are still heavily involved in the timber industry.

As the great rape of timbered lands began its final years, World War I came and went, allowing yet another opportunity for Redbone men and women from the dominant society to interact under the eyes of the U.S. military establishment.

With the clear cutting of the timber, large tracts of land lay nude throughout the region. The large corporate owners did not see the future potential of a regenerated forest; they saw only the tax burden. Therefore, the land became available at cheap prices. Llano del Rio Colony (Llano Colony), located in Penelope Valley California was looking for an opportunity to purchase a large tract of land. This commune wanted to relocate out of Penelope Valley with its inadequate water supply. In 1917, the Colony and its three hundred members moved by train to Stables, two miles south of Leesville, Louisiana. As the colony settled on its twenty thousand plus acres and began building, it renamed the community Newllano. Newllano was one of the more successful communistic colonies in the United States. At that time, the word "communist" was not a dirty word, and the depression of the 1930s made the concept and practice of such colonies

The Location

popular. Newllano thrived until it dissolved in 1937, due to political bickering. The location was solidly in Redbone territory. No study has been done to determine the reaction of Redbones to the colony.[240]

The Great Depression, coming at the close of the timber boom, acted to bring Redbones and the dominant society together. Louisiana was hit hard by this event, and no area was harder hit than southwest Louisiana. With the depression, eventually came federal programs designed to provide work for people who were now destitute. The "pump priming" efforts of the Roosevelt administration in the 1930s were lifesaving.[241] Chief among these pump priming efforts were the W.P.A. (Works Progress Administration) and the C.C.C. (Civilian Conservation Corps), both of which provided work on roads, the forests and other areas, under federal guidelines. The. C.C.C. program, with its communal living and somewhat regimented programming, did much to

---

[240] James N. Davidson, Newllano: *History of the Llano Movement* (Woodville: Dogwood Press, 1994.)

[241] The term pump priming was well understood by these country people who knew at the practical level that the old "pitcher pump" had to be primed before it could bring forth water. At the bottom of the pump was a system of leather valves that were positioned just above the water table underground. These leather valves dried out and shrunk when not in use and one had to pour water down the well to soak these valves so they would expand and allow the creation of a vacuum that would bring the water up.

prepare the men and the nation for the next major event – World War II. Even a cursory walk through a cemetery in Redbone communities reveals the military dead among them.

In the 1930s, the former Neutral Zone, with its timber clear cut, looked like a battle zone. The residue of the huge pine trees littered the landscape, and the area was burned each year for the benefit of livestock. This burning kept down unwanted brush, making way for fresh grass in the spring. In the process, it exposed the huge stumps and tree trunks left on the ground. It was here in 1940, that the United States Military decided to hold the largest maneuvers ever held. Camp Polk, now Fort Polk, was later built near Newllano. Some of the fort is on the land formerly owned by the colony, and some owned by Redbones.

World War II, perhaps more than any other event, by the size of the war effort, brought opportunity for mixing of the disparate groups all across America. With the war's end, came the GI Bill that provided assistance for education and training in colleges and vocational schools – again under federal auspices and guidelines. Following World War II, came the Korean Conflict and the Viet Nam and Gulf Wars, all demanding a mixing of races and ethnic groups. Also following World War II, automobiles and telephones came

The Location

into common use, making isolation of Redbones even more difficult to maintain.

It was during the depression years, also, that the radio began to appear in a significant number of homes. In rural areas, this was a welcome relief from isolation, and an opportunity for exposure to a wider world.

At about the time of the start of the Korean Conflict in 1950, television became more readily assessable to households in the country. This medium perhaps did more to expose relatively non-mobile rural populations to a broader world that any other development up to that time. In the Redbone community however, this medium likely had limited influence, as a large percentage of the population was of the Pentecostal faith, and thus many were prohibited from watching television at the time; further increasing the chances that they would retain a village mind with a limited worldview. Now, the Internet is the contender for the honor of exerting heavy cultural influence on isolated rural communities. Through the Internet, with its email, websites, and chat groups, Redbones can, and do, communicate with each other easily and freely. Redbones who live in a community of Redbones can communicate with those in another community of Redbones where once, only a few years ago, there was little communication between members of the various communities. Redbones who have moved away to nearby white communities or to another state can now easily remain in touch with friends and relatives. The Internet also provides an opportunity for Redbones to explore the non-Redbone world, and they can do it anonymously.

The net result to the strength and extremity of these communities is that, despite the erosion that has occurred, a core group remains in each of the Redbone communities. They carry on many of the old Redbone traditions, albeit in modified form.

Of these communities, Westport is the oldest, and still follows the old way of life more than others. Yet, it is here that members of the community seem more willing to talk about their history and way of life. It was here that interviews were easier to obtain than in the other Redbone communities. Lana J. Prejean was able to gain considerable cooperation, including interviews and photos for her thesis in the Westport Community. She wisely enlisted local church cooperation and involvement in seeking interviews.[242]

---

[242] Lana Jean Fagot Prejean, *Occupy Til I Come: The Redbones of Louisiana's No Man's Land*, (Thesis, MA Degree, University of Southwestern Louisiana, 1999).

The Location

William T Burke and **Fanny L Nelson** with daughters, Lillie and Luvenia. Fanny was the daughter of Valentine Garfield Nelson and Nancy Varner (couple pictured elsewhere here). Fanny was named for Valentine Garfield Nelson's mother, Fannie Goins Nelson Perkins. Bearhead Redbones. Courtesy, Marilyn Baggett Kobliaka

Elizabeth Doyle/Dial (included in the MtDNA study here) with her Goins grandchildren, Hazel, Lola, Herbert [Mano], and my mom, Roberta. Bearhead Redbones Courtesy Marilyn Baggett Kobliaka

REDBONE MIGRATIONS TO LOUISIANA

Redbones began their migration west after the end of the American Revolutionary War (1775-1783), and by the time of the Civil War, they had become well-established in Louisiana and east Texas. Following the Civil War, they continued to migrate, perhaps for different reasons. Not all Redbones, of course, migrated to the west; some stayed in the Carolinas and other southeastern states, while some stopped along the way for various reasons. Remnant groups in the Carolinas and other states have become so much a part of the mainstream dominant society, that in many cases, they are no longer recognized as Redbones.

The question of why Redbones migrated to the west, specifically to Louisiana and Texas, is difficult to answer with complete certainty, but some probable reasons arise. It is likely that there were multiple reasons for them to make the long and difficult journey to an unknown land, while others worked to push them out of their Carolina homes by exercising discrimination and legal challenges.

The usual reasons given for such movement in those days are: (1) that the land was worn out (fertilization of cultivated lands was little practiced), (2) they felt crowded by the encroaching population, (3) they were seeking adventure, (4) they were seeking cheap or free land, (5) they were running from the law, or (6) they followed friends or family to the new land. While many, if not all, of these reasons were likely applicable to Redbones as well as to other groups, there were other reasons that might have been more specific to them.

Great Britain acquired West Florida in 1763, and many residents of that area not wishing to remain under the "British yoke" began movement toward the west. Spain acquired the Louisiana Territory from France in 1762 and encouraged those who wished to move to come to the Louisiana Territory. This development, perhaps not directly involving a great number of Redbones, contributed to a general movement west attracting Redbones from the southeastern states.

Twenty years later, at the end of the American Revolutionary War, persons who supported the British against their fellow colonists, were often persecuted and harassed, and some had their property taken from them. Such was the case with some of the Ashworths, who became early Redbone settlers in Louisiana and Spanish Texas.[243]

Thirty years after the Revolution, the United States was at war with Great Britain again. The War of 1812 coincided with the new statehood of Louisiana. Many Redbones, no doubt, came from the southeast to New Orleans to participate in the new war. It is likely that some of them saw the land in the Neutral Zone and realized that it was remarkably similar to land they knew in South Carolina. They may also have known Reverend Joseph Willis, Josh Perkins, the Ashworths, Drakes and others who were in the area and might have had contact with old acquaintances.

Following this war, economic conditions on the east-coast were depressed, and the west offered cheap or free land.

Texas offered not only a glamorous enterprise with its land grants, but to mixed-blood people, it offered a more accepting environment. Louisiana's Napoleonic Code was more humane and acceptable than the harsh English Common Law legal system. The French were certainly perceived as more tolerant of persons of another race than were the British. As

---

243 Scott Withrow, *op. cit.*, p. 4.

harsh as the Spanish slavery system was, it was not equal in harshness to the system created by the British in the colonies of America and the islands to the south.

In 1821, the treaty transferring Texas from Spain to Mexico was finalized. The Mexican government was more accepting of new settlers coming to Texas than had been the Spanish, and it abolished slavery in 1828.

As discussed elsewhere in this book, laws about slavery and race changed frequently in the southeastern states. About the time Mexico abolished slavery, attitudes began to harden in the states. Slave owners became increasingly aggressive in imposing slavery on those whom they could subjugate. Definitions of who could be enslaved changed with increasing frequency, and the One Drop Rule became more and more liberalized, with persons possessing one sixty-fourth Black blood, or just being considered socially Black by neighbors, being enough to qualify one for slavery. When Redbones first came to Louisiana in 1800, Whites were still being enslaved in large numbers in the colonies. Redbones must have been acutely aware of this situation. Under the definitions of the time, anyone with an Indian or Black mixture was in even greater danger than Whites of being enslaved. So, it is little wonder that Redbones denied so vehemently any kinship to these groups. If Whites were being enslaved, anyone with a non-white mixture was in double jeopardy. They were fighting to keep their freedom.

During the Civil War, North Carolina virtually enslaved the Indians, now identified as Lumbee, from which many Redbone names can be traced. They were impressed to do menial work, while South Carolina enlisted them as white soldiers. The treatment of Lumbee's by North Carolina was at the root of the violent activities of the Lowery Band. The fear and bitterness engendered in this story likely was felt by the Redbones, some of whom migrated to South Carolina and elsewhere before migrating to Louisiana.

Before the Civil War, the major division of people in society was slave and free. After the war, as Gildermeister makes clear, the intermediate status of mixed-blood was mostly eliminated and the major divisions were Black and White.[244]

By the 1830s, the 1808 law prohibiting importation of foreign slaves was having the effect of reducing the supply of labor while the demand was increasing. Prices for slaves were

---

244 Enrique Eugene Gildemeister, Local Complexities of Race in the Rural South: Racially Mixed People in South Carolina (State University of New York, June, 1977).

rising. The planter elite began looking for new sources or ways to renew old sources of labor. The definition of who could be enslaved again reverted to a focus on social class. The poor White laborers could become enslaved and the stealing of children for enslavement increased.[245]

The 1850 compromise included a new fugitive slave law under which a slave owner or his representative could, and did, go into any state and apprehend an alleged runaway slave without due process. White and mixed-blood people who were free began to fear loss of their freedom. While Redbones had little or no history of being enslaved, the possibility always existed. So, there were multiple reasons to be concerned about one's racial identity beyond just a desire for social acceptance and a higher status. Freedom was at risk.

There is ample evidence, beginning with statements to offspring, to support the assertion that older settlers in the Louisiana and Texas Redbone communities wanted to hide their past. They often refused to discuss it and passed on little family history information to their offspring. The early

---

[245] Lawrence R. Tenzer, *The Forgotten Cause of the Civil War: A New Look at the Slavery Issue* (Manahawken: Scholars Publishing, 1997), p. 76.

Redbone Migrations to Louisiana

Louisiana Redbones developed a secretive and secluded lifestyle, developed a hostile attitude toward Negroes, and sometimes owned slaves. They maintained a sense of unity among themselves, even though they were not a highly structured society in a formal sense. Their communities or settlements had no formal boundaries and no formal government. As Crawford said, "they maintain the proposition that socially, all Redbones are equal; there is no nobility in the clan. In their ranks is frequent warfare, yet they quickly band together to fight a common enemy."[246]

In 1835, North Carolina ratified a new constitution which took away most of the rights of free persons of color, including the right to bear arms. Many Redbone ancestors migrated out of North Carolina into South Carolina and other states, including Louisiana.

Updated Information provided here that some, especially the Goyens, Perkins, Sherill, Mixon, Bird, Epsom, Lee, Willis, Weaver, Hall, Smiling, [Smirely] included as Francis "The Swamp Fox" Marion's Men aka Marion's Raiders had South Carolina births with a North Carolina/Tn. Migration.

---

246 Don C. Marler and Jane McManus, editors, *The Cherry Winche Country* (Hemphill, Texas: Dogwood Press, 1993), p. 2.

The Swamp Fox himself a mixed blood and born a Dwight,[247] in 1777 South Carolina, his mother or grandmother was a Goins (Guins) [248] we believe of the Goyens Clan and closely related to the James Guinns and Champness "Champ" Guins mentioned in the 1792 Franklin Co., TN. Census. George Waters, whose daughter Mary married Nimrod Perkins and removed to Louisiana. The Jeremiah Bass family (see also passport, migration to Louisiana with Wyndhams/Windhams, Hoos/ziers,) Smirely (Smiling), Tiptons, Ashurts (John) which may have been Ashworth, Driggers and others whose YDNA intermingled with a South Carolina birth to a North Carolina/TN migration after the Revolutionary War and formed most of the settlers at the Lost State of Franklin.

These males and several other related Redbone progenitors at Franklin Co., TN.[249] Remnant community of The Lost State of Franklin. See census records, The Watauga Petitions and information mentioned further here. These families appear to have a South Carolina birth, an older generation as

---

[247] Gravesite Details Francis Marion was born Dwight and adopted by his Uncle the Revolutionary Patriot when he was 15 years old so the Marion name could continue on with male heirs. Francis and Harriet Marion had 8 girls and no boys.

[248] The Alstons and Allstons of North and South Carolina" By Joseph Asbury Groves.

[249] See Attachments I, J, K.

identified in that census several are enumerated "old age" and migrated after the American Revolution to North Carolina's Lost State of Franklin, now part of Tennessee and North Carolina and purchased their bounty lands from their relatives and kin, the Overhill Cherokee. Some from Cheraw and NC/SC boarding Catawba Nation Reserve area.[250]

The 1830s brought the large-scale deportation of southeastern Indians known as "The Trail of Tears" and, in 1839, The Republic of Texas forced the Cherokee out of that country.[251] At the same time, the Choctaw in Mississippi were being driven out of that territory as their land was offered to Whites in yet another broken treaty.

On February 5, 1840, the Republic of Texas also passed an act that prohibited immigration of free Blacks and ordered all free Blacks living there to leave within two years *or be sold into slavery*.[252] (Emphasis mine). Here was the old threat to freedom that they had fled from earlier, arising once again. In 1840, three petitions from white citizens on behalf of two

---

[250] See Attachment L.
251 John Ehile, Trail of Tears: The Rise and Fall of the Cherokee Nation, (New York: Random House, 1989) and
Dianne Everett, *The Texas Cherokees: A People Between Two Fires 1819-1840*. (Norman: University of Oklahoma Press, 1990).
252 Nolan, Thompson, "Ashworth Act" in *The New Handbook of Texas*, (Austin: 1996), Vol I, pp. 267-268.

Ashworth families and a Thomas family, both living in the southeastern part of Texas, resulted in the passage of the *Ashworth Act [Goyens Act, and the Doyle Act]*. The act granted an exception to all free Blacks that were in Texas on the day of the Declaration of Texas Independence, and conferred residency [and character references] on David and Abner Ashworth who had immigrated after the declaration.[253] Despite this positive outcome, there were other Free Persons of Color, no doubt, living in the Republic who were Redbones or related to Redbones. Were it not for the *Ashworth Act*, they would have been forced to leave the Republic or be sold into slavery.

One who came under this cloud was William Goynes, a ~~quadroon from North Carolina~~, [We do not know he was a quadroon because no documentation exists as such. He was born in South Carolina as stated by the Republic of Texas original monument granted him in the 1940s by the Daughters of the Republic of Texas "DRT"] whose father had won freedom by serving in the American Revolutionary War, [No source for who his father was. The only provable relatives are by affidavits given in his estate records that William Goyens was a brother of Thomas Goyens, born ca

---

253 *Ibid.*, p. 268.

1774 in South Carolina, died Lafayette Parish Louisiana in 1825. Thomas Goyens widow, Nancy Johnson came to Texas by 1826, settled at Old El Orquisac, Liberty County, Texas[254]] and ~~whose grandmother was a free White~~. [we do not have a source for this information that his "Grandmother was a free white woman", unproven data[255]] He migrated to Texas in 1820 [with Old Thomas Williams family from Chief Bowles, Fields & Big Mushes Arkansas Cherokee camp.] Though William was said not to have had any children.[256] He did have two nephews Hadley, and Simon Goyens[257] named as heirs in his vast estate in 1856. Hadley Goyens inherited his freight hauling business. These male nephew's descendants have YDNA tested and their results are discussed later here among the Goyens Clan genetic studies, but we follow these lines of Goyens Clan more closely in the upcoming title, *Goins Book II*]. He may have migrated from ~~North to South Carolina and then on to Texas~~ [he probably

---

[254] Descendants inherited a league and labor at Liberty/Hardin and Polk counties Texas issued patent number 777, signed Sam Houston. The land is situated near Sam Houston's Grand Cane Plantation and the Isiah Sion Fields, Carriere, Aaron Cherry land along the Trinity River boardering all counties: Polk, Liberty & Hardin, Texas.

[255] much of the information here was taken from the Prince thesis which has since been proven inaccurate for reasons of falsifying source citational documents.

[256] Affidavits given in the Nancy Johson Goyens league & labor patent lawsuit, Hardin Co., Tx. 1887. Copy on file with editor.

[257] Nacogdoches County Probate Court, Hadley Goyens, appeared with Simeon aka Simon Goyens in August 1856 both recorded as "heirs and nephews" of William Goyens.

followed a South Carolina birth to the Lost State of Franklin (North Carolina/Tennessee) with now Missouri Arkansas Cherokee. William served in military campaigns in Upper Louisiana now Missouri, Illinois, and Arkansas before he arrived in Texas with other Tennessee Melungeon Cherokee Families] – that Mexican retreat from the degradation experienced by mixed-blood people all over the southeast. On January 4, 1823, the Mexican government passed a law that promised land to farmers who came to work the land and assured that there would be no "…buying or selling of slaves…"[258]

William, E/Oscar, John (of Fairfield, SC) and Simon Goyens along with YDNA genetic matched males: Old Thomas Williams, "his son" Leonardo Goyens Houston Williams (interchangeable used), John W. "Cherokee John" Williams, Wm "Old Bill" Williams, Brooks Williams born 1788 in Tennessee died at Fort Lacy, Cherokee Co., Texas on the crossing at the Sabine, in the Texican's Run-Away Scape by hostile Indians on the Louisiana side. He married Mary Ann Ellis, they had a son Robert Williams who married Vianna Mary Ashworth, and families migrated to Nacogdoches

---

258 H.P.N. Gammel, *The Laws of Texas* 1822-1987 (10 Vols., Austin, 1898, I), p. 28.

together from Missouri & Arkansas, each accused of being spies for the Mexican government.].

[William and an assumed brother, Leonardo Goyens aka Williams Houston, of Nacogdoches] both owned blacksmith businesses and gunsmith shops and [both] owned slaves. ~~While living there, he married a white woman, Mary Sibley; the wedding was performed by a Catholic priest.~~ [We are not sure where this information comes from, likely the Prince thesis, which again, has been proven inaccurate.] Mary "Maria Mary Lindsey Petra Mose Pate" was listed by these various surnames as an aggregated [259] slave in the household of William 1828-1835 Mexican censuses with "her son" Henry Sibley b.1800. Henry served in the Texas Rangers with William Goyens in 1838 when William ordered rations for both he and Henry and their horses for 60 days under order of Maj. T.P. Bush. Mary's granddaughters, Henriette, and Martha Sibley inherited half of Goyenses estate though no marriage record has ever surfaced and according to Mexican census records she was not recognized as Goyens's legal wife. It is also curious where the information comes from that in fact Mary was a white woman, as all records

---

[259] Slavery was not allowed by the Mexican Government, however, if the slave was free to hire themselves out and pay their owner a portion of earnings, then they were deemed "aggregated." *Mary or Maria Mary Lindsey Petra Mose (Moss?) Pate Sibley Goyens.*

indicated that she was a slave and her granddaughters (daughters of Henry Sibley) enumerated black, or mulatto in later census records. Granddaughters, Henriette "Conception" Sibley married Vital YBarbo grandson of the famous Antonio Gil YBarbo, who was associated with the Canary Islanders, the Cane River Creoles and, who served on the contraband court for No Man's Land Spanish land claims. He is mentioned throughout this publishing. Grandson Vital YBarbo served in the Civil War. Martha Mary Sibley married Manuel Victoria Sanchez and James Busey. Both granddaughters are listed on all located census records as Mulatto or Black. Henry Sibley was supposedly the son of Maria Mary Linsey Petra Mose Pate Sibley Goyens and Dr. John Sibley's son Henry Sibley also, who served as Indian agent Louisiana and quoted throughout this publishing, However, we have no confirmation of these facts have been produced to date that verify this relationship. And, no male heirs of Henry Sibley, son of Mary were reported.

Goyens was active in civic affairs, buying and trading land, and serving in law enforcement and served as an attorney for himself and others was frequently in court over loans and borrowed money. In 1826, Bele Yngles tried to force Goyens into slavery. Goyens, seeking to retain his freedom, paid a bribe and escaped enslavement ~~or re-enslavement~~ [there are no documents proving he was born a slave] only to face the same situation from another man who knew of the transaction. This time, Goyens appealed to the Mexican authorities and the matter was put to rest.[260] [**Family lore** passed down through the editor's family; that the pirates, Jean, and Pierre Laffite paid 5,000 cold coin for his safe release when Bill Yngles (English/Inglish) tried to enslave him. However, my family believed it had to do also with a negro winch and land which is what the documentations show that there was an exchange of land and "negrees wench." And, that his land on Nacogdoches' Half Moon prairie aka Goyens Hill where he built his plantation was the burial location of the lost Gutierrez-Magee expedition, 1812-1813 treasure. Supposedly Goyens had at his smithing shop at Nacogdoches, sealed the lids of the caskets which contained the expedition treasure. The expedition ended badly for them and Goyens had overheard their plans to bury the treasure for safe keeping and retrieve it later. Not very many years later Goyens placed his claim on the land and was

---

260 Diane Elizabeth Prince, *William Goynes, Free Negro on the Texas Frontier*, Thesis: (Stephen F. Austin State College, Nacogdoches, Texas, July, 1967), pp. 25-26. Most of the information here regarding Goyens comes from the Prince thesis. * It is with great trepidations that the editor allows the Prince, thesis citations to be republished. Her work has since been proven inaccurate and false. Those inaccuracies have been repeated many times over the years. For more accurate and up-to-date information concerning William Goyens of Nacogdoches, please see *Goins BookII and YDNA studies*, MEHRAssociation.

issued patent from Sam Houston, 1837. The treasure was never retrieved, or was it? Where did Goyens come by so much wealth? However, Goyens was not reported in Tejas 1812-1813 and was probably at Chief Big Mush or Bowels Arkansas Cherokee Camp. Perhaps he had something to do with that lost treasure later?]

Goyens served as Cherokee Interpreter and agent for Sam Houston who was exceptionally good friends with Goyens. They had probably known one another at the Lost State of Franklin and likely where both learned to speak Cherokee. Letters exchanged between Goyens and Houston prove a long friendship and relationship to the Cherokee. Houston stated Goyens was his "right-hand man" keeping the Cherokee from siding with the Mexicans during Texas Independence. In their personal exchanges, they discuss philosophical religious ideologies. Leonardo Goyens Houston Williams, a perfect YDNA matched lineage with other Goyens Clan descendants (Sweat, Perkins, Williams, Warwick, Powell) shared a business and Indian trading post in Texas with Sam Houston, Torres's Trading Post. Both he and Houston were present with Dr. Sibley at the Battle of Horseshoe Bend and who migrated from Tennessee to Louisiana and Texas.

Redbone Migrations to Louisiana

Thus, after Texas passed the new American legislation banning free colored citizens the old threat to liberty had moved west to haunt the mixed-blood people. One can only begin to imagine the fear, despair and anger that must have gripped Redbones in Louisiana and Texas, a large portion of whom were related to the Ashworth, Doyle/Dial (Bxton) and Goyenses as well as other mixed-blood people. Some had, no doubt, moved there while the territory was owned by Spain, and certainly while it was owned by Mexico. Many likely moved there because Mexico abolished slavery in 1828. Living near the border did have its advantages after all. They could cross back into Louisiana if the need arose.

William Goyens Republic of Texas monument once installed at his grave at Half Moon prairie (Goyens Hill) Nacogdoches, TX. vandalized by landowners, broken into 2 pieces, and pushed into the Ysleta Creek. Retrieved and restored by local philanthropist, Dr. Bright and placed at the top of Goyens Hill. Later, vandals shot it (rifle bullet holes and repairs are still visible) then pushed over and broken in 3 pieces by further vandals. The monument was once again repaired by Dr. Bright and moved to the Nacogdoches Co., courthouse where Goyens once ran his blacksmithing shop.

"His skin was black, his heart true blue"

Redbones of Louisiana

An early portrait of **Sam Houston** in full Cherokee regalia. Sam also spoke Cherokee and his legendary relationship with that tribe in Tennessee & North Carolina is widely accepted. He was the Indian Agent for Tennessee. Also notice the Turban type headdress of the Cherokee. Dr. Brent Kennedy identified the word used by the Tennessee Tsali Cherokee[261] word for "great leader" "Duwali" as Turkish. More details in the upcoming title, *GTT..Redbones Gone To Texas* and *The Goins Book II*.

---

[261] Tsali (Cherokee: ᏣᎵ), originally of Coosawattee Town (Kusawatiyi), was a noted leader of the Cherokee during two different periods of the history of the tribe. As a young man, he followed the Chickamauga Cherokee war chief, Dragging Canoe, from the time the latter migrated southwest during the Cherokee–American wars. In 1812 he became known as a prophet, urging the Cherokee to ally with the Shawnee Tecumseh in war against the Americans. Later, during the 1830s roundup of Cherokee for Indian Removal, Tsali, his wife and brother, his three sons and their families were taken by surprise and marched at bayonet point toward the Indian Agency on the Hiwasee River. Some marched to Tahlequah kept going and went passed the Rockies. This group reappeared in Missouri and Arkansas after the New Madrid earthquake predicted by Tecumseh. Temporary Chief John Looney, Tn. Chief Vann, Bowles and Fields were all leaders of this group who later showed up in Louisiana and Mexican Texas.

Portrait of an Ottoman Empire Turk in traditional clothing and headdress. Right, Sequoyah, a Native American polymath of the Cherokee Nation. In 1821 he completed his independent creation of a Cherokee syllabary, making reading and writing in Cherokee possible. He was born at Tuskegee and died in 1843, San Fernando, Mexico. He married Sally Benge. His parents were Nathaniel Gist & Tuskagee woman Wut-the. He was close allies with Chief John Ross, also a Redbone progenitor, his ancestry included Clark, Williams, Ward, Conrad, Fields, Miller.

Solomon Northrup, a Free Person of Color (born free) living in New York, was abducted from that state by slave traders and sold to plantation owners in central Louisiana. He ended up on a plantation less than a half-hour ride by horseback from Westport – a major Louisiana Redbone settlement. Northrup was enslaved from 1841-1853 when he was

Redbones of Louisiana

assisted to escape back to New York.²⁶² Plantation owners could enslave a person without due process as discussed elsewhere. By that time, Redbones were firmly established in the area and must have been aware of this mixed-blood person's free/slave status, either during his enslavement or shortly thereafter. This event, following closely the Texas threat, must have galvanized the Redbone settlement at the time and strengthened their resolve to remain silent, separate, and strong in defense of their freedom. It must have appeared to Redbones that here, as in the southeast, free mixed-blood persons who had never been slaves were under threat of becoming enslaved.

No evidence has been found that any attempt was ever made in Louisiana to enslave a Redbone. Anyone wishing to enslave one of them would have been asking for more trouble than he could have managed. Redbones had a history of freedom and autonomy, they had lived hard lives, many outside the law, and their culture accommodated violence; besides, they were "Marion Men" (~~some~~ many had served with Francis Marion "The Swamp Fox"), and were good guerilla fighters, so an attacker would have paid dearly for his trouble.

---

262 Sue Eakin, *Solomon Northrup's Twelve Years a Slave – 1841-1853*. Rewritten by Sue Eakin (Bossier City: Everett, Col 1990).

Redbone Migrations to Louisiana

If the theory that their migration west, their secretiveness, hostile stance and culture were all part of an attempt to preserve their liberty, are they not heroes in the tradition of the colonists who revolted against the Crown?

It should be kept in mind that in the early decades after the 1800, Territory of Orleans (now the State of Louisiana) was configured much differently from what it was later. The Neutral Zone was created in 1806, and new settlers were forbidden from moving there until 1821, yet; we see many moving into the area between the Calcasieu and Sabine Rivers during those years. That they did so in spite of the prohibition against it, is evidence of their spirit of independence, adventure, or desperation.

The El Camino Real (Kings Highway) ran from St. Augustine, Florida to Mexico City. Frank Mobley, in *El Camino Real*[263], discusses the part of the road from Natchez to Natchitoches in some detail. Some early settlers came to Louisiana by ship, some by the northern route entering from Arkansas, but the vast majority came by El Camino Real. They came to Natchez over the section we know as The Natchez Trace [some came via Tennessee, Magoffin Co., Ky.

---

263 Frank Mobley, *El Camino Real* (Dallas: Private Printing, 1995).

Redbones of Louisiana

To Indiana and Illinois Country or Upper Louisiana] and from Natchez to Natchitoches over the section known as Harrisonburg Road. Those coming over the Harrisonburg Road crossed the Red River at St. Maurice, which is between Montgomery and Natchitoches, Louisiana. From St. Maurice, they either proceeded through Natchitoches to western Louisiana and to what is now Texas, or they came south through Cotile (now Boyce) and from there to areas such as Hineston, Sugartown, Walnut Hill or Alexandria. While traveling up the Harrisonburg Road, many settlers wearied of the trail, no doubt, settled in the beautiful forests through which they were passing. Some with names that have been associated with Redbones and who are known to have lived near the old Harrisonburg Road were Adams, Basco, Brock, Byrd, Carter, Cloud, Collins, Curry, Evans, Davis, Dean, Dyess, Farris, Gibbs, Green, Hall, Harper, Harvey, Hicks, James, Jenkins, Jones, Johnson, Lewis, Martin, Mathis, Moore, Neal, Perkins, Pinder, Ray, Reeves, Roberts, Simmons, Smiling, Spikes, Sweat, Taylor, Thompson, Stanley, West, Walters, Williams, Wilson, Wise and Woods.

Natchitoches Parish extended east of the Red River back then, and the census shows many Redbone related names living in that parish in the mid-1800s. In 1850, according to one source, 63,000 immigrants passed through Natchitoches on their way to Texas.[264] Many of the Louisiana piney woods settlers had abandoned their cabins, they were "Gone to Texas." Many of the new immigrants, weary of the travel, settled into these abandoned cabins. "A countless number retired into the forest, built log cabins, and supported themselves by hunting, fishing, and occasionally herding cattle for the Texas drovers."[265]

Before getting to the settlers in Louisiana, a look at those in the nearby Natchez District is in order since many of them later migrated to Louisiana. By 1784, there were several persons living in the Natchez District whose names, or at least surnames are relevant. They are:

Gibson, Clark, Richard Curtis, Samuel Davis, Clemon Dyson, Thomas Evans, Elijah Flowers, Gidion Gibson, Ruben Gibson, Samuel Gibson, Richard Goodwin, Abner Green, Joseph Green, Thomas Green, John Griffin, Peter Hawkins, Jeremiah Hill, Sarah Holmes, Debdal Holt, Elijah Holt, Nathaniel Ivy, James Jackson, Isaac Johnson, John Jones, Russel Jones, Caleb King, Issac Lewis, Manuel Madden, John Martin, Nehemiah Martin, Thomas Osborn, William Owens, Jacob Paul, Joseph Perkins, Daniel Perry,

---

[264] B.H. Payne, Report on the Algiers and Opelousas Railroad, (New Orleans: 1851), p. 18.
[265] Shugg, *op. cit.* Some redbones were known as drovers in South Carolina and were listed on the Louisiana Census

Samuel Phipps, Thomas Reed, James Simons, David Smith, Zacheriah Smith, William Smith, Joseph Standly, Abraham Taylor, Sarah Welch, Cato West, John White, James Wilson, and Margaret Woods. [266] Some of the most common surnames were represented by many given names, so in some cases, only a representative surname is given here. (See the reference for a complete listing.)

By 1788, according to the Natchez Court Records Book B, there were also: Thomas Nash, Joel Bird, William West, John Coleman John Vaughn, John Curtis, Mark Cole, Asabel Lewis, William Collins, Jacob Nash and Samuel Levi Wells.

La Petites Nations

Alabama Muscogee

Jackson Doyle, the son of Nimrod, an Indian Countrymen[267] born 1790 at Broken Arrow Tribal Town, Creek Nation and died in 1846 in Texas & Susannah Isles/Islands Doyle born

---

266 Caroll Ainsworth McElligott, *Residents of the Natchez District: 1784*. Harleyville, S.C: Volume I of the Colonial Mississippi Series. Ainsworth McElligott Enterprises, 1988.

[267] Countrymen were in general prosperous Indian traders, and negotiators usually a white man who had mixed with Indian women. Most of these men, and their sons were headmen between the United States officials and tribal headmen. Most all of these men had a military background and were wealthy. The first documented "countrymen" came out of South Carolina, and included Vann, Martin, McIntosh, Weatherford, Blount, Ross and others.

1785 in Alabama. Susannah Isle's parents were Joseph Islands and Missy McIntosh, she died in 1854 in Nacogdoches, Texas.

Jackson Doyle, according to his petition made to the State of Texas, he was born the 8th of July 1816 at Creek Nation, Alabama. However, census records in Texas vary from an Alabama birth to a Georgia birth. He also states in the Doyle Act that himself, and wife and child crossed the Sabine from Louisiana in December of 1839. He served in 1840 in an Indian campaign on the Brazos as 1st Sergeant under his father, Nimrod Doyle, Captain. And, that he is by birth one half blood Creek Indian, and that he had never received land or headright for his service to the Republic of Texas.

Though Nimrod and Susannah had several more children, the family is highlighted in the book, *Belles of the Creek Nation,* by Scott Hodalee Sewell. Only Jackson, Winchester, and one daughter are named in his estate, in Texas. Thus, an inheritance court case sprung up in Texas when Nimrod passed away, leaving a large estate to his "free black" children. A vast sprawl of land, plantation, and personal property. However, at the time it was not legal for a "free black" to inherit anything, in fact they were not allowed to remain in the state. Thus, sprung the "Doyle

Act," and as Don has explained further here, these "Acts" in Texas (Goyens, Ashworth, Doyle Acts) forced free blacks to leave the state on pain of slavery. The Acts could be passed by good services to the Republic of Texas, and or character witness. Jackson Doyle asserted exception to this law through his, and his father's military contributions. He was awarded land and his father's estate in 1859. Jackson served as a Texas Ranger, Republic of Texas, and the Civil War. He was registered a "free Black" in Texas and married Puss Tayler (sic) born Alabama and died in Van Zandt, Texas. Winchester born 1828 in Alabama married Nancy Brewer born in Mississippi also received an exception.

Artwork depicting Nimrod Doyle, displayed in color on the cover of *Belles of The Creek Nation* by Scot Hodalee Sewell

TO ALL WHOM IT MAY CONCERN, Notice is hereby given that at the ensuing session of the Legislature of the State of Texas to assemble on the second Tuesday in January, 1879, Jackson Doyle will apply to said legislature for the passage of a special law granting him such lands as he may be entitled to as a citizen of the state of Texas—this Dec. 10, 1878

Jackson Doyle, in 1879 received land for his service as Texas Ranger.

Jackson Doyle
"Doyle Act" of Texas

Locations of Mvskoke Towns

Upper Creeks: Lived along the Coosa and Tallapoosa rivers in Alabama. Many Upper Towns were close to Ft. Toulouse and supported the French.

Lower Creeks: Lived along the Flint and Chattahoochee rivers in Georgia. Many Lower Towns were close to Florida and were friendly to the Spanish.

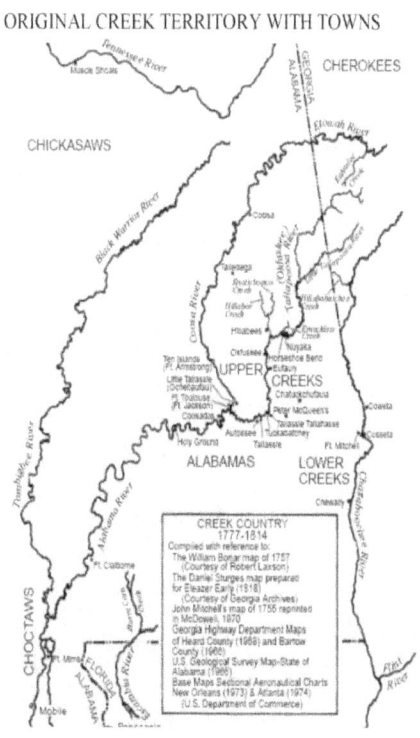

Red River Pakana Muscogee[268]

The Apalachee

The Apalachee, a "Petites Nations"[269] so called by the French government in 1763, when they petitioned for permission to relocate and settled in Louisiana. The delegation of Apalachee arrived in New Orleans from Tensas area around Fort Toulouse, prior to the transfer of the colony to Spain.

---

[268] LOC
269 Petites Nations": small, independent Southeastern Indian nations, many of whom relocated from east of the Mississippi River to colonial Louisiana to avoid English and American expansions.

Redbone Migrations to Louisiana

History of Apalachee Migrations from Florida

The Apalachee had lived in Florida and were among the first indigenous North Americans to be encounter by the European explorers. A strong tribe of more than 50,000 people, their villages centered around agriculture and organized under powerful chiefdoms. Spanish explorers found the Apalachee hostile and defensive of their territories. But the persistence of conflict and attacks by Spanish explorers along with virgin soil diseases brought by them brought about the death and destruction that swept through annihilating 1000s of Indians. The Apalachee numbers dwindled so drastically by the 17th century that those who did not die of explorer military aggressions, starvations or disease succumb to the European colonizers and were now bound to the Catholic mission system.

In 1702 a large Apalachee war party was severely defeated by Creek Indians assisted by some English traders, and in 1704 an expedition from South Carolina under Colonel Moore practically destroyed the nation. Moore claims to have carried away the people of three towns and the greater part of the population of four more and to have left but two towns and part of another. Most of these latter appear to have fled to Old Mobile Bay area, where, in 1705, they were granted land on which to settle around Fort Toulouse. The Apalachee who had been carried off by Moore were established near New Windsor, South Carolina, but when the Yamasee[270] War broke out they joined the hostile Indians and retired for a time to the Lower Creek settlements. Not long after, the English among the Lower Creeks became ascendant and the Apalachee returned to Florida, some remaining near their old country and others settling close to Pensacola to be near their relatives about the Mobile area.

By 1718 another Apalachee settlement had been organized by the Spaniards near San Marcos de Apalachee and close to their old country. In 1728 only two small Apalachee towns remained. Most of them gravitated finally to the neighborhood of Pensacola. In 1764, the year after all French and Spanish possessions east of the Mississippi passed into the hands of Great Britain, the Apalachee, along with several other tribes, migrated into Louisiana, now held by Spain, and settled on Red River, where they and the Taensa conjointly occupied a strip of land between Bayou d'Arro and Bayou Jean de Jean. Most of this land was sold in 1803 and the Apalachee, reduced to a small band, appear to have moved

---

[270] See Govinda Sanyal Chapter, *Carolina Genesis, Beyond the Color Line* for mtDNA research to Billy Bowlegs, Seminole Chief, the Yamasee and his maternal Gypsy ancestry.

about in the same general region until they disappeared. They are now practically forgotten, though a few mixed-blood Apalachee are still said to be in existence. A few accompanied the Creeks to Oklahoma.

Apalachee Population. Mooney (1928) estimates 7,000 Apalachee Indians in 1650, a figure which seems to me to be ample. Governor Salazar's mission-by-mission estimate in 1675 yielded a total of 6,130, and a Spanish memorial dated 1676 gives them a population of 5,000. At the time of Moore's raid there appear to have been about 2,000. The South Carolina Census of 1715 gives 4 Apalachee villages, 275 men, and 638 souls. As the Mobile Apalachee were shortly afterward reduced to 100 men, the number of the entire tribe in 1715 must have been about 1,000. By 1758 they appear to have fallen to not much over 100, and in 1814 Sibley reported but 14 men in the Louisiana band, signifying a total of perhaps 50 (Sibley, 1832). Morse's estimate (1822) of 150 in 1817 is evidently considerably too high.

Connection in which they have become noted. The Apalachee were mentioned repeatedly as a powerful and warlike people, and this character was attested by their stout resistance to Narvaez and De Soto. The sweeping destruction which overtook them at the hands of the Creeks and

Carolinians marks an epoch in Southeastern history. Their name is preserved in Apalachee Bay and River, Fla.; Apalachee River, Ga., Apalachee River, Ala.; and most prominently of all, in the Appalachian Mountains, and other terms derived from them. Tallahassee, the capital of Florida, the name of which signifies Old Town, is on the site of San Luis de Talimali, the principal Spanish mission center. There is a post village named Apalachee in Morgan County, Ga.

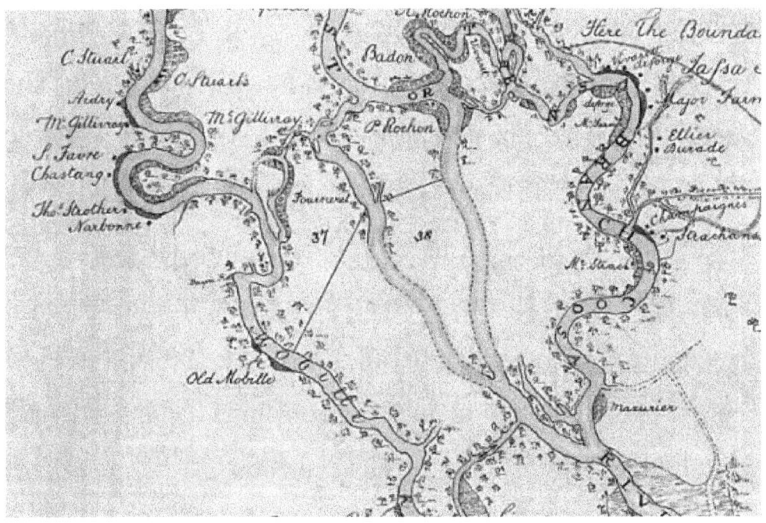

Thomas Strother, a progenitor Redbone in Louisiana's settlement at Old Mobile Bay area and the Aphallacha (sic) Indians also settlers' neighbors include, Chastang, Johnson, Hall, Sizemore, LeFevre, McGillivray, Narbonne (Darbonne), Stuart, Adry (Autry), Badon, Chastangs,

Champagnes, Cartier (Carriere), Sizemore all in the general area. Struthers male lines to Louisiana Redbone Families: Struthers, A., a merchant in Pensacola, West Fla., 1781., Struthers, James, trading between Port Glasgow and Montserrat, 1744, Struthers, William, born 1733, an Indian trader in Augusta, Ga., probate Ga. 1761, Struthers, William, a merchant in Mobile, West Fla., 1769.

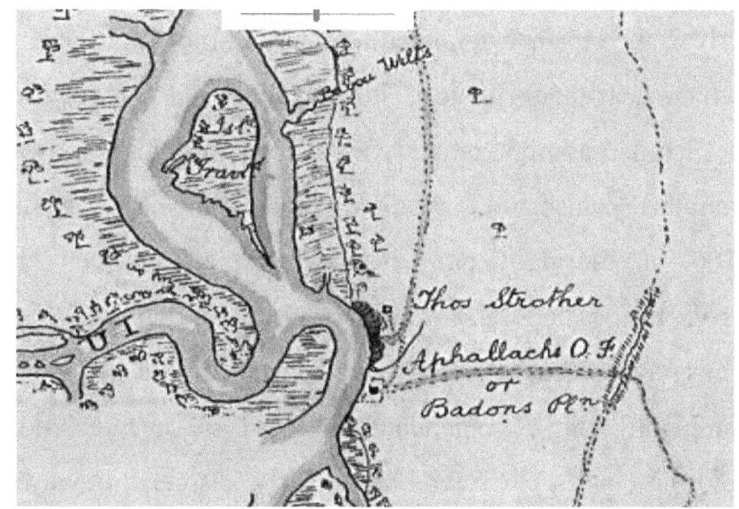

Thos. Strother & Aphallache (sic) at Badons Pt.

When the Apalachee petitioned the French Government at New Orleans, they provided the Apalachee Indians with boats, supplies, and guides to take them to their newly acquired land the on Red River, present day Rapides Parish. The land would lay about halfway between the Natchitoches post and the confluence of the Red and Mississippi Rivers

(Hunter 1994:4-5). See also map of 1770 settlers titled River Mississippi, from River Yazoo to the River Iberville presented later here which documents the Red River inlet.

However, not long after they had settled into their new lands, and built a village, cleared, and planted crops and were living autonomously until the Spanish Etienne Layssard arrived to serve as commandant of the district in 1767. Shortly after his arrival, the Apalachee helped to clear land for the Alabama Indians near their village. The Apalachee did not welcome the Spanish administrator. After all, they had turned away from the Spanish and toward the French in the early years of 1700 in Florida. Land disputes erupted between the Apalachee Indians and the encroaching settlers. One Mr. Vincent, a local French Cane River Creole lodged a complaint with Commandant Layssard for encroachment onto his land. The land was clearly disputed however, Vincent was allowed by Layssard use of the land until the Governor could consulted on the matter. A few mornings later, the Apalachee tribal leader, Martin and the entire Apalachee village arrived at Commandant Layssards plantation and began to fell trees and clear land for crops. When Layssard protested, tribal Chief Martin informed him that "since Vincent was allowed to use their land, they would take some of the commandant's in return" (Hunter 1994:5).

The Apalachee were known as a fierce and willfully independent tribe who quickly responded in asserting their sovereign rights, and after their altercations with Layssards, the Governor awarded them their own parish. The Parish of St. Luis des Appalages was established at the Apalachee village in 1764 (Hunter 1994:6). And, in 1765, they destroyed British supplies at Iberville. [271] Thus further stressing their relationship with the British, and I would venture to say why they petitioned the French Government to resettle outside West British Florida.

For the remainder of the later 18th century, the Apalachee and other La Petites Nations lived free and autonomously as sovereign people and nations in on the land given them by the French. Their neighbors surrounding them were Free People of Color, French Creoles, and other remnant Petite Nations with whom they formed close friendships, trade, and no doubt familial ties, including the Redbones in the area. Though some of their chief families spread out into other areas of Louisiana (Tribal leader Chief Etienne living near Shreveport) leaving to represent the Apalachee and their village was Louis, chief of the Taensa whose wife was

---

[271] The new régime, 1765-1767, Alvord, Clarence Walworth, 1868-1928: Carter, Clarence Edwin, 1881-1961, Croghan, George, 1720?-1782. Springfield, Ill., Illinois State Historical Library, 1916. Digital I.D. http://hdl.loc.gov/loc.gdc/gdclccn.16010691 pg. 186.

Apalachee, and who had settled with the Apalachee on Red River by 1788. Leaving their village lands unprotected from encroaching white settlers, outlaws, trappers & traders, merchants, and scoundrels thirsty to take from them their valuable Red River land.

After the Louisiana Purchase no peace would be enjoyed by these tiny nations of Indians. As traders, and Anglo settlers streamed into the area, so did the merchant lechers and land pirates. In about 1814, the merchant Alexander Fulton and William Miller attached a debt of 2,600.00 to the Apalachee Villagers and took their land in leu of that debt. Though some of the Apalachee headmen took accountability for the debt, others had not consented to them and in 1814 the Apalachee lodged formal complaints with the U.S. Land Office in Opelousas. The Apalachee charged that Miller and Fulton had never paid them for the land, they had "purchased" and the Apalachee further denied having been indebted to the merchants in the first place. Indian agent Dr. John Sibley supported the Apalachee cause, writing the U. S. land commissioners (January 20, 1814, ASP, PL, 1834, III:218) to refute the purported debt and sale of land to the merchants. Unfortunately for the tribes under his authority, Sibley was replaced as Indian agent shortly thereafter, due in part to his attempts to protect the rights of the Indian groups within his agency. At this time, the Apalachee village contained about 25 families who divided their time between hunting and agriculture (ASP, PL III, 1834:218).

The land commissioners did recognize a problem with the Miller and Fulton transaction and recommended in 1813 that title be confirmed to the merchants for the Taensa land only (ASP, PL II, 1834:796). Instead of awarding title to the Apalachee village site collectively to the tribe, however, the commissioners auctioned off the remainder of the tract as public land. It was purchased by Isaac Baldwin, who also purchased the Fulton and Miller claim. Baldwin established his plantation just below the Apalachee village and immediately began efforts to evict the disenfranchised Indians from their homes (Hunter 1985:26). Approximately 150 Apalachee and Taensa still occupied the Red River village at that time. Kenneth McCrummen who surveyed the land in 1819, located the "Indian burying ground" on the west side of the river near the village site. The Indians occupied both sides of the river, including the large point south and east of the burial ground on which McCrummen notes "Indians hold this part."[272] According to Spanish land deed

---

272 National Archives, Washington, D.C., Letters Received by the Office of Indian Affairs, 1824-1880. (Courtesy Donald G. Hunter)

records and U.S. patents, the Apalachee lands were surveyed, divided, and purchased by mostly white American settlers.

From this point forward, the Apalachee along with all Petite Nations would suffer intense persecution at the hands of the ever-increasing numbers of White or Anglo-American immigrants. Racism which seems to follow into the area with the White commitment to slavery and the wanton greed for the lush and fertile lands of Southwest Louisiana. However, with them they brought a brisk trade, and commerce which completed their dominance over the territory and the survival of such Petites Nations fell into a questionable future. And, with the Louisiana purchase, the La Petites Nations lost a great balance of peace they had enjoyed with the Spanish and French casta systems. All of which cost them dearly.

To escape their complete annihilation, the remaining Apalachee tribal families sought refuge in marginalized ecological and occupational safe zones in the Kisatchie Hills in Natchitoches Parish. Through the dispute over the village lands continued for several years, and in 1832, Indian Agent Jehiel Brooks recommended that title to the Apalachee lands undergo legal investigation and that the sale to Baldwin be canceled (Hunter 1985:28). Baldwin, however, persisted in his attempts to evict the Indians, boasting in 1826 that he had been able to evict all but five or six families. Indian agent George Gray stated in 1827 that depredations by Baldwin had driven at least ten families of Apalachee and Taensa into Texas (Hunter 1994:29-31).

Patents to part of the disputed tract had still not been issued by 1832, but the Apalachee had abandoned their village site by the time they petitioned the U. S. Senate and House of Representatives for reparations in 1834 (Bailey 1834).

> "The Apelatch (sic) Nation of Indians Residing in the State of Louisiana and parish of Rapides on the left Bank of Red River most Respectfully States, that they have inhabited the above-named place for the last 80 or 90 years, that we had made considerable Improvements in Bilding [sic] our Village besides Improving and cultivating the lands, that some time in the year of 1830 our lands was offered for sale at the land office . . . when one Isaac Baldwin became the purchaser of all our Village together with the land, shortly after which time our village was burnt, our farm lands wasted, and our women and children driven from our lands by the said Baldwin."

The last official census of the tribe made by Indian Agent George Gray in 1825 counted twenty men and twenty-five women (Hunter 1994:30). Ownership of the Apalachee village site remained in dispute for decades to come. Although part of the land was eventually awarded to an Apalachee descendent in 1853, her Anglo-American husband received patent to the land (Benguerel and Posey, March 18, 1857, GLO). The Apalachee then living in the Kisatchie Hills never learned of the final disposition of their tribal lands.

A group of Talamalia Band of Appalachee Indians around Kisatchi Hills

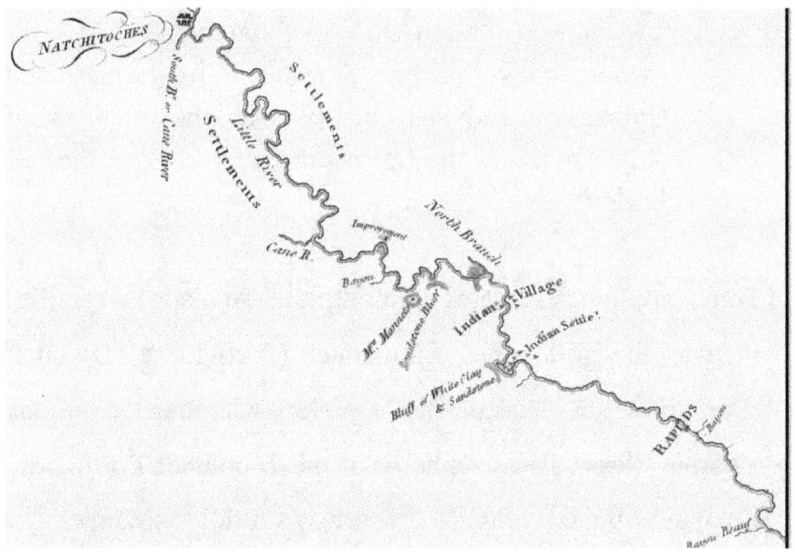

1760s Map illustrating settlements along the Red River including the Apalachee Indian Village identified here "Indian Village" between Bayou Boeuf and Natchitoches, Louisiana.

An excerpt from Miscellaneous Indians of North Carolina[273]

Georgia

In most of the counties along the northern border of this state are to be found many hundreds of people of part Cherokee descent . . .

> . . . It is reliably reported that a small group of 100 or more Cherokees and Creeks are at present in a settlement near Shellbluff Landing in Burke County, about Ten-Miles south of Augusta, and almost on the Savannah River. The family names are Clark, Woods, Shafer and Deal. Their settlement is sometimes

---

[273] Indian Communities East of the Mississippi, 1948; per a Report by the Smithsonian Institute

known as "Shafertown" or "Shafersville". . . . In earlier days Yuchi, Shawnee, Apalachee and Chickasaw Indians clustered in the vicinity of Augusta where the Savannah River crossed the fall line.[274]

Some common surnames among the Apalachee families include the following: Emmanuel (Portuguese), Bennett (Portuguese),[275] Martin, Basco, Valery who married into the Ybarbo. Please also see photos of the Tennessee Portuguese Emanuel/Manuel family courtesy Eddie Manuel, a Tennessee Melungeon.

The Pakana [Pakanatalaché]

Dr. John Sibley, the Louisiana Indian agent for the United States reported in 1805 only one hundred and fifty Pakana Muskogee's were living on Calcasieu Bayou, forty miles southwest of Natchitoches, Louisiana in the heart of Redbone country.

The Pakana like the Appalachee and Teanse settled near Fort Toulouse from Tallahassee area of Florida. From a letter

---

[274] Indian Communities East of the Mississippi, 1948; per a Report by the Smithsonian Institute. Accessed through website maintained by Vance Hawkins with direct link here: http://vancehawkins.blogspot.com/2013/03/indian-communities-eastof-mississippi.html

[275] http://sunnyokanagan.com/manuel/index.html My Manuel Family Tree 2010 Andrew Bennett

written by M. d'Abbadie, governor of Louisiana, April 10, 1764, we know that they emigrated to Red River at the same time as the Taensa and Apalachee.[276] He calls them "Pakanas des Alibamons," either from the name of the French post or from the fact that they were related to the Alabama Indians. Later these Pakana settled upon Calcasieu River in southwestern Louisiana, as shown in the following account given by Sibley:

"Pacanas, are a small tribe of about thirty men, who live on the Quelqueshoe [Calcasieu] River, which falls into the bay between Attakapa and Sabine, which heads in a prairie, called Cooko prairie, about forty miles southwest of Natchitoches. These people are likewise emigrants from West Florida, about forty years ago. Their village is about fifty miles southeast of the Conchattas; are said to be increasing a little in number; quiet, peaceable, and friendly people. Their own language differs from any other but speak Mobilian."

In about 1800 John Burgess, a so-called Frenchmen closely related to the Redbone families in Vernon and Calcasieu parishes staked his land in today's western Polk Co., Texas; called the Burgess Survey. In about 1813 there was a great Indian uprising, we do not have any details, except that John

---

[276] Amer. Antiq., XIII, pp. 252-253.

Burgess and wife Unknown Ash/Nash were killed leaving several orphan children, subsequently taken in and reared by the other Redbone families established in Calcasieu Parish, Louisiana. One of these orphans was Elizabeth Burgess, the great grandmother of the editor, and who was married to Leonard Covington Sweat, famed Rawhide Fight participant and Jayhawker. Legend is, he was ambushed and killed by his in-laws, the Nash/Ash family, and the Keefer Family. We do not know why but that he was shot, rode some distance, and died at a church near Jasper, Jasper Co., Texas and is buried in an unmarked grave.

John Burgess was married to a member of the Pakana Muskogee[277], and according to genealogical records and affidavits given in a marriage document of Elizabeth Burgess to Leonard Covington "LC" Sweat; Mr. Groves stated that Elizabeth was a daughter of "his wife's sister" who was a Nash/Ash, daughter of Thomas Nash/Ash. Thomas Ash/Nash, a progenitor forefather of nearly all Louisiana Redbone families.[278] Though her name is unknown to us now, it is though accounts of Texas Handbook history, that

---

[277]Texas Handbook, Online
https://www.tshaonline.org/handbook/entries/pakana-muskogee-indians.
[278] McManus, Jane. *A Backward Glance*. Pineville: Parker Enterprises, 1986.

states his wife was a "Pakana Muscogee" Indian from the Red River Indian's of Southwestern Louisiana.

According to the Texas Handbook, John Burgess invited other tribal members from his wife's clan to relocate to their survey in Texas, from Louisiana Red River region. There was a "Widow Burgeff" listed in the 1810 Opelousas census records next door to Thomas Ash, Gibson Johnson, Gideon Gibson, Thomas Goyens, Benjamin Goings, Benjamin Ash and Jean Baptists Laffite who we believe to be the same as the Pirate, Jean Laffite. John Burgess, laid survey on 640 acres of land along Kickapoo Creek.

The property was inherited by Burgess's wife and subsequently by other members of the tribe and became a permanent home for the Pakana Muscogee in Polk County. In 1859 Texas Governor Hardin appointed James Barclay to serve as agent for the Muskogee's, as well as for the Alabama and Coushatta who lived in Polk County. Responsibility for the Muskogee was included also in the duties of agents appointed for the Polk County Indians in 1861-65, 1867, 1868, and 1872. On November 12, 1866, the Texas legislature passed an act granting the Polk County Muskogee, 320 acres of land.

Matilda Sweat Mason Nash/Ash and son, **Guide Emmanuel Nash/Ash**, great grandfather, and great great grandmother of the editor. She was the daughter of Leonard Covington "LC" and Elizabeth Burgess Sweat Wife of and son of Emanuel "Command" Nash/Ash.

Unfortunately, the land was never purchased, and they continued to live on the John Burgess Survey without title. The population of this Pakana Muskogee community declined slowly almost from the date of the tribe's first appearance in Polk County: fifty were counted in 1859; forty-two were reported in 1882. The remaining probably died off because of illness and assimilations with the nearby Alabama and Coushatta. In 1899, persuaded by Creek Indians from Oklahoma, Chief John Blount and many of the Polk County Muskogees went to the Creek Nation in Oklahoma to live. Only a few-less than ten-Pakana Muskogees remained in their settlement on the John Burgess Survey.

An early chief of the Pakana Muskogee's, a Seminole Indian Chief Blount/Blunt, was awarded a silver medal of honor for his services as a guide to Gen. Andrew Jackson during the Seminole War in Florida. And, in 1834 John Blount/Blunt while en-route to Texas via New Orleans died in Louisiana. I am not sure at this writing if he in fact died in Louisiana and presented his medal or was passed to the chiefs of the tribe: David Elliott, Bill Blount, John Blount (grandson of the earlier chief with the same name), and Alex Davis and remains among their people to this day.

In a history account of Polk Co., Texas appeared the following article and picture by "Special Writer" Aline Thompson Rothe.

> "In a small trunk in the Log cabin of Jonas Davis in the Piney Woods of Polk County, some 14 miles

West of Livingston, there is a Sterling silver article that would probably occupy a place of honor against framed black velvet in a locked case if it were displayed in a museum. This rare piece of Sterling silver is an engraved eye shield presented by president Andrew Jackson to Jonas Davis is maternal great gran father John blunt, a noted Muskogee scout. It was given him in recognition of his service during the Seminole war, 130 years ago and bears the following inscription".[279]

"Andrew Jackson, president, U.S. of America to John Blunt, his faithful guide in the Seminole war."

Thirty plus years later, in 1834 the Pakana Muskogee's moved to a site on Penwau, translated from Creek means "Turkey"[280] Slough two miles east of its junction with the Trinity River in present Polk County, Texas. This location was on a high hill, generally believed to be the peninsula that extends into Lake Livingston and is known as Indian Hill.

[279] 1952: Houston Chronicle.
[280] S. Pony Hill

Redbone Migrations to Louisiana

Jonas Davis [son of Tilly Blunt, grandson of Chief William "Billy" Blunt[281]], descendant of a noted Muskogee Indian chief, proudly wears a silver eye shield presented by Andrew Jackson to his maternal great Gran father for his scouting services in the Seminole war.

The Redbones, and Petite's Nations share a most common migrations from the Florida's (East & West British Florida's) to Tensas and thence noted rush of Redbones to Rapides Parish Louisiana. Some later settling around Kisatchi Hills & Bayou, where Redbones had extensive land claims in the Neutral Zone, or No Man's Land.

---

[281] Steven Pony Hill, Strangers in Their Own Land: South Carolina's State Indian Tribes, 3rd Edition, Backintyme Publishing.

In about 1834, a Petitie's Nation associated with the Muscogee Creek of Alabama, the Pakana Muskogee, and the Apalachee Indians migrated from the Red River area of Louisiana boarder region. This small band of Pakana settled near Onalaska in western Polk County, Texas. The band originally living near Fort Toulouse, a few miles north of Montgomery, Alabama, and moved to Louisiana shortly after, or with the 1763 migration of Apalachee.

It is through the French Burgess, Strother/Strawther, Johnson, Hall, and Sizemore connection that the Redbones claim familial relationship with the Apalachee. Though I believe we can find some lineages with earlier ties through DNA studies to the Strothers, Hall, Sizemore, Johnson, Chastang, Martin, LaFantasy, and Portuguese Bennett and Emanuel families, Vallery and Ybarbo (Ebarb) families. Each following into Texas among the remnant Red River French La Petites Nations including the Coushatta, Pakana, Teanse, and Appalachee (sic).

The Pakana united with the Alabama living in Texas, where they are still remembered. The last survivor was an old woman who died many years ago. Her language was said to be distinct from Alabama.

Redbone Settlers to Early Louisiana

By 1770 a plat map appears to designate the landowners on the East side of the Mississippi River then controlled until 1793 by British Empire. This area which spanned between the Florida east coast to the Mississippi. At the time, this was a tenuous area of interest between Spain, France, Britain, and the United States.

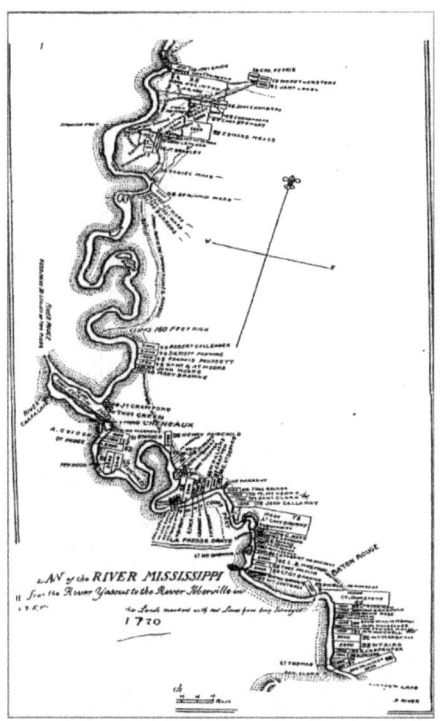

Plat map was collected at the Mississippi State Archives, Jackson, Mississippi, 2002 by the editor.

Settlers from Southern most portion at Ibberville to northern most settlers at confluences of the Yazoo rivers with the Red River merging about halfway between them.

McIntosh, John
Dan Clark
Lt. Thomas
Collins, (first initial illegible)
Carpenter, R.
Aird, Wm.
Marshall, Wm.
Mitchell, Wm.
Means, Howard
Illegible, John
Williams, David
Illegible
Illegible
Ross, David
Illegible, Bradford
Johnstone, Illegible (at Baton Rouge)
Nicols, Illegible
Outhhall, Wm.
Gower, Dan.
Brown, Lt, G.
Mims, Thos.
Illegible (Bastrop?), L.B.
Illigeble, Cuthbert
Browne, Lt. Wm.[282]
Warrant, Illegible
Illegible

Illegible
Conway
Marks
Reason
Hays, G or C.
Brown, Lt. Govr[283].
Gallaway, John
Clark, Daniel
McNeray
Gower, Thos.
Warrant (Warren?)
Derbone (Derbonne), C.Wm.
Crofton, C.
Williams, W.
Illegible
Illegible
Illegible (Marrow?)
Illegible
Illegible
Palmer, John
Illegible
Fairchild, Henry
Coles, Illegible
W/Hood, Mrs.
Hodge, D
DeVaugh, S.
Goidon, A.

---

282 west side below Point Coupe & adjacent of Illegible, Cuthbert
283 at Fort Point Coupe

Warrant (Warren), Illegible
Cheneaux, Thos
Green, Thos
Crawford, Js. (James)
River Chafalaia (sic)
Gowyn, Thos.
Browne, Mary
Moore, John
Moore, Wm. Wm. & A.
Fanning, Silvistra
Callender, Robert
"Cliffs 100 Ft. High"
Path to the illegible village
& Manshac (sic)
Burrows,
Ward, Jos.
Ward, Wm.

Ward, Benjamin
Ward, Daniel
Illegible, Dr.
Bradley, J.
Lefluer
McIntosh
Meass, Edward
Stewart, C. Wm.
Carrothers, S.
Chambers, Jams.
Clintons, E.
Fetherstone, Wm.
Lovel, Jams.
Petris. Geo.
Several Illegible at northern end.

A Settlement of Great Consequence

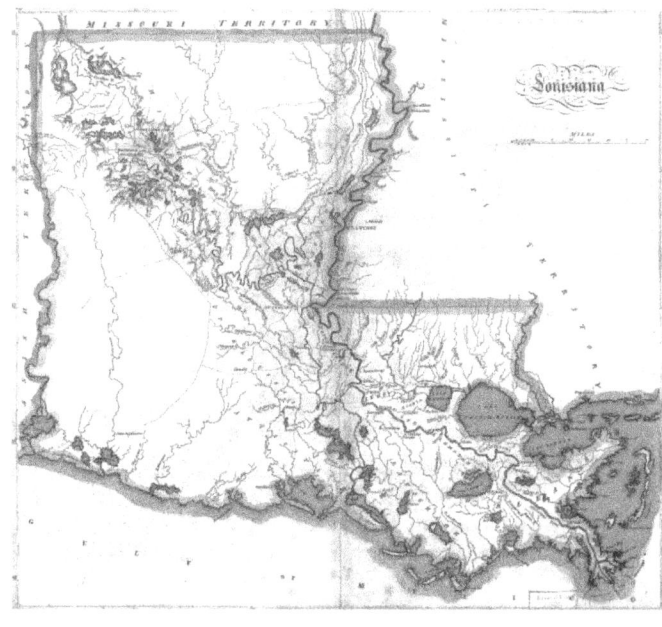

Collins & Other Redbone Progenitor Families

"John Friend, Sr. and Kerenhappuch 1763, Jul 14: On South Branch Potomac River, two Boys, Viz Collins & Sullivan, Killed and Scalped; Two Girls, named Delong."

"Collins, Elisha Collins, and Thomas these are the only Collins left in the county. Luke Collins had already left for Natchez, Ms." (Weaver 1998)

Earliest efforts at economic profit in British West Florida centered on the fur trade, with the central posts at Mobile and Pensacola enjoying a brisk business shipping furs to England as early as 1764. However, records for the Natchez District prove elusive, possibly because furs taken in the area were sold to the French and Spanish who paid higher prices than the English and shipped their skins from the port of New Orleans, outside British jurisdiction. A skin trade developed between Natchez and Manchac in 1773, and these goods may have gone either to New Orleans or Mobile. The West Florida fur trade represents an extensive and intricate relationship among Indians, trading companies, individual traders, and the governments of Britain, Spain, and France. As the initial endeavor of the British period, and one which represents initial contact between settlers and native groups, the fur trade deserves a brief examination and understanding from the point of waring Empires, and political struggles, of the period and area (Morris, George Galphin and the

Redbone Migrations to Louisiana

Transformation of the Georgia-South Carolina Backcountry 2014).

In September of 1779, The Battle of Baton Rouge broke out between the British who had hopes of controlling the fur trade in the Mississippi Basin, The Spanish governor of Louisiana, Bernardo de Galvez, had with his forces of Spaniards, Frenchmen, Germans, Acadians, free Blacks, Indians, and Americans, moved upriver from New Orleans. He tricks Lt. Colonel Dickson at Fort New Richmond into believing that they were preparing for an attack from the east, he opens fire at dawn with a roundshot volley from the south, and the British surrender within a few hours. Congress names John Adams to negotiate peace with England. Congress also names its president John Jay as minister to Spain. Spanish Governor Galvez of Louisiana captures the British gulf coast ports of Manchac, Baton Rouge and Natchez.

By 1781 however, the Spanish governor's attentions turn to distrust of the American's over negotiations with France, and all settlers of foreign origins, and unknown and suspect loyalties became his concerns.

A large group of early Virginia settlers, a group of South Carolina's Irish, and Welsh Indentured Indian Mixed Blood fur trader families settled in the Louisiana Districts trading between the British Gulf Ports of Natchez, Baton Rouge, and Manchac. A List of "Foreigners in the district of Opelousas, Attakapas, and in New Iberia was taken, including the trade settlement of dubious characters according to the Spanish Governor, Bernardo de Galavz. And in 1781 he ordered a list of foreigners taken, and an immediate surrender of arms.

MAY 15, 1781

> *"Etat du Rencensement General des Individus Etrangers lors du Desarmement dans le Partie des Attakapas, Opelousas et Nouvelle Iberie du 15 mai 1781.* (Gazette 1977, 152-194)

87 List of Foreigner's in the District of Opelousas and Attakapas and in New Iberia, who are to surrender their arms.

Luke Collins, Sr., William Hanchey, Samuel Allen, Charles Percy, John Kennedy, Roger West, Theophilus Collins, John Cotes, Jacob Miller, John Collins, Stephen Cotes, George Miller, William Collins, Abraham Roberts, Michael Ryder, Luke Collins Jr., Richard Rodney, John Orrey [Aury], William Wikoff, Amos Fairchild, Jack Crook, Samuel Wells, Michael Hunter, Michael Ryder, Cesar Archinard, Seth Hanchey, Thomas Priestman, Richard Ellis, Athanase Martin, Henry Bradley, John Ellis, Francis Daniel, Edward Tear, Thomas Murdock, Jacob Bihm, Zachery Martin, Raphael Bowker, Garret Harcourt, Edward Murphy,

Redbone Migrations to Louisiana

Evan Mill, James Cole, John McDonald, Gerard Brandon, Matthew Nugent, Jr., John Green, Robert Collingwood, Nathaniel Kennison, Edward Caslow, John Liver, James Clayton, Francis Little, Solomon Bernard, John Clark, Phillip Barbus, Henry Askeaiter, Robert Huxley, Joseph Wyble, Philip Howard, Patrick Clark, Charles Smith, John Tyson, Frederick Meyer, John Fitzpatrick, John Vaughan, Isaac Lewis, Joseph Ingrahm, Jacob Schnell, James Clark, Jacob Harman, Moise Cotter, John Bowels, James Brown, Mark Cotes, Peter McIntyre, Anthony Coskain?, Joshua Garret, John Ryan, Anthony Bennet, George Foreman, Francis Hoist, Benjamin Roth, William Brown, Nicholas Smith, Stephen Rhodes, Gabriel Martin, John Folse, Thomas Berwick, Matthew Nugent, Sr., Francis Stelly, Ephraim Hormelle, Edmund Nugent, Benjamin Malveau, Thomas Beard, Francis Roth, William Malveau, William Bundick, Joshua Wallace, Benjamin Anderson, Joseph Carr, Zachen Roth, Benjamin Fitz, John Brandon, Abraham Odom, Solomon Anderson, John Hair, David Odom ,Joseph Anderson, William McCullogh, Michael Haufpauir, James Anderson , Ebenazer Crene, Samuel Bell, James Yarborough, Cameron William, Fairbanks Thomas l, Yarborough Patrick, McCarty Luke, Folse John Leger, John Abshire, John Rider, Thomas Parr, Abraham Stuart, Matiquis Hayes, Adam Bridges, William Dickson, James Carlin Maxwell, Yarborough, George King.

In the Natchez District the local Petites Nations, as well as Choctaws, Creeks, and Chickasaws, exchanged deerskins for trade goods, with British trading companies Scrambling to keep local Indians in merchandise and Indians escalating their hunting practices to finance their demands for coveted trade items. The Indian-English fur trade became commercialized in the late 1700s and expanded throughout the entire English period. In addition to the Indian fur trade, individuals sometimes bartered skins with local merchants. The fragmentary account records of Newman and Hanchelle, Natchez merchants, note a deposit to a peltry account for Serah Truly. Truly brought three deerskins "in the hair" to Newman and Hanchelle on February 3, 1776 and received an account credit of $2.40, enough to purchase five quarts of rum or approximately seven yards of osnaburg fabric.

John Fitzpatrick, "Letter to Luke Collins, October 7, 1773 The Merchant of Manchac." pgs 30 & 31: "The war itself came to Natchez in 1778 when James Willing, one of the early merchants involved with the illicit trade to the Spanish, led an assault on the British along the Mississippi. Willing's mercantile venture had taken a turn for the worse as the Spanish under the new governor of Louisiana, Bernardo de Gálvez, favored trade with Americans rather than with the British. The occupation of Natchez went relatively smoothly, mainly because of a deal struck between Willing and a group of local planters. Shortly after his arrival in February 1778, Willing forced them to pledge that they would not "in any wise take up arms against the

United States of America or aid, abet, or in any wise give assistance to the enemies of the said States." Willing assured them that their "persons, Slaves, and other property of what kind soever [sic] shall remain safe & unmolested during our neutrality" and sent "a Flag of Truce to the Choctaw Indians to give out a talk with a Belt, to prevent the Indians falling on the Defenceless [sic] Inhabitants."

Pledge of the Natchez planters of the committee were Isaac Johnson, Luke Collins, William Hiern [Herron], Joseph Thompson, Charles Percy, and Richard Ellis. On trade and the relationship between the Choctaw and the British and United States.

"2 Mar 1768 Thomas HELM to Henry Heth 83 acres land granted to William & Hannah GILLIAM, corner of John MILBURN Wit: LUKE COLLINS-- Hampshire CO VA 2.25.1767 Luke Collins to Larence Hass & Sarah Hass wit: William Buffington and Samuel DEW – the Collins married into the William Buffington family in Hampshire CO VA.5.7.1759 Hampshire CO VA Luke & Sarah Collins to Stephen RUDDELL – wit: Gabriel Jones."

Luke Collins Records from Virginia to Louisiana

Collins, Old Homestead

> "Nov. 10, 1766 – Job Pearsall of Hampshire County to Luke Collins of Hampshire County, 323 acres on South Branch. Recorded Nov. 12, 1766."

Luke Collins had evidently been a military officer of the King in VA Colony, doubtless in the French War. He wrote to Major Luke Collins, "We had the happiness of joining in the sentiment in the Colony of Virginia, and as I may say, even wading through blood in supporting the cause of our country, heart in hand." He wrote to Arthur St. Clair, "I have in my little time in life taken the oath of allegiance to his Majesty seven times."

Creoles, according to genealogist and author Alex Lee of Beaumont, a direct descendant of Luke Collins. This group of mixed-bloods are self-defined as Creole.

Alice Collins, the daughter of Simon Collins and Elizabeth Pierre Boutte, both free people of color. Alice was married to Amede Olivier. Courtesy Alex Lee of Alex genealogy.

"COLLINS, Lucas, fils: commonly known as Luke COLLINS, (Jr.) was born circa 1760 in Hampshire County, Virginia to Captain Luke COLLINS, père, and Sara WHITE. His father served as a Captain during the French and Indian War. Luke Collins and his family settled in Opelousas, Louisiana prior to 1781. Shortly after their arrival, Luke fils (Jr.), was married on 17 Feb 1782 to Zoe COURTABLEU, daughter of Jacques COURTABLEAU and Marguerite KENTREK. Besides the legitimate children born to the union of his wife, he also had a lasting relationship with Nanette, GUILLAUME a Mulatresse libre [284] to which many COLLINS of color, in and around the Opelousas area descended." [285]

Chronicles of the South Carolina Scotch-Irish Settlement in Virginia Volume I AUGUSTA COUNTY COURT RECORDS.ORDER BOOK No. IV. (cont.)
(Additional Notes from Order Book IV. from beginning of Book IV. to March 21, 1754.)

AUGUST 16, 1753. Ludwick Franci South Carolina qualified Captain; Edward McDaniel, qualified Cornet; Jeremiah Scailer, qualified Captain; Luke Collins, qualified Ensign.

---

[284] Mulatrese, Female Mulatto. Libre, Free, free mulatto female.
[285] Alex Genealogy http://instagram.com/CreoleAlex

Brent Kennedy displaying photos of his great-uncle Will Collins/Gibson, Scott Co., Va. and Mother, Nancy Nash Kennedy. 2000 courtesy Dr. Brent Kennedy

"The Papers of George Washington" (U. S. Papers n.d.) index:
Collins, Luke, 1:20, 36; 7:5, 339, 340
Collins, —-: and George Mercer's lands, 10:203
Collins, —- (major), 9:248, 251

CHRONICLES OF THE Scotch -IRISH SETTLEMENT OF VIRGINIA; Vol 2, pp 420 – 429   by Lyman Chalkley
Land Insolvents and Delinquents, 1792:

"George Brooks, removed to Kentucky; Andrew Kinkead, to Kentucky; Wm. Russell, to French Broad; WilliamYoung, to Greenbrier; Christian Pery, to Kentucky; Robert Curry, to Kentucky; Robert Poage, to Kentucky; Robert Young, to

Kentucky; William and Andrew Young, to Kentucky; Daniel Brown, dead; Pat. Buchanan, to Georgia; Robert Christian, to Montgomery; James Campbell, to Penna.; John Gregory, to Philadelphia; Daniel Kidd, to Winchester; Ephraim McDowell, to South Carolina; Wm. McClintoc, to Kentucky; William Powers, in army; Henry Rutter, in army; John Sterling, to French Broad; James Bridge, Sr., to Amherst; David Boggess, dead; Luke Collins, to French Broad."

Older photo of **Will Collins**, great-uncle of Dr. Brent Kennedy. William "Will" born 1845, Scott Co., Va. Died 1931 in Knott Co., KY. He was the son of Elbert "Elbe" J.B. Collins and Catherine Kate Caty Gibson, 1795-1865. Elbe was born 1822 in Hancock Co., TN. And died 1905 in Floyd Co., KY. He was the son of Allen Collins and Rachel Nichols. Kate or Caty Gibson Collins was the daughter of Zacharia Gibson and Elizabeth Betsy McGee. Will married Martha Smith born 1856 in Jefferson Co., KY. And died 1937 in Knott Co., Ky. She was the daughter of Nicholas & Nancy Artie Johnson Smith, daughter of Thomas 1785-1828 & Philadelphia "Delpha" Carter Johnson 1787-1855 Surry, North Carolina.

1825 No Man's Land (Neutral Zone) Contraband Court

Spanish land claims arising out of the disputed land, the Neutral Zone. These cases were heard at Nacogdoches, Texas in 1825 between Mexican officials, Spanish officials (those who remained) and the United States Congress. Special court hearings called a contraband court to settle disputed (by the US Congress) land claims. Witnesses to your land claim/s would appear in (Nacogdoches, Tx.) to give affidavit as to all the particulars needed to establish your land settlement claim dates, acres cultivated, who settled the land previous and so forth. Your neighbors, relatives or business associates would testify on your behalf and likely yourself or elders in the community would give affidavit on behave of others claims. So, these contraband courts took some months. But just as curious and vague is why they called them contraband courts, unless we speculate the Baratarian angles as suggested by Redbone legends that survive to this day.

Most of the official Spanish Government was long gone by 1825 and with them they had removed, or someone had stolen documents needed to establish American land claims, in what had been the Spanish Empire. The Spanish had confiscated much of the documents from Nacogdoches, their government seat for the eastern outpost after the Mexican War of

Independence, 1821. Authenticating land titles was left to Pirate Pierre Laffite who served as "contraband officer" and authenticated claims and witness statements and details into to the character and reputation of those claiming land, and those giving witness. Antonio Gil YBarbo/vo also mentioned throughout this publishing, served as the Spanish official. As well, the famously known Lafitte associated families, the Cane River Creole's (Prudehomme) and Metoyer served on the Contraband Court.

Though Laffite scholars disagree in general that the Pirate brothers Jean & Pierre Laffite are the same men as Pierre, Jean (Jean Baptist[286]), Cezar, Louis Laffite family on the Sabine, in Texas and Bayou Pierre, Louisiana. And who are not the same family of men or aliases for the same, whose father was Paul Bouett "Babbitt" Laffite, according to the United States Land Claims. This family of Laffite's owned and operated a ferry between Nacogdoches and Natchitoches. The hostelry and ferry were located on the Texas side of the Sabin, now Gaines Ferry. Though many of the facts for my belief and assertion they in fact were the same family are not represented here. It is evident from these court cases that; Pierre Laffite, the pirate ensured many of our Redbones,

---

[286] Jean Baptist Laffite, 1810 Opelousas District Louisiana, enumerated neighbor of Thomas Nash/Ash along with other Redbone progenitors.

reputed Baratarians would indeed receive their Spanish land claims in the No Man's Land.

23rd CONGRESS 2nd Session

ON CLAIM TO LAND IN LOUISIANA.

The Committee Agrees:

"The committee do not believe the grants anything more than a bare permission to settle, nor are they aware that the lieutenant governor had any authority to make a title to the land. The committee do not, therefore, consider the applicant entitled to any more than other occupants and settlers in that section of the country; and they therefore report a bill allowing him two thousand acres of land, the quantity allowed by the act of the 3d (9sic) March 1801, to those settling by permission of the Spanish government, and which, if accepted by said Laffite, shall be in full satisfaction of all claim under said supposed grant."

Documents dated 1834 state the following, "That Pierre had lived in the area for more than 50 years".

Selected Land Claims, Louisiana

A full listing of claims in the No Man's Land and Contraband Court hearings transcriptions will be published in Don Marler's title, *The Neutral Zone: Backdoor to the United States from Backintyme Publishing*, Don Marler & Dogwood Press Collections at Amazon.

Claim # 923 NML Simon Goye' claims 640 superficial acres of land, situated on the right bank of Little River (later known as the Derbonne and present-day Calcasieu River), county of Claim # 923 NML Simon Goye' claims 600 acres of land, situated on the right bank of Little (later Calcasieu originally named Derbonne) River. The evidence of Manuel Derbonne, taken the 30th of July 1814, filed with the notice. The evidence of Manuel Derbonne, taken 9th October 1813 establishes that the first settlement was made twenty-five years ago by the claimant, who continued thereon three years, and then left it in charge of his hirelings, together with his stock, hogs, &s., that his hirelings have kept it up ever since.

No. 402 NML Claim #283. Thomas Goin, claims 640 superficial acres of land, situated on the right bank of Bayou Vermillion, in the county of Attakapas, bounded on all sides by vacant land. The evidence of James Dunman, taken the 15th of October 1812, states, that John Chavers built a camp on the land about fourteen years ago, where he continued three months; that it remained unoccupied from that time until 1810, when the claimant having purchased, deponent. believes, of (Chavers,) took possession, and has occupied and cultivated ever since.

Claim # 264 NML Drury Bunch, of the parish of St. Landry, filed his notice claiming, by virtue of inhabitation, occupation, and cultivation, a tract of land lying within the late neutral territory, situated on the west bank of the river Quelqueshue [sic], about ten miles above John Henderson's, and containing six hundred and forty acres. The claim is supported by the following testimony taken before the board: "John Stewart, being duly sworn, says that he knows the land claimed by Drury Bunch in his above notice: that said land is lying and situate as is therein described; that the same was inhabited, occupied, and cultivated by said Drury Bunch; by his living and growing corn, &c., thereon, on and previous to February 22, 1819' We are of opinion this claim ought to be confirmed, and in the abstract have classed it with claims of the third class.

241. Vincent Jackson, of the parish of Natchitoches, assignee of William Ash, filed his notice claiming, by virtue of occupation, inhabitation, and cultivation, a tract of land lying within the late neutral territory, situated on the east bank of the Sabine river, about two miles below the Cashata village, bounded on all sides by vacant land and containing six hundred and forty acres. The claim is supported by the following testimony taken before the board:

"Morris McLaughlin, being duly sworn, says that he knows the land claimed by Vincent Jackson in his above notice; that said land is lying and situated as is therein described; that the same was inhabited, occupied, and cultivated by William Ash, by his living and growing potatoes, peach trees, &c., thereon, sometime about the year 1810; that at that time said Ash had about seven acres cleared. Witness has never seen the place since." The rights of the claimant were lost by non-continuation of occupancy. —(See Nos. 121, 123, and 232.) We are of opinion this claim

ought not to be confirmed, and in the abstract, have classed it with claims of the "fourth class."
No.1061. Claimant: Robert Childress, 24 Mar. 1804. Rejected May 12, 1807. Robert Childress, a citizen of the Miss Ter., Adamas Co., legal representative of Thomas Ash, claims 160 acres in said county on the waters of Sandy Creek, by virtue of the said tract having been inhabited and cultivated by the said Thomas Ash in the month of October 1794, who was then the head of a family and continues in his possession until he conveyed the premises to Wilford Hoggatt, who sold the same to this claimant. The said land has been inhabited and cultivated ever since the year 1794 and is now the year claimed under section of the Act of Congress Regulating the Grants of Land.

1819 Joseph Grubb from Gibson Johnson 640 acres West side of Bayou Kisatchie witness Ethelred Smith and Major Smith that said tract was occupied cultivated and inhabited since prior to 1819. Claim was granted. Kisatchie Bayou. West of Pearl River, U.S. Land Claims, Library of Congress.

Redbones of Louisiana

Early Redbone Settlers in Louisiana

Date	Name	Origin / Destination	References[287]
By 1781	John Abshire	Unk	SGC[288]
By 1781	Luke Collins, Sr	Va.-WV	SGC
By 1781	James Clark	Unk	SGC
By 1781	John Bowels	Unk	SGC
By 1781	Adam Bridges	Unk	SCG
By 1781	Richard Ellis	Unk	SGC
By 1788	Simon/Simeon Goye'(Goyens)	SC Calcasieu	CC[289]
By 1770	Benjamin Gower	Unk Opelousas	1770 Map
By 1770	Daniel Gower	Unk Opelousas	1770 Map
By 1770	Thos. Goywn,	Unk @Atchafalaya	1770 Map
By 1770	Collins	Opelousas	1770 Map
By 1770	Ward, Jos.	Village Manchac	1770 Map
By 1770	Ward, Wm.	"	"
By 1770	Ward, Benjamin	"	"
By 1770	Ward, Daniel	"	"
By 1793-5	Daniel Boon	Opelousas	Epp 33-35
By 1790s	John (Joshua) Dial	SC Rapids, (sic) La.	EW 188a
By 1798	Tapley Dial	SC Natchez	EW 118-119

---

[287] The Key to these references are as follows:
JM = Jane McManus, *A Backward Glance* (Pineville: Parker Enterprises, 1986).
EPP = Jean L. Epperson, *Lost Spanish Towns: Atascosito and Trinidad De Salcedo* (Woodville: Dogwood Press, 1996)
EW = Erbon W. Wise, *Sweat Families of the South* (Sulphur: Private, 1998, Revised 2002).
HEI = Paul Heinegg, Free African Americans of North Carolina, Virginia, and South Carolina: From the Colonial Period to About 1820 4th Edition Genealogical (Baltimore: Publishing Co. 2001).
[288] Editor has added early settlers to the Districts of Opelousas, Attakapas & New Iberia as "SGC," (Settlement of Great Consequence).
[289] The editor has updated the following list and added reference to the contraband court as CC. I also use NML to identify Spanish land claims within the No Man's Land (Neutral Zone).

Redbone Migrations to Louisiana

By 1798	John Chavers	Va./Attakapas	Bayou Vermillion	
By 1800	Jeremiah Bass	NC	Natchez	JM29
By 1800	William Ash	Ft. Kaskaskia	Natchitoches	NML
By 1804	Ephraim Sweat	NC	St. Landry	EW 10b-11
By 1804	Gilbert Sweat	NC	St. Landry	EW 10b-11
By 1804	Peter McDaniel	SC	St. Landry	EW10b&13
By 1804	John McDaniel	SC	St. Landry	EW 13
Aft1804	Thomas Nash	NC/Natchez	St.Landry	JM
By 1805	John Aaron Drake	UN	Atascosita	Epp. 33-35
By 1810	Jesse Ashworth	SC	St. Landry	HEI 72
BY 1810	George Perkins		St. Landry	HEI 72
By 1810	Polly Ashworth	SC	St. Landry	HEI 72
By 1810	Tapley Dial	SC	St. Landry	EW 188a
By 1810	John Bass	NC	St. Landry	JM43 EW113
By 1810	James Groves, Sr.	NC	Natchitoches	JM 237
By 1813	George Orr	PENN	Atascosita	EPP 80ff
By 1815	Philip Goin(s)		Natchitoches	JM 239
By 1815	Keziah Nash		Natchitoches	JM 476
By 1816	Moses Ashworth	SC	Calcasieu	NML
By 1818	Gibson Johnson		Calcasieu	NML
By 1819	Drury Bunch	KY	Calcasieu	NML
By 1819	Rees Perkins	SC	Calcasieu	NML
By 1819	James Ashworth	SC	Choupique	NML
By 1820	Amos Avery	Conn	St. Landry	EW 113
By 1825	Thomas Goyens	SC	St. Landry	Probate
By 1826	William Taylor	VA	Atascosita	JM 472
By 1828	Leonard Covington Sweat		St. Landry	JM 472
By 1828	Moses Bass		Calcasieu	NML/JM 217

Passport issued for these persons-April 5, 1799 to Natchez

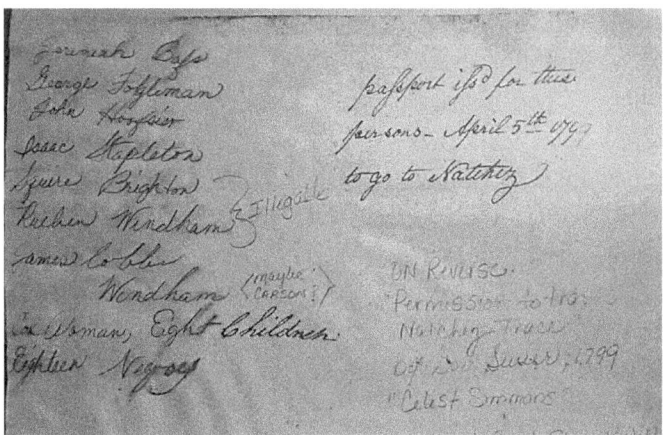

Jeremiah Bafs (Bass)
George Fogleman
John Hoosier
Issac Stapleton
Squire Brighton
Rueben Windham
James Cobb
Illegible Windham
Cox Woman, Eight Children
Eight Negroes
Signed Governor Sevier, 1799

The above Jeremiah Bass and others were enumerated in the Lost State of Franklin, later Franklin, TN. 1792 census. The land was associated with the Watauga Petition and inadequately represented here. Some Redbones to Louisiana were part of the formation of that Lost State, prior to The Free State of Jones. Pioneering Revolutionary War, mixed bloods who sought to set up their own state first being allowed by North Carolina, and later denied by the United States Congress. It was then divided up into present day Tennessee and North Carolina. The land was originally purchased from relatives among "Over the Hill" (Overhill) Cherokee and was mostly in the North Carolina Colony. See "Attachment I."

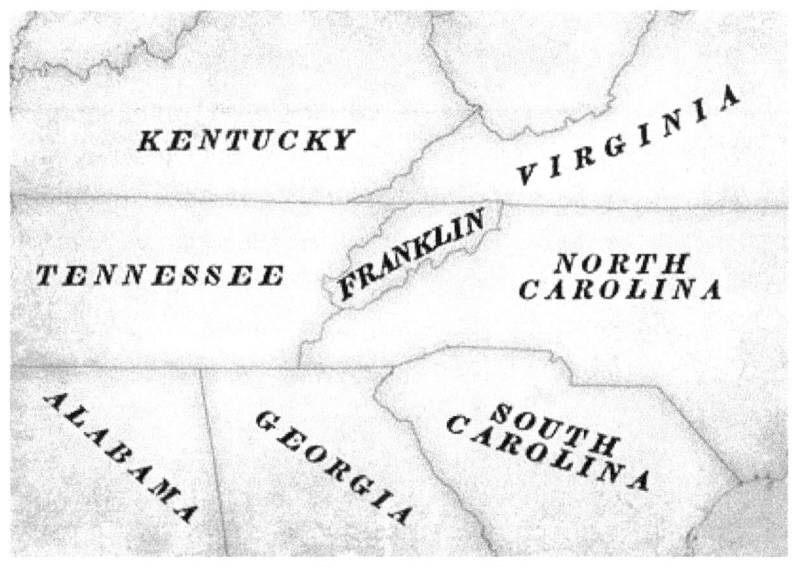

Lost State of Franklin

Author Erbon Wise, in *Tall Pines II*, lists early settlers in Ward Five of what is now Vernon Parish without identifying when they came into Louisiana. His list includes Alexander Calhoun, James Going (YDNA case study here), John Graham, Gibson Johnson, Joshua Johnson, Frederick McMullen, Jourdan Perkins and William Pinchback. These persons all got early land grants. Jep Beesen was said to be the first settler in what is now known as Pitkin. By the 1850s there were others. Elias Weldon, Bill Mathis, John Jeter and Dave Morrison.[290]

Author Judson Shook in, *Beauregard Parish at the Millennium*, cites early settlers in Beauregard Parish but does not precisely cite their arrival in Louisiana.

> *It is said that Beauregard Parish was first populated by way of the Calcasieu River, not by the Sabine River. Some say that "Saddler" Johnson was the first settler in Beauregard Parish. He arrived there about 1815. According to tradition the next to arrive were Edward Escobas, Demsey Iles, John L. Lyons, Joseph W. Moore, E. Shirley, James Simmons, William B. Welborn, Ezra Young and G.W. Corkran-sometime around 1825.[291]*

In 1805, John Aaron Drake migrated to Texas from Opelousas, Louisiana. It is not known when he came to Opelousas, and the Drake families must have returned to Opelousas, because John Aaron III married Sarah Ashworth there in 1831. On the 1807 Spanish Census of Camp

---

[290] Erbon W. Wise, *Tall Pines II: A History of Vernon Parish, Louisiana and its People* (Sulphur: Privately Printed, 1988). In the chapter "Pioneer Settlers of Ward 5," unfortunately the pages are not numbered.
[291] Judson Shook, *Beauregard Parish at the Millenium* (Privately printed, 2000), p. 10.

Orcoquisac – Atascosito, Drake is listed as Juan Eromdreque, and his wife, Charity Smith, was listed as Serafina Esmitt.[292]

George Orr was another who moved to the Atascosito area from Opelousas. It is not known when he came to Opelousas, but he participated in the Magee-Gutierez Campaign in 1813. He married Delphine Berwick, who was born in Opelousas in 1802, and moved to Atascosito in Mexican territory, where he was a leader in civic affairs. See the Epperson book for a discussion of this interesting man.[293]

In 1835, Santa Anna moved against the Texians when they decided to declare independence from Mexico. The rest is history, as the saying goes, with the battles of the Alamo and San Jacinto as evidence. Further evidence is the victory of the Texians and creation of the Republic of Texas. Some of the soldiers who participated in the Battle of San Jacinto had names familiar to those who lived in and around the Neutral Zone. It is logical that some Redbones who lived in the Neutral Zone area would break the boredom of daily life with

---

[292] Jean L. Epperson, *Lost Spanish Towns: Atascosito and Trinidad De Salcedo* (Woodville: Dogwood Press, 1996), p. 39. The Magee-Gutierrez Campaign was one of the many ill-fated expeditions designed to "liberate" the people of Texas from Spanish rule – to capture Mexico. Many of them started in New Orleans or Natchez and were staged in the Neutral Zone.
[293] *Ibid.*, p. 80ff.

a little excitement on the battle-front, and the prospect of free land was a likely inducement for them to join the Texians. Many of those involved received land as payment for their services and no doubt stayed in the country. Soldiers involved include those with the surnames:

Bailey, Barton, Bell, Bennett, Berry, Bond, Boyd, Brooks, Brown, Burch, Clark, Cole, Coleman, Colins, Craft, Crawford, Crier, Cumba, Curtis, Davis, Faris, Fields, Gill, Goodwin, Green, Hall, Harper, Harvey, Henry, Holmes, Hunt, Johnson, Jones, Lee, Legg, Lewis, Manuel, Martin, Miller, Moore, Nash, Orr, Osborne, Page, Parker, Powell, Price, Reaves, Reed, Roberts, Robinson, Scott, Self, Smith, Taylor, Teal, Thompson, Tyler, Vaughn, Watson, Welch, Wells, Wilson, Wily, Wood and Wright.[294]

Almost every mixed-blood family moving to the southwest part of Louisiana in the first decades of the 19th century had at least one female member named Keziah or some variation of that name. It was a favorite name of Gypsies and Indians. Many of the mixed-blood families also had daughters named "Dicey" and sons named Joshua or "Josh."

Dr. Tommy Johnson, of Natchitoches, Louisiana, long a student of the history of Redbones, became interested in the

---

[294] Wallace L. McKeehan, "Alphabetical List of San Jacinto Veterans" Sons of Dewitt Colony Texas – website.

Redbone Migrations to Louisiana

Melungeon story as told by Brent Kennedy, and began studying the relationship between them and Redbones. He refers to Louisiana Redbones as "Louisiana Melungeons" – a practice not followed here. Most of the census data given in this section is from Johnson's work, which he has graciously given permission to use. Anyone interested in this aspect of the history should consult his informative books; *They Came West* and *From the Chattahoochee to the Calcasieu*, for more data.[295]

Johnson used Kennedy's list of Louisiana Redbone surnames to identify people of possible Redbone extraction who had moved to the area. He made no attempt to verify the Free Persons of Color status of any of them, so no definite interferences can be made, nor conclusions drawn, but a sense of the movement of people with these surnames is evident. As stated elsewhere, not all Redbones settled in small, isolated communities. These data support that assertion to the extent that these names represent Redbones. They were scattered over a large area of the state as well into Texas.

---

295 Tommy G. Johnson, From the Chattahoochee to the Calcasieu: The Story of Charles Lewis and His Wife, Nancy Riley 1836-1880. (Natchitoches: Private Printing, 1997), and
Tommy G. Johnson, *They Came West* (Natchitoches: Private Printing, 1996).

In addition to the Opelousas Parish 1810 data, Johnson surveyed the data of the St. Landry Census (Opelousas Parish) 1820; Rapides Parish data for 1820, 1850 and 1860, and Natchitoches Parish data for 1850. A portion of what he found is as follows:

Opelousas Parish 1810 – Territory of Orleans.
Selected heads of households are listed in chronological order. Some names are identical but represent different individuals.

1. George Boland
2. Murtough (?) Collins
3. Joshua Perkins
4. Philip Goin
5. James Ashworth
6. John Clark
7. Abijah Clark
8. William Clark
9. James Goin
10. John Cole
11. Jesse Clark
12. Gabriel Robinson
13. John Robinson
14. Solomon Cole
15. James Reeves
16. William L. Collins
17. Tapley Dial
18. Charles Smith
23. Lawrence Taylor
24. William Moore
25. William Moore
26. John Collins
27. Gibson Johnson
28. William Turner
29. William Johnson
30. Venue (?) Luke Collins
31. Charles Moore
32. Robert Taylor
33. William Moore
34. Edmund Johnson
35. Joseph Willis, Sr.
36. John Johnson
37. Isaac Perkins
38. Gilbert Sweat
39. William Dalton
40. John Bass

19. Andrew Marish
20. John Taylor
21. John Marsh
22. Benjamin A. Smith
41. Sarah Johnson
42. Andrew Weaver
43. John Jackson
44. Thomas Ash (Nash)

By 1820, this list for Opelousas Parish had more than doubled to 105 names.

Rapides Parish census data for 1810 listed only 13 names using the Johnson criteria and on the 1820 census, there were 28 – a trend was beginning to develop – the population was moving to the north and west. The Rapides Parish names found, using the Johnson criteria, had also more than doubled in 10 years.

Rapides Parish 1850 (Number in front of the name is the household). Johnson found more than 250 names meeting his criteria – of which those below represent a selected sample.

402	James Johnson, age 72	b. Virginia
419	E.B. Carter, age 28	b. South Carolina
422	Rev. Joseph Willis, age 98	b. South Carolina
448	James Orr, age 40	b. North Carolina
487	Melinda Perkins, age 50	b. Tennessee
494	Lewis Perkins, age 57	b. South Carolina
523	Russell Smith, age 40	b. Tennessee
527	Nancy Perkins, age 60	b. South Carolina
----	Elizabeth Perkins, age 55	b. South Carolina

528	James Bunch, age 37	b. North Carolina
574	Lebum C.K. Scott, age 33	b. Tennessee
588	Daniel Curry, age 45	b. North Carolina
626	John Dyal, age 47	b. North Carolina
630	Isaac Perkins, age 61	b. South Carolina
641	Willis Perkins, age 60	b. South Carolina
644	Z. Gibson, age 50	b. South Carolina
651	Sally Strother, age 63	b. South Carolina
659	Thomas Dyal, age 80	b. South Carolina
660	Edgarton Willis, age 65	b. North Carolina
738	Robert W. Smith, age 63	b. South Carolina
788	Thomas Smith, age 63	b. South Carolina
814	Evan Coleman, age 37	b. South Carolina
825	George W. Evans, age 42	b. South Carolina
838	Nancy Turner, age 39	b. Kentucky
840	George E. French, age 32	b. Virginia

Natchitoches Parish 1850

3	Morris Johnson, age 38	b. South Carolina
24	John Johnson, age 27	b. North Carolina
26	Joseph Martin, age 45	b. North Carolina
27	John Martin, age 26	b. North Carolina
57	J.G. Campbell, age 38	b. South Carolina
63	James Wood, age 63	b. North Carolina
69	L.P. Williams, age 38	b. South Carolina
70	Thomas Nash, age 97	b. North Carolina
72	Lewis Hall, age 45	b. North Carolina
126	John Freeman, age 73	b. North Carolina
131	Tyrus Bell, age 51	b. South Carolina

Redbone Migrations to Louisiana

214	E.P. Martin, age 49	b. South Carolina
230	Will Williams, age 49	b. South Carolina
243	Henry Hill, age 36	b. South Carolina
246	C.D. Buxton, age 40	b. Tennessee
247	B.B. Gibson, age 39	b. Tennessee
296	R.H. Williams, age 48	b. Tennessee
308	W.W. Powell, age 30	b. South Carolina
319	Noah Cloud, age 50	b. Kentucky
324	Wood Bell, age 39	b. South Carolina
325	Rachel Williams, age 85	b. South Carolina
326	James Williams, age 47	b. South Carolina
336	Margaret Adams, age 27	b. Tennessee
363	J.M. Williams, age 29	b. South Carolina
380	Laura Powell, age 53	b. North Carolina
---	Will Parsons, age 22	b. South Carolina
394	Jesse Jones, age 56	b. North Carolina
411	William Whitted, age 53	b. North Carolina
---	William Whitted, Jr., age 27	b. North Carolina
---	Levi Whitted, age 26	b. North Carolina
435	Sam Clark, age 43	b. Tennessee
486	Richard Williamson, age 36	b. South Carolina
539	Robert White, age 29	b. South Carolina
540	Giles Berry, age 34	b. South Carolina
557	James Clark, age 55	b. South Carolina
581	William Smith, age 38	b. Kentucky
594	Lawrence Cox, age 30	b. North Carolina
600	Elisha Green, age 41	b. Kentucky
609	Luther Stewart, age 39	b. Kentucky
659	William Robinson, age 38	b. Kentucky
664	Newton Coffee, age 39	b. Kentucky
724	E.H. Jones, age 29	b. Virginia
731	John Powell, age 29	b. South Carolina

758 R.W. Campbell, age 48   b. Kentucky

Rapides Parish 1860
(Names from the 1850 Census are not repeated)

59	Mary Jones, age 20	b. Kentucky
100	Henry Adams, age 50	b. South Carolina
112	M.H. Stanley, age 36	b. North Carolina
134	Gadi Sweat, age 82	b. South Carolina
190	Samuel Clark, age 72	b. South Carolina
242	David Evans, age 64	b. South Carolina
252	Zedakiah Gibson, age 60	b. South Carolina
285	K.P.F. Powell, age 52	b. North Carolina
294	Hugh Johnson, age 30	b. South Carolina
327	Mary S. Johnson, age 71	b. South Carolina
334	Nancy M. Williams, age 63	b. North Carolina
---	Edward F. Williams, age 26	b. Tennessee
---	Emily J. Williams, age 25	b. Tennessee
343	Nathanial S. Williams, 27	b. North Carolina
375	Joseph Nichols, age 41	b. North Carolina
405	Vicey Turner, age 18	b. Kentucky
421	John Goines, age 42	b. South Carolina
443	Elizabeth Lawson, age 37	b. Tennessee
503	George James, age 38	b. Kentucky
519	Nathan Perkins, age 58	b. South Carolina
539	C.L. Williams, age 27	b. Tennessee
583	Powhatten Clark, age 21	b. Tennessee
---	Francis W. Smith, age 22	b. Virginia
693	Harrison V. Nash, age 32	b. South Carolina
706	Ruel Cumba, age 44	b. South Carolina
771	Nathan J. Orr, age 25	b. Tennessee

Redbone Migrations to Louisiana

777	Charles W.V. Clark, age 21	b. Kentucky
788	Henry Robertson, age 42	b. Virginia
917	J.S. Green, age 28	b. Tennessee
1001	William H. Osborn, age 30	b. North Carolina
1002	John A. Kennaday, age 35	b. Tennessee
1267	David Collins, age 46	b. South Carolina
1303	E.K. Davis, age 40	b. North Carolina
1471	S.R. Wright, age 35	b. South Carolina
1496	George M. Graham, age 53	b. Virginia
1527	Thomas D. Martin, age 35	b. Tennessee
1535	Catherine James, age 70	b. Virginia
1686	Howell, Orr, age 52	b. North Carolina
1741	J.W. Johnson, age 45	b. Virginia
1751	R.J. Cumba, age 43	b. South Carolina
1770	James T. Nichols, age 39	b. Tennessee
1777	William Clark, 33	b. Tennessee
1778	Robert Clark, age 33	b. Tennessee
1794	A.J. Johnson, age 38	b. Kentucky

Of the 113 names listed with place of birth:

South Carolina	46 persons	41 percent
North Carolina	26 persons	23 percent
Tennessee	21 persons	18 percent
Kentucky	12 persons	11 percent
Virginia	8 persons	7 percent

Author Edward Price did examine the census for the purpose of identifying Free Persons of Color.[296] He found that the Rapides Parish census takers usually chose to call the

---

296 Edward T. Price, Jr., Mixed-Blood Populations of Eastern United States as to Origins, Localizations, and Persistence (Ph.D. Dissertation, University of California, 1937).

Redbones White by omitting the color symbol opposite their names. The designations with spellings and use of lower case will be given as written by Price. From the Price dissertation:

Families with Redbone Names or Other Names of Interest Taken from Louisiana Census Records

1810

Avoyelles Parish

Clark, white
Johnson, white

Opelousas County (later St. Landry Parish)

Clark, white
Johnson, 3 free colored, 2 white (one holding slaves)
Nelson, free colored
Perkins, 2 free colored
Sweat, free colored (holding slaves)
Thompson, white
Willis, free colored (holding slaves)
Goin, 2 free colored
Going, free colored
Ash, 2 free colored
Bass, free colored

Rapides Parish

Clark, white and free colored (same family)
Thompson, white

1820

Natchitoches Parish

Thompson, white

Rapides Parish

Clark, white
Perkins, white
Ware, white
Willis, white

St. Landry Parish (including most of southwest Louisiana)

Ashworth, 4 free colored
Clark, one free colored, one white (holding slaves)
Johnson, one free colored, 2 white (1 holding slaves)
Nelson, one free colored, one white
Strother, white (holding slaves)
Sweat, 4 free colored
Thompson, 2 white (holding slaves)
Wisby, free colored
Going, free colored
Dial, 3 free colored
Bass, free colored
Chavers, free colored
Bunch, free colored

1830

Rapides Parish

Ash, white
Perkins, 3 white   }
Willis, white   } All listed on same page
Johnson, white   }

Swet, 2 white   }

St. Landry Parish

    Quelquesui (present Calcasieu Parish)
    Johnson, free colored
    Buxton, free colored
    Ashworth, 4 free colored
    Perkins, 5 free colored
    Gowens, 2 free colored
    Clark, free colored
    Willis, free colored

Bayou Mallet Township

    Chavis, free colored

Bayou Teche

    Chavis, free colored
    Dial, 4 free colored
    Sweat, 2 free colored
    Johnson, free colored
    Bass, free colored
    Nelson, free colored

1850 Calcasieu Parish (including a much larger area than today)

    Perkins, 6 mulatto, 6 white
    Ashworth, 5 mulatto
    Pinder, 1 white
    Johnson, several white
    Goodman, 1 mulatto
    Clark, 1 mulatto, 1 white

Redbone Migrations to Louisiana

Bunch 1 mulatto
Bass, 2 mulatto, 1 white
Goan, 3 mulatto
Buxston, mullato
Thompson, several white
(above families for the most part closely grouped)

Rapides Parish

Perkins, 3 white
Willis, 3 white
Buxton, white
Strother, white
Swett, white

1880

Calcasieu Parish

Bass, 2 mulatto
Ashworth, 8 mulatto, 1 white
Clark, 5 mulatto
Pinder, white
Doil, 4 mulatto
Wisby, mulatto
Johnson, mulatto
Buxton, 3 mulatto, 1 white
Perkins, 13 mulatto, 1 white
Dial, 2 mulatto
Nelson, 2 mulatto
Thompson, mulatto

Rapides Parish Ward 6

Dyel, 6 white
Perkins, 5 white

Nelson, 1 white
Sweat, 1 white
Dyle, white
Johnson, 8 white
Strother, 6 white
Dyes, 1 white
Willis, 6 white
Ware, 2 white
Buxton, white

Ward 5 Apparently, a few Redbones were located in this ward also, but the lack of concentration make any assumptions unsafe.[297] Also from the Price dissertation:

Summary of Names Occurring in Association with Louisiana Redbones and Elsewhere as Mixed-Blood or Free Colored Louisiana
Name Elsewhere (as mixed-blood or free colored)

Goins   Melungeons,
Drake County, SC 1830 (Kershaw and Sumter Districts) and now.
Chavis South Carolina, 1990 (Cheraw, Edgefield, Orangeburgh) 1830 (Barnwell, Edgefield, Richland, Sumter) & now.

297 *Ibid.*, pp.123 a-c.

Bunch Melungeons, South Carolina 1790 (Berkley, Orangeburgh), and now

Dial	Croatans (in North Carolina on SC border)
Swett	S.C. – 1790 (Cheraw), 1830 (Chesterfield, Marlboro, Sumter)
Strother	S.C. – 1830 (Abbeville, Fairfield)
Nelson	S.C. – 1830 (Fairfield)
Clark	S.C. – 1790 (Lancaster, Richland),

Present mixed-bloods of Rockbridge Co, VA[298]

Tommy Johnson relates a story told him by the late Reverend Karl Mayo regarding a wagon train to Louisiana and Texas.

The story as recorded by Johnson is as follows:

Starting in late 1856 or early 1857 a giant push to the West began in the Wiregrass area of Georgia, Alabama, and Florida. This area was composed of the counties of Randolph, Early, Baker, and Decatur in Georgia; counties of Walton, Holmes, and Washington in Florida; and counties of Barbour, Henry, Pike, Dale and Coffee in Alabama. As plans began to formulate, one can anticipate the eagerness to get under way

---

298 Ibid., p. 124a.

to the new State of Texas; that wild land flowing with milk and honey.

Chosen to lead the huge wagon train of 100 wagons was none other than Alfred Franklin Mayo, Sr. believed by most historians to be the father of most Louisiana Mayos and those of East and Central Texas. In the oral history of the families of Mayo, Perkins, Lewis and Harville riding with him is a Cherokee woman described as the Indian woman – with rifle on horse – our Nancy Riley Lewis, wife of Charles Lewis. Joining them were other progenitors of Central and Western Louisiana people. Allen Lewis of Baker Co., Georgia; John Mack Nichols, Sr., James Turner, Sr., Jesse Register, Solomon Criel (Creel), all of Washington Col, Florida; Elias Bird Leavines and Ruel Cumbaa of Holmes Co., Florida. Mayo was also of Holmes Co., Florida.

A typical wagon Train in the 1800s

Also, this writer's [Johnson's] paternal G-G Grandfather Levi Johnson and his wife Nancy French Johnson joined the train from Henry Co., Alabama as did John Joseph Nichols, his brother Brittan Nichols, Jr. Others were John Milton and Millard Fillmore Cauthorn, Basil and James Gray, Horatio Nelson Gray, and Pleasant T. Patterson. Still other family groups joined such as: Blackshear, Welch, Bennett, Stanley, Ray, NesSmith, and Cooper to name a few. They traveled the Lone Star Trail or 3 Notch Trail [Natchez Trace] through Alabama and Mississippi to Natchez (this is present day U.S. 84). Whether they used the ferry at Natchez or the one at Rodney, Mississippi and Waterproof, Louisiana is not known. But regardless of the place, just imagine the massive task of getting the one hundred wagons across the mighty river. If they crossed at Natchez, they then proceeded west along the old Indian trail to Vidalia, Clayton, and Sicily Island; if they crossed at Rodney, they proceeded along the road still known as the Texas Trail, [Harrisonburg Road] to the Tensas River and on to Sicily Island. From this point they crossed the Ouachita River at Harrisonburg, turned south to Manifest and Jena and then West to Rochelle (near Georgetown), to Packton, and finally to St. Maurice on the Red River near Natchitoches. By this time, it had over 100 wagons, and was probably backed up five miles. (Rev. Carl Mayo of the Hicks Community in Vernon Parish estimates it took over one week to cross the Red). When this was accomplished, it moved through Cotile Landing (present day Boyce, Louisiana). Here, Alfred Mayo asked about his sons Martin, Eziekel, and Samual and their families. They had moved to the area about three years prior: he was told they lived about 25 miles to the West; they were sent for and upon their arrival led the train via McNutt Hill and to Valentine (present day Gardner, Louisiana). According to Bertha Terrell Mayo and this writer's Uncle Neil Harding Johnson, a secret meeting of the young men and elder members was held. Uncle Neil states that his grandfather Martin Jasper Nichols told him before he died that it was at Valentine.

The women, girls and small boys were left in camp and the men folk went into the woods for a secret meeting. It was discussed that many were wanted by the law and had a variety of things to live down (for example, the Nicholses were whiskey runners and had helped to stir up the Indians that led to the Creek Indian War of 1836 in Alabama) they "swore" secrecy and would tell no one who they were. Ms. Bertha and Uncle Neil both state this is why it is so difficult to find out about our ancestors – they would not talk. However, thanks to a few tongues loosened up, we are able to piece a past together. It was at Valentine that many started leaving the wagon train, others dropped off at places such as Simpson,

Hicks, Laurel Hill, and Walnut Hill while others crossed the Sabine River at Burr's Ferry and went on to the wonderland of Texas.[299]

The second wagon train came west in 1868-69 after the Civil War. One of Dr. Johnson's relatives, Mary Jane Lewis Rougeou, provided some of the information on this second groups' journey west. Johnson's story continues:

They lived near the communities of Coffeyville, Bladon Springs and Aquilla in Choctaw Co., Alabama and the Indian

---

299 Tommy G. Johnson, From the Chattahoochee to the Calcasieu: The Story of Charles Lewis and His Wife, Nancy Riley 1836-1880. (Natchitoches: Private Printing, 1997), pp. 7-8.
Alfred Franklin Mayo is buried at the Mayo cemetery in Hicks, Louisiana. The cemetery was untended with no grave markers until Reverend Karl Mayo had the parish scrape the area with a road grader. He then got local old-timers to identify where some of the old graves had been. Rev. Mayo had a headstone erected for Alfred Franklin Mayo, which is inscribed:
Alfred Franklin Mayo, Sr.
1792 S.C. 1854
Vet War 1812
Dr. Johnson was contacted by telephone on 11/11/2002 for an explanation of the discrepancy between the date the wagon train came with mayo as its leader and his date of death on the marker. He said that he does not know what happened. Reverend Mayo said that someone had said 1854 was the death date and that had been put on the headstone. He thought Alfred F. Mayo died shortly after he led the train west. The 1860 Rapides Parish census lists the wife of Alfred Franklin Mayo, Catherine Youngblood, as a widow. She died in 1862; and she too was born in South Carolina. Reverend Mayo also said that Alfred Franklin had come to the Neutral Zone around 1825 to scout out the country for a move to it and had decided that the area was still too wild. Hicks is in Vernon Parish which did not become a parish until 1871.

Grandmother from Louisiana came to get them. This would be Nancy Riley Lewis and she would join forces with George Washington Mayo and his wife Adeline Cumbie (Cumbaa) in leading the second big wagon train to Louisiana after the Civil War. Adeline was a sister to Ruel Cumbaa who was the blacksmith on the 1857 train led by George's father Alfred Franklin Mayo and the Indian woman, Nancy Riley Lewis.

The Indian Grandmother would ride ahead and scout the trail and lead the wagon train to the best campground near clear running streams. She would actually hide the train in order to avoid roving bands of carpetbaggers and thieves. Bad weather and the winter of 1868-69 caught them; she helped them camp for the winter and raised a crop the following spring before proceeding west. Ms. Jewel (Jewel Rougeou Kelly, Mary Jane's daughter) said her mother stated that the Indian Grandmother rode a black horse. So we now have a better description of her, "Indian woman on a black horse with rifle". (Nancy Riley Lewis, b. in probably Davidson Co., North Carolina in 1814 must have been a fantastic woman and one tough "cookie") The group finally arrived in Louisiana in late 1869.[300]

---

300 Tommy G. Johnson, From the Chattahoochee to the Calcasieu: The Story of Charles Lewis and His Wife, Nancy Riley 1836-1880. (Natchitoches: Private Printing, 1997), p. 9.

Redbone Migrations to Louisiana

These stories illustrate the idea that some settlers came to Louisiana because family and friends were here and, also, perhaps someone in the group saw the area during the war of 1812. At least one person, Alfred Franklin Mayo, fought in the war, though we do not know if he was at the Battle of New Orleans.

Why did some Redbones who migrated west terminate their journey in communities known to be dominated by other Redbones while some did not? These communities were located in and near the Neutral Zone. The reasons for choosing the Neutral Zone for their settlements were discussed previously. Examples of these communities are those located at Westport, Pitkin, Elizabeth, DeQuincy, Starks, Fields, Bearhead, and Merryville, in Louisiana and Newton, Texas.

It should be recognized that not all identified with, lived in, or associated with such communities. It is likely that many more settled along the way than settled in communities of like-minded families. Some, we know, started living within these communities but later moved away in an effort to hide their Redbone affiliations, as many early Redbones settlers hid their Black and Indian ties. Some spread out into the surrounding dominant community. This surrounding community was so sparsely settled, one could easily lose a mixed-blood identity in it.

A casual drive through of much of central Louisiana, east Texas and rural Arkansas or Mississippi, looking at names on mailboxes reveals a familiar pattern of names found in the established Redbone communities. Though this is admittedly not a scientific or systematic way to study populations, it does suggest that perhaps not all Redbones or people with Redbone-related surnames settled in identified Redbone communities, and yet they survived.

Coming to a new country with a different culture must have been an experience that produced considerable anxiety. Joining an old friend or family member would no doubt have provided support and comfort. It would have been natural to advise friends and relatives back home, who were anticipating making a move, that they had a place to which they could come. Furthermore, a leader with a stature of Reverend Joseph Willis, who had prepared the way, may have been an enticement for other mixed-blood people to join him. Yet, these are not reasoning enough. After all, others, both mixed-blood and non-mixed blood, had made a similar trip and had followed family, friends, and leaders, but had not developed communities that were armed camps, as was virtually the case with numerous Redbone communities.

Many of these communities had their beginnings before the Civil War when the risk of enslavement was still a real threat. Redbone families had been persecuted in other settings and some were running from the law. In possession of a past they vowed to submerge and forget, they felt a need for protection, and living unto themselves in a wilderness was, in their judgement, the best way to gain such needed protection. Those who banded together must have known that they would be identified as a separate group and therefore become a visible target. Perhaps this was an openly discussed subject with some disagreeing with the plan and refusing to join. What is known is that not all joined in, and some that did, left for life outside the Redbone world.

Soon Redbone communities were a reality, just as the Maroon Societies had been before them. The success of such separated groups as the Seminoles in Florida and the Lowery Band in North Carolina might have served to inspire, motivate, and guide them.

They adopted a hostile and defensive stance toward the dominant society that widened the gap between them and

White groups. Their violent and defensive behavior became a lifestyle – an entrenched part of their culture. Did the Redbone communities in southwest Louisiana serve essentially as did the "Cities of Refuge" of Biblical times? In the Biblical City of Refuge, if one could make it to the city, he was safe from retribution from those who were pursuing him?[301]

Following the Civil War, the threat of enslavement was no longer present. Radical Reconstruction was a harsh reality and might have prolonged the unease and unrest. At any rate, the pattern of hostile reaction and separateness had been established. The west had cheap land and family members had already moved there. Many followed families, and besides, the timber boom had started, and work was plentiful.

Now that violent responses or a protecting city were no longer needed, and might indeed have become counter-productive, was it nonetheless difficult to relinquish such responses? Was it difficult to take down the walls of the protective cities?

---

301 *Holy Bible*, Numbers 35:6.

Redbone Migrations to Louisiana

L to R Front (Children): Benjamin Franklin (Buddy) Calhoun, Jessie J. Calhoun, Elijah Calhoun, Mary Almiranda Calhoun, William Reason
L to R Middle: Merle Wilburn Calhoun, Almiranda Johnson Nash, Octavia Nash Calhoun, Unknown Henderon (Hen) Calhoun
L to R Back: William R. (Bud) Calhoun, Unknown, Unk. Nash, Unk. Nash, Joseph Martin (Dank) Calhoun, Uknown

Wm. Harrison Nash 1869 Rapides Parish, La. And died 1958 in Lufkin, Angelina Co., Tx. He was the son of Joseph "Big Joe" & Martha A. Williams Nash. He married Sarah A.

Gore in 1894 in Newton Co., TX. Grandson of Benjamin "Penashes" and Hannah Perkins Nash/Ash.

Ed (son of 1. Nancy Simmons Allen Nash/Ash), **Guide** (son of 2. Matilda "Tilley" Sweat Mason Nash/Ash) **& Eli** (son of 1. Nancy Simmons Allen Nash/Ash) all sons of Manuel "Command" Nash.

NATURE/NURTURE

Definition and Identity

The age-old issue of the relative influence of nature and nurture – genes and environment – is still open in the Redbone community. In order to avoid confusion and make the following discussion meaningful, perhaps we should begin with a definition of Redbone, Redbone Community, and Culture.

> *A Redbone is a person whose biological heritage is some combination of at least two of the following: Caucasian, American Indian or Negro – and who is a member of a group that identifies itself as a Redbone group or Redbone Community, holding certain values, beliefs, and worldviews.*
>
> *A Redbone Community is composed of a group of people who identify as Redbones and live apart from the dominant society, propagating its own set of beliefs, traditions, value system and worldview.*
>
> *Culture is the community of ideas, attitudes, practices, beliefs, and values to which we are exposed as we mature and in which we presently live.*[302]

---

302 Community can be a geographical location or a group of people who share criteria for membership, whether formal or informal. And it

Culture is not defined here as how refined we are (as in a highly cultured person), but rather our immediate nurturing environment. For this discussion, cultures are simply different – not necessarily better than another.

The proposition of this book is that the essence of a Redbone is his/her culture, not his/her racial/ethnic heritage.

Let's assume for purposes of discussion that the racial/ethnic heritage is any one of the several combinations:

Indians/White
Indian/Black
White/Black
Indian/Black/White

(White includes Portuguese, White Moors, Spaniards, Turks and others.)

can be a group of people who have a network of communication and who may live in several different geographical locations. There can be several geographical locations in the larger community. For example, Starks, DeQuincy, Merryville, Fields, Pitkin and Westport are separate locations, yet, considered by some as primarily Redbone communities. In numbers, perhaps, and by influence, almost certainly, these are Redbone communities. Yet, together they form a larger Redbone community.

Nature/Nurture

The question arises immediately "who is not of one of these combinations?" Almost everyone has one or more of these combinations, so if being one of these combinations is the criterion for membership into the Redbone group, then almost everyone is a Redbone. Under that circumstance, is the term not meaningless? It certainly is not, then, in that case, a functional term for identifying a specific group of people.

Likely, the most socially acceptable of the above categories is Indian/White. Can we honestly say that all persons who have this mixture are Redbone? If not, which ones are, and which are not? Is the determining factor a mixture of certain Whites and certain Indian tribes, and if so, which ones? What percentage of the mix is necessary and what of those who are of a tri-racial mix?

Let us assume for discussion that there were three brothers in South Carolina in 1880 who were Indian/White and they lived apart from the dominant society – they were Redbones. Brother #1 married a lady from that group and continued living there. This group was oriented toward the Indian culture. Brother #2 married a woman from a close-knit community who was identified as Black. Brother #3 married a woman from the dominant (White) group, lived there and adopted their customs. The brothers now live in three separate cultures; all three have the same parents. Each brother and his family are accepted in the culture/community of his choice.

Are each of the brothers Redbone? Yes, because they had the same upbringing, but what will their descendants be? Brother #1's descendants are likely to (in an effort to preserve their heritage) maintain the genetic purity of the group for much longer than those of brothers #2 and #3. The children of Brother #1 will be identified as Redbones; they will think of themselves as such. The children of brothers #2 and #3 will see themselves as Black or White respectively, even though they still have the required mixed blood.

The descendants of each brother are likely to marry members of the group they have joined. One of the differences between the descendants of Brother #1 and those of #2 and #3 is that the marriage choices for those of Brother #1 will be much smaller than those of the other two brothers – increasing the chances that descendants of Brother #1 will marry relatives.

The descendants of Brother #1, who were reared in a "Redbone Community" and who shared its way of life and beliefs (culture), have experiences that are distinctly different from those of brothers #2 and #3, who were reared in a different culture. The descendants of Brother #1 are members of a more narrowly defined and more isolated group, one with a smaller population than that of either of the other groups. *The isolated group then has a more distinct and unique identity.*

On the other hand, the descendants of the three brothers are all still of mixed-blood but each is now self-defined as Redbone, Black or White.

Let us complicate this model further by having each brother adopt one of three siblings (babies) of a family in Sweden. These children take the father's name and are respectively reared in the home/community of each of the three brothers. When they are eighteen years of age, what identity do they possess? Are they likely to see themselves as members of the group into which they were adopted? How important is their biological heritage likely to be to them? How important are the ideas, way of life and values of the community? Is it not obvious that they will possess the views, values and world outlook of the community in which they were nurtured and that their views, behavior, and values, will be largely unaffected by their biological history?

Prominent in pioneer lore is the story of Cynthia Ann Parker, stolen by Indians when she was a child eleven years of age. Her response to being brought back to her hearth culture after spending twenty-five years of living as an Indian may be instructive. Her blue eyes and genetic heritage mattered not – she wanted to return to her Indian family and Indian lifestyle. She made several unsuccessful attempts to do so and mourned the loss of her Indian family – the Comanche.[303]

Most of us have several identities – personal and group, i.e., identity as a son, daughter, husband, wife, father, mother, American, Redbone, resident of a Redbone Community, employee, Baptist, Democrat. *How important is it then, that one have a group identity (such as Redbone) apart from his personal identity?* The answer to this question is personal and varied. For some, the identity might be either personal or group or both. Obviously, for some Redbones, such an identity is a negative, and they have avoided it by denial, leaving the community, passing away, getting lost in a larger and more diffuse group, or maintaining social and physical distance in personal ways. They have rejected Redbone as an identity at either the personal or group level; they don't live

---

[303] Cynthia Ann Parker was captured by Indians from her Texas home at the age of eleven years. She later married an Indian and was the mother of Quanah Parker, who became a well-known Comanche Chief.

Nature/Nurture

in a Redbone group and do not identify as a Redbone. For some, being identified as a member of a Redbone Community is a positive and provides a way to stand out from the crowd (larger society) as a member of a unique group; they live in the group and also claim membership at the personal level. For some, it is possible to live apart from the group and still claim a positive identity as a Redbone. In other words, being identified as a Redbone is very important for some, but not to others, and being a member of a Redbone Community is important to some but not to others.

If an identity as a Redbone is important, what is the most important element in the identity: nature or nurture – genetics or culture? The above discussion supports the view that culture is the salient factor, but many Redbones believe that genetic history is the most compelling factor.

Genetics is often the first thought as to why they behave in certain ways or believe certain things. This is a somewhat fatalistic view. A tendency toward violence and family feuding, for example, is seen as a result of the genes. We do this or that because of our genes, so there is nothing we can do about changing it. The idea that their violent culture might be the result of learned behavior passed on generation after generation through the acculturation process is relatively strange to many Redbones.³⁰⁴ This idea is discussed further elsewhere.

There are millions of Americans who are some mixture of Indian, Black and White who have never heard the term Redbone, are they therefore, Redbones, nonetheless? They are not Redbones; they have not been exposed to the Redbone culture. It is primarily the culture that produces the unique qualities of a Redbone. In Mexico or New Mexico, a Redbone would be physically indistinguishable from the other citizens. He would not be known as a Redbone unless he self-identifies as a Redbone. If one knows the Redbone culture from which he came, he might surmise he is a Redbone after learning his cultural values and views.

The result of the recent DNA study done for Melungeons show that Melungeons are a self-defining population. They are not a genetically narrowly defined group. The sample testing the male lineage reveals a widely diverse range – wider than for all of the hundreds of samples taken in England.³⁰⁵ Given the similarities between Redbones and

---

304 When this idea was presented to the Redbone Internet Group, members had difficulty accepting it, but eventually struggled through to a view that their behavior, values and worldviews are a combination of nature and nurture.
305 Jones, *op.cit*, 2002.

Nature/Nurture

Melungeons, there is no reason to believe a DNA test for Redbones would show anything different for them. Genetically, they are an amalgamation of many genetic strains. While many Redbones combine to give an impression of certain physical characteristics, the physical differences within the Redbone group are perhaps as varied as in any other group. The incidence of blue, hazel, gray and green eyes in this usually, but not always, dark-skinned, dark-eyed people, is extraordinary.

Ephraim A. Dial/Doyle Photo courtesy of Larry Keels

Male Doyle/Dial/Dyal descendants are exact YDNA to the BUXTON male surname lineage. You can read the case study in *The Journey: A Genetic Genealogy and Handbook with Case Studies.*

Redbone country in southwest Louisiana.
Unless otherwise noted, they are from the James
Albert Johnson Collection.
The photos were furnished by Beverly Jackson.

Gerald Buxton & wife

Photos

Wm. H. Foster
And **Mame Perkins Ashworth**

Buxton Family

Photos

Carroll Marcantell and
Odelia White Marcantell

Lucile Clark Spell

Georgia Dial/Doyle Tubbs

Photos

Creasy Drake Clark

James Mitch Johnson and
Lillie Ashworth Johnson

Photos

Nettie Doyle/Dial

Lillie Says Smith

Photos

Eunice McLeod Clark and **Eva McLeod Smith**

Mary Elizabeth Perkins

Photos

Howard Goins
While in a CCC Camp at Leesville, La.
1930's

Curley Perkins

Photos

Left George **Washington Manuel** (Emanuel) born 1867 and died 1952. Right wife **Dora Lee Gwinn** (Goin) born 1881 died 1926.
Courtesy Eddie Emanuel
Below Portuguese **Emanuel Family**, Virginia.

Below **Eddie Emanuel "Manuel"** YDNA positive to the Royal Emanuel family of Portugal King Emanuel I & II

Portuguese Emanuel Family. Courtesy Eddie Manuel

THE REDBONE CULTURE OF VIOLENCE

Despite the moderating influence of Reverend Joseph Willis, who established churches in many of the communities dominated by Redbones, they established early on a reputation as a people quick to avenge a perceived wrong by violent action. They were quick to protect their heritage and reputation from questions and their community from intrusion by non-Redbones. They also developed a reputation for committing acts of violence toward each other more frequently than is perceived as normal. Though they may fight with each other, when threatened by non-Redbones, they quickly band together against a perceived common outside enemy. While this proclivity toward violence is less today than in the past, it does still exist. Its pervasiveness and persistence have caused some modern Redbones to question whether the original Redbone settlers moved to Louisiana just ahead of the law. For many Redbones today, this culture of violence is a matter of pride – a major criterion for identifying who they are. Prejean, in her study of Redbones, found that they accept violence as a major part of their identity.[306]

Some modern Redbones recognize that the violent aspect of their culture is cause for an uneasy pride. It is evidence that their forefathers did not passively accept abuse from the dominant society; but, as a major cultural identifier, it makes it more difficult for Redbones to discard violence in its entirety as the need for it diminishes. As the dominant society becomes more tolerant and accepting, modern Redbones are caught between their culture and tradition and this very tolerance. The choices they have in responding to this development are to view the proclivity to violence as "in the blood", which implies that it cannot be changed, or as part of a learned culture in which case, it can be changed. The latter view is much more difficult to accept and its implications for change more difficult to implement. In talking with Redbones today, it is evident that they are struggling with the old traditional nature *vs.* nurture issues both in concept and in practice. Along with acceptance of the culture as a behavioral determinant, comes the responsibility for change. To accomplish change, one would likely have to challenge

---

306 Lana Jean Fagot Prejean, *Occupy Til I Come: The Redbones of Louisiana's No Man's Land*, Thesis for the MA Degree, University of Southwestern Louisiana, 1999, pp. 89-90.

and uproot old beliefs, attitudes and worldviews and would also have to challenge family and neighbors. Few in any society have the fortitude to make such a challenge, especially since Redbones have historically survived by solidarity among members of the group – which makes challenge more difficult. And though violence is perhaps still greater in the Redbone community than in society in general, it is lessening there also.

A few brief accounts of violent episodes involving Redbones, some apparently instigated by them, are illustrative of the history of this culture of violence.

THE RAWHIDE FIGHT occurred in 1850 or 1851 near Walnut Hill, which is between Leesville and Hineston. This fight was not between Redbones and Whites, but neighbor against neighbor. A new school was deliberately burned before it could be occupied. There had been allegations and accusations about who burned the school. At a meeting of citizens called to discuss the matter, a fight broke out during which several people were wounded and five killed. So many people were killed or hurt, they ran out of blankets to put them on or cover them with, and they brought rawhides from the local trading post to use as substitutes, thus, the name Rawhide Fight. Prior to the meeting, the tension was known to be high, so everyone was asked not to bring guns; they brought knives and clubs instead.[307]

THE WESTPORT FIGHT occurred at Westport, located in Rapides Parish approximately ten miles from Hineston. This was perhaps the most famous altercation to ever occur between Redbones and Whites in Louisiana. Long after the account of the Westport Fight was mostly forgotten by the Whites, an unpublished typescript detailing it was being circulated among Redbones. Marler and McManus published this story in 1993 and it continues to be popular among Redbones.[308]

Occurring in December 1881, several people were killed during the fight and in its aftermath. As people came to the Hatch and Moore store to buy supplies for Christmas, the Redbones were reportedly prepared to ambush the Whites. The ambush failed because the Whites were informed ahead of time. At the store, Gordon Musgrove, a man who identified with Whites but was himself part Indian, started the fight. There had been a horse race at Hineston that resulted in a dispute over whether the winner was a horse owned by a

---

307 Don C. Marler and Jane McManus, editors, *The Cherry Winche Country* (Hemphill, Texas: Dogwood Press, 1993), p. 65.
308 Ibid.

White or one owned by a Redbone. It was still fresh in the minds of the people. Musgrove used this dispute to goad the Redbones into a fight. The comments of Musgrove touched off the Redbone tinderbox, and a fistfight led to a gunfight in which several people were killed.[309]

FAMILY FEUDS among Redbones have been numerous. Illustrative of them is one that occurred in the Wisby family in the 1930s. The ambush and killing of Leonard Covington Sweat, in Texas by extended and close family; Nash/Ash & Keefer's. People were killed and the strong feelings engendered in the event prevent its free discussion, even today.

THE BEARHEAD FIGHT unlike the Westport Fight, which occurred earlier, has been largely forgotten. Perhaps it was forgotten because no one wrote an account of it, as did Crawford of the Westport Fight.

The Bearhead community was located in a part of Old Imperial Calcasieu Parish, now known as Beauregard, which was created by the state legislature in 1912. The location at

---

309 Ibid.

which the fight occurred is approximately 20 to 25 miles northwest of Lake Charles.

Again, Redbones fought Whites in this August 1891 fight, in which seven people were killed. The newspaper accounts of the day clearly took sides with the Whites and used language regarding Redbones that would be totally unacceptable for a newspaper today. The idea and practice of newspaper people reporting the facts objectively was seldom found in those days – they chose sides, called people derogatory names and engaged openly in racism and class struggles.

Because the old newspaper accounts are poor microfilm copies, this account will be transcribed here rather than photocopied. It is a sample of the kind of reporting common for the time. No corrections or changes have been made in language, punctuation, or word usage.

REDBONES RAMPANT

FURTHER ACCOUNT OF THE BATTLE OF SUNDAY

The Leaders of Both the Factions Shot Dead and Their Followers Fiercely Contest the Ground

THE OFFICERS CONFESS THEMSELVES POWERLESS AT PRESENT

Redbone Culture of Violence

A Bad Class of Citizens to Deal With and Much Trouble May be Encountered in the End

Lake Charles, La., August 4. – A Post reporter was detailed to procure the full particulars of the wholesale killing which occurred on Lock, Moore & Co.'s tram twenty-two miles from here, Sunday morning and afternoon, of which the Post had an exhaustive report this morning.

There is a class of people who live in a settlement known as "Bear Head Country" on Lock, Moore & Co.'s tram about twenty-five miles from here and who are known as "Redbones." They are supposed to be a mixture of white, negro (sic) and Indian blood, and have a redish cast which suggests the name.

The Ashworths, Dials, Dysons, Murcles and Perkins families are the recognized leaders of the "Redbones." These men receive employment from the Lock, Moore & Co. and McDonald trams, and only work sufficiently to give them money for drink, and it is said that they obtain their living by depredations upon the better class of people in that section.

They (the Redbones) have always looked upon the whites, who obtained and profited by steady employment, with envy.

Redbones of Louisiana

The cause of the immediate trouble occurred last week, when Hooker Morris, one of the foremen, questioned one of his men as to where were those "Redbones" who ought to be driving those wagons? Mr. Morris was not aware at the time that these men objected to the nickname applied to them, and which has been in common use in this community for years, and on last Friday Mr. Morris was surprised by a gang of Redbones, led by Austin Ashworth who came to his house and ordered him to come out and receive a whipping and then leave the country.

Upon his refusal to come out, Ashworth informed him that they would 'lay for him' the next day. Morris went to the woods Saturday with his men, as usual, but was careful to arm himself before going, and in consequence was not molested that day.

Sunday morning at about 10:30 o'clock Hooker Morris, Jesse Ward, Jesse Killen, Jim King, Sam Fulton, Jim Baggett and two others left their camp and went down to Dupree LaComb's saloon about one and one-half miles from the camp, to get some whisky.

At this moment Jesse Dyson emerged from the saloon and said: "I am the best man on the ground," and followed up the remark by pulling his six-shooter, when Jesse Ward of the camp crew pulled his gun and shot Dyson through the head.

Redbone Culture of Violence

Immediately a fusillade (sic) began. Seven out of ten of the Redbones were shooting. When the shooting began, Jesse Hellen [elsewhere given as Kellen] Jim King, Sam Fulton, Jim Baggitt and Buck Elliot, whose gun would not work, took to their heels, leaving Hooker Morris, Jesse Ward and the two others to do the fighting. And well did they fight, killing five of the Redbones, and carried off the body of one of their own men, Jesse Ward, who lingered on till yesterday morning, when he expired. Ward said to Dr. A.J. Perkins, the coroner, just before he died, that he wanted the bullet extracted from his body as soon as dead, because he did not want "to be buried with a Redbone bullet in his body."

In the fight Hooker Morris had his left ear burned by a rifle bullet from the gun of the opposing faction.

Dupree LaComb, the bartender, was shot in the leg and his eight year old boy, Louis Lacomb, was shot in the knee. Neither of these wounds are serious.

After the battle a report was received at the mills that the "Redbones" were murdering men, women, and children up at the tram and a reinforcement went up to aid the camp boys. Among the latter was an old man by the name of T.T. Swan, who insisted on going up to the saloon, contrary to the advice of his friends, and when he was about a quarter mile from the camp was shot dead by one of the "Redbones" in ambush.

Mrs. Lacomb took her children and ran to the woods and remained there until after dark. She said to The Post reporter that upon returning she found the bodies of Lee Perkins and Andrew Ashworth (Redbones) lying in the saloon and the body of their leader, Jesse Dyson, lying on the step. Marion Murcles' body was lying under the gallery of Josh Perkins, an old negro (sic) living near by, and the fifth man, Owen Ashworth, was rolling in agony over the hill about twenty-five yard distant but was dead on Monday morning. She stated further that on Sunday [Monday?] morning, at sunrise, about twenty-five Redbones armed with rifles and shotguns came and carried off their dead.

Dr. A.J. Perkins, the coroner, was interviewed and stated that he was telephoned Monday morning to go out and hold an inquest upon the bodies, but was unable to find any bodies, except those of Ward and Swann. He said that he did not make a very vigorous search, because he did not know but what some one might shoot from an ambush again, and that he did not care to make a target of himself. He had to summon two juries before he could hold inquests upon the two bodies that he did find.

Deputy Sheriffs Joe Courtney and E. Lang Clark went to the scene and arrested Hooker Morris and the two men above mentioned whose names are unknown, all of whom are now in jail at Lake Charles.

Redbone Culture of Violence

The Post reporter interviewed the gentlemen arrested and they substantiate the above report.

When Coroner Perkins arrived on the scene he found five or six men with shotguns on guard over the bodies of Ward and Swann.

More trouble with this gang of Redbones may be expected at anytime as they are of a tough element and will not be arrested without making a strong resistance.[310]

It is easy to see that the newspaper account has many inaccuracies and is plainly biased. The white men are gentlemen, and the Redbones are a gang of outlaws. The Redbones are not expected to surrender to arrest, and more trouble is predicted. It is curious that there were two Whites who were unknown to everyone else. One of the two "unknowns" was Rufus Mouton, son of ex-Senator and ex-Governor, Alexandre Mouton. (Rufus' brother Paul lived in Lake Charles at the time of this event). The other white man was identified by the *Lake Charles Commercial* as Olley Gloss, a Texan.[311]

---

310 "Redbones Rampant," *The Post*, August 4, 1891.
311 "Result of an Old Feud," *Lake Charles Commercial* August 8, 1891, Vol. II No. 7, p. 3, col. 3 – located in Southwest Louisiana Genealogy Library, Lake Charles, Louisiana. Microfilm Roll No.9).

A total of seven men were killed in this affair, but Owen Ashworth was not one of them. *The Echo* reported a few days later that a man named Willis died on the following Wednesday from wounds he received in the fight. So, the dead were: Willis, Lee Perkins, Andrew Ashworth, Jesse Dyson, Marion Murcles, T.T. Swan (Swann) and Jesse Ward. Three of the remaining Redbone leaders were arrested without the further trouble predicted by *The Post*, which later reported the correction about Owen Ashworth and identified Mouton. It also reported that three of the most desperate Redbone leaders had been arrested: Amen Ashworth, Austin Ashworth and curiously, Josh Perkins. Were there two people in the area named Josh Perkins? Previously, *The Post* had identified Josh Perkins as an "old negro who lived nearby," but then he is listed by the same paper as one of the most desperate Redbone leaders.[312]

THE GRABOW FIGHT occurred in 1912 at the community of Grabow, Louisiana, located in the heart of the Redbone community. A group of sawmill workers and the mill's owners and managers got into a gun battle over efforts of the workers to unionize the plant. There was one death and

---

312 The article quoted here from *The Echo, The Post* and *The Lake Charles Commercial* may be found at the Southwest Louisiana Genealogy Library, Lake Charles, Louisiana.

some of the workers were jailed. Despite facts to the contrary, the workers were blamed with the entire incident and many of them were placed in jail. None of the owner/manager group was charged, though it was a worker who was killed, and it was the managers who started the fight.[313]

THE ELIZABETH PLANT/UNION FIGHT occurred in more modern times at Elizabeth, Louisiana. Workers, a majority of whom were perhaps Redbones, got involved in a labor dispute with a paper manufacturing plant during which there was much violence. The dispute involved the use of dynamite that was readily available at the time. Central and southwest Louisiana, having been heavily forested with southern yellow pine, had remnants of these trees in the form of stumps that dotted virtually the entire landscape. In the late 1940s, plants were developed in the Elizabeth and Oakdale areas to render these stumps into naval stores – turpentine and related products. The stumps were, in many cases, huge. They were pushed out of the ground with large bulldozers and holes were drilled in them where dynamite was inserted.

---

313 Don C. Marler, *The Neutral Zone: Backdoor to the United States* (Hemphill, Texas: Dogwood Press, 1995), pp. 191-197.
Arthur L. Emerson, father of actress Faye Emerson, eventually became famous as an actress and wife of President Franklin Roosevelt's son, Elliott, and later the wife of orchestra director, Skitch Henderson. She was born at Elizabeth, Louisiana.

They were then blown apart, making them easier to load on trucks for transport to the plant. Redbones lived in the area and were well adapted to such work. They worked in all phases of this large reclamation project and therefore knew how to secure and use dynamite.

Two plants, one for making paper and one for making products from the paper, were established in the Elizabeth, Louisiana area. The companies, Calcasieu Paper Co. and Southern Industries, Inc., were owned by McGehee Industries, Inc., of Florida. The trouble started when the AFL (labor union) struck the plants in September 1952. The strike continued for over a year, and the plants were eventually closed. No one was killed, but several were seriously wounded. The level of violence was perhaps unprecedented in the history of such conflicts. The total number of incidents is unknown but at month thirteen of the conflict, the following tally was published. There were 109 violent acts including: dynamiting – the natural gas line was hit 40 times, cars and trucks 28; booby traps 3, houses 2, railroads 2, beer hall 1; burnings – houses and barns 11, picket shacks 8; shootings – at plants, houses, pickets 20, at cars from ambush 9. There was one report of a pasture poisoned so cattle could not use it. Gov. Kennon refused to declare martial law, but

Redbone Culture of Violence

scores of state troopers were assigned to the area to assist the local deputies of three parishes.[314]

The plants were in Redbone country and Redbones made up a large part of the work force. They found themselves in what was described by some as a virtual civil war – brother against brother, neighbor against neighbor. One paper reported:
Strikers and non-strikers said some of the violence has been stirred up because of old feuding habits in this once wild territory, the center 100 years ago of runaway slaves, Indian tribes and adventurers.[315]

In hindsight, one could have predicted that given the Redbone history of violence and the frequent practice of confrontation often practiced by labor unions, the strike that has come to be known as the Elizabeth Strike would have turned so violent.

Even in the pre-terrorist days of the 1950s conventional explosives such as dynamite were not usually readily available, but the activities involved in gathering the old pine stumps made it easily obtained. This only compounded an

---

314 *State Times* (Baton Rouge), November 2, 1953.
315 Unidentified newspaper article.

Redbones of Louisiana

already complex situation, and in some instances, likely provided cover for carrying out old feuds.

The following are accounts of outlaw groups or activities in which Redbones might have been involved.

JOHN MURRELL, the infamous land pirate from Tennessee, is reputed to have extended his organized group of outlaws to Louisiana. There is some evidence that Redbones were connected to this organized mayhem in Louisiana in the 19th century. The Murrell Clan smuggled contraband goods, ran slaves, murdered, robbed, counterfeited, raped, and pillaged in the Neutral Zone. His men in the Louisiana contingent included some familiar names: Baley, Beverly, Bluren, Boalton, Bryant, Coper, Cotton, Depont, Deris, Duncan, Hunt, Johnson, Jones, M'Cart, M'Nut, Miller, Moss, Muret, Parker, Pase, Pelton, Phelps, Ray, Read, Rhone, Robinson and Willis.[316]

THE WEST AND KIMBRELL CLAN accounts for another tale of organized violence, perhaps unsurpassed in the annals of crime in America. They operated around the

---

316 Augustus Q. Walton, *The Life and Adventures of John Murel: The Great Western Land Pirate*, (Woodville: Dogwood Press, 1994) p. 55. This is a reprint of the original 1834 publication.

time the Civil War ended and a few years thereafter. Their headquarters were at Wheeling, Louisiana – located between Winnfield and Montgomery. The Clan had members from Mississippi to Mexico who watched for travelers with money, reporting them to the leaders. The leaders were John West, the Justice of the Peace and Sunday School Superintendent of the local Methodist Church, and Dan Kimbrell, Deacon of the church and owner of the local boarding house. Wheeling and the boarding house were on the Harrisonburg Road, over which immigrants from the southeast came to Texas and the Neutral Zone. These outlaws killed, perhaps, more people than any other group in American history. So many people were killed, disposing of the bodies was a problem. In order to solve the disposal problem, the Clan dug a well every mile for forty miles. Bodies of victims were placed in these wells as the need arose.

Some of the immigrants, weary of the road, settled along the Harrisonburg Road and no doubt some were of Redbone stock. See the chapter on "Redbone Immigration" for more on the immigrants who came over this road. A list of names of those affected by these outlaw activities reveals that some families were on both sides of the law. Many of the names are of interest to Redbones. The following names are from one source.[317] Associated with the outlaws were: Adams, Beall, Binion, Carter, Collins, Crew, Frame, Harper, Hicks, Ingram, Kimbrell, Maybin, Mitchell, Thompson, Williams, West and Vines.

Associated with law abiding citizens were: Albright, Barr, Bird, Bostick, Brock, Carter, Curry, Davison, Dean, Durham, Evans, Fergerson, Hicks, Hutto, Jones, Kelly, Lewis, Mathis, Martin, McIlwain, McCain, Mitchell, Neal, Patten, Robins, Shelton, Simmons, Spikes, Straughn, Teagle, Turner, Wilson and Woods.[318]

JOSH PERKINS (there were several) according to Redbone lore, while living in Louisiana, was such a proficient outlaw that the U.S. Government hired him to assist in catching other outlaws in the area.[319]

In situations where an antagonist is overwhelmed by the resources of a foe, the antagonist often resorts to hit and run or ambush tactics. The lore of Redbones reflects such practices. The hero of old time Redbones was Francis Marion, the Swamp Fox. General Marion and his men

---

317 Richard Briley, III, *Nightriders: Inside Story of the West and Kimbrell Clan* (Hemphill: Dogwood Press, 1998).
318 Ibid.
319 Two different sources related this information. Their names are held in confidence.

invented and perfected guerilla warfare in South Carolina.[320] This South Carolina, born-and-bred officer put his extensive knowledge of the swamps to good use in the American Revolutionary War. He and his men operated at night under heavy secrecy and stealth. After their brief, fast, surprise attacks on the regimented British, they moved back into the swamps. These hit and run clandestine operations decimated and demoralized the British troops moving the colonies far forward in their quest for victory. Special Forces, including the Navy Frogmen (SEALS), Rangers, Green Berets, etc., have claimed Marion's tactical success in guerilla warfare as the model for modern day special warfare.

One of the earliest Redbones to come to Louisiana, Reverend Joseph Willis, was with Marion's band. Willis said he and his friends, Ezekiel O'Quinn and Richard Curtis, were proud to be called "Marion Men."[321] Among Louisiana Redbone men, the names Francis, Marion and various combinations of these names have been popular through the years. Throughout the United States, there are numerous towns and counties named Marion in honor of the general.

---

320 Noel B. Gerson, *The Swamp Fox, Francis Marion* (New York: Doubleday, 1967).
321 Internet material from Reverend Randy Willis, Great Grandson of Reverend Joseph Willis.

Author Boddie has developed a list of 2500 men who served with Marion. The list is incomplete; containing mostly names of men who made claims for financial assistance. Joseph Willis never made the list. The following names should be of interest to those interested in possible Redbones who served as Marion men. Note that some surnames had so many representing the name, not all are listed here – see the book for the complete list. It is not suggested that all in the Boddie list were Redbones, but it appears that many were. Some of those in the list with names familiar as Redbones were:

George Bird, William Bird, Evan Boyd, John Boyd, Jacob Buxton, Samuel Buxton, John Byrd, Sutton Byrd, Abner Cain, John Cain, John Clark, James Clark, Joseph Clark, Thomas Clark, Anthony Clark, David Cole, James Cole, John Cole, Richard Cole, Abner Coleman, Charles Coleman, Francis Coleman, Jacob Coleman, John Coleman, William Coleman, Edmund Collins, Daniel Collins, Gary Collins, Jonah Collins, John Collins, Lewis Collins, William Crawford, John Day, Garret Dial, John Dial, John Dick, John Doyal, William Drake, Juluis Driggers, Burwell Evans, William Fountain, Gideon Gibson, Gilbert Gibson, Richard Goodwin, William Green, James Hall, Solomon Harper, John Hicks, James Jenkins, Gilbert Johnson, James Johnson, James, Jolly, Thomas Jones, John Keels, Thomas Knight, Joseph Lewis, Robert Lewis, James Mathis, John Mathis, Samuel Mixon, John Mixon, James Moore, Daniel Morrison, Isham Nettles, Jesse Nettles, William Orr, James Owens, David Perkins, John Parker, Matthew Paul, William Paul,

Redbone Culture of Violence

Lewis Perkins, John Roberts, John Smiley, Jeremiah Smith, Thomas Stokes, George Strother, Edward Thomas, Leonard West, William West. Jonathan Wise, Alexander Wood, Francis Wylie, William Wyndham and Matthew Young.

Several names stand out on the list, one of whom is Isham Nettles, who was a fellow minister with Reverend Joseph Willis.[322]

IN SUMMARY

Violence, as discussed elsewhere in this book, is often seen by Redbones as an identifying trait and a source of pride, albeit an uneasy pride. There seems to be an almost constant tension among family members, with violence or the threat of it, ever present. Females manage children and the household, while men work and manage money, the family's relation with the broader community including politics, and relationships between families. As one informant said: "When the violence starts, you have to join in. You are drawn in or forced out. The control over you is tremendous. Many people have moved out of the community and refuse to live there again. Moving away is a major way of avoiding the violence; if you live there, you cannot avoid it."

---

322 William Willis Boddie, *Marion's Men* (Heisser Printing, Co., 1938).

In politics, block voting is common. This is achieved usually by a dominant male who pressures family and friends to vote as he wishes. Some family tension is related to this control of behavior.

Bearhead Redbones, **Hester Amanda Buxton Perkins** and her daughters, **Lettie** and **Nettie Perkins**. Amanda is daughter of James Toby Buxton and Catherine Doyle. Amanda married William Vincent Perkins.
Courtesy Marilyn Baggett Kobliaka

OLD SAYINGS, BELIEFS, PRACTICES AND LEGENDS

Many of the following "old sayings" and words were common to the rural south, if not all of America. Historically, throughout the South, there is found a love of storytelling, recounting old sayings and "playing on words." Migration from the east to the west and the commonness of these cultural artifacts has obscured their origins so they can be attributed, or claimed by, any group wishing to do so.

There is no way to determine definitely which, if any, are of Redbone origin. Many of them were provided by members of the Redbone Internet Discussion Group after a request for them was issued over the internet; so, they were in common use in the Redbone community at some fairly recent period; some are still used.

Older Redbones are known to have a tendency to corrupt words and to create special use for them. These sayings reflect wisdom, earthiness, ignorance, humor and charm. Here is a sampling of those "old sayings" and words – furnished with explanations when appropriate.

WORDS that are most likely of pure Redbone origin are: *Now Aaah*. In the 1940s and 50s, Redbones in southwest Louisiana had a saying that may have been of their own creation. When asked a question to which they did not know the answer, or did not wish to answer, they simply said – "Now aaah." They pronounced it with a short a, as in "at".

B'live. Believe

Cherry Winche. The Cherry Winche Creek, near Westport, is said to have received this name due to a corruption of the phrase Cherokee Wench. The legend is that a Cherokee chief lived alongside this clear freshwater creek in a cabin with a black woman – commonly referred to in those days as a wench. When he died, the woman continued living in the cabin near the creek. Over time, the creek came to be known as the Cherokee Wench's creek, that was corrupted by Redbones to Cherry Winche Creek. Whether it is a true story or not is unknown, but it is a fine example of an old time Redbone linguistic concoction. Today, some refer to that area of the state as the Cherry Winche Country.

WORDS used by Redbones; some, possibly of Redbone origin:

Batry. Battery.
Boogers. Another word for gremlins.
Borry, Borrow
Carry. A substitute for take. As in, I will carry you to town.
Chunk. To throw.

Old Sayings, Beliefs, Practices and Legends

Clum. Climbed.
Clur. Clear.
Copacetic. OK or alright. As in, everything is copacetic.
Coner. Corner
Crunk. Cranked.
Deef. Deaf.
Directly. Soon. I'll be back directly. Sometimes pronounced "dreckly".
Drap. Drop
Et. Ate
Faut or faught. Fought.
Fixin. Getting ready. As in, I am fixin to leave for work.
Flub. Fail or make a mistake. As in, I flubbed that test.
Gallery. The porch.
Gallueses. Suspenders
Gaum. To some, it means to mess up something; to adhere to or "latch on to" something as in Gaum on to it.
Heah. Hear.
Heap. Many – much.
Hep. Help.
Hern. Hers.
Hisen. His.
Het. Heated.
Hit. It.
Holt. Hold.
Hope. Help.
Howsomever. However.
Jist. Just.
Lak. Like
Loud. Allowed, as in "he loud (allowed) that he was too old to make the trip." One definition of allowed is to admit or concede.

Mash. Push or Press.
Mout. Might.
Nigh. Near.
Nur. Near.
Onest. Once.
Onusual. Unusal.
Peers. Appears.
Pert near. Close.
Pore. Poor.
Puore. Pure.
Pizzen. Poison. Pronounced "Pie-zin."
Raineyfield. Looks like it might rain.
Ranch. A wrench.
Rench. Rinse.
Retch. Reach.
Riled. Angered.
Seed. Saw, as in, I seed him do it.
Sot. Set, as he is sot in his ways.
Spect. Expect.
Sposed. Supposed.
Tarn. Torn
Tollable. Tolerable, moderately good. How are you? Answer: Tollable.
Tump. Turn. You are going to tump over that pot.
Turtle Hull. Car trunk.
Vye dock. Railroad overpass.
Winda. Window.
Winder. Window.
Yore. Your.

SAYINGS used by Redbones, some possibly of Redbone origin:

Old Sayings, Beliefs, Practices and Legends

Gotta lick that calf again. One has to do the job over again and better.

The buzzards laid you on a stump and the sun hatched you.

Cut on the lights.

Crank the car. This is a holdover from the days when one used a hand crank to start the car.

Don't bark woman till I pull your chain.

They served cold coffee. They were cold, rejecting or unfriendly.

She looks like she's been rode hard and put up wet.

Lord willin (willing) and the creeks don't rise. A variation is – Lord willin and the Creeks don't rise – meaning the Creek Indians.

I'd rather be looking for dead people than have them looking for me.

Dumber than a post.

Busy as a one-eyed man at a burlesque show.

Jumpy as a long-tailed cat in a room full of rocking chairs.

Busy as a cat on a hot tin roof.

Madder than an old wet hen.

Light a shuck. Means get away quick – hurry.

He was shaking like a dog shittin a peach seed.

He can eat a settin of eggs. A brooding hen is one ready to set on her eggs until they hatch. She was called a settin (setting) hen. A setting is 16 eggs.

Lower than a snake's belly in a wagon rut.

I am going to jerk a knot in your tail.

I have to catch my bath water. This likely comes from the old custom of putting a tub under the "eaves" (dripline of the roof) to catch rainwater as it fell from the roof.

Happy as a dead pig in the sunshine.

Happy as a pig in slop.

It's raining like a tall cow peeing on a flat rock.
That old dog won't hunt. Meaning the item in question will not work or I don't believe in it.
He has gone around the bend. He is mentally ill. He has lost his mind.
Every tub must sit on its own bottom. This saying has the same meaning as *Everyone must paddle his own canoe.*
He would pee in your pocket and tell you it was raining. He was a charmer and would lie to you.
We can't dance, and it's too wet to plow.
Pleasure bent. A bowlegged girl.
She was so bowlegged she couldn't hem a hog up in a ditch.

Well, that is enough of these old sayings. The hunt is over, "let's pee on the fire and call the dogs."

REDBONE CUSTOMS have received little attention. The following is a beginning at recording them.

Local Whites and Blacks shared many of the beliefs included here. Indeed, some of them sound like African or West Indies voodoo. Some, no doubt, have English or Irish roots and some are still practiced today. A questionnaire asking for old beliefs and practices was posted for the Redbone Discussion Group on the Internet. The questionnaire could be completed and returned without self-identification. The respondent was asked only to indicate whether or not he/she was a Redbone. Only five were completed and returned – not one of which

Old Sayings, Beliefs, Practices and Legends

was completed by a person who indicated that he/she was a Redbone. Yet, members of the Redbone Discussion Group did communicate some old beliefs by email and in person, which has resulted in a collection of some interesting items. These, along with others found in a few written sources, are given below.

One frequently given example of a belief and practice is the reading of the scripture Ezekiel 16:6 to stop bleeding. Only special people are supposed to know and practice this. It is supposedly passed from father to son, but recently an elderly Redbone lady claimed she has the power to stop bleeding using this method. It is still practiced, and several members of the Redbone Discussion Group still believe in its efficacy. This belief is still present among Whites and Blacks, as well as Redbones.

Sam Stasby, a now deceased resident of southwest Louisiana, was said to be able to prevent babies from dying from "Boll-Hives," a form of "infected heat." The process had to be implemented before the baby was ten days old. The tools used were a razor, a blue quinine bottle, a sulfur match, and a silver spoon. An "X" was cut on the baby's back with the razor, then the match was struck and placed in the bottle. The mouth of the bottle was placed over the cut, and the burning match created a suction that drew out a few drops of blood. This blood was put in the silver spoon with a few drops of the mother's milk and this was fed to the baby.[323]

Another man, whose surname was Doyle/Dial/Doyal, "cured" the asthma of his young daughter by putting a lock of her hair in the split branch of a willow tree. As the tree grew and healed, she outgrew her asthma.[324] In a variation of this, a hole was bored in a picket fence, and a lock of the child's hair was put in it. When the child grew above the hole, the asthma was cured.[325]

Babies with "thrush" or "thrash" mouth were often treated by having a man who never knew his father blow into the child's mouth. This practice is still performed by some.

---

323 Interview with Doris McMain Vaughn, now deceased, a relative of Mr. Stasby. The practice is also reported by Kadlecek and Bullard, in *Louisiana's Kisatchie Hills*, p. 491. It was practiced among Natchez Indians as reported by Du Pratz and quoted in Swanton, *Indian Tribes of the Lower Mississippi Valley and Adjacent Coast of the Gulf of Mexico*, p. 81. The Natchez doctors did this in a less elaborate manner on adults. They used a flint knife and sucked the blood or used a Bison horn to draw the blood. The process was more like the practice of bloodletting than the process described by Vaughn and was perhaps to release evil spirits.
324 Interview with Mary Cleveland of Leesville who witnessed this act.
325 Email from Donny McCorquodale who was a witness to this act – November 18, 1999.

Old Sayings, Beliefs, Practices and Legends

Perhaps the most mentioned old remedy, and that one that many people living today has experienced, is that Chicken Pox can be cured by having chickens fly over the child's head. This was to cure the Pox or assure that no scar was left. The trip to the chicken house was sometimes done before daylight. It was enough to scare the Pox out of a child.

Until modern times, cattle were allowed to roam the open range in the areas of Louisiana where most Redbones lived. Redbones were good cattlemen, but they had a few practices that were apparently not based on sound reasoning. Among these were the practices of splitting a sick cow's tail and rubbing salt into the wound and cutting off the horns or boring holes in the horns of the sick cow. These practices were based on a diagnosis of hollow tail or hollow horn respectively. Since these actions were deemed necessary, mostly at times when forage was scarce, it is suspected that a proper diagnosis would have been hollow belly – not enough good food. Both procedures were still practiced a few years ago and may still occur. The only result is a tendency for worms to get in the wounds (especially when the horns are cut off), which sometimes complicates the animal's problems.

BELIEFS AND PRACTICES that were or still are observed by some people in the Redbone community.

> Cure earache in a baby's by blowing cigarette smoke in the baby's ear.
>
> A person who dies a painful death is thought to have been a sinner.
>
> At funerals, each person throws a handful of dirt on the casket after it is lowered into the ground.
>
> Putting tobacco on a sting will bring out the poison.
>
> It is considered bad luck to receive an open knife and return it closed.
>
> All crops must be planted by the signs of the Zodiac.
>
> Your hair should be cut by the signs of the Zodiac.
>
> It is bad luck to walk across the floor with one shoe off or to open an umbrella in the house.
>
> Dreaming of muddy water is a bad sign.
>
> Hearing a hen crow or rooster cluck is a bad sign.
>
> The number 13, walking under a ladder and breaking a mirror are bad signs.

Old Sayings, Beliefs, Practices and Legends

Put a penny in your shoe for good luck.
If you allow someone to sweep under your feet as you set in your chair, you will never marry.

It was bad luck to sweep trash over the threshold after dark.

Don't do your laundry on New Year's Day because you might wash a family member out that year.

If a young girl can peel an apple without a break in the peel, she should swing it over her head to the right three times and let go. When the peel lands, it will form the initials of the man she will marry.

A pregnant woman should not wash her hair or take an allover bath during pregnancy.

Many illnesses can be cured by "sweating out" the poison. If a rooster crows before daylight, it is an omen of death in the community.

Cure headache by binding the head as tight as possible.

When saying goodbye, it is bad luck to watch someone walk or drive away until you can't see them anymore.

When you get a burn, certain people can keep a blister from forming by passing their hand over it, blowing on it and saying some words under their breath – this is called drawing fire. Drawing fire is a frequently referenced practice of the present day.

If you were born with a veil over your face, you may have special powers. The veil, of course, is the amniotic sac that retains the fluid in which the fetus rests. When the sac breaks prematurely, as it sometimes does, it collapses over the face. This sometimes restricts oxygen causing brain damage or other problems. The child then often acts differently from others who have experienced a more normal birth and becomes, in the eyes of the community, a special child with unusual powers.

One of the most common old beliefs is "water witching." Certain people are supposed to have the ability to use a forked stick (or modern metal rods) to find underground water. The person walks over the ground holding the two ends of the stick with the single end pointing out. When he reaches the spot of underground water, the stick bends down. This practice is still quite common today among those hunting water and treasure.

Kadlecek and Bullard tell of a practice in the Kisatchie Hills known as "frauding." There was a certain place in the hills

Old Sayings, Beliefs, Practices and Legends

that people gathered to watch men fight for sport. On occasion, these men would cut a vein in their wrist and drink the blood until they were ready to fight. Through this practice, they were "pumped up" and ready to fight. These fights did not involve guns or knives, and the participants usually left as friends.[326] There is no evidence that this practice was widespread or common in either the Redbone community or the general society, but Redbones do still get together in a least one community fight for sport.

Some Redbones report that they have premonitions – visions or feelings – of coming events. Some recognize in these events "warnings" and "signs" of things to come. In some instances, they report these "feelings" are related to things that have already happened but are not yet common knowledge.

Many Redbones (and many Christians generally) believe God personally attends each individual's needs and requests. Some believe there are angels, and some believe that these angels are assigned to protect people. Some people believe in witches, ghosts, and spirits – good and bad. Most modern

---

326 Mabell R. Kadlecek and Marion C. Bullard, *Louisiana's Kisatchie Hills: History Tradition and* Folklore (Alexandria: 1994), p. 310.

Louisiana Redbones, who belong to a church, are Baptist or Pentecostal.

RECREATION, WORK and SOCIALIZATION of Redbones were not significantly different from that of the surrounding communities. In the era of the 1930s to 1950s, gospel singing was a favorite form of socialization and recreation in the rural south, and it was especially popular among Redbones. Local churches sponsored "singing schools" during the summer months. Such schools usually lasted two to three weeks and featured learning to use "shaped" notes – seven different shapes (squares, triangles, circles, etc.) representing the notes on the scale. In addition to providing knowledge of music, these singing schools provided an opportunity for the young people to "court" and form friendships, and it provided an opportunity for young and old to sing in public.

The knowledge and talent gained at singing schools was tested at "singing conventions" which followed. These conventions were all day affairs also sponsored by the local churches. There was singing for several hours with "dinner on the ground", and then more singing. At these affairs, anyone who wished to do so could lead the assembled group in singing gospel songs. There was opportunity for all to sing

Old Sayings, Beliefs, Practices and Legends

solo, duet, in trio, or quartet as they desired. Some were very good singers or musicians and some, very bad. No one was denied opportunity regardless of talent or lack thereof. The following is an example of shaped note music.

While many in the Redbone communities went to the usual "Saturday Night Dances" during the 1930s, the Baptists considered this a sin, so they created a substitute known as "Play Parties." The dances involved fiddle music and use of "fiddle sticks." A fiddle stick was a long stick – often a long bone knitting needle. One or two of these sticks were held in the hand, and the player would tap out a rhythm on the body of the fiddle as the fiddle player played.[327] At the Play Parties, the young people sang hymns without music and

---

327 Lenox Antony, "Calcasieu Parish Folklore: DeQuincy (sic) Section," FWP files folder 89. This material is used here by permission of the Cammie Henry Research Center, Northwestern State University, Natchitoches, Louisiana, p. 2.

played dance games such as "Marching to Jerusalem." They also had taffy pulling and played various "forfeit" games.[328] Redbones have historically been excellent stockmen. In South Carolina, they were drovers, and some pursued this vocation in Louisiana and Texas. Until the mid1900s, there was open range in central and southwest Louisiana. The area where Redbones resided was one of the last to be closed by law to stockmen. Redbones had traditionally been allowed to run livestock on publicly owned land and land owned by large timber companies. The closure of these lands caused much strife and violence in the Redbone communities.

Herds of hogs and cattle that became essentially wild were managed with the aid of horses and dogs. The favorite stock dog was the Catahoula Cur (sometimes called a Blue Leopard or Catahoula Hog Dog). According to legend, DeSoto (or his men), left some of those dogs with the Catahoula Indians, who lived near Catahoula Lake, and they have been kept as a pure breed since then.

Horseracing was a popular past time in rural southwest Louisiana in the mid1800s and after the Civil War. The racetrack at Hineston was said to have featured a race where a dead goose that had been picked clean of feathers and

---

328 *Ibid.*, p. 5.

Old Sayings, Beliefs, Practices and Legends

greased was hanged by the feet at the end of the track. The winner of the race was the person who could get to the goose first and pull its head off. Now, the rodeo is a most popular sport.

The most plentiful natural resource in the area where Redbones lived was several varieties of Southern Yellow Pine. In approximately 1800, large companies from the northern states bought huge tracts of timberland and brought in mills capable of processing the timber into lumber. Steamships had been plying the Sabine River since the 1830s, but it remained for the railroads to make this industry viable. Redbones benefitted through the labor this industry provided. The timber was so vast that the activity necessary to cut it out lasted fifty years. Redbones were, because of their previous experience, excellent in the use of teams of oxen and mules used to skid the logs to the small gage railroad (called spurs) that had been built from the mainline right into the woods. The men driving teams of oxen were called "bull punchers" and those driving mules were known as "mule skinners." The men who cut the logs (the sawyers) were known as "flatheads." The origin of the term flathead is uncertain. There was, early in the log-cutting days in Louisiana, and perhaps across the south, a type of hat used to keep falling limbs from hitting the heads of workers. This hat was made of a hard cardboard and was flat on top. It was similar to the "safari" hat that came later. Thus, the term "flathead" was applied to the sawyers who wore such hats and eventually to all who cut logs.[329]

LEGENDS often reveal or reflect an underlying belief, and efforts at social control. The following legends were recorded in the early 1930s as part of the Federal Writer's Program (FWP) in which writers were hired to record local color stories. Such stories were often told as entertainment and to keep young children from venturing astray.

THE WILD PEOPLE

> *Somewhere on an unused almost forgotten road, miles out of DeQuincey (sic) it is rumored that the town of Wild People still exists. Formerly, when the old road was still used, this town was the terror of travelers. For on the approach of a stranger, all of the inhabitants would desert their homes and hide in the forest. Finding a deserted group of houses, all furnished, the traveler, puzzled, would perhaps take to his heels and flee from the accursed town. But, if weary of the road, he decided to stay, his doom was sealed. As he lolled in the twilight, resting, he would perhaps hear strange rustles in the surrounding*

---

[329] Information provided by Mr. Cecil Gill who has worked for the Crowell Lumber company for 52 years.

Old Sayings, Beliefs, Practices and Legends

forest, sometimes even sounds that seemed to be laughter or voices. Then as darkness fell, silence would grip the whole forest world. Lulled, the traveler would retire.

No sooner was he asleep, then the Wild People would return on silent padded feet to peer into the cabin where the stranger slept. Again there would be soft laughter, and whispered words. Then abruptly a shot would ring out in the night and the traveler would be no more.

"It was the most ungodliest place this side of hell," Calcasieu old folk say, describing the town, "They would shoot you down just to see you kick."

But memory of their murderous ways is not the only quality of the Wild People that survives in local legend. Some of the Wild People, used to have one eye on one side of their head, one eye on the other, "jest like an ox". One of the wild women, it is related, had the habit of running through the forest, a knife in her hand, killing the farmer's sheep. Another woman was so powerful she could wrestle with alligators. Some of the men had such huge appetites they could eat a whole sheep at one meal and the distinguishing trait of one of the wild men was said to have been his jaws. "He had the powerfulest jaws in the world," the story goes and his hair was just as red as blood and his eyes were red too." This man could crack hickory nuts with his teeth and once during a fight he bit a man's arms completely off.

> *Who the wild people were, where they came from will never be known, it is added, since in addition to their hatred of strangers, there was an insurmountable barrier of language, since the Wild People spoke only in the Screech Owl Language.*[330]

Was this story of a fierce people who lived apart from everyone else, who were not always welcoming to strangers, who looked different, spoke differently from others and whose origins were unknown, a metaphor for Redbones?

One final legend will end this section.

THE MATRIARCH

> *The tale of Susan Hoosier, known as The Matriarch, is still told [early 1930s] in Starks, Green Island, Lunita (Rabbit Town), Perkins, and many other tiny hamlets lying north and west of DeQuincey (sic). Susan, it is related, was a wonderful woman, blessed with the strange miraculous (sic) power to replenish barren and unfruitful fields. When a farmer's crop withered or failed or his land grew unfertile, he would send for The Matriarch and she would come, her much thumbed Bible in her hand, to bless his fields. Always, it is said, that after the blessing the ground would once more yield fine crops.*

---

330 Anthony *op. cit.*, pp.7-9.

Old Sayings, Beliefs, Practices and Legends

So grateful were the farmers that in spite of Susan's objections, gifts were showered on her. These, Susan always distributed among the needy of the villages.

Of a very opposite nature was a witch woman who once lived in this same territory. Possessed of as strange a power as The Matriarch, she turned these powers to the use of evil. One of her most potent secret charms was said to be so strong as to enthrall the person against it was so much that the bewitched one would bring the witch woman all his property. [This confused sentence was copied as it appeared.] *She is said to have kept a retinue of followers constantly poor by her mystic powers.*[331]

POLITICS have been of interest to Redbones at least since the mid1800s. Their involvement was curtailed in the early years after their move west because only free white male property owners could vote. The "white" component could change when necessity arose. Shugg, in *Origins of Class Struggle in Louisiana*, related that:

Although suffrage was constitutionally restricted to white freeman, local elections were sometimes so closely contested that rival candidates enlisted the aid of free people of color. The most notorious cases in the Old South, long since forgotten, occurred in

---

331 *Ibid.*, p. 9.

Rapides. Here in the so-called "Ten-Mile Precinct," lived a hundred or more mulatto families...the terror of their poor neighbors. But relations were not so unfriendly as to prevent considerable miscegenation, for the color of their progeny was admitted to be no clue to their race. Whig politicians first marched these Negroes to the polls in 1838 and entered public land in their names so that they might qualify to vote as if they were white men...The scandal was aired by the American party in a desperate effort to defeat Colonel Robert A. Hunter, Democratic candidate for State Treasurer in 1857. ...But "Ten-Mile Bob", as his opponents dubbed him, carried Rapides by sixty-eight ballots....[332]

Louisiana is a wonderfully diverse cultural environment. In the mind of the public, the state is divided into the south Louisiana Catholics and the north Louisiana Protestants, with Alexandria being the dividing line between the two. While this division is useful, it is not the entire story. The state is seasoned by several small ethnic groups, many of which have maintained their own culture or parts of their culture. Louisiana, rather than being a melting pot, is more like a salad bowl where the different ingredients retain their own unique color and flavor, while contributing to the whole. Such is the Redbone culture.

---

332 Shugg, *op. cit.*, p. 144.

Old Sayings, Beliefs, Practices and Legends

While most such ethnic groups in south Louisiana are heavily influenced by the French Catholic culture, Redbones are an exception. They are culturally akin to the Protestants of north Louisiana. They are primarily rural hard-working farmers, tradesmen, timber workers and stockmen. They are almost all Baptist or Pentecostal, and few are Catholic. Redbone families are close-knit and matriarchal.

FUNERAL AND BURIAL practices are wonderful indices of old cultural practices, and a look at Protestant and Redbone cemeteries is instructive. Cemeteries that serve Redbone communities reflect the influence of the Redbone's Protestant choice. Catholic cemeteries are declared sacred ground and a forest of crosses and other religious icons on the tombs or graves immediately identifies them. In breaking away from the Catholic Church, Protestants rejected the heavy emphasis on icons, and their cemeteries are usually not declared sacred ground though they are highly respected. As Jordan in his seminal study of Texas cemeteries said:

> *Southern cemeteries, in keeping with British dissenter Protestant tradition, do not occupy sanctified ground. John Wesley, for example, opposed the consecration*

of burial grounds as 'a mere relic of Romanish superstition."[333]

While a few crosses are evident in Protestant cemeteries, the usual icons found there such as lambs, doves and open Bibles, are muted and sedate.

The non-Catholic cemetery might be associated with a church and share the name of a church. More often, the name derives from a family, community, or natural landmark, such as a creek, and therefore carries that name. Many are even more secular, such as the "Little Hope Cemetery" of Wood County, Texas.[334] In the parts of Louisiana commonly associated with Redbones, the following cemetery names are examples: Woods, Hunt, Collins, Cooley, Blue Branch, Glass Window, Holly Springs, Good Hope, Monk Hill, Willis Flat, Pine Island, Mt. Pleasant, Canaan, Plunkaway, Antioch and Silver Creek.

An analysis of the data on the 123 cemeteries in Vernon Parish is instructive.

---

333 Terry G. Jordan, *Texas Graveyards: A Cultural Legacy*, (Austin: University of Texas Press, 1982), p. 33.
334 Ibid.

Old Sayings, Beliefs, Practices and Legends

CEMETERIES BY NAME AFFILIATION

Religious/Church	14
Family	64
Community	11
Natural (Hills, Creeks, etc.)	19
Other (mixture, neutral such as Friendship)	15
Total	123[335]

These cemeteries are often located on a well-drained hill of sandy loam soil, and trees; cedar, crepe myrtle and magnolia, are highly preferred. Jordan draws a connection between the ornaments, flowers, shrubs and trees in Protestant cemeteries and old Pagan customs. The rose is the most frequently found flower in southern cemeteries. The rose is associated with the Mediterranean Mother Goddess and the many depictions of her such as Isis and Demeter – the prototype of Mary.[336] The rose is associated with motherhood and "Mother's Day." These ancient connections are lost to the consciousness of people today, but nevertheless may be influential.

---

335 Jane McManus, *L'est We Forget: Cemeteries of Vernon Parish, Louisiana*, (Alexandria: Parker Enterprises, 1996), Vols. I, II, III. These data were compiled by use of the three volumes of the McManus work.
336 Jordan, *op. cit.*, p. 28. See this book for much more on the interesting discussion of the Pagan connection and possible meanings of the various flora found in our cemeteries.

Graves in Protestant and Redbone cemeteries are laid out in the traditional east-west pattern with the feet to the east. A smaller stone at the foot counterbalances the headstone. Occasionally, a grave is laid out north to south. This usually signifies the person so buried was an outlaw or had done something the community or family highly disapproved. In the 19th century, there were occasions when serious outlaws pretended to bury someone, but instead buried treasure in the official grave and disposed of the body intended for the grave in another place. These graves were often laid out in an unconventional manner, marking them for future visitation to retrieve the treasure. Burial of married couples in Redbone cemeteries usually follow the conventional practice of the wife buried on the south side of the husband.

Redbones usually keep their cemeteries in excellent condition. The method of maintenance of Protestant and Redbone cemeteries in Louisiana has changed drastically since World War II. Before the advent of the war, these cemeteries were kept clean of grass. The grass was scraped or hoed and removed or burned. Traditionally, a day was set aside for the "Graveyard Working." This project was a community affair; everyone gathered and began the rather hard and difficult work. The work, however, was similar to the work they did every day; at home they hoed the fields and their own yard. Jordan suggests that this may account for their preference for the term graveyard over cemetery. The elongated mounds over the graves were similar to the mounds of the rows in the fields that were hoed clean of weeds or grass. The grave mounds were kept especially clean and repaired. If sinking had occurred, or if rain had washed dirt away, this dirt was replaced, and the dirt on the mound refreshed.

The people working the graveyard told stories about the deceased and renewed their memory of the departed. There was "dinner on the ground" and socializing all day.

Families often reserved a plot of ground so their members could be buried near each other. Various items were and are placed on graves such as toys, flowers, and shells.

Markers in the early days were made of wood that rotted or was eaten by termites. If the cemetery was not kept scraped, the frequent forest fires burned the wooden markers. Concrete was eventually used with names and dates crudely added. Professionally engraved headstones (made of stone) gradually became common as they became available at affordable prices. Now, new technology allows photographs to be permanently embossed on the headstone in bronze or ceramics, and these are seen with increased frequency.

After the war, power lawn mowers were more readily available. The traditional scraping of the cemeteries and the tradition of the day set aside for this activity gave way to the cemeteries covered with grass, which could be mowed. The most common grasses in cemeteries in southwest Louisiana are the native Carpet grass, St. Augustine, Bermuda or Centipede Grass. These grasses are mowed by someone paid by the "Cemetery Association" or by a person dedicated to keeping the cemeteries maintained. Many graves are now covered with concrete, effectively eliminating the need for scraping. Many graves, especially in the "Perpetual Care" cemeteries, are flat and level with the ground and the marker is a bronze plaque lying flat – allowing the mower to pass over it smoothly. Some communities still have graveyard workings in a modified form. A day is set aside for a general clean-up of the cemetery and a reunion of people associated with the cemetery. Some come from long distances for the annual event. This practice is as much for a reunion as for the cemetery cleanup. Brenda Bass, a member of a Redbone community, believes that the day set aside for the "Graveyard Working" is still important to families represented at the local cemetery.

With the passing of the "Graveyard Working", a quaint tradition is dying. In its absence, the family reunion has gained in popularity since World War II. While no study of family reunions has been found, it appears that these events are more numerous, better organized and attended than in the past. These reunions are often now used to share genealogy information. The Internet has digitized the search for family history information, and perhaps by extension, it has digitized one of the main functions of graveyard working. It is not too much of a stretch to say that family reunions and the Internet have replaced the "graveyard working." The modified graveyard workings may be a transition from the old days when the scraping and removal of grass required much labor.

Chickasaw Redbone Treasure Cave, A Legend

On the northern bank of the Tennessee River, in an area near Muscle Shoals, Alabama, lies a hidden limestone cavern containing an incredible multi-million-dollar fortune in gold, silver, and jewels. Known as the Spanish treasure cache of Redbone Cave, the history of this great lost wealth goes back to around 1540, the time of Spanish explorer Hernando De Soto's march into the New World.

In 1538, Charles V of Spain had given De Soto permission to conquer Florida at his own expense, and the Spanish explorers sailed with a richly equipped company of 600 men, 24 ecclesiastics, and 20 officers. The expedition landed at the Bay of Espiritu Santo, now Tampa Bay, and the Spaniards first marched north as far as the Carolinas.

Here, legend has it, De Soto and his men came upon the sacred mountain city of the Cherokees. The Indians were hostile, but the Spaniards subdued them, took their gold and other treasures, and pushed on westward to Alabama, then back through Tennessee to Alabama.

Since fall was over, and cold weather was coming on, the Spaniards began constructing a winter camp. Chickasaw Indians who lived on the south side of the Tennessee River proved friendly until spring came. At that time, De Soto, who was breaking camp for a trek into Mississippi, arrogantly demanded that the Chickasaw chief furnish several hundred pretty maidens to accompany the Spanish expedition.

This high-handed request was an indignity the Indians could not ignore, and a night-time attack on De Soto's camp was the result. The Spaniards, taken by surprise, were forced to flee. In doing so, the great treasure they had taken from the Cherokees was left behind. In his retreat, De Soto's guides led him into swamps and trackless forests where great numbers of his men perished.

Turning south along the river, he headed toward the Gulf of Mexico, but he never made it. At a place called Chickasaw Bluffs, he was seized with fever and died. Fearing that the hostile Indians would find his grave and mutilate his body, his men buried him in the Mississippi River. Only a handful of the remaining expedition ever succeeded in reaching the Spanish settlements on the Gulf.

Once the Spaniards had been driven away, the Chickasaw chief had some of his braves take the discarded treasure to a point on the north bank of the Tennessee River, where there were large limestone caverns. In one of these the treasure was concealed.

For 180 years, the story of the great treasure in the river cave was handed down from one Indian chief to another. All but forgotten otherwise, the treasure site lay undisturbed until 1720. Then, one day in the summer of that year, a tall and handsome white trapper appeared at the Chickasaw village. A friendly man, he asked permission from the chief to trap game on tribal lands. Impressed by this act, the chief readily agreed. However, this was not the only reason for the chief's ready acquiescence.

He had only one child, a beautiful daughter. For some time, he had been trying to marry her off, since he needed a grandson to succeed him. The girl, however, would have none of the braves who were brought before her for approval. But once she laid eyes on the handsome trapper, she lost no time in letting her father know he was the man she wanted.

Unaware of what was going on, and unmindful of the fact that the chief's daughter was watching him constantly, the trapper accepted the quarters offered by the chief and quietly went about his business of trapping. A month passed, and one night he was awakened by two braves. Before he could fully awaken from a deep sleep, he found his hands being tied. He started to resist but when the Indians softly told him they meant to do him no harm, he let himself be blindfolded.

All that night and the following day, he was led through the cool dark forest. Several times the group rested, and he was given something to eat and drink. On one of the occasions the blindfold slipped from one eye, and before the Indians could readjust it, he managed to see a river and white cliffs. Since he had been up and down the river many times, he thought he

Old Sayings, Beliefs, Practices and Legends

recognized the area which lay many miles from the Indian village.

Shortly afterwards, he was led into a canoe, and the party moved across the river. Alighting, they went up an embankment. Then the ground began to slope downward, and he felt sand under his feet. From the change in the air, he knew they had entered a large cavern. At this point, the Indians told him to walk stooped, so as not to hit his head on low-hanging rocks. On several occasions, he heard a bat or bird wings near his head and instinctively ducked.

After a while, the party stopped, and the trapper's hands were untied, and the blindfold removed. Frightened and confused, he rubbed his eyes and wrists. Two Indians held torches to dispel the darkness, and, to his amazement, he saw that one of them was the Chickasaw chief himself, while the other was the tribal medicine man. Then he looked around the cave.

Reaching from the cavern floor to its ceiling were stacks of gold and silver bars, while rotted chests spilled jewels and other objects across the floor. The trapper could only shake his head in wonder. Where had all this wealth come from? He listened with open mouth as the old chief told him the story of the Spaniard De Soto and how the Chickasaw tribe had gotten the treasure many moons ago. But after being hidden for all these years, the trapper wondered why it was now being shown to him.

It was simple, explained the chief. If the trapper would marry the chief's daughter, all the treasure he now saw would be given to him. And if he did not want to marry the daughter, what then? The old chief sadly shrugged. Since the trapper had been blindfolded and did not know where the treasure cave was located, he would be allowed to leave in peace.

While the chief was talking, the trapper was doing some quick figuring. All this wealth would be his if he married the daughter, but, if he had to live in the wilderness with the Indians, he might as well not have it. If he refused to marry the daughter, he would be allowed to leave unharmed. The old chief had said so, and he believed him.

Trying to hide his anticipation, the trapper told the chief that he would have to think about his decision for a few days. Since he already had a wife and family in one of the white settlements, he lied, he just could not make up his mind that quickly. The trapper was blindfolded again, and the return trip was accomplished until the three men were once again in

Old Sayings, Beliefs, Practices and Legends

the great forest near the Indian village. The old chief was tired, so the men made camp for the night.

Later, as the two Indians lay sleeping, the trapper killed them both and threw their bodies into the nearby river. Thus, he made certain that he could leave the area. The next morning, he departed and soon showed up at Fort Rosalie, where he enlisted the aid of a friend to recover the treasure.

Hiding in caves by day, and looking at night, the two men spent several months in searching. Finally, the friend grew disgusted and returned to the settlements where he later died of yellow fever. Alone now, the trapper took a chance and returned to the village of the Chickasaw. He was greeted warmly, and, to his surprise, heard nothing about the two men he had killed. Apparently, no one had ever known about their taking him to the treasure cave. This was just what he had counted on.

Searching out the old chief's daughter, the trapper told her that he wanted to marry her and did so. In a roundabout way, he soon found out that she only knew her father had disappeared. It was apparent that she knew nothing of the treasure cave, nor did any other member of the tribe it seemed.

Under the guise of trapping trips, the trapper continued his search for Redbone Cave. But try as he might, he could never find the right place.

In 1729, the trapper's wife died, and he returned to Fort Rosalie. But the place lay in ruins, the settlers having been massacred by the Natchez Indians. As the years passed and he grew older, he would sometimes tell the riverboat men at Natchez-under-the-Hill about the lost treasure cave. Maybe in time some lucky treasure hunter will find this lost cave and the multi-millions still hiding there.[337]

Details related to me from another source, while researching the Natchez Trace. Specific location finds associated with the Redbone treasure hunting.

Close by the Natchez Trace Bridge in Colbert County, in 1971, two men discovered a gold ingot about the size of a brick, a farmer working a field south of Smithsonia in Lauderdale County found a gold bar that had either Indian or Spanish markings. Many people believe that both discoveries were from the treasure in Redbone Cave;

---

[337] http://www.thunting.com/smf/cache_hunting/where_is_the_lost_treasure_of_redbone_cave-t22802.0.html

Old Sayings, Beliefs, Practices and Legends

however, there are many others that believe they came from different sources.

Don Marler and Chickasaw Redbone **Gary "Gabe" Gabehart** our only "Redbone chief" 2002 Redbone Heritage Foundation Conference, Alexandria, Louisiana

GRAVEHOUSES constitute a mystery. Many commonplace practices do not get discussed in writing until it is too late. Oral tradition does not have the permanence needed as the collective memory often fails. Such may be the case with these mystery structures. Knowledge of their origins, purpose and function is now elusive. Geographer, Jordan, says they are more common in the upper south than in the lower south. This form of grave covering may have originated in Africa or Britain or with Native Americans. They were more popular with Indians than anyone else and more popular with Whites than Blacks.[338] Native Americans might have viewed them as "Spirit Houses." Others might have seen their function as protecting graves from roaming animals in the days of open range and before cemeteries were fenced. They might have served to protect the graves from elements and to keep grass and weeds from growing.

These houses or shelters were often built over a special grave, such as that of a child or person who was much beloved, famous, or outstanding. Some houses covered more than one grave. They were usually made of wood with varying levels of skill in workmanship and were semi-open with a lathe across the sides and ends to which were attached pickets, often decoratively shaped. The roof was made of split (rived) boards, usually of cypress. Many of these dating back to the mid-19th century have rotted and fallen, and now have been removed. Some 19th century specimens still survive. Some have been built in the 20th century, and those tend to have

---

338 *Ibid.*, p. 34ff. Jordan cites evidence for an African, British and American Indian origin for gravehouses and he comes down on the side of an Indian origin. Jeane, on the other hand, cites strong evidence for a British origin. It is possible that they had multiple origins as they also existed in Africa; or, perhaps, this is an example of ancient cultural sharing.

Old Sayings, Beliefs, Practices and Legends

metal as part of the structure. Vernon Parish, Louisiana has the honor of having one of the largest collections of grave houses in the South. The Talbert, or Pine Grove Cemetery, has fifteen grave shelters.[339] McManus did a reading of this cemetery and described what she saw.

> *"...the most unique feature is that at first glance the site resembles a small village. In three separate rows, each burial has an individual metal roof over the grave such as you might see in a small house or shed. Each roof has wooden eaves [gables?] at the front and back, and a wooden ceiling. Most of these sheds also have a wooden picket fence, about 4' tall, that completely surrounds the grave. All the burials under roof also have white shells that cover the graves."*[340]

Terry Jordan stated the social and cultural importance of cemeteries well:

The message of the folk cemetery, for those who would read it, is that there is a lot of European, a fair amount of African, and more than a trace of Indian in all southerners, regardless of their skin color. In the cultural sense, the people of the South have much in common with each other. For three

---

[339] Donald Gregory Jeane, "Southern Graveshelters and English Lychgates: The Search for Culture Trait Origins", *Tributaries*, Vol. III, Alabama Folklore Association.
[340] McManus, *op. cit.*, p. 290

centuries the three groups have exchanged ideas and genes, creolizing the culture to a remarkable degree. Nowhere is that blending more apparent than in the places we have set aside for our dead. These traditional graveyards are not merely repositories for our dead, but museums full of reminders from our ancient past and distant, diverse ancestral homelands.[341]

L to R, Alpha Gibson, Bella Allen Mathews, Lula Allen Reed. Front Row L to R, Charlie Nash, Pinkney Allen, Jesse (Jesus) Maria Garza Rapides Parish, La. to No Zulch, Madison Co., TX.

---

341 Jordan, *op. cit.*, pp. 39-40.

Gravehouse Photos

Walnutt Hill Cemetery Gravehouse
Vernon Parish, La.
Photo by Jane McManus

Close up view of a gravehouse at the Pine Grove Cemetery
Photo by Jane McManus.

Cemetery, courtesy Farah Norton
Talbert-Pierson Cemetery, Vernon Parish. La. Courtesy, Farah Norton.

Gravehouse Photos

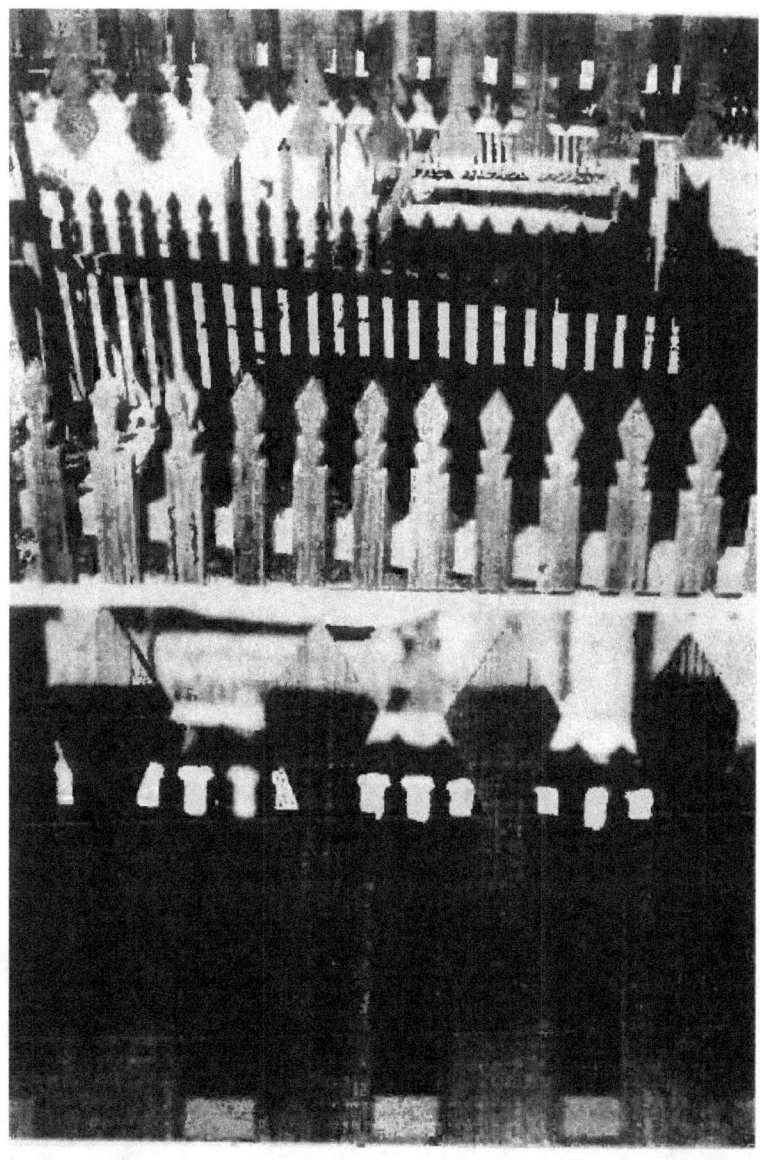

Detail of fretwork on the fences of gravehouses at the Pine Grove Cemetery. These are Talbert Family courtesy Jane P. McManus.

Cherokee Indian Graveyard near Stillwater, Oklahoma. The small shelters were built by Cherokee for use of the spirits. Courtesy April Mullins Mela. Presented 2002, Melungeon Heritage Association Conference, *Providing Necroethnic Clues for Cultural Continuity Among Mixed Racial Populations In Appalachia*. Kingsport, TN. Photo taken 1929 by Arthur B. Cozzens.

Russell County, Virginia, burial date 1954 courtesy April Mullins Mela

Gravehouse Photos

Below Seminole Gravehouses, Seminole Nation, Indian Territory (IT).

Christian Creek Indian Gravehouses, Okaloosa County, Florida

Talbert-Pierson Cemetery, Vernon Parish, Louisiana.

Tilley Family Gravehouse, Vernon Parish, La.

The cemetery was established by members of the Talbert and Pierson families, pioneers who first settled in the area in the 1860's. Thirteen graves are covered with unique grave houses. The origins of grave houses are uncertain – some tracing the beginnings to European or Native American roots. Other sources simply attribute the custom to a form of protecting the graves before cemeteries were commonly fenced. Grave houses were a part of the Upland South tradition; the custom also included decorating the graves with shells. Tradition demanded that the grave house was to be built before sunset on the day of burial. Talbert-Pierson Cemetery was listed on the National Register of Historic Places in 2003. Adjacent to the cemetery is Pine Grove Methodist Church established on April 10, 1887 as part of the Sugartown circuit. The first church was located approximately one mile from the present church, which was built in 1921

Photos

This is a typical home in this area in the early part of the 20th century Pictured, **Jessie Willis**. **Nancy Doyle/Dial Willis**, **Leonard Doyle/Dial**

Following Contributed by Stacy R. Webb

Guide E. Nash Cabin, Burke/Diboll, Texas son of Command Nash & Matilda Sweat Mason Nash/Ash
Guide E. Ash/Nash & daughter **Maxine Ash/Nash Stringer**

Joseph C. and **Hannah Dearman Nash/Ash Family** cabin near Rapides Parish La. Son of James Nash & Mary Polly Perkins Nash/Ash Family portrait below.

Photos

Sena Goyens Nash/Ash 3rd wife of Command. Children Rob, Eli (sons of Matilda Sweat Mason Nash/Ash), Jewell (babe on lap), Lilla, Ralph Nash.

Emanuel "Command" aka "Many" Nash 1843-1917 born in Rapides Parish Louisiana and is buried at Trinity Co., Tx. son of James & Mary Polly Perkins Nash/Ash (both pictured elsewhere here). He married 1. Nancy Jane Simmons Allen, 2. Matilda "Tilley" Sweat Mason, 3. Sena Goyens. He fathered close to or at least 30 children but raised more than 50 at No. Zulch, Madison Co., TX. He made application, 1896 to Cherokee Nation. He served in the Civil War.

Mandy Nash/Ash Vincent daughter of Command & Sena Goyens Nash/Ash. Zwolle, La.

Lilla Mae Nash/Ash Cootie daughter of Command & Sena Goyens Nash/Ash. Zwolle, La.

Photos

Emily Nash/Ash Allen Author daughter of James Nash & Mary "Polly" Perkins Nash/Ash. Born Rapides Parish, La. Died Nash Settlement, North Zulch, Madison Co., TX.

Bull Punchers hauling logs.
Varice Clark, Griffin Adams, Charlie Gillis

Mule Skinners skidding logs using a slip-tongue cart.
Ira Dickerson & Unknown.

Photos

Louisiana Redbone **Powell**

Texas Redbone **Powell**

Exact YDNA Matched Male Lineage: Left: L.C. Sweat, Jr. son of L.C., Sr. "Raw hide fight/Jayhawker" La.-ETX Right: William Collins Goyens, La-ARK-OK-TX-Missouri. Regardless of Surnames, these men are exact YDNA matches to one another.

Jesse Doyal born in Bayou Chicot 1810 blacksmith son of Aaron Dial who was brother to Tapley Dial and Keziah Dial Ashworth. Married (1) Patsy Johnson, (2) Mary Ann Bass (3) Louisiana Davis.

Photos

Newly Discovered Headstone at Nash Cemetery, No Zulch, Madison Co., Texas next to Benjamin Nash/Ash thought to be that of his wife Hannah Perkins Nash d/o Nancy Perkins, (Buried Glass Window Cemetery, Vernon Parish, La.). Carving design appears Native American in style. No legible lettering, shaving cream used to identify faint carved markings. It is of interest; this cemetery is not East/West burials. Her MtDNA was passed from Nancy Perkins and a detail of MtDNA results elsewhere here.

Worked footstone with bat wing shaped bottom and concaved side. Found some distance (shown below picture, white item pictured is a regular sized notebook) directly below newly discovered headstone thought to be Hannah Perkins Nash. It could be another headstone, but the shape is concaved appearing to be a footstone. Dowsing area predicts only one grave but unproportionally long and indicated an adult female burial.

Photos

Son of James & Mary Polly Perkins Nash/Ash (pictured elsewhere here). Applied Cherokee Nation, 1896 and lived remainder of his life in Oklahoma.
He served in the Civil War.

Benjamin Nash/Ash "Penashes" born 1809 probably Mississippi though later census records indicate a Louisiana birth. Mistakenly, not the son of Old Thomas Nash, as previously thought. Example of incorrect or misleading documentation in Mexican Texas stating Benjamin was Thomas's son. Though autosomal results would lead us to believe he could be the son of Thomas's wife, Anna Goins Nash. YDNA results prove he could not have been his son, though closely related male descendants. He was the son of Wm Jr. and William "Old Billy" Nash/Ash.[342] His YDNA biology is an older sample than that of Old Thomas Nash/Ash (even though his age is younger). Benjamin signed the Treaty of Dancing Rabbit, Crowders Stand @ Big Black (Eli & Patsy Goings (1) Crowder discussed elsewhere here) and gave permission for the "whites to settle on Cushatty land" in Texas, 1838. He settled at No Zulch, Madison Co., Texas and was an Austin's Colony settler. 1826 he is next door to Aaron Cherry Atascosita District, Tx., 1830 Natchitoches, La., 1840 & 50 Rapides Parish, La., 1860 Alexandria, La. 1870

---

[342] See Attachment N.

Photos

Leon Co., TX, 1880 living with son Calvin at Madison Co., Tx.

1969 Starks, Calcasieu Parish, Louisiana. Bearhead / Ten Mile Redbones, **Jasper C. Stanley** son of Wm L. & Mama Pearl Bass-Stanley Sr. (pictured elsewhere here) **Shirley J Perkins Gill** daughter of John O. Gill, Morris, Al & Virginia Janie Perkins Gil, Starks, La. Family. Courtesy Brent "Peppy" Stanley.

William Lockett & Pearl Bass Stanley, Ten Mile Readbones. Courtesy, Peppy Stanley

Photos

Brothers, Jasper, Charlie, Edgar, Etzelray "Uncle Shorty" Stanley. Ten Miler "Stanley's Precinct" Redbones.

Virginia Janie Perkins

Peppy Stanley

Shirley Gill, Virginia Janie Perkins Gill, Dorothy Perkins, Rosemary Perkins (d/o Charlie Perkins).

GENETIC STUDIES

Haplo Study

Since this publishing, the Redbone Heritage Foundation and MEHRA (multiethnic historical research association) have conducted extensive DNA studies among the descendant members of the Redbone Heritage Foundation. To document and study the origins, migrations and matched lineages of the families known as Redbone. Following are the results from Y-DNA, passed father to son in an unbroken chain, or that no illegitimacy/adoption/orphan or an uncustomary inheritance of a surname, i.e., Matriarchal society social structure, passing Mother's maiden name, which might or might not have been inherited by her in a customary fashion father to child or multi generations of surname's inherited in an uncustomary fashion. Unless otherwise specified a different surname but the same Y or Mt DNA genetic results.

Once the YDNA (or MtDNA) results are completed Y or Mt DNA are assigned a "haplo" assignment. The haplo assigned is basically "where" the oldest known sample of that DNA has been located, or a geographic location of oldest known or ancient sample. As humans migrated out of their ancient origins, wherever they went they picked up DNA from others, and left behind the same (bread crumb trail or technical term SNP's). Your bread crumb trail of that ancestral lineage is assigned geographic coding known as "markers." Haplo assignment is nothing more than a study of your lineages marker results and or, the breadcrumb trails we can now follow throughout the world. Haplo assignment studies are nothing more than the study of a human origin and migration throughout the world to you (YDNA father to son, or MtDNA mother to child).

Overall Participant Haplo Origins
Legend in B&W Read Clockwise

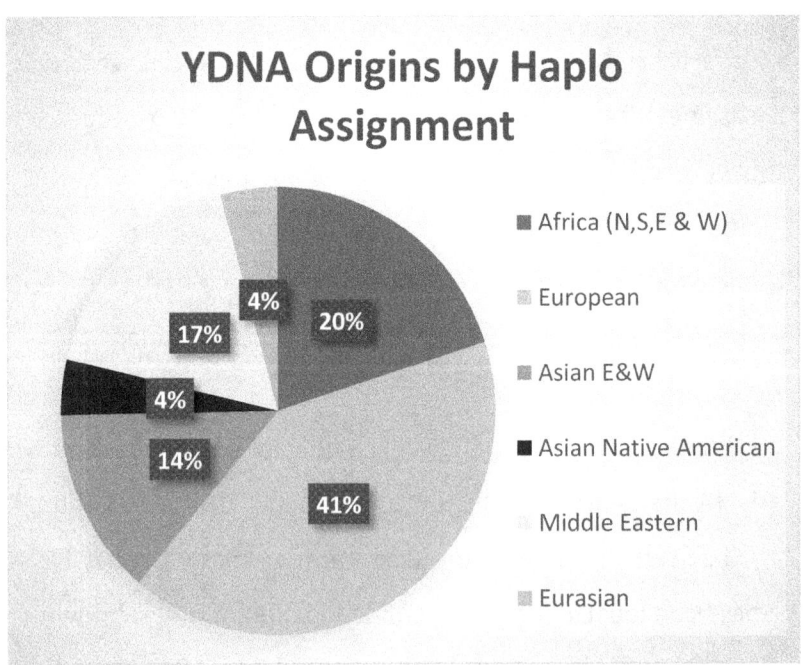

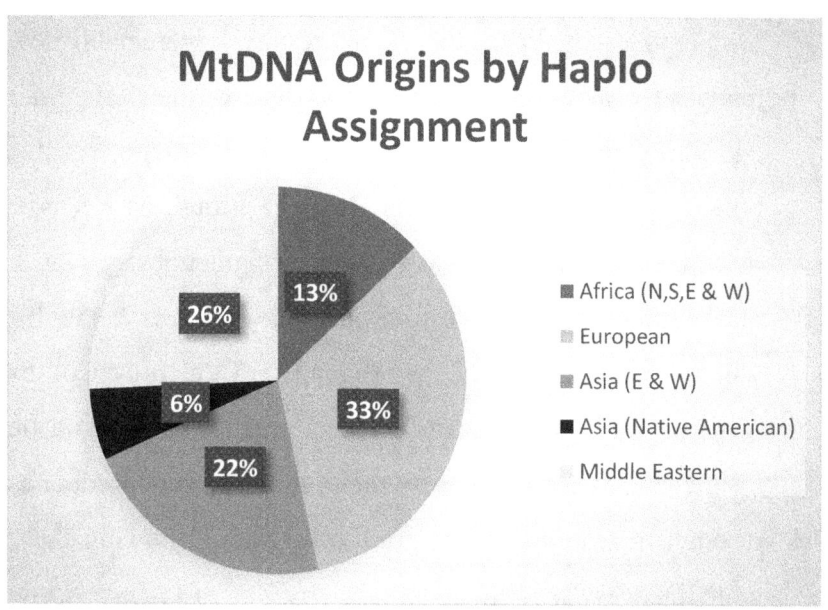

Case Studies Y-DNA

YDNA study of the **COLLINS** surname have confirmed an exact YDNA matched lineage in progenitor male Luke Collins, an early Louisiana settler and beyond further to Texas, Missouri, and Arkansas and that to Nvarrah "Vardy" Collins a founding forefather of most Vardy Valley Melungeon Colony (Newman' Ridge) and who is mentioned throughout this publishing.

In a surprise turn of events, Valentine Collins, who was also a Vardy Valley progenitor, and thought to be the son of or brother to Vardy. When the YDNA results[343] were published, many were shocked and confused to discover he (Valentine) and Vardy did not match YDNA. These contradicting results, however, did not surprise the Redbone group, as we have been dealing with this male progenitor(s) phenomenon since the beginning of DNA testing our male Y lines. Though I will not speculate on who the progenitor of Valentine Collins was, his haplo assignment[344] details are fascinating and tie his male line specifically with the Melungeons and Redbones through migrations and migration origins. Following these male lineages "specifically" I mean by way of 1. Their origin 2. Their migration at the same time; together to these shores.

Undoubtably, the following men (or, their progenitors), though **NOT the same YDNA** lineage; they share only an exact haplo assignment, or geographic origin (came from the same place) and, share an exact migration at the exact same

---

[343] https://www.familytreedna.com/groups/collins/dna-results

[344] Haplo assignment is basically a geographic code assigned to a set of DNA markers which follow the Y line, or father to son through human migrations throughout the world. The haplo origins follows from the oldest known or documented human markers or "original origins" location, perhaps 10s of 1000s of years old. As mummies, and archeological remains are discovered, and tested positive for those specific male human Y markers, then that haplo assignment is updated with a new/or other set of further geographic markers or "geographic location code" assigned to those males wherever their markers are located, geographically. Therefore, early estimates that all "E" haplo assignments were/are Black African in "recent" origins was grossly misunderstood by testers and scientist.

time (traveled together from the same origin) with one another to these shores. They share haplo origin E-P278 updated to more specific geographic origin **E-CTS10652** not to confuse but this haplo is a child of **E1b1a-M2**. Haplo E along with all haplo assignments are ancient being 10s of 1000s of years old. We can determine this E haplo arises out of East Africa anciently but share an Asia migration nearly as old.[345] This haplo POD (CTS10652) is not well defined or documented to date, as to exact origin migrations. The highest frequency is Haiti, Jamaica and matched DNA found in Barbados. E-M96 (Haiti 69.1% and Jamaica 66%) and represent the predominant Y-lineages in both populations, a higher degree of genetic diversity is observed in Jamaica than in Haiti, with the former population possessing a total of 41 paternal haplogroups, whereas the latter is character-ized by only 28 patrilineages. Haplogroup E1b1a-M2, a genetic signature of the Bantu expansion throughout South-Saharan Africa (Ber- niell- Lee et al., 2009), is present at elevated levels (63.4% in Haiti and 60.4% in Jamaica) in both populations analyzed. ... However, it appears from this study, best estimates currently are *Southwest Asian* origin, with a

---

[345] Trombetta, Beniamino et al. "Phylogeographic Refinement and Large-Scale Genotyping of Human Y Chromosome Haplogroup E Provide New Insights into the Dispersal of Early Pastoralists in the African Continent." Genome biology and evolution vol. 7,7 1940-50. 24 Jun. 2015, doi:10.1093/gbe/evv118

diaspora perhaps through an east India slave trade? Their closest genetic matched haplo is Barbados.

The Following Male Lineages Tested Positive/share markers for haplo migration "CTS10652" but who are **NOT biological male matches** for one another.

Warning, these are self-reported *oldest known progenitor, the genealogical data may or may not be correct. The lineages presented here are based on the biology of those self-reporting oldest known progenitors.

Matches positive for **E-CTS10652.**

Below in ORDER OF BIOLOGY-

1. **Valentine Collins** b. 1786, Wilkes Co., NC. (Morgan Co., Ky.)
2. **John Bunch/Punch** b. abt 1630
    His progeny (according to tester submitted genealogy, and biological pedigree; not in any order of "age" of ancestors):
    a. John Bunch b. c1641 d. 1700
    b. John Bunch b. c1621
    c. John Bunch b. c. 1662 450ac on New Kent Co., Va.
        Their progeny
        d. Solomon Bunch b. 1783 d. 1870
        e. Henry Bunch Bertie Co., NC
    Their progeny
        f. Lorenzo Dow Bunch
        g. Elza Bunch

3. **George Nelson** b. ca 1812, Claiborne Co., TN d, 1888 Greenup County, KY. (no other details if the Redbone Nelson's matched this Nelson. Still in search of participants to verify or rule out this potential match).

4. **Phillip Goings (1) clan oldest biology progenitor** b. ca 1792 d. aft 1813 La. (Texas, Arkansas & Oklahoma progenitor). Phillip may also have died at same time as above brother James. He married (1) Luchia Lawson (Lumbee), 2. Oti Montroe (Choctaw), 3. Keziah Nash/Ash (Redbone). We lose trace of Philip after 1815 when in Natchitoches Parish, La. He and Keziah Nash/Ash legitimize their children, Michael, and Rebecca Goings (1) clan.[346] His son Jeremiah Goins, son of second wife Oti Montroe/Monroe migrated to San Antonio area. His known male progeny are Jeremiah b. 1792 Natchez District, Mississippi, he married Sarophina Drake and Michael Leroy b. 1808 in Mississippi he married Hardena Taylor.

   James Goings (1) clan oldest biology progenitor b. ca 1794 died in Indian Territory "IT", Big Black Band of Choctaw Redbones to Calcasieu Parish, La. Progenitor of Louisiana Bearhead community, he died at Mayhew Mission, Boggy Mountain Depot, Big Black Band of Choctaw arrival at Choctaw Agency uprising, buried mass grave near Boggy Mountain Depot. James married Elizabeth Betsy Perkins and his male progeny include William Moses b. 1809 in La. married Charlotty Nelson, Joshua b. 1810 La. M. Sarah Perkins, J. Aaron b. 1830 La. He married Salize Perkins. Both males are thought to be the sons of Old William Goings born probably North Carolina and died in Louisiana, he is enumerated in the household of James in the 1820 census in Calcasieu Parish, La. and who was married to "Mama Cherokee".

---

[346] Gary "Mishiho" Gabehart, a descendant of Phillip and 1. Oti Montro/Monroe (Choctaw).

The following male' lines are in some way biologically descended from above progenitors, to date, James, and Philip Goings (1) samples who carry the oldest biology of all males tested for this cluster of male matches (YDNA). All others fall below in order of biological connection to the *oldest known progenitor, despite generations, despite physical age or perceived "generation" of oldest known male progenitor. "Their progeny"

    Their progeny
- a. James Goins b. ca 1792 Moore Co., NC
- b. William Goins b. ca1825 prob Surry Co., NC
- c. Levy Goins b. 1796, Ga.
- d. George Washington Goins
- e. Cornelius Keife/Keef/Keiffe or Keith of Stafford Co., Va. Born ca. 1675 and died ca. ca 1730 in Lunenburg, Virginia he married Dianna Cockarill. They had a daughter Mary, who married John Frederick Goins. I am not sure what happened here. If this is an example of bad genealogy and the assumption/adoption of surnames? "John Frederick" Goins, or John F. and his "son in law" are exact YDNA match to one another. 200 years difference above oldest biology, and both fall into "the descendant" roll below James and Philip Goings (1). Which would confirm bad genealogy, or a surname exchange/adoption, further research is encouraged.[347]
- f. John Goins b. ca. 1730, Fairfax Co., Va. Married Mary Keife daughter of Cornelius Keife and Mary Cockrill, above but who carry the exact same YDNA genetics.
- g. Michael Goins b. ca 1738 d. ca 1798

---

[347] https://www.familytreedna.com/groups/goins/dna-results

    h. Lewis Fuel Goins b. ca 1817-1905, KY.
    i. Fuel Goins b.ca 1828 Va., d. ca 1864 Patrick Co., Va.
    j. Michael Gowing b. ca 1806, d. 1873

MALES Matching Exact YDNA to above but with "other" surnames:
    k. Lawson, no details
    l. Bell, no details.
    m. Carr, no details
    n. Harrison, James Sr. b. ca 1750, d. 1830 Sumner Co., TN.

Back to the Collins Match YDNA
Nvarrah & Luke, Sr. Collins perfect YDNA Matched Males

Tracing the male lineage in an unbroken chain (father to son unchanged for 10s of 1000s of years) from the Redbone settler Luke Collins, who now reside in Texas, Louisiana, Missouri, and Arkansas we discovered a perfect YDNA matched lineage, descendants of Nvarrah "Vardy" Collins.

The recent testing and results have been a real breakthrough for mixed ethnic groups of early Virginia history. Each group with reputed Native American ancestry. These groups related maternally and paternally scattered about the fledgling country and so it would appear assuming or assigned different ethnic monikers but who are of the same male genealogical YDNA lineage.

This group of Collins males share a haplo origin assignment of R-M512. Though this male haplo pod is newly discovered and undocumented, we can determine a migration out of Western Asia, or perhaps the Middle East. A map is provided here of the wide spread of haplo R-M512 (R1a1a) through western Europe, Eurasia, and the middle East. To break down the haplo origin even further, some have tested extended markers which resulted in an upgraded origin location, called a POD. The POD returned with an R-YP1433. This is a newly discovered POD and is undocumented as to its latest origin location and migration. However, R1a, like its brother branch R1b, may have had its origins in Western Asia (Near/Middle East). R-YP1433 is known exclusively as a Middle East origin. It is well represented in Scandinavia through North African Berber migrations and Central and Eastern Europe. To a lesser extent, it shows up in Western Europe.[348] Some hints recently show this male lineage's last known origins before reaching these shores to be perhaps, Italy or the Mediterranean rim area which also falls within the same

---

[348] Melungeon YDNA Core Project at Family Tree DNA. https://www.familytreedna.com/public/coremelungeon/default.aspx?section=yresults

geography and corresponds with the findings from the progenitor wife, Peg Gibson Collins, and her mitochondrial results.

"There is also a little bit of very old R1a-M198 (M417-), and some R1a-Z93, notably the Y15121 subclade found in Iran, India and the Middle East, and which could have come with the Scythians or other Iranic steppe tribes. Little data is available for neighboring Macedonia, but it includes at least L1029 (under M458) and L366 (under CTS1211)."[349]

Pitfall of matching YDNA males. No documented trail of genealogy between the testing males and their oldest known progenitor, and or no genealogy between male line matches. I encourage everyone recording their genealogy to do their own research, cross reference your male lineages with YDNA results already posted via online, if possible, or what we call "stubby pencil" genealogy. Document all your sources properly and be at the ready to defend your findings to the public and other descendants.

---

[349] https://forums.familytreedna.com/forum/paternal-lineages-y-dna/y-dna-haplogroups-snps-basics/15797-italian-man-r-m512

Redbones of Louisiana

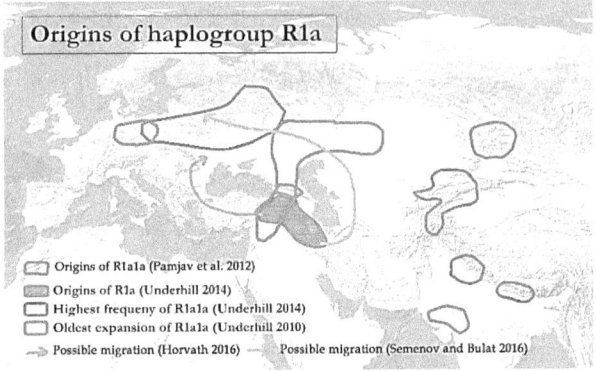

Origins of R1a1a (Nvarrah Collins) with migrations highest-lowest frequency locations[350] The shaded zone shows the origin at its highest peak in modern day Syria/Iraq & Iran (Persia).

Case Study MtDNA

In the biggest stroke of luck to date between the Redbones and Melungeon's, the Lumbee and the Cherokee! This match was the first to link the Melungeon's, to the Redbone's in a confirmed and undeniable biological relationship. To say the least, we were elated. In 2007, a participant in the initial DNA studies through Sorenson Labs in Houston, TX. A Bearhead Redbone who showed an exact maternal match to a living female Cherokee at Tahlequah, Oklahoma. This participant traced her female MtDNA lineage in an unbroken chain to Obedience, Biddy Collins Cole married Wm. M. Anderson Cole born 1791 in North Carolina and died 1885 in Kentucky,

---

[350] By Joshua Jonathan - Own work, CC BY-SA 4.0, https://commons.wikimedia.org/w/index.php?curid=49855114

a daughter of Nvarrah and Margaret Gibson Collins, also known as "Spanish Peg."

Along with her husband Vardy Collins, wife Spanish Peg Gibson Collins also finds exact mitochondrial DNA (shortened to MtDNA) throughout these ethnic groups as well as Cherokee lineages. To date we have identified and confirmed through exact mitochondrial matches (passed mother to child unchanged for 10s of 1000s of years) between the following ethnic groups: Lumbee, Cherokee, Redbone, and the Melungeon. A newly acquired match, contacted participants just prior to this publishing from the Rom Gypsy community. However, no details yet on her maternal lineage. We will try to update this as newer information and matches are made, through the *Redbone Chronicles*.

The confirmation of these lineage was groundbreaking discovery, as it confirmed Peg's MtDNA as the "oldest known progenitor" to date. However, some suggest her mother was Matilda Collins born about 1750 and died 1850 in Virginia. We could not confirm this information at publishing.

This MtDNA includes but is of course not limited to the following surnames and families:

The link to the Melungeon Gibson and Collins's daughter, Bitty Collins Cole, Magoffin Co., Ky. And included: Whitekiller (Tahlequah, OK), Musgrove (Nancy, Magoffin Co., Ky.), Perkins (Magoffin & Floyd Co's., KY), Duvall, Nickells (Floyd Co., KY McIntosh Co., OK). Anderson (NC to KY), Brooks & Barnett (Goochland, Va., Handcock Co., TN), Hurdt (North Carolina), Wright, (Greenville, SC).

The matched **Redbone MtDNA** traces their lineage to the Drake & Chavis (unknown origins to Attakapas District, La., St Landry La., Calcasieu Parish., La., San Antonio, TX.), Bloodwoth, Doyle, through a Goings (1) clan descendant (previously mentioned here in the YDNA study (E-CTS10652 matches). The second matched Redbone lineage was a Clark who traces her lineage surnames as: Clark, (Bearhead, Calcasieu Parish, La.), Bloodworth and Dial/Doyle (Calcasieu Parish, La.), Redd & Clemont (Reserve Parish, La.), Fontenot, Chapman (Lake Charles, La.).

The **matched Lumbee** associated mitochondrial lineages match traces her MtDNA through the surnames: Lowery, Brewer, Brooks, Ransom, Jacobs, Oxendine, Strickland, all multi generations of Robeson, NC Lumbee Indians. Kara Brewer Boyd related an amazing story about her great grandmother after learning their "Royal" Gypsy descent which is discussed further below.

"In about 1930, our grandmother was a patient in a hospital giving birth to a child. While a patient there, she was approached by a band of Gypsies who had caravanned outside the hospital. They attempted to entice her to come with them, as they wanted to make her the Queen of their Gypsy tribe. Of course, shocked and confused she declined the offer. However, met with more powerful persistence and threat of kidnapping, they explained…. That their queen had recently died and that they were in search of a new Queen which had led them to her. Of course, she rejected their attempts to kidnap her and their family a bit bewildered all these years". Once the results were discovered, all that happened made a lot of sense. But, how did they know, we assume some way they had kept track of their Royal Gypsy lineages and identified Kara's Grandmother as a potential Queen.[351]

Marie Vaspurkan K(h)alderash Gypsy Markers The matched mitochondrial DNA is traced to the haplo origin assignment of H7a1a. This haplo assignment has been

---

[351] Interview., Kara Brewer Boyd, 2012

identified as anomalous and exclusively Gypsy mitochondrial haplo assignment. However, the MtDNA is also positive for a set of specific markers, known only among Gypsy's called the Kalderash Sleewi and or the Marie Vaspurkan Khalderas which originates in India, migrated to Iran and were the priestess of the ancient Persian religion Zoroastrian.[352] Famous people like the lead singer of Queen, Freddie Mercury family are Iranian Zoroastrians.

Though the Mitchell Gypsy clan none are known matched MtDNA, however, they are positive for the Kalderash Sleewi or Marie Vaspurkan Kalderash, markers for the "royal" Gypsy lines of India and Iran. This positive markers between the Mitchell/Marks family means that sometime in the very distant ancient times, they were in fact descended from the same mother.

We have traced this MtDNA haplo H7a1a assignment origins last known migration from Macedonia area to these shores. According to demographic data from the register in 2002 (latest work on the discovery) the population of the Republic

---

[352] **Zoroastrianism** is an ancient Persian religion that may have originated as early as 4,000 years ago. Arguably the world's first monotheistic faith, it's one of the oldest religions still in existence.

of Macedonia is 2,022,547 with 64.2% ethnical Macedonian, 25.2% ethnical Albanians, 3.9% ethnical Turks, 2.7% ethnical Romanies and a small percentage of other ethnic groups.

People in this region of the world, from different ethnic communities rarely have marriages between each other due to their national and religious determination.[353] Whether or not this influences the distribution of mitochondrial lineages has yet not been studied for Macedonia. An earlier study described mitochondrial (mt)DNA control region variation for ethnical Macedonians, which brought a similar haplogroup distribution to other West-Eurasian populations.[354] Here, we describe MtDNA control region variation in carefully selected samples of the three other major ethnic groups (148 Albanians, 150 Turks and 146 Romanies) and thus add a total of only 444 MtDNA lineages to the body of world-wide MtDNA database.[355] Only 13 lines

---

[353] Forensic Science International: Genetics, 13 (2004) 1-2; Science *Direct Mitochondrial DNA control region analysis of three ethnic groups in the Republic of Macedonia.*
https://www.fsigenetics.com/article/S1872-4973(14)00131-8/pdf
354 Zimmermann B., Brandstätter A., Duftner N., Niederwieser D., Spiroski M., Arsov T., Parson W. Mitochondrial DNA control region population data from Macedonia. Forensic Sci. Int. Genet. 2007;1:e4–e9.
355 Mitochondrial DNA control region analysis of three ethnic groups in the Republic of Macedonia. Renata Jankova-Ajanovska,a Bettina

of this mitochondrial DNA have been reported in the United States, to date. Six of these samples can trace their MtDNA through mixed ethnic and Native American groups as follows: Redbones, Lumbee, Melungeon, Marks/Mitchell/McMillan Gypsy tribes, Cherokee, Choctaw, and MOWA to date. No participants were located from the known Ben Ishmael Tribe of the Grasshopper Gypsy clan to date. We would be curious to see if they also carry lines of this specific MtDNA and or that of the Kalderash royalty lineage markers?

A few quotes connecting the Gypsy and the Native American.

"A Cheyenne cemetery is in the same direction as where my mother told me she watched gypsies camp through her west window as a girl, about ½ mile from that house. I have reverently walked though that Cheyenne cemetery as early as ten, looking at the headstones and wondering who they were and where they came from. I did not know then, that in that cemetery were descendants from the Sand Creek Massacre." Pioneer family of Sand Creek Colorado.[356] Black Kettle[357]

Zimmermann,b Gabriela Huber,b Alexander W. Röck,b Martin Bodner,b Zlatko Jakovski,a Biljana Janeska,a Aleksej Duma,a and Walther Parsonb,c,

[356] Bury My Heart at Wounded Knee: An Indian History of the American West (Arena Books) Paperback – December 1, 1987 by Dee Alexander Brown

[357] Black Kettle was a prominent leader of the Southern Cheyenne during the American Indian Wars. Born to the Northern Só'taeo'o /

" There was a time when my curiosity about Cherokee people peaked. My father was a Baptist preacher, and we didn't grow up with Cherokee people. We didn't grow up in the culture other than things that Daddy taught us. We were never around other Indian people. We were called gypsies. I grew up in Tennessee and it was something that I had to seek out for myself." Rita Coolidge, Cherokee, singer songwriter, 2011 interview, *I have no Indian Name.*

Kalderash Tabor Gypsy The specific set of DNA markers were carried down from Spanish Peg [Oldest known female progenitor to date] to living descendants and known as the "Kalderash Sleewi" or the Marie Vaspurakan and the Armenian Kalderash Gypsies who claim descent from the House of David, Daniel or Zerubabbel his Chief Magi [358] These specific markers seem to follow what the Gypsies call their "Royal" lineages and in biology they must have known which lineage was which lineage or who carried these markers and who did not. Qualifying them for tribal leaders, or not. It is a set of specific markers passed by MtDNA and is on the rarer side of their genetic pool with not all Gypsy females passing this onto their offspring. The

---

Só'taétaneo'o band of the Northern Cheyenne in the Black Hills of present-day South Dakota, he later married into the Wotápio / Wutapai band of the Southern Cheyene.

[358] To find out more about the Roayla Khalderash Sleewi DNA aka "Marie Vaspurankan Khalderash markers, please visit
https://parrotsgrl.wordpress.com/my-red-bones/roma-gypsy/gyspy-mitchell-clan/

word Kalderash is also a name of a sleeve designed costume worn by the males and females of this specific "Royal" lineage.

Kelderars/Khalders/Kalders (Kotlyars) They made caldrons and baking trays on mobile anvils or mended leaking dishes. Initially they traveled through Danube principalities[359], but after 1856 headed to neighbor countries. Soon the Kotlyar Tabors[360] arrived in Poland, Russia, France, Spain, and England.

Gypsy Children Sand Mountain, near Attala Alabama, ca 1940s

---

[359] Danubian Principalities was a conventional name given to the Principalities of Moldavia and Wallachia, which emerged in the early 14th century. The term was coined in the Habsburg Monarchy after the Treaty of Küçük Kaynarca in order to designate an area on the lower Danube with a common geopolitical situation.

[360] small drum, especially one used simultaneously by the player of a simple pipe.

Kalderash Roma Camp, 1902 Gypsy wearing his Kotlyar Tabor costume. It is of interests that the Gypsy word for non-gypsy peoples is "Gadji (female), Gadjo (male)" which interpreted means "civilian".

A Kalderash sleeve worn by some Gypsies to represent their "royal" status. Here you can see the designed sleeve in a female and male costume.

Perfect MtDNA Matches: Marilyn Baggett Kobliaka (Bearhead "Redbone Queen"), Private (Cherokee), Obedience Biddy Collins Cole (Melungeon daughter of Spanish Peg Gibson Collins) and Kara Brewer Boyd (Lumbee). We believe they favor one another besides sharing exact mitochondrial DNA.

Case Review Perkins Y-DNA A calamity of various matches and no matched YDNA results between several lines of Perkins to Louisiana and E. Tx. among the Redbone participants. All claiming descent from one man or claiming as their oldest known progenitor, Joshua Old Jock Perkins who married Mary Polly Black Carter County, TN. These lineages and YDNA facts being a hotly debated issue currently.

To date there is at least **five (5) Joshua Perkins**. A Sr. Roan and Johnson counties, Tn. He is enumerated 1836 and perhaps another Joshua Perkins who married a Nolen (Nolen/Nolin surname also mentioned in the 1792 Lost State of Franklin census) and who settled at Carter Co., TN Roan Mountain area and a Jr. previously unrecognized by family historians or miss recognized as "Old Jock Perkins" who had his plantation and estate at Perkins Hallow, Carter Co., TN, and married M. Polly Black. Mary, who may have been a Bradford married to a Black first, and a sister to Mary Bradford who married Rvrd. Joseph Willis also a Marion's Men.

Two other Joshua Perkins, also called "Old Jock" Pee Dee River, Cheraw South Carolina who married Mary Mixon in 1818, Perquimans, North Carolina (her father was also a

Marion's Men, he had many native mixed blood wives concurrently) and who is thought to be the same as Joshua "Old Jock" who married Francis Pettyjohn 1785 in North Carolina.

Still another contemporary to Old Jock, Sr., Joshua "Old Jock" born 1744 at Cheraw's who married Mary Sherrill in 1756 and a Joshua who married Rebecca Sherrill in 1795 in North Carolina, cousins to one another but both likely cousins already to Joshua Perkins and migrated from Accomack Co., Va. to Cheraw South Carolina with grandparents Wm "The Conestoga Trader" Sherrill family.

The Sherrill's were the first to forge the Catawba River. There is a book written titled Misty, Misty Morn by David Oaks which related the story of the Sherill and Perkins migration to Cheraw from Spesutie Baltimore, Maryland and recorded Richard and Mary "Esther" [big hint] Perkins born Mosquito Creek, Maryland lineage. Please see attachments L & M migration maps. However, a document trail exists between the Senior Joshua Perkins at Roan and Carter counties, Tennessee and great great grandfather, George Oaks. You can read more on this in the title *Redbone Chronicles*. We heavily suspect a relationship and or descendants of the first *Twenty and Odd*, by Katherine

Hall Knight, the first Portuguese slave ship at Jamestown. And that of the tail of Margaret Cornish Goins Sweat related in Paul Heinegg's material, *Free African Americans.*

YDNA Results Perkins

To date there are **four (4) YDNA results** among the Redbone Perkins males: **First** is a "white Spaniard or Portuguese type" haplo assignment and comes out of New Jersey, New Hampshire upper Delaware and Maine, to Rowan and Craven counties, North Carolina. This YDNA lineage matches the lines of Oliver Perkins born 1805 New Hampshire died 1860 Rapides Parish, Louisiana they match surname **Reed**. Their closest genetic match is Albania, England, Germany & Ireland.

Second Perkins lineage is North African which is matched to the **Goyens Clan** YDNA to the surnames, **Sweat, Williams, Warwick, Powell**. These lineages are identical for each other and are direct descendants of the Egyptian Pharaonic line of King Rameses III. Their closest genetic matches are, Argentina at 2.1% of population males tested 41, Armenia at 0.2% of population males tested 982, Portugal (Azores) at 0.2% of population males tested 2140.

Third Perkins YDNA Results is an East African haplo whose closest genetic match is to the Island of Cyprus[361] in the Mediterranean and attached to the Carter Co., TN. Perkins families. This YDNA lineage is a match to the **Driggers/Rodriguez** (thought to be a Spaniard or Portuguese) a **Doyle** (Louisiana), **Perkins** (Accomack Co., Virginia) but still several genetic distances between these samples of self-reported "oldest known progenitors" 1. Nimrod Perkins who married Betsy (not laughing)[362] Waters and 2. John Perkins born 1817 in Pennsylvania or West Virginia (conflicting birth records) and died 1902 in Aiken, Minnesota. Some of whom are enumerated in the Lost State of Franklin, 1762 attachment I. The Doyle sample, which is the oldest biological sample are not proven lineages to Louisiana. This group to Louisiana claim from Esther Perkins and attach Old Jock Joshua Perkins Carter Co., TN. Married Mary Polly Black Perkins and who also

---

[361] Cyprus, officially called the Republic of Cyprus, is an island nation in the eastern Mediterranean Sea. It is the third largest and third most populous island in the Mediterranean and is located north of Egypt; northwest of Lebanon, Palestine, and Israel; west of Syria; southeast of Greece; and south of Turkey.

[362] The "laughing" was a joke, all be it not a funny one made by the Nash Network and got carried into people's genealogies. It was suggested Betsy Waters was an Indian and the Network decided that for Nimrod to have married an Indian he must have been drunk and deemed her "laughing Waters."

claim her as their MtDNA lineage. But how could this be accurate? It cannot be correct, biologically.

Paul Heinegg's Free African Americans Documentation on Esther Perkins. A document was published in his work on Esther Perkins who was fined by a court action against her for having "illegitimate" children. Unfortunately, without thinking much about how YDNA results are inherited (father to son unchanged for 10s of 1000s of years), many have attached this lineage to Joshua "Old Jock" Perkins who married Mary Polly Black.

This all creates real problems with finding the progenitors of each line when all *think they are correct. Biologically, we know not all these lines came from the same Joshua Perkins or "Old Jock." And we hold no value in the popular Paul Heinegg's documentation concerning Esther Perkins, who's court records document a bond "bastard bond" imposed for having children out of wedlock. One Thomas **Blair**, esquire[363] showed up in court and paid her fines.

Beyond the romantic spin these researchers attached to those records asserting Ester Perkins was a slave and

---

[363] The title esquire or Esq. after his name would infer he was an attorney, lawyer or otherwise a representative of the court.

Thomas Blair, Esq. was her slave owner. Nowhere in that document did it state either of those facts, this was made up sensationalism for whatever reasons. And not to be too long winded about all this affair, quite simply put… Esther was a female who passes down MtDNA, it is impossible for her to pass YDNA to her sons and their male heirs. YDNA is only inherited and passed down father to son. If Esther Perkins were the mother of Old Jock Perkins, she could not pass down Perkins YDNA from her father. If Esther was married to a Perkins, then who was she and who was her Perkins husband? This scenario would not lend any relatedness to "bastard" children if she were married. Again, if this is the case, Heinegg's documentation is still rendered invaluable. Why did Thomas Blair, Esq pay Esther's fines? Was Thomas Blair the father of her children? If Thomas Blair was the father of her children, this might explain one lineage of the male Perkins YDNA debacle.

Fourth YDNA Perkins results and I believe a major key to the entire fiasco. We have a YDNA line of the **Cornelius** surname members who also matched the, **Perkins**, **Reed** and **Blair** surnames from around Hazard County, KY to Horse Cave, Hart Co. Ky. These families are associated with the Ben Ishmael Grasshopper Gypsies and Caramel Indians of Indiana and Ohio. Some ended up in Michigan. As Don has stated here, there are several Redbone Joshua Perkins.

However, the group pushing the agenda of Esther Perkins being the mother of Joshua "Old Jock" Perkins refuse to understand their scenario is of course biologically impossible. Which all proves these lines are not thoroughly researched and making any judgements on which Joshua was which YDNA impossible, short of digging them up and testing their remains. And those factions ascertaining they can prove which Joshua was theirs or who is who through autosomal (cousins matches) are shooting in the dark or believing in hocus pocus based on the Redbones history of endogamy. These methods of appropriate matching are methodically laid out in our Genetic Genealogy Handbook & Guide with Case Studies, *The Journey*. We follow more closely some of the male Perkins lineages in the upcoming *Goins Book II* but we will certainly consider a Perkins Book in the future.

So, you can see why we encourage further research into each Redbone progenitor lineage, and to examine each male

YDNA independently and then as a tribal people carefully and without bias or predetermined conclusions.

Endogamous tribal people name their children for one another and females passed their surnames on to male heirs, which would cause a break in the chain of father to son YDNA and explain the many Perkins YDNA results among us. If Esther Perkins was a SISTER of Old Jock, daughter of Richard and she had children with a **Blair**, then this would identify one, and perhaps two of the male YDNA lineages.

Identical YDNA Matched lineage It is also worth mentioning here, the DIAL/DOYLE/DYAL etc. spelling surname males and the BUXTON surname males are identical YDNA for one another. The oldest known progenitor is Jude BUXTON. There is a detailed pedigree and YDNA results included in the title *The Journey*: A genetic Genealogy Handbook and Guide with Case Studies by Stacy R. Webb and previously mentioned throughout this publishing.

In conclusion

Valentine Collins (or whoever his progenitor was), **John Bunch/Punch** (or whoever his progenitor was), **James &**

Phillip Goings (1) Clan (or whoever their progenitor was), **George Nelson** (or whoever his progenitor was) migrated together from the very same place and at the very same time. Their closest genetic matches are from Barbados and a Palestinian Bedouin their oldest origin genetic match.

The haplo study proved both Nvarrah and Spanish Peg were of typical Gypsy origins in India and, or Iran. And, though Nvarrah Collins haplo origin is likely Middle Eastern the migration is proper with the Ottoman Empire period migrations.

Peg's MtDNA is specifically known as a Gypsy mitochondrial lineage with migration out of India to Iran. We can also trace with good confidence to date; that both Nvarrah Collins haplo migrations markers and those of his spouse, Spanish Peg Gibson Collins, from their last known origins to the area now known as Macedonia. These markers show their haplo evidence documents the migrations were both via the Middle East, and that would conclude both spouses last origins were Macedonia area and or the geographic region of Macedonia.

The Gypsies defy the conventional definition. As a population, they have no nation-state, speak different languages, belong to many religions, and comprise a mosaic of socially and culturally divergent groups separated by strict rules of endogamy[364]. Referred to as "the invisible minority," the Gypsies have for centuries been ignored by Western medicine, and their genetic heritage has only recently attracted attention. Common origins from a small group of ancestors characterize the 8–10 million European Gypsies as an unusual trans-national founder population, whose exodus from India played the role of a profound demographic bottleneck. Social and economic pressures within Europe led to gradual fragmentation, generating multiple genetically differentiated sub isolates. The string of population bottlenecks and founder effects have shaped a unique genetic profile, whose potential for genetic research can be met only by study designs that acknowledge cultural tradition and self-identity. (BioEssays 27:1084–1094, 2005).

These conclusions are based on the evidence to present date. However, though DNA facts are stubborn things despite the wishes, inclinations, dictation, or declaration of our passion, they cannot alter the factual evidence. DNA study is a fluid

---

[364] the custom of marrying only within the limits of a local community, clan, or tribe.
BIOLOGY the fusion of reproductive cells from related individuals; inbreeding; self-pollination.

one, which can change haplo origin details with ferocious speed as new evidence arise with archeological discoveries. So, taking that all in and piecing the genealogies back together by biological exact matches, and establishing generations by biology is a little confusing, if you do not have a good grasp on basic pedigree (genealogy) understandings, or skill set. There is a great lack of understanding of YDNA, MtDNA and autosomal paths and how those are passed (inherited) down by mainstream participants. Here are the challenges we find the most concerning currently.

DNA Challenges for Redbone Studies

MEHRAssociation found the biggest effort was educating our community on the science of DNA along with the public at large. And endogamy is a serious obstacle. Nevertheless, we preserver. And, bottom line, if you descended from any one of these mixed-ethnic racial isolates, free people of color, mulatto, "other" etc. classification for race, or monikers: Redbones, Melungeon, Dominicker, Brass Ankles, Lumbee, etc. The truth is...We are not all the same and should be examined independently with verified Y and MtDNA comparisons with matched maternal and paternal lineages identified. Context is important because of distance in relationship. Example, most racial groups have no real genealogical documentations, because likely those never existed and or large gaps in undocumented generations. Be not surprised if your grandfather, or mother may or may not actually be who their genealogy has been attached to in past efforts. I do not believe any of that was nefarious or "purposeful" perspective, but likely "best guesses" or, "processes of eliminations," type of attachments. Neither are good genealogical research habit and take experienced and unbiased study. However, those unwilling to accept the biology of the matter are of a frustrating variety. Clinging to the old brick and mortar mistakes of the past where DNA has unblocked new paths.

DNA Brings New Research, Genealogical Challenges & Previously Unrecognized Complex Family Units

The obstacles with current DNA studies for our people are:

1. **Endogamy**[365] - Rendering the popular autosomal[366] DNA testing comparisons useless in identifying ancestors through multiple matches. Therefore, rendering admixtures estimates also relatively useless.

---

[365] the custom of marrying only within the limits of a local community, clan, or tribe. BIOLOGY the fusion of reproductive cells from related individuals; inbreeding; self-pollination.
[366] DNA-based test which looks at specific locations of a person's genome, in order to find or verify ancestral genealogical relationships or to estimate the ethnic mixture of an individual as part of genetic genealogy.

Each of these obstacles require a different, unconventional, and meticulously organized study approach to research in genetic genealogy of the people known as Redbones, and other endogamous mixed ethnic isolates.

2. **Migration to these shores.** Not many, if any paternal (unlike MtDNA where we see many matches in other countries/continents of origin and migrations) matched YDNA participants in country of origin. To put this simply, male YDNA sampled results among us rarely jump the pond to Africa or Europe. This phenomenon could be as simple as there are no participations in the country of last origin or migration who have tested. Or more complex phenomena; a result of slavery, Cromwellian genocide and outcasts, [367] or religious outcasts from Europe? Whereby no matching male YDNA lineages remain in their country or geographic regions of origins. Ireland is a great example of this phenomenon where there are known male families that became completely extinct during periods of the British' Empire's expulsions of white indentured servitude (white slavery) and Australian penal colony systems.

3. **Adopted European Surnames.** As in the case of Valentine COLLINS who obviously had a close relationship with Nvarrah Collins. It appears, Valentine adopted the surname COLLINS, perhaps

---

[367] The Cromwellian conquest of Ireland and Scotland or Cromwellian war in Ireland was the conquest of Ireland by the forces of the English Parliament, led by Oliver Cromwell, during the Wars of the Three Kingdoms. Cromwell invaded Ireland with his New Model Army on behalf of England's Rump Parliament in August 1649.

from Nvarrah, (who also might or might not have landed on these shores with a North European surname) and would not have arrived on these shores with a European surname. This was a common practice among our people. And in later YDNA results, we can see that *some non-European origin participant males, closely related otherwise appears, a "set" or several "sets" of non-European origin males and one of a European origin male with European surname, though not paternally related but who are related to one another otherwise and would have taken/adopted their relative's surname. **Inherited surname phenomena** from outside a father to son relationship. Such as Indians and Slaves would not have inherited a European surname from their father and father before them. Those would have been adopted from someone else and or passed down in unconventional ways. Such as adopting a surname from an owner, married into family member, admired character, or what we experience most, a matrilineal inherited surname.

4. Tribal & marginalized ethnic group **assimilations.**

5. **Nomadic lifestyles**: hucksters, Indian trader elements, trade element females (Lawson's mixed-blood Cheraw & Catawba Indian Trade Girls) who are fiercely un researched.

6. **Polygamy** Mixed-blood Fur Trader element, who shared multiple wives, and or, concubinage. This was never so well documented with our Redbone

forefathers, as with the group of our men who ended up in Wyoming's Wind River area.

Polyandry Mixed-blood, free woman of color, slaves, fur trader elements, Indians [matriarchal society] and other cultural women who shared more than one husband, and at the same time; can also be an example of endogamy, marrying into or within the same line male family for multiple generations.

7. **Documentation and Genealogy**: Though we can make leaps and bounds in genetics, matching progenitor YDNA and female MtDNA. We are still unable to make the leaps needed with documenting the genealogy to and from our matched lineages, or progenitor/s (huge gaps of many generations with little or no paper trails). This is in general the case with most mixed-ethnic and marginalized populations. Further research between matches is encouraged to break the gaps and fill in the correct lineage(s).

8. **Incorrect Genealogy, Agenda Narratives, Preferred Ancestor(s) Phenomena,** genealogical descendants pushing a family genealogy into a position preferred by a subjective path of history. Usually without any proof, documentation, or DNA results. Example: Perkins descendants pushing a certain path of YDNA results (there are many male progenitors among these lines) to their preferred "oldest known progenitor" family without any proof and contradicting or disregarding all other proof of YDNA facts.

9. **Documentation vs. Complex family Units** & previously unknown relationships: Family Units rearing children from multiple generational sources (rearing male offspring of cousin's or their children, children's children, uncles, nephews, etc) Example: Documenting through enumeration" as one family unit" but whose DNA results revealed complex relationships within one family grouping whose documented vital records were incorrect according to biological matches.

   Example: Progenitor, Stephen Goyens (m. Edith Ida Perkins) family unit enumerated 1850 with a particular set of children/ages. Steven Goyens (m. Adeline Sampson or Johnson) enumerated in 1860 with the same basic named children but irregular/unexpected birth years for parents and children. Though always *thought to be the same couple, perhaps two different wives (Edith "Ida" & Adeline could be the same woman) they appear not to be the same men/couples, at all. This fact only made apparent through extensive YDNA study of all the male descendants located from those male's enumerated within the households. **Biological Conclusion:** The males listed in those households as family units (father/sons/brothers) could not have been brothers to one another. But that leads us to a more critical crises in the genealogical efforts. Though these males were closely descended from the same progenitor male their "generations" from each other biologically made it impossible that they were in fact brothers from the same father. So, then, onto the next new crises...who was the Progenitor really was Stephen their father, or was Steven their father? Why is the youngest son in age closer related to the progenitor than *some of the other males listed as brothers? Age and relationship in genetics have nothing at all to do with biological "order." As demonstrated in this chapter, on YDNA matches. Also, example of Benjamin Nash/Ash, though documented in Mexican census as son of or living with Old Thomas Nash and Anna Goins, their biology proves he could not be the son of Old Thomas Nash/Ash. Therefore, documentation that is widely accepted like census records can and are incorrect but only discovered through DNA testing.

10. **Stepfamilies** sometimes going by or using the same name as their stepfather, etc. As in the case with William Billy Powell, Jr. "Oceola." We know his father was not the man his mother had subsequent children with (Powell) but he took his name. All the children born to Polly Coppinger (mother of Oceola) who had about a dozen children in all, most born after Wm Billy Powell, Sr. left for Missouri with two daughters by her, but all subsequent children carried his surname, Powell.

11. **DNA understanding**; educating the public at large.

    a. **Race & Admixture**; According to biology neither race, nor admixture exist. Both are political and social constructs and are not based in human biology whatsoever. Therefore, we find it incredible difficult to help others navigate their DNA results and that of our collective genetic pool when these facts are not fully understood by and or promoted by mainstream consumer corporations. DNA is simply put, a study of human migration, and anything else is guessing game to appease consumers and promote further DNA kit sales.

These are significant hurdles and obstacles to overcome in the coming years. With the help of DNA, we can achieve so much more than we understood in the past. But with it brings different questions, difficulties in genealogy and a need to now revisit facts we took for granted in the past.

Jennie & Ivey Nash/Ash
Children of Lud & Lula Gibson Nash/Ash.

Albert Goings (1) Clan with children, Alberta, Roberta, Hazel, Forest Gochie, and Lola. Herbert Mano is behind Alberta. Albert, son of James "Jim" and Apalona Perkins Goings (1) Clan Calcasieu Parish, La. Albert's YDNA is included here. Courtesy Marilyn Baggett Kobliaka.

Manuel & Sena Goyens Nash/Ash children, Zwolle, La.

CONCLUSIONS
By Don C. Marler, original to this title. Which we feel relevant even now.

Success in reaching the goals set for this book is uneven. While most objectives were met, a major disappointment arose around efforts to get more information on Redbone culture, both past and present. Request for completion of questionnaires met with complete failure, and requests for interviews received minimal response. Thus, an opportunity to record the most extensive aspects of Redbone culture has been lost. Nevertheless, a few cultural items have been identified and discussed throughout the book, particularly in Chapter 12. Prejean secured interviews more readily for her thesis by working through a church group in the geographical area she chose for her study. Reliance for needed information was based on personal contacts developed over the last ten years and on the Redbone Internet Discussion Group. The difference in response to these two approaches may be instructive for future investigators. When the reluctance of Redbones to share cultural information directly became evident, the effort to get these data was abandoned.

With the increasing frequency of changes in the laws affected mixed-blood people on the east coast of America, which limited their status and rights as citizens, and more

Conclusions

importantly, threatened their freedom, they began to move to the west. North Carolina, especially in the 1830s, passed laws that, no doubt, alarmed many mixed-blood people, so they began movement to South Carolina, Florida, Georgia, and eventually to Alabama, Mississippi, Louisiana, and Texas. Some came by the northern route through Tennessee to Missouri and Arkansas and then to Texas and Louisiana. A central tenet of this book is that one of the reasons mixed-blood people moved west before the Civil War was to escape being enslaved.

By the 1850s, they were coming to Louisiana and Texas in wagon trains over the Natchez Trace and the Harrisonburg Road to Natchitoches. Some stopped along the way, settling in the pine forests of central to north-central Louisiana. From Natchitoches, some went on to Texas, while others moved southwestward to the Neutral Zone, forming the small, isolated communities that would become known as Redbone communities. These communities would assume a defensive posture – developing essentially an armed camp mentality.

Being loosely organized as sparsely populated rural communities, it is remarkable that they remained as unified as they did. Their success as an ongoing cohesive society, lasting 200 years, no doubt reflects the seriousness with which they perceived the threat to their freedom. The American 19th Century South was determined to possess adequate slave labor regardless of color, and the freedom of poor whites again became threatened. This threat put mixed-blood people in double jeopardy. Redbones, whose history, with few exceptions, included no slavery, would have none of it. Spanish/Mexican-owned Texas provided a haven for mixed-bloods, or so it seemed. The Neutral Zone, from 1806 forward, offered options to them; those residing there could move back and forth between Texas and Louisiana, as the need might arise.

Since their entry into the area, Redbones have survived events that have threatened to diffuse their communities including upheavals, surrounding ownership of Texas, the Civil War, rape of the timberlands, World War I, and the Great Depression, which brought federalized work/relief programs such as the WPA, NYA and CCC. Then came World War II, the Korean Conflict, the Viet Nam War and the Gulf War.

These major events, along with the more gradual development and availability of radio, television, Internet, rapid communication and transportation, and the high mobility of the general population have taken their toll on

Conclusions

membership in Redbone communities. Furthermore, society at large, though not free of prejudice, is now much more accepting of various ethnic groups, reducing the need for the defensiveness, secretiveness, and exclusiveness of Redbone communities. While it appears that the realization of this fundamental change is beginning to take hold in the minds of many Redbones, many still strive to maintain a closed community. An apparent value is placed on the existence of the Redbone community as a separate and distinct entity, apart from any objective perceived need for such separateness. The self-identity and self-esteem of some Redbones seem to be tied closely with the identity of the community, albeit an identity as a community that is too comfortable with violence.

In this book, an attempt has been made to describe things as they were or are without passing judgement on them. This non-judgmental standard was consciously abandoned in the discussion of the issues surrounding slavery.

Whether change in the Redbone culture is in order or not is for Redbones to decide; it is not within the purview of this book to suggest or discuss this, and any suggestion to the contrary is not intended.

Now Louisiana Redbones are taking pride in the name and heritage. If this book contributes to that positive development, it will have accomplished its goal.

By the Editor

I believe the original work by Don, and the updates contained here further enlighten and educated descendants, and the public at large concerning the people known as Redbone; their history, genetics, migrations, and oppression as a people. Though I disagree in some regard with the further literature and opinions formed concerning the "Redbone Culture of Violence." It is the conscience of the Redbones the need to document these occasions of social frustrations, prying interests, query, and examinations as well as the clashes of violence. After that, it is up to the reader to be informed that as it appears from the abundance of historical accounting of social outbursts of violence, those are in many regards the only accounts which survives multiple and hundreds of generations. It appears from my perspective, as a Redbone based on thousands of hours of dedicated research; that we as a cultural and tribal people were historically and continue to be proactive in defense of our long and difficult journey navigating the paths of many racial fires and excessive use of social, racial, and political

Conclusions

injustices against us which spurred on the sojourners of our people.

We carry in us a true sense of self and familial preservation. Which has obviously led us to violence and vengeance measures over our history. I believe a people maligned, harassed, degraded, denied, and stripped generationally of their wealth, freedom and rights are nothing short of reactionary assaults against racism and the legal retaliations of the "Triumph of the One Drop Rule.[368]" Self-preservation methods regardless of outside opinion are nothing more than the mere results of decades of defensiveness which engrained within us a strong pride in our culture and heritage. The truth about Redbones, we lack any compassion for the outsider's opinions of us, and regardless of our historically and modernly perceived reputations, we are sure you would not understand unless you are one. And therefore, we reject any form of judgement of reputations assigned us. We are proud of our heritage, whatever survives, and we will continue to regard the truth as a measure of justice, not shame.

---

[368] Sweet, F. W. (2005). Legal History of the Color Line: The Rise and Triumph of the One-Drop Rule. Paml Coast, Florida: Backintyme Publishing.

Redbones of Louisiana

Our family structure does not fit within the module given here by Don. We in fact are a more matriarchal society, where the men in most instances are the bread winners but who tend to allow the females to rule the home, religion, finances, discipline, and most times the political view and social activities.

The need for further genetic genealogy participants, their DNA testing results, and education is paramount to moving forward in discovering the complex and diverse nature of our mixed ethnic, social, religious, and cultural tribal people. Participation of testers who are genuinely related to and descended from Redbone ancestry, find ourselves in a struggle with current sentiments or mind set of "inclusiveness" that "all mixed-race people" were Redbone, or Melungeon or Brass Ankles, Seminole, etc., a real and valid obstacle in the path of genetic studies. In short, the Mayflower society does not allow members who are not descendants of the Mayflower to be members of their societies, and those who are must also prove their lineage. More urgently, and in a biological sense, the genetic study of Redbone descendants who can prove their relatedness is a much-needed policy to discovering the true genetics and extent of those related for proper recording of ethnic

Conclusions

backgrounds, history, migrations, and culture of the people known as Redbones as well as other related ethnic groups.

We reject definition, as it is obvious to us if you descended from a particular set of families then likely your ancestral heritage should be included in the genetic studies as Redbone. We have developed multiple groupings of racial isolate communities and families where we are able now with genetics to determine unequivocally if a participant is somehow related. We use these panel comparisons, as a determining factor for inclusiveness in our studies.[369]

With forthcoming books from Backintyme, we hope to publish these genetic studies, the results of comparisons, and ethnic origins of our progenitors and progenitor couples in the: *The Progenitors*, and *Goins Book I, II, The Perkins* and other publishing's like the *Redbone Chronicles*. We hope you will continue to join us on our genetic genealogy journey.

Deep pockets and communities identified and, or, mentioned here with little or no proper research to date.

Port Gibson, Redbone settlement (Samuel Gibson) and dealing through the slave trade which was created and existed

---

[369] https://www.familytreedna.com/groups/mehra-project/about/background

through the No Man's Land Baratarian pirate activities in the Gulf of Mexico. Settled by Samuel Gibson, Dr. Thomas Goings, the Dean, Wise and Durant families.

Tangipahoa Parish, Louisiana Redbones, not represented here but are represented in forthcoming titles, *The Goins Book I & II.*

Jackson, Mississippi, Redbone settlement at Warren Co., Ms. Originally settled by the Tobias Gibson, who was also an itinerant Baptist preacher along the Clinch River with Father of the Opelousas, Reverend, Joseph P. Willis.

Fields Community, Louisiana. Though the community is mentioned here, little if no research that ties the Redbones to Cherokee Chief George Fields (Tennessee/North Georgia) has been completed. Though application affidavits exist that tie the two groups together, through the Cherokee Nation. And, with confirmed ancestral ties to those families through DNA autosomal results.

Fields Settlement, Old El Orquisac, Liberty, Liberty Co., Texas spoken of briefly here in "Update; Baratarians." These families were obviously associated with the Baratarian Redbones and Chief Bowels Arkansas/Missouri Cherokee.

Conclusions

Related Groups

By Autosomal DNA Results

Canary Islanders or Isleños are an ethnic group living in Louisiana, consisting of people primarily from the Canary Islands. In Louisiana, the Isleños originally settled in four communities which included Galveztown, Valenzuela, Barataria, and San Bernardo. In general, were brought from the Northwestern coast of Africa to Louisiana by the Spaniards to support the Catholic Mission System.

The Canary Islanders of Texas, arrived to South Texas in 1731 and founded San Fernando de Bexar (later San Antonio).

Further research is encouraged to establish genealogical links to the DNA results.

Ancient Canarians "Guanches"

The Guanches are related to the indigenous Berbers of neighboring Morocco. The Guanche language is firmly in the Afro-Asiatic family of languages and is a dialect of the Berber subfamily therein. In 2017, the first genome-wide data from the Guanches confirmed a North African origin and that they were genetically most similar to modern North African Berber peoples of the nearby North African mainland. It also showed that modern inhabitants of Gran Canaria carry an estimated 16%–31% Guanche autosomal ancestry.

Canary Islanders, or Canarians (Spanish: canarios), are a Romance people and subgroup of the Spaniards. They are indigenous to the Canary Islands, an autonomous community of Spain near the coast of northwest Africa and descend from a mixture of Spanish settlers and aboriginal Guanche peoples. The distinctive variety of the Spanish language spoken in the region is known as habla canaria (Canary speech) or the (dialecto) canario (Canarian dialect). The Canarians, and their descendants, played a major role during the conquest, colonization, and eventual independence movements of various countries in Latin America. Their ethnic and cultural presence is most palpable in the countries of Uruguay, Venezuela, Cuba, Dominican Republic, and the United States territory of Puerto Rico.

Common Surnames [370]

Rodriques, Gonzalez, Hernandez, Perez, Garcia, Santana, Martin, Diaz, Suarez, Sanchez, Lopez, Babrera, Ramos, Medina, Fernandez, Morales, Marrero, Delgado, Alverez, Ramirez, Alonso, Herrera, Jimenez, Dominquez, Gomez/s, Gutierrez, Reyes, Cruz, Acosta, Torres, Martinez, Leon, Vega, Sosa, Rivero, Moreno, Mendez, Quintana, Navarro, Trujillo, Afonso, Luis, Padron, Armas, Ortega, Guerra, Gil, Castro, Brito, Ruiz, Melian, Mendoza, Perdomo, Mesa, Ojeda, Pena, Romero, Benitez, Falcon, Betancor, Vera, Dorta, Deniz, Dorta, Deniz, Castellano, Padilla, deLeon, Santos, Quintero, Estevez, Batitsta, Alamo, Toledo, Santiago, Chavez, Vazquez, de-la-Cruz, del Pino.

---

[370] https://forebears.io/spain/canary-islands#pedigrees

GLOSSARY

Alabama Cajan: This group is now known as the MOWA Choctaw Tribe. They are recognized as a tribe by the state of Alabama. The term Cajan was considered by them as derogatory. MOWA is an amalgamation of Mobile and Washington after the two primary counties in which they are located.

Cajun: People of principally southern Louisiana who descended from the Canadian French and who were ejected from Acadia by the English. Cajun is a corruption of Acadian.

Calcasieu River: (Cal-ca-shoe) A river in Louisiana that served as the eastern boundary of the Neutral Zone.

Cane River Creoles: Known as Free Gentlemen of Color, these people were a combination of Negro and Spanish or French. They rejected all categories and lived apart from Negroes or Caucasians, making a separate society for themselves. Cane River located south of Natchitoches, Louisiana was created when the Red River changed its course.

Coon-Ass: A term given the Acadians or Cajuns because of their practice of wearing coon skin caps with the tail still attached.

Creole: There is no more difficult term to define as its definition has changed with changing time and circumstances. In this book, when used by the author, it means persons of Spanish or French and Negro heritage that were born in America.

Culture: Culture as used in this book is the community of ideas, attitudes, practices, beliefs, etc. to which we are exposed as we are growing up and in which we live.

Frauding: The practice of cutting the wrist and drinking the blood before a fight.

Free Issues: This term is essentially the same as Issue and Old Issue. It simply differentiated between the mixed blood progeny (issue) of slave owners that were freed from slavery and those not so freed. Issues were not a community or settlement of people. The term related to the progeny of slave owners wherever they lived. (See Old Issue)

Griffe: A term used primarily in Louisiana to refer to a person who was ¾ Negro and ¼ White.

Impress: Impress refers to the practice of kidnapping people and forcing them to work against their will. This was a favorite practice of the British who kidnapped people of the streets in the British Empire and forced them to work on ships and come to the West Indies and colonial American. After the Revolutionary War, they continued kidnapping Americans and forcing them to perform duties as sailors

Glossary

against their will. This practice was one of the precipitating events in the War of 1812.

Manumission: The act of freeing a slave.

Maroon: A person who ran away from slavery and lived in isolation. Can also refer to a community of such people.

Melungeon: (pronounced Muh-luhn-juhn) A mixed-blood people the original group of whom were located on Newman's Ridge in what is now Hancock County, Tennessee. Their heritage is now hotly debated. They are likely a wide mixture of Turks, Scots, Indian, Portuguese, Negro and Sittis from India. There may be a close relationship between Melungeons and Redbones.

Metisage: The action of racial mixture.

Miscegenation: A law created during the Civil War and repealed in 1967 prohibiting interracial marriage. There were no miscegenation laws before the Civil War and therefore mixed marriages and mixed relationships were common then.

Natchitoches: (Na-ca-toush) The a is short, as in "at". The oldest continuously occupied settlement in Louisiana.

Neutral Zone or Neutral Ground: The territory in western Louisiana that was in dispute between Spain and the United States after the Louisiana Purchase. The dispute was over the boundary. The generals in the field signed an agreement that neither side would send troops or peace officers in, nor would new settlers be allowed in, until the two countries could settle the dispute. The agreement lasted from 1806 to 1821.

Octoroon or sang-mele: In Louisiana, this term referred to a person who was 1/8 Negro and 7/8 White.

Old Issue: While there is no clear definition of this term, it was apparently created after the Civil War to identify those persons who were freed before the war and who were the progeny (issue) of slave owners. This term then would have been useful in contrasting from the newly freed slaves (those freed by the war). Redbones likely objected to the term because they maintained that they had never been slaves – which with few exceptions was true. (See Free Issue)

Quadroon: As used in Louisiana, quadroon referred to a person who was ¼ Negro and ¾ White.

Redbone: A Redbone is a person whose biological heritage is some combination of at least two of the following: Caucasian, American Indian or Negro, and who is a member of a group that identifies itself as a Redbone group or Redbone community, holding certain values, beliefs and worldviews.

Redbone Community: A Redbone community is composed of a group of people who identify as Redbones and live apart from the dominant society, propagating its own set of beliefs, traditions, value system and worldview.

Red Man: A name first applied to the Beothuk Indians of

Glossary

Newfoundland because of their habit of painting their bodies and possessions with red ocher. Later it was applied to Native Americans.

Red Sticks: Creek and Seminole Indians displayed red sticks when about to go to war. They were then known as "Red Sticks".

Sabine River: (Sa-bean), The emphasis can be on the first syllable or, as is usual, equally on both. The a in Sa is short, as in at. The most common pronunciation is with both syllables muted. This river, which now divides Louisiana and Texas, served as the western boundary of the Neutral Zone.

Six Miler: Mixed-blood people, otherwise known as Redbones, who live in the territory drained by Six Mile Creek in southwest Louisiana. It is an old term used instead of Redbone and was once a more acceptable term. Its usage, never as prevalent as Ten Miler, is declining as the term Redbone becomes more accepted.

Ten Miler: Mixed-blood people, otherwise known as Redbones, who live in the territory drained by Ten Mile Creek in southwest Louisiana. It is an old term used instead of Redbone and was once a more acceptable term. Its usage seems to be dwindling.

Redbones of Louisiana

Tri-Racial Isolate: People who were a mixture of Caucasian, Negro and Indian, and were physically and socially isolated from the dominant society are sometimes referred to as "tri-racial isolates". The term is resented by some members of mixed-blood groups because they interpret it as implying that they are interbred. For some, it is also resented because they deny there are Negro genetics in their bloodline.

ATTACHMENTS

Attachment A
List of Seminole Indians

Abraham, (black interpreter)
Billie, Charlie
Billie, Ingraham
Billie, Johnny
Billy, Girtman
Billy, Miami
Blount, John
Bowers, Joe
Bowlegs, Billy (black interpreter)
Bowles, Lucy
Brown, Andrew J.
Buster, Johnnie
Caballo, John
Franklin, Ben
Garden, Tom Devil's
Gopher, Jim
Hall, Charlie Dixie
Harney, Billy
Hicks, John
Homespun, Henry
Ingraham, Charley
Jim, George Hendry
Jim, Miami
Jimmy, Miami
John, Willie
Jones, Sam
Osceola, John
Parker, Dan
Parker, Old Polly
Parker, Ruthie
Payne, Adam
Perryman, Thomas
Poole, Billy
Powell, Billy
Riley, Joe,
Roberts, Nuff-kee
Sanders, Calvin
Shore, Frank
Smith, Billy

Attachments

Charley, Jackson	Joseph, W.F.	Snaps, Ginger
Charley, Miami	John Josh	Stranahan, Frank
Chipco, Tallahassee	Jumper, John	Tiger, Ingraham
Clay, Henry	Jumper, Old	Tiger, John Miami
Conepatchie, Billy	Kibbetts, John	Tigertail, Charley
Coven, Tom	Kidd, William	Tom, Blind
Cowkeeper, Chief	King, Lena	Tommie, Smallpox
Daniles, Elijah	King, Willie	Tommie, T.B.M.
Dixon, Charlie	Lee, Charles	Ward, Charlie
Doctor, Little	McKinley, William	Ward, John
Elliott, Davy	McQueen, Peter	Washington, George
Factor, Jim	Micco, John	White, John
Factor, Pompey	Motlow, Billie	Wilson, Lake
Frank, Stanley	Osceola, Charlie	

Source:

List compiled from a variety of sources, but the main source is: James W. Coventon, *The Seminoles of Florida*. (Gainesville: University of Florida Press, 1993).

Attachment B
List of Lumbee Names

The following is a partial list of Lumbee names. These names are a compilation from materials by several authors.

Allen	Dare	Powell
Barton	Demery	Quick
Bell	Dial	Ransom

Bennett	Graham	Revel (Revell)
Berry	Goins	Sampson
Blanks	Hagans	Sanderson
Braboy (Brayboy)	Hagins	Scott
Brewer	Harris	Smith
Bridger	Harvey	Stevens
Briger	Harvie	Strickland
Brooks	Howe	Strong
Broom	Hunt	Taylor
Brown	Jacobs	Thomas
Bullard	Johnson	Tyler
Burnett	Jones	Vicars
Canady	Lasie	White
Carter	Locklear	Wilkins
Chapman	Lowry (Lowery, Lowrie)	Williamson
Chavis	Lucas	Willis
Clark	Martin	Wood
Cole	Mathis	Wright
Coleman	Maynor	
Cooper	Mitchell	
Cumba	Nash	
Cumbo	Oxendine	
Cumbow	Paine	
Cumming	Patterson	

Sources:

Adolph L. Dial, The Only Land I Know: A history of the Lumbee Indians. San Francisco: The Indian Historian Press, 1975. W. McKee Evans, To Die Game. Nashville: Parthenon Press, 1971.

Attachments

Brent N. and Robyn Vaughn Kennedy, The Melungeons: TheResurrection of a Proud People. Macon: Mercer University Press, 1994, Revised 1997.

Attachment C
Melungeon and Melungeon Related Names

The list of Melungeon and Melungeon related names has been compiled using information from the writings of Kennedy, Elder and others. Many of these names are common across Redbones, Brass Ankles and Turks.

Adams	Coles	Gann	Maloney	Sizemore
Adkins	Colley	Garland	Martin	Stallard
Bales	Collier	Gibson	Miner	Stanley
Barker	Collinsworth	Gipson	Minor	Steel
Barnes	Colyer	Glass	Miser	Stewart
Bean	Counts	Goings	Mizer	Sweat
Beckler	Cox	Goins	Moore	Swindall
Belcher	Coxe	Goodman	Morely	Tackett
Bell	Crow	Gorvens	Mosely	Taylor
Bennet	Cumba	Gowan	Mullins	Tipton
Berry	Cumbo	Gowen	Nash	Tolliver
Berry	Cumbow	Goyen	Nichols	Turner
Biggs	Curry	Graham	Noel	Vanover
Bolen	Davidson	Gwinn	Orr	Watts
Bolton	Davis	Hale	Osborn	White
Bowlin	Denham	Hall	Osborne	Whited
Bowling	Dooley	Hambrick	Perry	Williams
Bowman	Coxe	Hammond	Phelps	Willis
Branham	Crow	Hendricks	Phipps	Wilson
Brogan	Cumba	Hendrix	Polly	Wright

Bullion	Cumbo	Hill	Powers	Wyatt
Bunch	Cumbow	Hillman	Pruitt	
Burton	Curry	Hopkins	Ramey	
Byrd	Davidson	Ivey	Reaves	
Campbell	Davis	Jackson	Rhea	
Carrico	Dorton	Jones	Horton	
Carter	Dula	Keith	Rice	
Casteel	Dye	Kennedy	Riddle	
Caudill	Ely	Kiser	Rivers	
Chavis	Evans	Kyle	Roberson	
Clark	Fields	Lawson	Robertson	
Coal	Fleenor	Lopes	Robinson	
Coffey	Freeman	Lovins	Sexton	
Cole	French	Lucas	Shephard	
Coleman	Gallagher	Maggard	Short	

Attachment D
Plecker Letters

W.A. Plecker, M.D., the state of Virginia's first Registrar of Vital Statistics, waged a bureaucratic paper war against mixed-blood populations in that state in the mid1900s. He was invited to speak to or present papers to professional and governmental groups as early as the 1920s, and he wrote letters in his capacity as Registrar advocating drastic measures. His ideas were similar to those espoused in Nazi Germany regarding Jews and Gypsies. He may have influenced the German attitude in regard to race purity.

Attachments

That Plecker was allowed, and even encouraged, in his work and supported by Virginia laws is evidence that this man was not significantly out of step with his time. That his ideas were encouraged, and his behavior permitted, only sixty years ago is cause for dismay, but that they would not be well received today is heartening.

A sampling of his writing follows. The spelling and punctuation are as they were written. Darlene Wilson and others have posted these materials on the Melungeon Home Page and in other places. Melungeon researcher Ms. S.J. Arthur found these letters and called attention to them.

Commonwealth of Virginia
Department of Health
Richmond
I.C. Riggin, M. D.
Commissioner
Bureau of Vital Statistics
W. A. Plecker, M. D. Registrar

August 5, 1942
Secretary of State,
Nashville, Tennessee.

Dear Sir:

Our bureau is the only one in any State making an intensive study of the population of its citizens by race.

We have some of the counties of southwestern Virginia a number of so-called Melungeons who came into that section from Newman's Ridge, Hancock County, Tennessee, and who are classified by us as of negro origin though they make various claims, such as Portuguese, Indians, etc.

The law of Virginia says that any one with any ascertainable degree of negro is to be classified as colored and we are endeavoring to so classify those who apply for birth, death and marriage registrations.

We have a list of the free negroes, by counties, of the 1830 U. S. Census in which we find the racial origin of most of these Melungeons classified as mulattoes. In that period, 1830, we do not find the name of Hancock County, but presume that it was made up from portions of other counties, possible Grainger and Hawkins; where we find considerable numbers of these Melungeon families listed.

Will you please advise as to that point and particularly which of these original counties Newmans Ridge was in.

Attachments

Thanking you in advance and with kindest regards, I am

Very truly yours,

W. A. Plecker, M. D.

State Registrar.
Commonwealth of Virginia
Department of Health
Richmond
August 12, 1942

W. A. Plecker, M. D. Registrar

State Registrar
Bureau of Vital Statistics
Richmond, Virginia

My dear Sir:

The Secretary of State has sent your letter to my desk for reply. You have asked us a hard question. The origin of the Melungeon has been a disputed question in Tennessee ever since we can remember.

Hancock County was established by an Act of the General Assembly passed January 7th, 1844 and was formed from parts of Claiborne and Hawkins counties.

Newman's Ridge, which runs through Hancock county north of Sneedville, is parallel with Clinch River and just south of Powell Mountain. The only map on which we find it located is edited by H. C. Amick and S. J. Folmsbee of the University of Tennessee in 1941 published by Denoyer-Geppert Co., 5235 Ravenswood Ave., Chicago, listed as [TN 7S]* TENNESSEE. On this map is shown Newman's Ridge as I have sketched it on this little scrap of paper, inclosed. But we do not have the early surveys showing which county it was originally in. It appears that it may have been in Claiborne according to the Morris Gazetteer of Tennessee 1834 which includes this statement:

> "Newman's Ridge, one of the spurs of Cumberland Mountain, in East Tennessee, lying in the north east angle of Claiborne County, west of the Clinch River, and east of Powell's Mountain. It took its name from a Mr. Newman who discovered it in 1761."

Early historians of East Tennessee who lived in that section and knew the older members of this race refer to Newman's Ridge as "quite a high mountain, extending through the entire length of Hancock County, and into Claiborn County on the west. It is between Powell Mountain on the north and Clinch River on the south." Capt. L. M. Jarvis, an old citizen of Sneedville wrote in his 82nd year: "I have lived here at the base of Newman's Ridge, Blackwater, being on the opposite side for the last 71 years and well know the history of these people on Newman's Ridge and Blackwater enquired about

Attachments

as Melungeons. These people were friendly to the Cherokees who came west with the white immigration from New River and Cumberland, Virginia, about the year 1790...The name Melungeon was given them on account of their color. I have seen the oldest and first settlers of this tribe who first occupied Newman's Ridge and Blackwater and I have owned much of the lands on which they settled. They obtained their land grants from North Carolina. I personally knew Vardy Collins, Solomon D. Collins, Shepard Gibson, Paul Bunch, and Benjamin Bunch and many of the Goodmans, Moores, Williams and Sullivans, all of the very first settlers and noted men of these friendly Indians. They took their names from white people of that name with whom they came here. They were reliable, truthful and faithful to anything they promised. In the Civil War most of the Melungeons went into the Union army and made good soldiers. Their Indian blood has about run out. They are growing white.... They have been misrepresented by many writers. In former writings I have given their stations and stops on their way as they emigrated to this country with white people, one of which places was at the mouth of Stony Creek on Clinch river in Scott County, Virginia, where they built a fort and called it Ft. Blackamore after Col. Blackamore who was with them.... When Daniel Boone was here hunting 1763-1767, these Melungeons were not here."

The late Judge Lewis Shepherd, prominent jurist of Chattanooga, went further in his statements in his "Personal Memoirs", and contended that this mysterious racial group descended from the Phoenicians of Ancient Carthage. This was his judgment after investigations he made in trying a case featuring the complaint that they were of mixed negro blood, which attempt failed, and which brought out facts that many of their ancestors had settled early in South Carolina when they migrated from Portugal to America about the time of the Revolutionary war, and later moved into Tennessee. At the time of this trial covered by Judge Shepherd "charges that Negro blood contaminated the Melungeons and barred their intermarriage with Caucasians created much indignation among families of Phoenician descent in this section."

But I imagine if the United States Census listed them as mulattoes their listing will remain. But it is a terrible claim to place on people if they do not have negro blood. I often have wondered just how deeply the census takers went into an intelligent study of it at that early period.

I have gone into some detail in this reply to explain the mooted question and why it is not possible for me to give you a definite answer. I hope this may assist you to some extent.

Attachments

Sincerely,

Mrs. John Trotwood Moore

State Librarian and Archivist

August 20, 1942

Mrs. John Trotwood Moore

State Librarian and Archivist

State Department of Education

Nashville, Tennessee

Dear Mrs. Moore:

We thank you very much for your informative letter of August 12 in reply to our inquiry, addressed to the Secretary of State, as to the original counties from which Hancock County, Tennessee, was formed.

We are particularly interested in tracing back, as far as possible, to their ultimate origin the melungeons of the Newmans Ridge section, especially as enumerated in the free negro list by counties of the states in the U. S. 1830 census. This group appears to be in many respects of the same type as a number of groups in Virginia, some of which are known as "free issues," or descendants of slaves freed by their masters before the War Between the States. In one case in particular which we have traced back to its origin, and which we believe to be typical of the others, a slave woman was freed with her two mulatto sons and colonized in Amherst County in connection with a group of similar freed negroes. These sons were presumably the children of the woman's owner, and this seemed to be the most satisfactory way of disposing of them. One of those sons became the head of one of the larger families of that group. All of these groups have the same desire, which Captain L. M. Jarvis says the melungeons have, to become friends of Indians and to be classed as Indians. He referred to the effort which the Melungeon group made to be accepted by the Cherokees, apparently without great success. It is interesting also to know the opinion expressed by Captain Jarvis that these freed negroes migrated into that section with the white people. That is perfectly natural as they have always endeavored to tie themselves up as closely as possible either with the whites or Indians and are striving to break away from the true negro type.

We have a book, compiled by Carter G. Woodson, a negro, entitled "Free Negro Heads of Families in the United States in 1830," listing all of the free negroes of the 1830 census by counties. Of the names that Captain Jarvis gave, we find included in that list in Hawkins County, Solomon Collins, Vardy Collins, and Sherod (probably Shepard) Gibson. We find also Zachariah Minor, probably the head of the family in

Attachments

which we are especially interested at this time. We find also the names of James Moore (two families by this name) and Jordan and Edmund Goodman. In the list for Grainger County we find at least twelve Collins and Collens heads of families. This shows that they were evidently considered locally as free negroes by the enumerators of the 1830 census.

One of the most interesting parts of your letter is that relating to the opinion of the Judge mentioned, in his "Personal Memoirs," who seemed to have accepted as satisfactory certain evidence which was presented to him that these people are of Phoenician descent from ancient Carthage, which was totally destroyed by Rome. We have in Virginia white people, descendants of Pocahontas, who married John Rolfe about 1616. About twelve generations have passed since then, and we figured out that there was about $1/4000^{th}$ of 1% of Pocahontas blood now in their veins, though they seem to be quite proud of that. If you go back to the destruction of Carthage in 146 B. C., or to the destruction of Tyre by Pompey in 64 B. C., when all characteristic features of national life became extinct and with it racial identity, you will see that the fraction of 1% of Phoenician blood would reach astronomical proportions and be totally lost in the various mixtures of North Africans, with which the Carthaginians afterwards mixed. The Judge also speaks of the inclusion of Portuguese blood with this imaginary Phoenician blood. It is a historical fact, well known to those who have investigated, that at one time there were many African slaves in Portugal. Today there are no true negroes there but their blood shows in the color and racial characteristics of a large part of the Portuguese population of the present day. That mixture, even if it could be shown, would be far from constituting these people white. We are very much afraid that the Judge followed the same course pursued by one of our Virginia judges in hearing a similar case, when he accepted the hearsay evidence of people who testified that they had always understood that the claimants were of Indian origin, regardless of the documentary evidence reaching back in some cases to or near to the Revolutionary War, showing them to be descendants of freed negroes.

We will require other evidence than that of Captain Jarvis and His Honor before classifying members of the group who are now causing trouble in Virginia by their claims of Indian descent, with the privilege of inter-marrying into the white race, permissible when a person can show his racial composition to be one-sixteenth or less Indian, the remainder white with no negro intermixture. We have found after very laborious and painstaking study of records of various sorts

Attachments

that none of our Virginia people now claiming to be Indian are free from negro admixture, and they are, therefore, according to our law classified as colored. In that class we include the melungeons of Tennessee.

We again thank you for your care in passing on this information and would be delighted if you ever visit in Virginia and in Richmond if you will come into our office. Miss Kelley and I would be greatly pleased to talk with you on this and kindred subjects and to show you the work which Miss Kelley is doing in properly classifying the population of Virginia by racial origin. She is doing work which, so far as I know, has never before been attempted.

Very sincerely yours,

W. A. Plecker

State Registrar
Commonwealth of Virginia
Department of Health
Bureau of Vital Statistics
Richmond

January 1943
Local Registrars, Physicians, Health
Officers, Nurses, School Superintendents
and Clerks of the Courts
Dear Co-workers:

Our December 1942 letter to local registrars, also mailed to the clerks, set forth the determined effort to escape from the negro race of groups of "free issues," or descendants of the "free mulattoes" of early days, so listed prior to 1865 in the United States census and various types of State records, as distinguished from slave negroes.

Now that these people are playing up the advantages gained by being permitted to give "Indian" as the race of the child's parents on birth certificates, we see the great mistake made in not stopping earlier the organized propagation of this racial falsehood. They have been using the advantage thus gained as an aid to intermarriage into the white race and to attend white schools, and now for some time, they have been refusing to register with war draft boards as negroes, as required by the boards which are faithfully performing their duties. Three of these negroes from Caroline County were sentenced to prison on January 12 in the United States Court at Richmond for refusing to obey the draft law unless permitted to classify themselves as "Indians".

Some of these mongrels, finding that they have been able to sneak in their birth certificates unchallenged as Indians are now making a rush to register as white. Upon investigation we found that a few local registrars have been permitting

Attachments

such certificates to pass through their hands unquestioned and without warning our office of the fraud. Those attempting this fraud should be warned that they are liable to a penalty of one year in the penitentiary (Section 5099 of the Code). Several clerks have likewise been actually granting them licenses to marry whites, or at least to marry amongst themselves as Indian or white. The danger of this error always confronts the clerk who does not inquire carefully as to the residence of the woman when he does not have positive information. The law is explicit that the license be issued by the clerk of the county or city in which the woman resides.

To aid all of you in determining just which are mixed families, we have made a list of their surnames by counties and cities, as complete as possible at this time. This list should be preserved by all, even by those in counties and cities not included, as these people are moving around over the State and changing race at the new place. A family has just been investigated which was always recorded as negro around Glad Springs, Washington County, but which changed to white and married as such in Roanoke County. This is going on constantly and can be prevented only by care on the part of local registrars, clerks, doctors, health workers, and school authorities.

Please report all known or suspicious cases to the Bureau of Vital Statistics, giving names, ages, parents, and as much other information as possible. All certificates of these people showing "Indian" or "white" are now being rejected and returned to the physician or midwife, but local registrars hereafter must not permit them to pass their hands uncorrected or unchallenged and without a note of warning to us. One hundred and fifty thousand other mulattoes in Virginia are watching eagerly the attempt of their pseudo-Indian brethren, ready to follow in a rush when the first have made a break in the dike.

Very truly yours,

W. A. Plecker, M. D.

State Registrar

of Vital Statistics

(NOTE: This letter is attached to a list of surnames organized by counties and cities; both were typed on a similar, if not identical, typewriter.) this note is from Darlene Wilson, who posted this letter and list.

Attachments

SURNAMES, BY COUNTIES AND CITIES (illegible) VIRGINIA FAMILIES STRIVING TO PASS AS "INDIAN" AND/OR WHITE

Abermarle:

Moon, Powell, Kidd, Pumphrey

Amherst: (Migrants to Allegheny and Campbell) Adcock (Adcox), Beverly (this famiy is now trying to evade the situation by adopting the name of Burch or Birch, which was the name of the white mother of the present adult generation), Branham, Duff, Floyd, Hamilton, Hartless, Hicks, Johns, Lawless, Nuckles (Knuckles), Painter, Ramsey, Redcross, Roberts, Southwards (Suthards, Southerds, Southers), Sorrells, Terry, Tyree, Willis, Clark, Cash, wood.

Bedford:

McVey, Maxey, Branham, Burley (See Amherst County)

Rockbridge:

(Migrants to Augusta) Cash, Clark, Coleman, Duff, Floyed, Hartless, Hicks, Mason, Mayse (Mays), Painters, Pults, Ramsey, Southerds (Southers, Southards, Suthards), Sorrell, Terry, Tyree, Wood, Johns

Charles City:

Redbones of Louisiana

Collins, Dennis, Bradby, Howell, Langston, Stewart, Wynn, Custalow (Custaloo), Dungoe, Holmes, Miles, Page, Allmond, Adams, Hawkes, Spurlock, Dogett

New Kent:
Collins, Bradby, Stewart, Wynn, Adkins, Langston

Henrico and Richmond City:
See Charles City, New Kent, and King William

Caroline:
Byrd, Fortune, Nelson (See Essex)

Essex and King and Queen:
Nelson, Fortune, Byrd, Cooper, Tate, Hammond, Brooks, Boughton, Prince, Mitchell, Robinson

Elizabeth City & Newport News:
Stewart (descendants of Charles City families)

Halifax:
Epps (Eppes), Stewart (Stuart), Coleman, Johnson, Martin, Talley, Sheppard (Shepard), Young

Norfolk County & Portsmouth:
Sawyer, Bass, Weaver, Locklear (Locklair), King, Bright, Porter

Westmoreland:
Sorrells, Worlds (or Worrell), Atwells, Butridge, Okiff

Greene:

Attachments

Shifflett, Shiflet

Prince William:
Tyson, Segar. (See Fauquier)

Fauquier:
Hoffman (Huffman), Riley, Colvin, Phillips. (See Prince William)

Lancaster:
Dorsey (Dawson)

Washington:
Beverly, Barlow, Thomas, Hughes, Lethcoe, Worley

Roanoke County:
Beverly (See Washington)

Lee and Smyth:
Collins, Gibson, (Gipson), Moore, Goins, Ramsey, Delph, Bunch, Freeman, Mise, Barlow, Bolden (Bolin), Mullins, Hawkins. – Chiefly Tennessee "Melungeons."

Scott:
Dingus (See Lee County)

Russell:
Keith, Castell, Stillwell, Meade, Proffitt. (See Lee and Tazewell)

Tazewell:
Hammed, Duncan. (See Russell)
Wise: See Lee, Scott, Smyth, and Russell Counties.

Redbones of Louisiana

VIRGINIA'S ATTEMPT TO A ADJUST THE COLOR PROBLEM*

W. A. Plecker, M. D., FELLOW A.P.H.A.
State Registrar of Vital Statistics, Richmond, Virginia

*Read at the joint session of the Public Health Administration and Vital Statistics Section of the American Public Health Association at the Fifty-third Annual Meeting at Detroit Michigan, October 23, 1924. This copy from the American Journal of Public Health, 1925.

The Settlers of North America came not as did the Spanish and Portuguese adventurers of the southern continent, without their women, bent only on conquest and the gaining of wealth and power; but bringing their families, the Bible, and high ideals of religious and civic freedom.

They came to make homes, to create a nation and to found a civilization of the highest type; not to mix their blood with the savages of the land; not to originate a mongrel population combining the worst traits of both conquerors and conquered. All was well until that fateful day in 1619 when a Dutch trader landed twenty negroes and sold them to the settlers, who hoped by means of slave labor to clear the land and develop the colony more quickly.

Few paused to consider the enormity of the mistake until it was too late. From this small beginning developed the great slave traffic which continued unto 1808, when the importation of slaves into America was stopped. But there were already enough negroes in the land to constitute them the great American problem. Two races as materially divergent as the white and the negro, in morals, mental powers, and cultural fitness, cannot live in close contact without injury to the higher, amounting in many cases to absolute ruin. The lower never has been and never can be raised to the level of the higher.

This statement is not an opinion based on sentiment or prejudice but is an unquestionable scientific fact. Recently published ethnological studies of history lead to this conclusion, as do the psychologic tests of negro and negroid groups, especially the tests made by the United States Army for selective service in the World War. It is evident that in the hybrid mixture the traits of the more primitive will dominate those of the more specialized or civilized race. It is equally obvious that these culturally destructive characteristics are hereditary, carried in the germ plasm, and hence they cannot be influenced by environmental factors such as improve economic, social and educational opportunities. On the contrary, such opportunities often accelerate the inevitable decadence. Dr. A. H. Estabrook in a recent study, made for the Carnegie foundation, of a mixed group in Virginia many of whom are so slightly negroid as to be able to pass for white, says, "School studies and observations of some adults indicate the group as a whole to be of poor mentality, much below the average, probably D or D- on the basis of the army intelligence tests. There is an early adolescence with low moral code, high incidence of licentiousness and 21 percent of illegitimacy in the group."

When two races live together there is but one possible outcome, and that is the amalgamation of the races. The result of this will be the elimination of the higher type, the one on which progress depends. In the mixture the lower race loses its native good qualities which may be utilized and developed in the presence of a dominant race.

The mongrels are superior in mental power to the lower race. They are more cunning and more capable, but they lack the creative power of the higher race and cannot sustain a lasting civilization that will rank with the best of the world.

Attachments

History affords many examples. Egypt in the day of her greatness was white. But the white Pharoahs began to extend their dominion south into the negro land, and to bring back multitudes of captives for laborers and soldiers, special mention being made also in their records that women in large numbers were included. Interbreeding with these negroes began and continued through many centuries until the country became largely negroid.

The climax was finally reached when one of the Pharoahs took to himself a negro wife and his mulatto son Taharka succeeding to the throne. The color line had vanished and with-it Egypt's greatness. Assyrian invaders met with no effective resistance. From that day to this Egypt has been a mongrel nation, incapable of initiative, and now dependent upon foreign protection and leadership.

India affords a parallel example. Four thousand years ago the invasion of India by Aryans occurred. These came into contact with a mixed population of white-yellow-black composition. The conquerors attempted to prevent their own amalgamation with the natives by establishing a rigorous caste system, which was not like the present one based upon occupation, but upon color. This system failed, and though caste is still in force in India the reason for it no longer exists.

Modern South Africa is a melancholy example of what may occur when the intermixture which inevitably results is hastened by fanatical religious teaching and misguided legal interference from the mother country. Major E. S. Cox, who spent years in that region and in other countries studying race conditions, in his book "White America," (White America Society, Richmond, VA) gives a graphic account of the struggle made by the determined colonists against the imposition. They lost out, and the population of Cape Colony province is today largely mixed, showing how quickly this condition results when the natural process is speeded up by negrophilism and the law.

Let us return now to our own country, and, as we are considering Virginia, to that state in particular.

There are about twelve million negroes; of various degrees of admixture in the Union today. Of the population of Virginia, nearly one-third is classed as negro, but many of these people are negroid, some being near-white, some having succeeded in getting across into the white class.

The mixed negroes are nearly all the result of illegitimate intercourse. The well known moral laxity resulting from close contact of a civilized with a primitive race makes illegitimate intermixture an easy matter. This is illustrated by

Attachments

the fact that the illegitimate birth-rate of Virginia negroes is thirty-two times that of Rhode Island, while the District of Columbia rate is thirty-seven times, and that of Maryland forty-six times.

In the days when slavery was still a blight upon our state, it was quite a common occurrence for white men to father children born to the negro servants. The history, as related to me, of at least one colony of people known as "Issue" or "Free Issue," now spread over several counties, is that they originated in part in that manner.

It was considered undesirable to retain these mulattoes on the place, bearing the family name, and a number from one county were given their freedom and colonized in a distant county. These intermarried amongst themselves and with some people of Indian-negro-white descent, and received an additional infusion of white blood, either illegitimately or by actual marriage with low-grade whites.

At present these people are claiming to be white, or Indian, and under the former law when a person with one-sixteenth negro blood could be declared white, they were able in some instances to establish their claim legally.

These mixed breeds are not classed as white by the people of the community, and they will not associate with the genuine negroes. Five hundred or more in number they thus constitute a class of their own, and a serious problem in that county and to others to which they migrate. If refused classification as white they claim to be Indian, and as such have been accepted in the birth reports to avoid listing them as white. In a recent test case, the court upon evidence submitted from our birth records reaching back to 1853, and from the testimony of old residents, decided that these people under the new "Racial Integrity" law cannot be permitted to intermarry with whites.

Another large colony which extends over into North Carolina probably has a similar origin. We have also compromised with these, and accept certificates as Indians, which indicates to us that they are not white.

In another county are about forty descendants of an illegitimate mating of a negro man and white woman four generations back. All of these have formerly succeeded in being classed as white. Though under the new law our office has supplied to the clerks who issue marriage licenses, school authorities, commonwealth's attorneys, physicians and local registrars, a complete family tree, with the injunction to class them as colored.

Attachments

Similar conditions exist in other localities, though not yet so far advanced. A case was recently discovered where a white man married a mulatto woman (probably in another state), and now has nine children, four of them being reported to our office as white. Investigation revealed the fact that two other women bearing the same family name had mated with white men and were raising large families of children.

Another man whose birth was reported in 1878, both parents being registered as colored, had the court declare him a white man under the one-sixteenth law; married a white woman, and has four children reported as white by physicians.

The question of their color was referred to our office by the school authorities when the facts were discovered, and the white school advised under the new law not to receive them, though they engaged a lawyer to assist them.

These examples illustrate the fact that even in Virginia where the questions of race and birth receive as much attention as anywhere in the country, the process of amalgamation is nevertheless going on, and in some localities is well advanced. Complete ruin can probably be held off for several centuries longer, but we have no reason to hope that we shall prove the one and only example in the history of the world of two races living together without amalgamation.

In Mexico, much of South America and the West Indies the process is practically complete, the mixture being Spanish or Portuguese, Indian and negro. Some portions of southern Europe have undergone a similar admixture. Immigrants from these lands to this country, while really negroid, are classed as white.

Several South American countries, or portions of them, still retain a considerable degree of race purity, which is being maintained by European immigration.

The immigration law recently passed by our Congress will stop the legal admission of Mongolians and will check much of the negroid immigration from elsewhere in the old world, but it will not prevent negro and negroid immigration from other parts of the western hemisphere. It is estimated that there are today from 500,000 to 750,000 Mexicans in the state of Texas alone, and that Mexicans compose more than half of the population of Arizona.

We now come to the question of a solution to the problem.

There is but one absolute solution which is acceptable and feasible, and that the one advocated by Lincoln and other far-seeing statesmen of the past – the separation of the races by gradual repatriation of the colored races. This measure is still possible, but the longer it is deferred the greater the task.

In the lifetime of some now living, we may expect the present twelve million colored population to increase to twenty or possibly thirty million, and that perhaps to one hundred millions during the next century, to say nothing of the prolific Mongolians who are already firmly established upon our western coast. With the competition of this large number of people of low ideals and low standards of living, and the great effort to secure the means of maintaining a family up to the desired standard, the white population will to that extent be crowded out.

Virginia has made the first serious attempt to stay or postpone the evil day when this is no longer a white man's country. Her recently enacted law "for the preservation of racial integrity" is, in the words of Major E. S. Cox, "the most perfect expression of the white ideal, and the most important eugenical effort that has been made during the past 4,000 years." Of course, this law will not prevent the illegitimate mixture of the races although a law requiring the father to share with the mother the responsibility of the birth would have a deterring effect. When more than one man is involved, all should be held equally responsible in sharing the cost, as I am informed is the case in Norway.

But it is possible to stop the legal intermixture, and that Virginia has attempted to do so in the above-mentioned law, which defines a white person as one with "no trace whatsoever of blood other than Caucasian," and makes it a felony punishable by confinement for one year in the penitentiary to make a willfully false statement as to color.

Clerks are not permitted to grant licenses for white persons to marry those with any trace of colored blood. It is needless to call attention to the sad plight of a white person who is thus imposed upon or of a white woman who under such circumstance would give birth to a child of marked negro characteristics, as will occur from time to time under Mendel's law.

The new law places upon the office of the Bureau of Vital Statistics much additional work, but we believe it will be a strong factor in preventing the intermarriage of the races and in preventing persons of negro descent from passing themselves off as white.

Attachments

We are greatly encouraged by the interest and cooperation of physicians, local registrars, clerks, school authorities, the general public, and even the midwives. Our success during the first four months of the enforcement of this law, in securing more accurate statements as to color on our birth certificates and in correcting previously existing errors is far beyond our expectation.

The states which now permit free intermarriage of the races, as listed in "American Marriage Laws", (Russell Sage Foundation, New York 1919) are: Connecticut, District of Columbia, Illinois, Iowa, Kansas, Maine, Michigan, Massachusetts, Minnesota, New Hampshire, New Jersey, New Mexico, New York, Ohio, Rhode Island, Pennsylvania, Vermont, Washington, Wisconsin, and Wyoming. The most urgent need is the speedy adoption by these states and the District of Columbia of a law forbidding the intermarriage of the white and colored races.

We are all interested in reducing the death rate from preventable diseases, and of increasing our birth rates. Is that however, the only thought that may occupy the mind of health workers? Is it not of greater importance to the welfare of the state to give some thought to the quality and value of its future citizens than to lavish all of its energies an money upon prolonging the lives and increasing the number of the unfit, who are already increasing far more rapidly in proportion than the more desirable?

The white race in this land is the foundation upon which rests its civilization and is responsible for the leading position which we occupy amongst the nations of the world. Is it not therefore just and right that this race decide for itself what its composition shall be, and attempt, as Virginia has, to maintain its purity?

This is working no hardship and no injustice upon the other races; for the same effort tends at the same time to maintain the purity of their races as well.

That the mongrel races are liable to perpetuate the undesirable qualities of both their constituent stocks is abundantly demonstrated by a study of the larger and older of the mongrel groups in Virginia, as well as upon a study on a far larger scale in various other parts of the world.

The colored races therefore should be equally zealous in preventing both the legal and illegal admixture of the races. We are glad to say that the true negro of Virginia is beginning to appreciate this point and is agreeing to the wisdom of this movement. Our chief trouble is with some of the near-whites who desire to change from the colored to the white class.

By firm adherence to the standard which has been set, we believe that it is possible within a reasonable time to secure through our office an adjustment of the larger number of racial differences, and by constantly securing correction of our vital statistic, and by stopping all further legal and much of the illegitimate intermixture, at least to hold the situation in check until Lincoln's real remedy can be adopted.

This, however, is but the beginning, and our efforts will be of less avail until every state in the Union joins in the move to secure the best marriage laws possible, and a wholesome public sentiment on this the most important of all questions confronting us as a nation.

Four hundred years ago there were nations whose ships sailed the waters of the world and whose armies and navies made England tremble with fear. They claimed continents as their own, they grew rich upon their vast trade in slaves, selling thousands of them in a day from one block.

These slaves have disappeared, not by transportation, but by assimilation. Today families of the old type are rare, and these peoples are scarcely thought of in the councils of nations.

Today the eyes of the world are turned with envy upon us, and millions crave the privilege of landing upon our shores.

We are now engaged in a struggle more titanic, and of far greater importance than that with the Central Powers from which we have recently emerged.

Many scarcely know that the struggle which means the life or death of our civilization is now in progress and are giving it no thought.

What odds will it make in the year 2500 or 3000 to the few Caucasic remnants of our present day – Americans, when they look around upon the half billion or perhaps more brown skinned descendants of the races now occupying our land, whether the typhoid death rate of 1924 was one, or one hundred, per 100,000?

What they will find in that day will depend upon how we of today think and act. The very existence of our race in that time is dependent upon the thought and action of us today. Let us then accept our responsibility and meet its demands with wisdom and courage.

Attachments

[Author's note: Plecker here reflects a belief often expressed in the 1800s that "black blood" was dominant over "white blood"]

Attachment E
List of Surnames from Barbados

In 1997, Brent Kennedy posted on the Internet a list of names of person coming to the United States from Barbados. He commented that:

> "These surnames are virtually a directory of Melungeon surnames and can potentially play a major role in demonstrating how specific English and Scotch-Irish names popped up among the various Melungeon populations. It also reaffirms how the official U.S. census records can be misleading regarding race, ethnicity, and actual origin. These people were all legitimate "English" and "Scotch-Irish" settlers and would have passed this heritage along to their offspring. But ethnically, they were of mixed European, Middle Eastern, Indian, and African origin. One more lesson in the flaws of unquestionably accepting the written census record as "fact."

Many of these names are, of course, also found in the Redbone community. For further information on the people moving from Barbados to America see:

John Camden Hotten. *The original lists of persons of quality, emigrants, religious exiles, political rebels, serving men sold for a term of years, apprentices, children stolen, maidens, pressed, and others, who went from Great Britain to the American plantations, 1600-1700. New York: Empire State Book, Co. [n.d]*

Freedmen

Clark	Weaver
Hall	White
Kennedy	Williams
Phipps	Willis
Reeves	

Portuguese Jews

Atkins	*Miner*
Cole	*Sizemore*
Isham	

Prisoners

Adams	*Dyer*

Attachments

Atkins	*Greene*
Bennett	*Hall*
Collins	*Hill*
Cooke	*Hillman*
Cox	*Lockbeare (Lockleare)*
Crow	*Moore*
Dale	*Mullins*
Denham	*Nash*
Dennis	*Osborn*

Attachment F
Redbone Surnames

This is a tentative list based on years of reading and personal knowledge. Some of these names appear here because they have appeared on lists developed by others. As always, one needs to keep in mind that many of these names are common and a person with one of these names is not necessarily a Redbone – that is a given. For example, just because some Ashworths are Redbones does not mean all Ashworths are Redbones.

Abel	Chavis	Eaves
Ashmore	Clark	Epps

Redbones of Louisiana

Ashworth	Cloud	Faris
Baggett	Cole	Farris
Baham	Coleman	Farrell
Bailey	Collins	Fee
Basco	Cooley	Franks
Bass	Cooper	Free
Bedgood	Creel	Garland
Bennett	Cumba	Gibbes
Berwick	Davis	Gibbs
Bolin	Dowden	Gibson
Boling	Doyal	Gipson
Bolton	Dial	Gill
Boyd	Doyle	Glass
Bunch	Drake	Goins
Buxton	Droddy	Green
Bynog	Dyal	Hall
Capp	Dyer	Harmon
Cain	Dyess	Harper
Carter		
Harvey	Newman	Stanley
Hatch	Nichols	Starnes
Ivey	Orr	Stokes
Jacobs	Owens	Strother
James	Pack	Stukes
Jeane	Paige	Sweat
Jenkins	Page	Swindall
Johnson	Parker	Thompson
Jones	Paugh	Townley
Knight	Paul	Turner
Laird	Peavy	Wagley
Lambright	Pender	Walters
Laurence	Perkins	Weatherford

Attachments

Lard	Perry	Weeks
Legg	Peters	Wells
Lewis	Phelps	West
Lucas	Potts	White
Maddox	Porter	Whitman
Mancil	Powell	Williams
Mansell	Price	Willis
Mathis	Ray	Windham
Maricle	Reeves	Wright
Mathis	Reid	Wisby
Markle	Rivers	Wise
Martin	Roberts	
Mayo	Sandel	
McFatter	Sanderson	
Mishoe	Scott	
Mims	Self	
Monk	Short	
Moore	Smalls	
Morrison	Smith	
Mullens	Spears	
Mullins	Speirs	
Nash		

Attachment G

Cherokee Surnames

Adams	Bowling	Cook	Guin
Akin	Brady	Cooper	Hagan
Allen	Branch	Copeland	Hall
Anderson	Brantley	Cosby*	Harrington
Ashley	Briggs	Couch	Harris

Ashmore	Brooks	Cox	Harrison
Atkins	Bryant	Crawley	Hart
Austin	Bunch	Crowley	Hayes
Ayers	Burgess	Curtis	Haynes
Bailey	Burris	Daughterty	Head
Ballard	Byers	Davis	Hicks
Barclay	Caldwell	Day	Hodges
Barnes	Capps	Dean	Holder
Barnett	Carpenter	Denam	Holt
Barnhart	Carr	Dixon	Hooks
Bates	Carroll	Drake	Hudson
Bayles	Carter	Dyer	Hughes
Bean	Carver	Elliott	Ivy
Beebe	Chastain	Ellis	Jackson
Bell	Cheek	Estes	Jacobs
Bennett	Cherry	Evans	Jarvis
Berry	Christian	Fields	Jeffers
Beverly	Clark	Foster	Johnson
Bird	Cloud	Freeman	
Black	Cody	Galloway	Jones
Boles	Cole	Garrett	Kellar
Boling	Coleman	Gentry	Kennedy
Boswell	Collins	Graham	King
Bowie	Combs	Gregory	Lawrence
Bowles	Coody	Griffin	Lawson
Lee	Perry	Terrell	
Long	Peters	Terry	
Love	Phelps	Thompson	
Lowery	Pope	Thorn	
Martin**	Porter	Trammell	
Massey	Powers	Travis	
Mathes	Prather	Tucker	

Attachments

Mathies	Price	Walker
Mathis	Puckett	Ward
Matthews	Ray	Ware
Mattox	Reed	Waters
May	Reid	Watkins
McDaniel	Rice	Watson
McFarland	Riley	Webb
McKinney	Ritchie	Wells
McNutt	Ritter	West
Merrill	Robinson	White
Miller	Rogers	Whitmire
Moore	Sanders	Williams
Morgan	Scott	Willis
Neal	Sells	Wilson
Nelson	Shaw	Wisner
Newton	Sheppard	Wolf
Nichols	Shirley	Womble
Nugent	Sills	Wood
Nunn	Simpson	Woodward
Osborn	Sizemore	Wright
Owen	Spears	Young
Owens	Stagg	Youngblood
Pace	Starnes	
Parker	Starr	
Parks	Swearingen	
Parsons	Sweat	
Paul	Taylor	

*Comedian, Bill Cosby descended from Henry Parsons, a Cherokee. In Charles White, *Hidden and Forgotten* (Buckingham County Virginia, 1985), as reported by, Horace

R. Rice, *The Buffalo Ridge Cherokee: A Remnant of a Great Nation Divided* (Heritage Books, 1995), p. 77.

**Comedian, Steve Martin descended from Robert Washington Martin, who lived in what is now Vernon Parish, Louisiana and served as a Home Guard Captain in the Civil War. See Don C. Marler, "The Louisiana Redbones", paper presented at First Union, at a meeting of Melungeons at the University of Virginia at Wise, Va., 1997.

Attachment H
List of Names
Of the
Lost Colony of Roanoke

Surnames in italics were among the Croatans in 1891. People representing forty-three percent of these names were found living among the Croatans in 1891.

MEN

Allen, Maurice
Archard, Arnold
Arthur, Richard
Bailey, Roger
Bennett, Mark
Berde, William

Colman, Thomas
Cooper, Christopher
Cotsmur, John
Dare, Ananias
Darige, Richard
Dorrel, Henry

Attachments

Berry, Henry
Berry, Richard
Bishop, Michael
Borden, John
Bridger, John
Bright, John
Brooke, John
Browne, Henry
Browne, William
Burdon, John
Butler, Thomas
Cage, Anthony
Chapman, John
Cheven, John
Clement, William
Hynde, James
Johnson, Henry
Johnson, Nicholas
Jones, Griffin
Jones, John
Kemme, Richard
Lasie, James
Little, Peter
Little, Robert
Lucas, William
Martyn, George
Myllet, Michael
Mylton, Henry
Newton, Humphrey
Nichols, William
Paine, Henry
Pattenson, Hugh

Dutton, Willian
Earnest, John
Ellis, Thomas
English, Edmund
Farre, John
Fernando, Simon
Florrie, Charles
Gibbes, John
Gramme, Thomas
Harris, Thomas
Harris, Thomas
Harvie, Dionys
Hemmington, John
Hewet, Thomas
Howe, George
Tomkins, Richard
Topan, Thomas
Tydway, John
Viccars, Ambrose
Warner, Thomas
Waters, William
White, Cutbert
White, John
Wildye, Richard
Wilkinson, Robert
Willes, William
Wotton, Lewes
Wright, John
Wyles, Bryan
Wyles, John

WOMEN

Phevens, Thomas
Powell, Edward
Prat, Roger
Rufoote, Henry
Sampson, John
Scot, Thomas
Shabedge, Richard
Smith, Thomas
Sole, William
Spendlove, John
Starte, John
Stevens, Thomas
Stilman, John
Sutton, Martin
Taverner, Richard
Tayler, Hugh
Taylor, Clement

Archard, Joyce
Chapman, Alice
Colman _____
Dare, Eleanor
Glane, Elizabeth
Harvie, Margery
Jones, Jane
Lawrence, Margaret
Mannering, Jane
Merimoth, Emma
Payne, Rose
Pierce, Jane
Powell, Winnifred
Tappan, Audry
Viccars, Elizabeth
Warren, Joan
Wood, Agnes

BOYS AND CHILDREN

Archard, Thomas
Ellis, Robert
Howe, George
Humfrey, Thomas
Prat, John

Sampson, John
Smart, Thomas
Viccars, Ambrose
Wythers, William

Source:

Stephen B. Weeks, "The Lost Colony of Roanoke: Its Fate and Survival", Papers of the American Historical Association, Vol. V., New York: Putnam, 1891., pp. 476-77.
This list is as published by Professor Weeks except the last name has been placed first and the list alphabetized.

Attachments

The Lost State of Franklin (also the Free Republic of Franklin or the State of Frankland) was an unrecognized and autonomous territory located in what is today Eastern Tennessee, United States. Franklin was created in 1784 from part of the territory west of the Appalachian Mountains that had been offered by North Carolina as a cession to Congress to help pay off debts related to the American War for Independence. It was founded with the intent of becoming the fourteenth state of the new United States.

Franklin's first capital was Jonesborough. After the summer of 1785, the government of Franklin (which was by then based in Greeneville), ruled as a "parallel government" running alongside (but not harmoniously with) a re-established North Carolina bureaucracy. Franklin was never admitted into the union. The extra-legal state existed for only about four and a half years, ostensibly as a republic, after which North Carolina re-assumed full control of the area.
— Benjamin Franklin, Letter to Governor John Sevier, 1787[8]

On May 16, 1785, a delegation submitted a petition for statehood to Congress. Eventually, seven states voted to admit what would have been the 14th federal state under the proposed name of Frankland. This was, however, less than the two-thirds majority required under the Articles of Confederation to add additional states to the confederation. The following month, the Franklin government convened to address their options and to replace the vacancy at Speaker of the House, to which position they elected Joseph Hardin. In an attempt to curry favor for their cause, delegation leaders changed the "official" name of the area to Franklin (ostensibly after Benjamin Franklin). Sevier even tried to persuade Franklin to support their cause by letter, but he declined, writing. Associated Documents, Watauga Petition Signers, Settlers of Watauga, attachment J. December 1787. 1792 census Franklin Co., TN for remnants of Redbones remaining in the Lost State of Franklin included here Attachment I.

Attachment I
1792 Franklin Co., TN List of Taxables
"The Lost State of Franklin"

List of the taxable property of Alex Andrew Greers Company in the year 1792

Name, Land, Pole

Jacob Hendrick, 300, 1
J Michael Smith Peters, 750, 1
Thomas Duncan son, , 1
Aleson Greer, , 1
Christan Shoults Joner (Jr.), , 1
Jeremiah Bass, ,9

Attachments

Jacob Hendrick, Jr., , 1
Valentines Sevier, Jr., ? , 1
Richard Cox, ,1
Joseph Brown, ,1
John Arnold, , 1
Thomas Greers, , 1
Robt Johnston, , 1
John Carter, , 3
Charles Burden, ,1
Jarret Burden, 100,1
Solomon Holbert, 233, 1
Elisha Humphreys, 125,1
John Parker Moore, , 1
Christian Shooths, Sr., ,1
Gutradge Garland, 130, 1
Godfrey Carriger,Sr. , 2727, 1
Nicholes Carriger, 500,0
Michael Carriger, 500, 1
Michael Carriger, , 1
Landon Carter, 2930, 6
William Driggar, 200, 1
James Ivy, 100, 1
Leonard Bowers, 20, 1
Peter Nasie? (Nash), 150,1
Abraham Nasie ? (Nash), , 1
Abraham Sevier, 100, 1

Joseph Sevier, , 2
Valentine Sevier, Sr., 350,
Pharo Cobb, 1000, 10
Joseph Large, , 1
John Kerr, , 1
Isaac Tipton, , 1
Thomas Tipton, 550, 1
John Garlands, 200, 1
Steven Redmond, , 1
John Worley, 100,1
John Nowland, , 1
Ephraim Murry, ,1
Isaac Kite, 200,2
Joseph Greer, 400, 3
Christopher Peters, , 1
Isaac Lincoln, 350, 1
John Gillum, , 1
James Wright, , 1
Abraham Helton, ,1
Michael Dary, ,1
Arnold Helton, ,1
John Musgrove, ,1
Humphrey Garland, , 1
John Robison, 50,1
Christian Stover, ,1
Jame sMilsap, 100, 1
Andrew Greer, Sr., 2150, 4
Robert Hooker, , 1

A List of Taxable Property taken by Richard White for the year, 1792.
Name, Land, Free poles, Slaves

Samuel Yates, , 1, 0
James Milsaps, , 1, 0
James Simerly (Smilie), 200, 1,0
George Water (written in later, Walters), , 1, 0
John Wilson, Sr. 60, 1, 1
David Waggoner, 572, 1, 3
Joseph Gentry, 110 1, 0
William Wilson, 0, 1, 0
John Wilson, 70, 1, 0
William Cook, 0, 1, 0
Mathew Waggoner, 0, 1,2
Lewis Jones, Senr. "Over age", 100, 0, 0
Adam Snider, 115, 1, 0
Champness Guinn (Goyens Clan), 0, 1, 0
James Guinn "over age", 250, 0, 0
Joseph Ford, 375, 1, 1
Euina Heatherly "over age", 95, 0, 0
George Perkins, 200, 1, 0
Mathew Lindsat "over age", 176, 0, 0
Joab Wilder "over age", 50, 0, 0
William Baker, 0, 1, 0
Aaron Wallace, 0, 1, 0
John Ashurst (Ashworth ?), 100, 1, 0
Aaron Wallace, 0, 1, 0
James Graves 0, 1, 0
Samuel Wilson, 225, 1, 0
Peter Snider, 132, 1, 0
Peter Kane, 0, 1, 0
Edward Smith "over age", 600, 0, 0

Note: 2 pages of Richard White's List misplaced, not copied here-see original.

Attachments

Attachment J

Watauga Petition Signers

Petition of the Inhabitants of the Western Country. In Senate, December, 1787. Read and referred to Court on Public Bills. (N. C. St. Rec., XXII, 705-714.)

John Corson	John Jameson
Benja. Gist	David Gewel
Henry Brumley	John Galbreath
James English	Dan'l Rawlings
Thos. Bromley	Thomas Bell
Simon Ridgs	(Illegible)
William Hannah	William Jinkins
Hugh Beard	Thomas Rodgers
Joseph Donn	James Watson
Peter McNamee	Robert Smith
Samuel Beard	Anthony Kelly
Allen Bellew	(Illegible)
James Shanks	Wm. Howard
James Millikin	Thos. McMackin
Rows Potter	William Goings
David Robinson	Joshua Tadlock
Robert Orr	George Davies
John Norton	James Hays
Robert Allison	Robert Hayes
Searling Bowman	Nathaniel Davies
Aaron Norton	David Carr
Isaac Davis	Thomas Johnson
Rich'd Woods	Samuel Davies
Aaron Rider	Joseph Garrison
James Mitchell	Francis Johnson
Robert McCall	John Lowe

William Gillehan
Joseph Wilson
Stephen Strong
Js. x Huston
David Brown
Michael Rawlings
William Brown
Donnell Cremor
Jas. Henry
Nath. McMeno.
John x Huston
Alexr. Potter
William La- (?)
William Reynolds
(Illegible)
Lanry Armstrong
David Reynolds
Wm. Morrow
William Hennidge
Aaron Been
Charles Ramsey
John Armstrong
William Wilson
(Illegible)
Andrew English
Thos. Thomson
John R. (?)
Nathaniel Hayes
David Rankin
Peter Nowels
Daniel Leming
John Lee
James Millikan
John Williams
Sam'l Vance
Thomas Millikan his
Rd. Kerr
Thomas Dicson
Robert x Miller
Samuel McPherson
Redman McDaniel
Matthew Rue
Nathaniel Witt
(Illegible)
Joseph Lusk
Rich'd Dunn
Andrew Jackson
Wm. Dunn
William x Rust
Jos. Gest
Thomas Call mark
Jos. Newberry
Joseph Blair
H. Call
Wm. Magill
Thomas Williams
Joseph N. Newport
Oton Clark
Henry Styers
Wm. W. Newport
John Gibson
John Greer
Reuben Gibson
Thomas x Tadlock

Attachments

Absolem Greer
William Adkins
Thomas Springer
Thomas Fryar
William McPick
Levy Springer
John Lyon
Botholmu Odeneal
Thomas Wolfe
William Brownin
Conrod Wolfe
Rich'd Wood
Shadrack x Hale, Jr.
Philip Suibb
James Pickins
Henry Easter
Robert Bettey
Daniel Denny, Jr.
William Eatster
George Black
John Wear
Simeon Craine
Reuben Riggs
Ashael Rawlings
Harmon Nowel
George Hayes
Henry Earnest
James Patton
William Hill
James Patterson
Robert Patton
Henry Richardson

Francis Hughes
John Fout
Shiffell Goodlop
Robert Hood
Peter Fout
John Shane
Harman Kennedy
Miller Doget
Wm. x Francis
Moses Long
Christy Miers
Coonnas Miller
John Miers
Thomas McKee
William Owins
Patrick x Kirkpatrick
And. Wray
Thomas Owins mark
Wm. Wood
John Jarrett
John Tadlock
Gordon Potter
Thomas Pickny
James Davis
Wm. Peck
James Stump
Benn Brumley
Thomas Mosely
Leonard Hopkins
Mary Webster (?)
Henry Mosely
Martha Gahee

George Kirkpatrick
Philip Rudolph
Patrick Gahee
Thomas Jones
Wm. Stubblefield
Jeremiah Smith
William Jones
Thomas Baits
Robert Sample
Reuben Simmon
John Keller
Anthony Moore
Archibel Alexander
Moses Keller
James McCammis
Moses Kelsay
William Fergosen
Thomas McCammis
Robert McCall
Adam Fergosen
William McCammis
Joseph Alexander
Ralph Hogan
Adam McCammis
Wm. Cocke
William Hogan
Henry H. Hammer
Archibald Roan
Richard Webb
Franses Castel
Elias Witt
Josiah Epperson

Jacob Meek
Thomas Witt
Humph'y Montgomery
Thomas Miller
Alex. Lowry
Carmack George
Robert Pain
Jno. McClelland
Charles Wilson
Joseph Hamilton
Solomon Reed
John Johnston
Robert Kerr
Uriah McClellennon
Samuel Gilbertson
John Sellars
James Stinson
Samuel McMinn
Wm. Moore
Alexander Street
Auborn'" (?)
Joseph Ray
James McPherson
Anson Rit
John Prim
Nuness Potter
Thomas x Baley
Jacob Smelser
John Noman (?)
Joshua Kidwell
Peter Nuless
Moses Moore

Attachments

Samuel Jameson
James W. Begses (?)
Joseph Lachlen, Sen.
John Brumley
Dalton Ridgs
Joseph Lachlen, Jur.

William Davidson
James Jack
Edward Crunt (?)
Wm. Boyd
John Adkins
James Crunt

The following names are taken from the back of the petition:

Nicholas Hayes
Alexander Cavitt
Forrester Mercer
Sam'l Hayes
Moses Cavitt
Bryce Russell, Sen.
Jno. Mitchell
Jacob Jobe
Bryce Russell, Jr.
James Hammer Henry
Nathan Jobe
James Pickens
Hokimer Geo. Martin
Joseph Birdwell
Phil. Grafford Pierce
David Moore
Geo. Birdwell
William Gewil
Henry Winterberger
James Smith
Charles Parker
Jos. Winterberger
Moses Russel
Antony Agee
Saml Winterberger
Conrad Shepley

John Sawyer
Joseph Lusk
John Comin
Joseph Moore
Thos. Wood
Walker Barren
John Yancy
Joseph Gest
John Bell
Richard Shipley
William Gest
William Carson
W. Cage
Joshua Kidwell
Robert Christian
Timothy Huff
Thomas Davie
Abraham Tittsworth
George Christian
John Kidwell
Benjamin Walb'" (?)
Deness Murfee
Charles Kidwell
Green Chote
Isaac Thomas
Whaley Newby

John Goad, Jun.
William Massengill
Craven Dunear
George Vincent
John Tulley
Alexr. Lowrey
Henry Heckey
Thos. Easterlin
James Stinson
Owen Atkin
William Copeland
Adam Guthrey
Nicholas Mercer
Rich'd Gamon
Wm. Craige
Richard Mercer, Sen.
John Spurgin
Benjamen Henslee
Arch'd McHaughan
Thos. King
Abel Morgan
Edward Mercer
Roger Gibson
Thomas Vincent
John Black
James Adam
Jno. Chester
John Hunt, Jr.
Geo. Gabriel (black)
Patrick Morrison
Basset Hunt
John Yokley
Stephen Easley
Reuben Hunt
John Woolsey
Jackal Light
Thomas Tipton

James Arbutton (?)
Robert Easley
Jonathan Hunt
Martin Roller, Jr.
Henry Sullivan
James Cooper Isaiah
Joseph Blair
John Light
Waldrew Lewis
Hunt
David Arwin
William (?)
Moses Robinson
James Smart
Thos. Taylor
Adam Stoaks
William Light
James Smith
Joseph Waldrep
William Light, Sen.
Joseph Smith
Mattw. Caruthers
Thomas Easley
John Duncan
Gilbert Christian
William Goad
Wm. Berry
John Pryor
Jesey Holland
Isaac White
Moses Looney
James Walb'" (?)
Samuel Cox
Macajah Adams
William Wilson
James Wheeler
James McLern

Attachments

Moses Kennedy	David Taylor
John Cottrell	John A. Caft
Alexander Caright	Peter Fin
Hermon King	Benj a. Gist
Hugh Gentry	D. Wright
Benj. Burdwell	John Hunt
Joseph Screat	Joseph Huson
Valentine Rose	Adam Stake
John Dean	William Bailey
Lewis Tadlock	Mikill Borders
Eli Shipley	William Shewmaker
William Holland	George Smith
Thomas Tadlock	Alx. Pethrow
Thomas Shipley	Gabriel Goad
William Morroson	Jacob Joab
Joshuaway Padfield	Oystan Hewtower
William Childress	Peter Easley
John Morroson	William Cooper
Joshway Hampton	Wm. Davies
James Morroson	Jacob Cox
Thomas x Bennet	Wm. Jackson
Christurphur Cross	John Noris
Samuel Bofman	William Bucknell
Benjamin Aze	Ephraim Joab
David Merryon	Robert Hayes
Moses Kelsay	Haley Bucknell
Reuben Hunt	William Mehallm
Richard Morell	James Hayes
John Anderson	Preley Bucknell
Ellecander Moore	Charles Bacon
Dudley Rutherford	William Sippard
James Richardson	Shadrick Haile
Martin Roller	John French
John Bradford	

ATTACHMENT L

Catawba Indian Reservation, straddling the North and South Carolina Boarder.[371] Ceded to South Carolina in 1771 in exchange for 11-mile strip East of Catawba River.

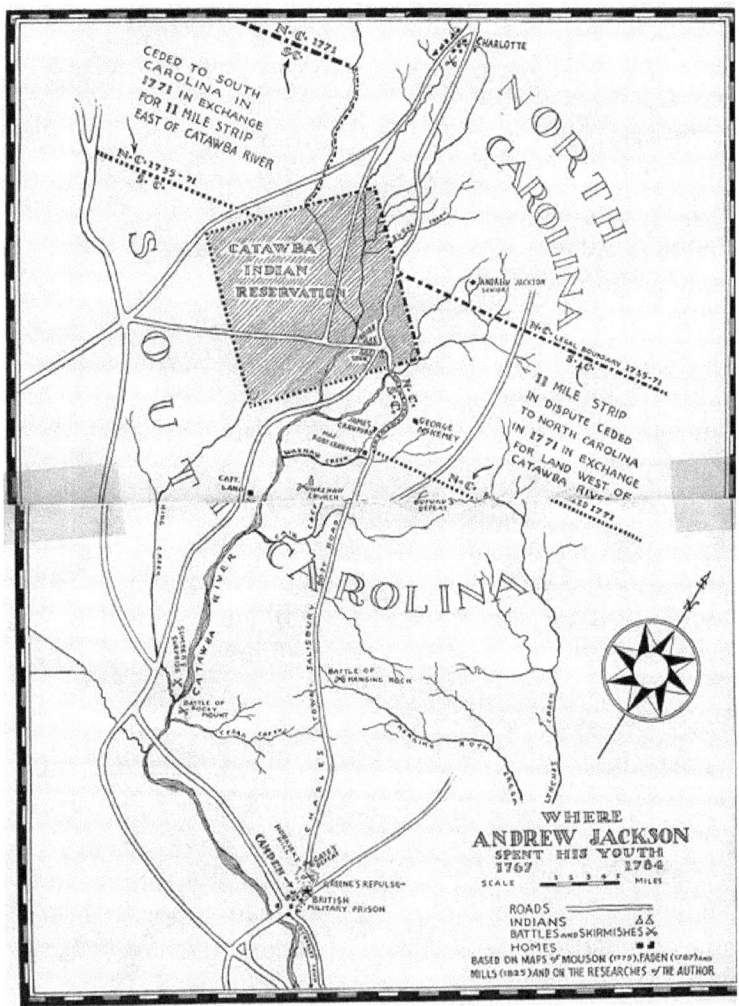

[371] Map Title "Where Andrew Jackson Spent His Youth 1767-.1784

Genetic Studies

ATTACHMENTS M

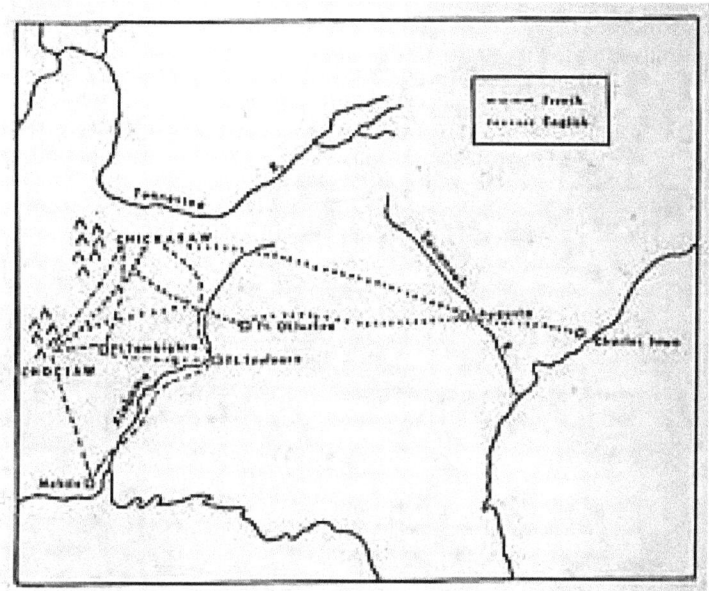

English and French Fur Trade Map

Migration Map of Perkins and Sherrill Families through the Shenandoah Valley and along the Blue Ridge Mountains Welsh Settlement to the Catawba River. The Sherrill's were descendants of the famous "Shipwreck Sherrill" and William the Conestoga Wagon Maker.

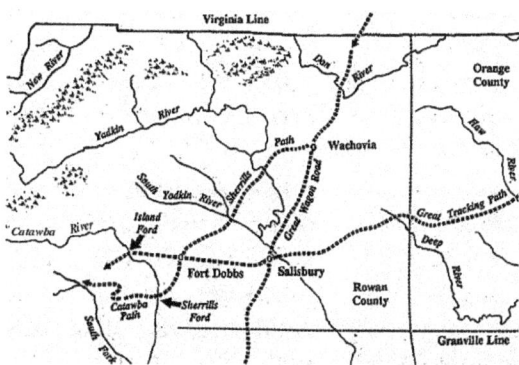

Redbones of Louisiana

Settlement Routes & Extensions, Island Ford Road, Sherrill's Path ca. 1747 to Sherrill's Ford Catawba River and further to Gastonia, Georgia Road ca. 1750 to Charlotte, Mecklenburg Co., 1762

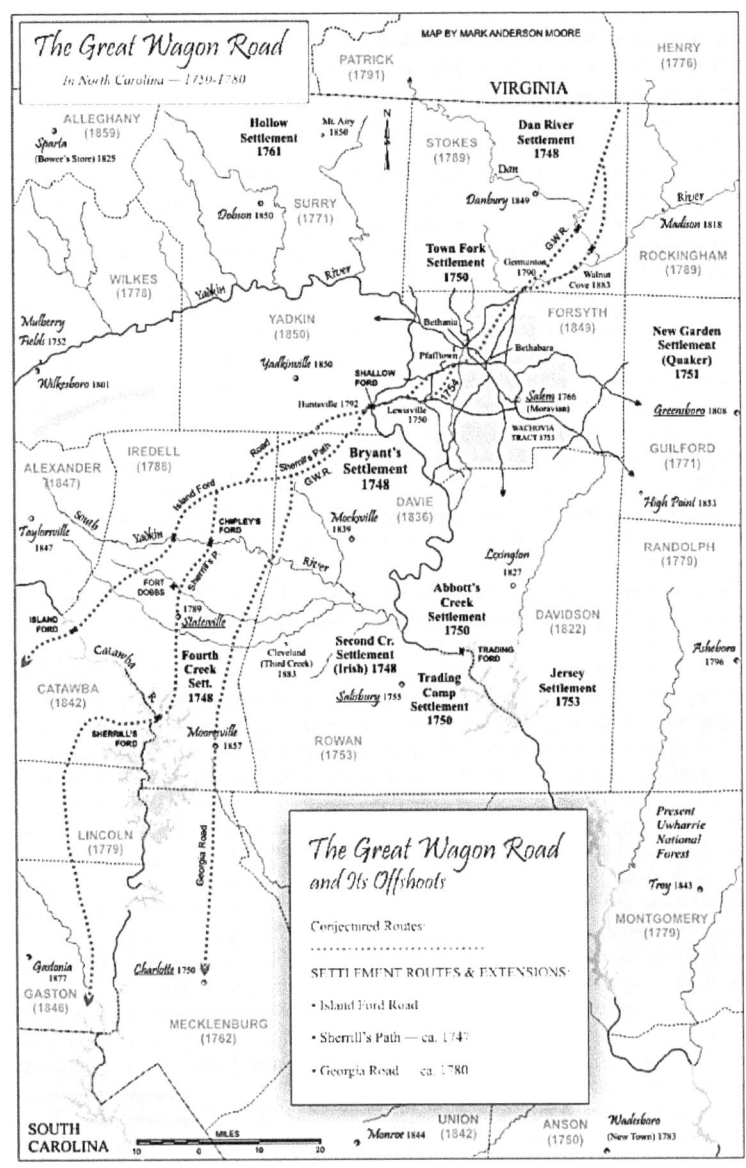

Genetic Studies

Attachment N

Handwritten Note from Enis Goyens Clan, son of Wm T. & Deliah Nash/Ash Goyens Clan

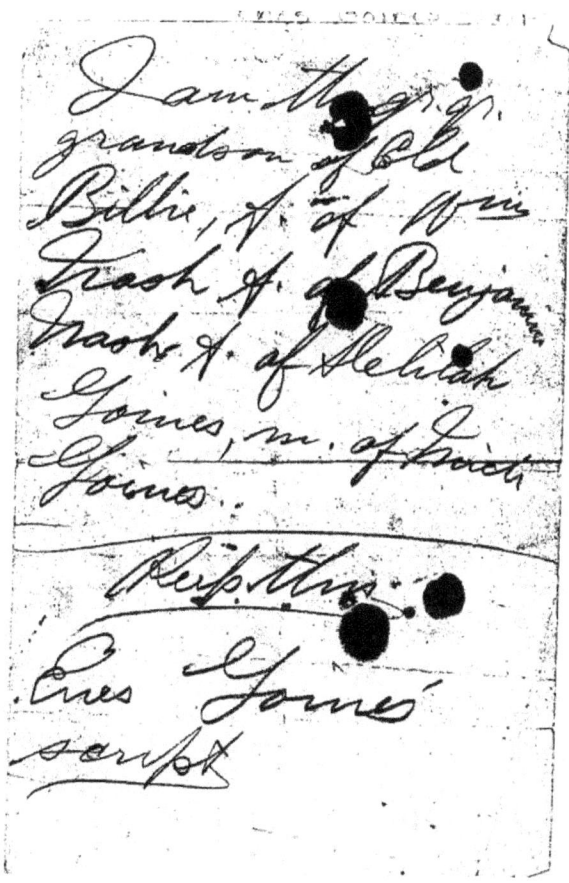

"I am the gr.gr.grandson of Old Billie, & of Wm. Nash & of Benjamin Nash & of Delilah [Nash/Ash] Goins (Goyens Clan) Keep this Enis Goins script." William T. & Delilah Nash/Ash Goyens named all 13 of their sons, William something. We follow the YDNA family of these Goyens Clan males more closely on the upcoming Goins Book II. Courtesy Marilyn Baggett Kobliaka.

18th century copy of an ancient Turkish Map naming Indian Tribes down the East Coast and all across the United States to West of the Mississippi. The original map is lost and only a few tribal names have been translated, most are illegible. We hope by publishing a copy here to encourage further study into the details and transcription of this map.

BIBLIOGRAPHY

Books and Published Articles

Ball, Bonnie. *The Melungeons: Their Origin and Kin*, 8th edition, 1984. No other publication data given.

Ball, Bonnie. *The Melungeons: Notes on the Origin of a Race*. Johnson City: The Overmountain Press, 1992. This is a revision of the above listed book by Ball.

Ball, Edward. *Slaves in the Family*. New York: Farrer, Straus and Giroux, 1998.

Barnett, Richard D. "Polydactylism in the Ancient World." *Biblical Archaeology Review*, Volume 16, Number 3, May/June 1990, pp. 46-51.

Beers, Henry Putney. *French and Spanish Records of Louisiana: A Bibliographical Guide to Archie and Manuscript Sources*. Baton Rouge: LSU Press, 1989.

Bergeron, Arthur W. Jr. Dennis Haynes and His "Thrilling Narrative of the Sufferings of...the Martyrs of Liberty of Western Louisiana", *Louisiana History* Vol. XXXVIII, No. 1 1997, pp. 29-42.

Berry, Brewton. *Almost White: A Study of Certain Racial Hybrids in the Eastern United States*. New York: Macmillan, 1963.

Bertrand, Alvin L. *The Many Louisianas*: Bulletin No. 496 Louisiana State University, June 1955., pp. 27-28.

Boddie, William Willis. *Marion's Men*. Heisser Printing Co., 1938.

Boland, Charles Michael. *They All Discovered America*. New York: Doubleday, 1961.

Bridenbaugh, Carl and Roberta. *No Peace Beyond the Line: The English in the Caribbean, 1624-1690*.

Briley, Richard, III. *Nightriders: Inside Story of the West and Kimbrell Clan*. Hemphill: Dogwood Press, 1998.

Brooks, Richard D., Groover, Mark D., and Smith, Samuel C. *Living on the Edge: The Archaeology of Cattle Raisers in the South Carolina Backcountry.* Occasional Paper of the Savannah River Archaeological Research Program, South Carolina Institute of Archaeology and Anthropology, University of South Carolina, paper number 10.

Brown, Sharon Sholars. *Four Generations of the Marino Basquez Family.* Jonesboro, La., 1983.

Brues, A. *People and Races.* New York: McMillan, 1997.

Bynum, Victoria E. *The Free State of Jones: Mississippi's Longest Civil War.* Chapel Hill: University of North Carolina Press, 2001.

Callahan, Jim. *Let We Forget.* Johnson City: The Overmountain Press, 2000.

Cambiarie, Celestin Pierre, Ph.D. *Western Virginia Mountain Ballads, The Last Stand of American Pioneer Civilization.* London: The Mitre Press, 1935.

Carmer, Carl. *Stars Fell on Alabama.* New York: Farrar and Rinehart, 1934.

Carver, Ada Jack. "The Redbone", Harper's Magazine, CL (Feb. 1925), 257-70.

Channing, Edward. *History of the United States.*

Cohen, Felix. *Handbook of the Federal Indian Law.* Washington: Government Printing Office, 1942.

Conrad, Glenn R. *A Dictionary of Louisiana Biography.* Vols 1&2. New Orleans, Louisiana Historical Association, 1988.

Council Journal, No. 21, p., March 3rd, 1753, S.C. Archives.

Coventon, James W. *The Seminoles of Florida.* Gainsville: University of Florida Press, 1993).

Crane, Verner W. "A Lost Utopia of the First American Frontier," (*The Sewanee Review Quarterly*, Jan-Mar, 1919, pp. 48-61.

Cupit, John. *A Brief History of Vernon Parish.* Typescript-no date.

Davidson, James N. *Newllano: History of the Llano Movement*, Woodville: Dogwood Press, 1994.

Bibliography

Deacon, Richard. *Madoc and the Discovery of America.* New York: George Braziller, 1966.

DeMarce, Virginia E. "Very Slitly Mixt" Tri-Racial Isolates of the Upper South – A Genealogical Study" *National Genealogy Society Quarterly* Vol. 80 No. 1 March 1992, pp. 5-35.

DeMarce, Virginia Easley. "Review Essay: The Melungeons" *National Genealogical Society Quarterly*, Vol. 84, No. 2, June, 1996, pp. 134-149.

Deville, Winston. *Rapides Post on Red River: Census and Military Documents for Central Louisiana, 1769-1800.* Ville Platte: Provincial Press, 1985.

Dial, Adolph L. *The Only Land I Know: A History of the Lumbee Indians.* San Francisco: The Indian Historian Press, 1975.

Douglas Frederick "The Future of the Colored Race." *North American Review*, 142 (May 1886): 437-40.

Du Bois, W.E.B. *Black Reconstruction in America.* New York: Russell and Russell, 1935.

Dugger, Shepherd M. *The War Trials of the Blue Ridge.* Banner Elk: Puddingstone Press, 1932 reprinted 1974.

Dulles, Foster R. *Labor in America, A History.*

Drake, Samuel G. *Book of the Indians.* Boston: Antiquarian Bookstore, 1832, reprinted by AMS Press, 1976.

Eakin, Sue. *Solomon Northrup's Twelve Years a Slave – 1841-1853.* (Rewritten by Sue Eakin) Bossier City: Everett Co, 1990.

Ehile, John. *Trail of Tears: The Rise and Fall of the Cherokee Nation.* New York: Random House, 1989.

Ericson, Carolyn. *Natchitoches Neighbors in the Neutral Strip*, Nacogdoches: Ericson Books, 1993.

Etienne-Gray, Trace "Black Seminole Indians" *The New Handbook of Texas.* Austin: The Texas State Historical Association, 1996, Vol. 1, p. 571.

Evans, W. McKee. *To Die Game.* Nashville: Parthenon Press, 1971.

Everett, Dianna, *The Texas Cherokees: A People Between Two Fires, 1819-1840*. Norman: University of Oklahoma Press, 1990.

Elder, Pat Spurlock Melungeons: *Examining An Appalachian Legend*. Blountville: Continuity Press, 1999.

Farley, Gloria. *In Plain Sight: Old World Records in Ancient America*. Columbus: ISAC Press, 1994.

Fell, Barry. "Christian Messages in Old Irish Script Deciphered from Rock Carvings in W. Va." *Wonderful West Virginia* (Charleston: State of West Virginia Department of Natural Resources, March 1983, pp. 12-19.

Fernandez, Carlos A. "La Raza and the Melting Pot: A Comparative Look at Multiplicity" in Maria P.P. Root, Editor, *Racially Mixed People in America*. Newbury Park: Sage Publications, 1992, p. 128-29.

First Settlers of the Louisiana Territory: Orleans Territory Grants From American State Papers, Class VIII, Public Lands. Vol. I. Nacogdoches: Ericson Books, 1983.

First Settlers of the Louisiana Territory: Orleans Territory Grants From American State Papers, Class VIII, Public Lands, Vol. II. Nacogdoches: Ericson Books, 1983.

Fletcher, Mary Dell. *The Collect Works of Ada Jack Carver*. Natchitoches: Northwestern State University, 1980.

Forbes, Jack D. *Africans and Native Americans: The Language of Race and the Evolution of Red-Black Peoples*. Urbana: University of Illinois Press, 1993.

Furman, McDonald. "The Privateer Redbones". *The Watchman* and *Southron*, May 27, 1896.

Furman, McDonald. "Old Issues vs Redbones" A letter to the Editor of *The State* in longhand. It is item #46 in the Furman collection in the South Caroliniana Library. The letter was published in *The State* on July 16, 1896.

Furman, McDonald. "Old Issue" *The Register*, May 9, 1998. Located in the South Caroliniana Library. Charles James

Bibliography

McDonald Furman Papers, South Caroliniana Library, The University of South Carolina.

Furman, McDonald. "Old Issues" *The Register* May 9, 1898. Located in the Furman Collection in the South Caroliniana Library.

Furman, McDonald. "Certificate" Correspondent *Charleston News & Courier & Columbia State*, March 3, 1902. Handwritten copy in The South Caronliniana Library-Furman Collection.

Gallagher, Ida Jane. "Light Dawns on West Virginia History" *Wonderful West Virginia* (Charleston: State of West Virginia Department of Natural Resources, March 1983), pp. 7-11.

Gallegos, Eloy. *The Spanish Pioneers in United States History: Santa Elena*. Knoxville: Villagra Press, 1998.

Gallegos, Eloy. *The Spanish Pioneers in United States History: The Melungeons*. Knoxville: Villagra Press, 1997.

Gammel, H.P.N. *The Laws of Texas 1822-1987*. (10 Vols. Austin: 1898, I).

Gerson, Noel B., *The Swamp Fox, Francis Marion*. New York: Doubleday, 1967.

Gilbert, William. Harlan, Jr., *Surviving Indian Groups of the Eastern United States*. Publication No. 3974, U.S. Printing Office, 1949.

Gilbert, William. Harlan, Jr., "Memorandum Concerning the Characteristics of the Larger Mixed-Blood Racial Islands of the Eastern United States, *Social Forces*, May 1946, pp. 438-447.

Gillis, Charles F. "Early Starks History and the Logging Camps. *No Man's Land*. Starks: Starks Historical Society, Publishers, Vol. I No. 1, March, 1993., pp. 25-27.

Goins, Jack. *Melungeons: And other Pioneer Families*. No Publisher Listed, 2000.

Gordon, Cyrus H. *Before Columbus*. New York: Crown, 1971.

Grant, Bruce *Concise Encyclopedia of the American Indian*. New York: Random House, 1994.

Greene, Glen Lee. *House Upon A Rock*. Alexandria: The Parthenon Press, 1973.

Groneman, Bill. *Alamo Defenders: A Genealogy*. Austin: Eakin Press, 1990.

Griffin, John Howard. *Black Like Me*. Boston: Houghton Mifflin, Co., 1960.

Hall, Gwendolyn Midlo. *Africans in Colonial Louisiana: The Development of Afro-Creole Culture in the Eighteenth Century*. Baton Rouge: LSU Press, 1992.

Hancock, Ian. *The Pariah Syndrome*. Partin Web Journal edition, 1999.

Handlin, Oscar and Mary F. "Origins of the Southern Labor System", *William and Mary Quarterly*, April 1950.

Heinegg, Paul. *Free African Americans of North Carolina, Virginia, and South Carolina: From the Colonial Period to About 1820*. 4th Edition Genealogical Baltimore: Publishing Col, 2001.

Hickey, Donald R. *The War of 1812: A Forgotten Conflict*. Chicago: University of Illinois Press, 1989.

Hodes, Martha. *White Women, Black Men: Illicit Sex in the 19th-century South*. New Haven: Yale University Press, 1997.

Hoffman, Michael A. *They were White and They Were Slaves*. Coeur d'Alene: Independent History & Research Co., 1991.

Hollandsworth, Skip "The Curse of Romeo and Juliet", *Texas Monthly*, Vol. 25, No. 6, 1997, pp. 82-112.

Hook, Jonathan B. *The Alabama Coushatta Indians*. College Station: Texas A&M Press, 1997.

Hopkins, Harry, *Fortune Magazine*, July, 1935.

House of Representatives Journals 1789-1790. Part Two, pages 92-93, 107, S.C. Archives. January 20th, 1790.

Hudson, Charles. *The Juan Pardo Expeditions*. Washington: Smithsonian Institution, 1990.

Bibliography

Huyghe, Patrick. *Columbus Was Last*. New York: Hyperion, 1962.

Jacobs, Curtis. "The Early History of the Starks Area", *No Man's Land*. Starks: Starks Historical Society, Publishers, Vol. I, No: I, March, 1993. pp. 28-30.

Jameson, W.C. *Buried Treasures of the Ozarks and the Appalachians*. New York: Promontory Press, 1993.

Johnson, James A. "Starks", *No Man's Land*. Starks: Starks Historical Society, Publishers, Vol. I, No: I, March, 1993. pp. 17-23.

Johnson, Tommy G. *From the Chattahoochee to the Calcasieu: The Story of Charles Lewis and His Wife, Nancy Riley 1836-1880*. Natchitoches: Private Printing, 1997.

Johnson, Tommy G. *They Came West*. Natchitoches: Private Printing, 1996.

Josephy, Alvin M., Jr. *The Indian Heritage of America*. Boston: Houghton Mifflin, 1968.

Kadlecek, Mabel R. and Bullard, Marion C *Louisiana's Kisatchie Hills: History Tradition and Folklore*. Alexandria: 1994.

Katz, Willilam Loren. *Black Indians: A Hidden Heritage*. Antheneum: Macmillan Publishing Co., 1986.

Kennedy, N. Brent and Kennedy, Robyn Vaughn. *The Melungeons: The Resurrection of a Proud People*. Macon: Mercer University Press, 1994, Revised 1997.

Kevles, Daniel J. *In the Name of Eugenics: Genetics and the Uses of Human Heredity*. New York: Alfred A. Knoph, Inc., 1986.

Kindall, Elaine. *Los Angeles Times*. September 1, 1985.

King, J. C. *The Biology of Race*. Berkeley: University of California Press, 1981.

Klevan, Miriam. *The West Indian Americans*. New York: Chelsea House Publishers, 1990.

Kniffen, Fred B., Gregory, Hiram F., and Stokes, George A. *The Historic Indian Tribes of Louisiana*. Baton Rouge: LSU Press, 1987.

Knight, Ethel. *The Echo of the Black Horn*. No publisher listed, 1951.

Kupperman, Karen Ordabl. *Roanoke: The Abandoned Colony*. Savage, Md.: Bowman & Littlefield, 1984.

Kurlansky, Mark. *The Basque History of the World*. Toronto: Knoff, Canada, 1999.

Langdon, Barbara. *The Melungeons: An Annotated Bibliography: References in Both Fiction and Nonfiction*. Hemphill, Tx: Dogwood Press, 1998.

Laubey, Almon Wheeler. *Indian Slavery in Colonial Times Within the Present Limits of the United States*. Williamstown: Corner House Publications, 1913.

Leyburn, James G. *The Scotch-Irish: A Social History*, Chapel Hill: University of North Carolina Press, 1962.

Leaming, Hugo P. "The Ben Ishmael Tribe: A Fugitive "Nation" of the Old Northwest" in *Gone To Croatan: Origins of North American Dropout Culture*, Eds. Sakolsky, Ron and Koehnline, James, New York: Autonomedia, 1993.

Lindahl, Carl, Owens, Maida, and Harvison, C. Renée. Editors. *Swapping Stories: Folktales From Louisiana*. Jackson: University Press of Mississippi, 1997.

Lipscomb, Terry. "The McDonald Furman Papers, 1889-1903". *USCS Newsletter*, Spring 1997.

Lockett, Samuel H., (Post, Lauren C., Editor), *Louisiana As It Is*. Baton Rouge: L.S.U. Press, 1969.

Marler, Don C. *Historic Hineston*, Second Edition, Hemphill, Tx: Dogwood Press, 2001.

Marler, Don C. and McManus, Jane, Editors. *The Cherry Winche Country*, Hemphill, Texas: Dogwood Press, 1993.

Marler, Don C. *The Neutral Zone: Backdoor to the United States*, Hemphill: Dogwood Press, 1995.

Matte, Jacqueline A., *They Say the Wind is Red: The Alabama Choctaw, Lost in Their Own Land*. Montgomery: New South Books, 2002.

Bibliography

Mayo, Karl and Doris. *The Henry Jeter Family*. Leesville: No publication data.

McCrary, Mary Jane. *Transylvania Beginnings: A History*. Easley, S.C.: Southern Historical Press, Inc., 1984.

McDowell, Bart. *Gypsies: Wanderers of the World*. Washington, DC: National Geographic Society, 1970.

McElligott, Carroll Ainsworth *Residents of the Natchez District: 1784*. Harleyville, S.C.: Volume I of the Colonial Mississippi Series. Ainsworth McElligott Enterprises, 1988.

McManus, Jane. *Pioneers West of Appalachia*. New Orleans: Polyanthos, 1984.

McManus, Jane. *A Backward Glance*. Pineville: Parker Enterprises, 1986.

Mills, Gary B. The Forgotten People: Cane River's Creoles of Color. Baton Rouge: Louisiana State University Press, 1977.

Mira, Manuel. *The Forgotten Portuguese: The Melungeons and Other Groups*. Franklin: Portuguese-American Historical Research Foundation, 1998.

Mobley, Frank. *El Camino Real*. Dallas: Private Printing, 1995.

Mooney, James. *History, Myths and Sacred Formulas of the Cherokees*, Asheville: Historical Images, 1992.

Morrison, Samuel Eliot. *The European Discovery of America: The Northern Voyages, A.D. 500-1600*. New York: Oxford University Press, 1971.

Mullin, Mela, April. Presented 2002, Melungeon Heritage Association Conference, *Providing Necroethnic Clues for Cultural Continuity Among Mixed Racial Populations In Appalachia*. Kingsport, TN.

Murphy, Laura Frances. *The Cajans of Mobile County, Alabama*. Thesis Searitt College June, 1935.

Murphy, Laura Frances. "Mobile County Cajans" *Alabama Historical Quarterly*, Vol I, No. 1, pp. 76-86, 1930.

Nardini, Louis R. *No Man's Land*. Gretna: Pelican Publishing, 1961.

Nolan, Thompson. "Ashworth Act" *The New Handbook of Texas*, Austin: 1996, Vol. I.

Northrup, Solomon. *Twelve Years a Slave* - 1841-1853. (Rewritten by Sue Eakin) Bossier City: Everett Co, 1990.

Osborne, J. H. Researcher: Melungeons "Self defining", *Kingsport Times – News*, June 21, 2002.

Olmsted, Frederick Law. *A Journey Through Texas: Or A Saddle-trip on the Southwest Frontier*. Austin: University of Texas Press, Reprint of 1857 edition.

Orr, Evelyn McKinley. "The Origin of Name Melungeon-Wider World Views" *Gowen Research Foundation Electronic Newsletter* September, 2000. Vol. 3, No. 9, p. 2.

Parenton, Vernon J. and Pellegrin, Roland J. "The Sabines: A Study of Racial Hybrids in a Louisiana Coastal Parish", *Social Forces*, 29 (1950), pp. 148-154.

Payne, B.H. *Report on the Algiers and Opelousas Railroad*. (New Orleans: 1851).

Paxton, W.E. *A History of the Baptists of Louisiana from the Earliest Times to the Present*. St. Louis: C.R. Barns Publishing, Co., 1888.

Penn, Willilam S. *As We Are Now*. Berkeley: University of California Press, 1997.

Perdue, Theda. *Native Carolinians: The Indians of North Carolina*. Raleigh: North Carolina Department of Cultural Resources, 1985.

Perdue, Theda. *Slavery and the Evolution of Cherokee Society, 1540-1866*. Knoxville: University of Tennessee Press, 1979.

Phares, Ross. *Cavalier in the Wilderness*. Gretna: Pelican, 1998.

Philips, Ulrich B. *Life and Labor in the Old South*.

Price, Richard. *Marron Societies: Rebel Slave Communities in the Americas*. Baltimore: The John Hopkins University Press, 1996.

Bibliography

Pyle, Robert L. "A Message From The Past" *Wonderful West Virginia*. Charleston: State of West Virginia Department of Natural Resources, March 1983, pp. 3-6.

Pugh, Ellen. *Brave His Soul*. New York: Dodd, Mead & Co., 1970.

Relethford, John H. *Genetics and the Search for Modern Human Origins*. New York: Wiley-Liss, 2001.

Rice, Horace R. *The Buffalo Ridge Cherokee: A Remnant of a Great Nation Divided*, Heritage Books, 1995.

Root, Maria P.P., Editor. *Racially Mixed People in America*. Newbury Park: Sage Publications, 1992.

Rouse, Parke, Jr. *The Great Wagon Road*. Richmond: Dietz Press, 1995.

Sakolsky, Ron and Koehnline, James. *Gone to Croatan: Origins of North American Dropout Culture*. New York: Autonomedia, 1993.

Sandel, Luther. *The Free State of Sabine and Western Louisiana*. Many: Jet Publications, 1982.

Schechter, Patricia A. *Ida B. Wells-Barnett and American, 1880-1930*. Chapel Hill: University of North Carolina Press, 2001.

"Scotch Indians in Scotland" *Quarterly Journal of the Society of American Indians*. Vol. 2, 1915.

Shook, Judson. *Beauregard Parish at the Millennium*. Privately Printed, 2000.

Shugg, Roger W., *Origins of Class Struggle in Louisiana*, Baton Rouge: LSU Press, 1939.

Sibley, John. *Indian Notes and Monographs: A Report From Natchitoches in 1807*. Hemphill: Dogwood Press, 1996.

Sider, Gerald M. *Lumbee Indian Histories: Race, Ethnicity, and Indian Identity in the Southern United States*. Cambridge: Cambridge University Press, 1993.

Sivad, Doug "African Seminoles" in Sakolsky, Ron and Koehnline, James. *Gone to Croatan: Origins of North American Dropout Culture*. New York: Autonomedia, 1993.

Smith, Velmer R. *The Best of Yesterday...Today: A History of the Sabine River and No Man's Land*. DeRidder, VBS Enterprises, 1994.

Spencer, Rainier, "Race and Mixed Race" in Penn, William S. *As We Are Now*. Berkeley: University of California Press: 1997, p. 126-139.

Spikard, Paul R. "The Illogic of Racial Categories" in Root, Maria P.P. Editor, *Racially Mixed People in America*. Newbury Park: Sage Publications, 1992.

State v. Davis, State v. Harmon 2 Bailey 558, Dec. 1831.

Statutes of the Virginia Assembly, Vol. 2, 1860.

Strong, Robert C. *North Carolina Reports Vol. 169: Cases Argued and Determined in the Supreme Court of North Carolina*, W. B. Goins, et al.

Strother, Greene W. *About Joseph Willis*, New Orleans: Baptist Bible Institute, 1934, Thesis.

Stuart, Jesse. *Daughter of the Legend*. Ashland: Jesse Stuart Foundation, 1993.

Swanton, John R. *Indian Tribes of the Lower Mississippi Valley and Adjacent Coast of the Gulf of Mexico*. New York: Dover, 1998 and is an abridge version of the 1911 publication.

Sykes, Bryan. *The Seven Daughters of Eve: The Science That Reveals our Genetic Ancestry*. New York: Norton & Co., 2001.

Tenzer, Lawrence R. *The Forgotten Cause of the Civil War: A New Look at the Slavery Issue*. Manahawken: Scholars Publishing, 1997.

The Oklahoma United Methodist Contact. Vol. 130, Number 32, January 13, 1984.

The New Handbook of Texas. Austin: Texas State Historical Association, 1996, Vol. 1.

The State. Unsigned newspaper article dated March 18, 1928.

Thomas, J.A.W. Handwritten letter to McDonald Furman from J. A. W. Thomas dated May 17, 1893. This letter to Mr.

Bibliography

Furman is found on the Internet in several sources and in the Furman Collection at The South Caroliniana Library.

Thompson, Nolan, "Ashworth Act" *The New Handbook of Texas*. Austin: 1996, Vol. I, pp. 267-268.

Tillery, Caryle. *Red Bone Woman*. New York: Avon Books, 1950.

Touchstone, Samuel J. *Louisiana History of Sabine Parish*, Princeton, La: Folk-Life Books, 1997.

Tracy, Houston, Jr. "Chronology of Joseph Willis" CLGSQ Vol. 10, No. 1 pp.34-40.

Trillin, Calvin "U.S. Journal: Sumter County, S.C. – Turks" *The New Yorker Magazine*, March 8, 1969.

Vandervelde, Isabel. *Other Free People in Early Barnwell District*. Aiken: Art Studio Press, 2001.

Vandervelde, Isabel. *Aiken County: The Only South Carolina County Founded During Reconstruction*. Spartanburg: The Reprint Company, 1999.

Vaughn, Emily E. *Index of Black Churches and Cemeteries, Sumter County: Headstones and Inscriptions*. New York: Copy in the Sumter County Genealogical Society Museum Library.

Walton, Augustus Q. *The Life and Adventure of John Murel: The Great Western Land Pirate*, Woodville: Dogwood Press, 1994.

White, Charles *Hidden and Forgotten*, Buckingham County, Virginia, 1985.

White, Laura. *Journal of Southern History*, I. 1935, p. 47 as reported by Richard Price.

Williams, Eric. *From Columbus to Castro: The History of the Caribbean*, 1492-1969, 1970.

Wilson, Terry P. "Blood Quantum: Native American Mixed Bloods" in Root, Maria P.P. Editor, *Racially Mixed People in America*. Newbury Park: Sage Publications, 1992, pp. 108-125.

Wise, Erbon W. *Sweat Families of the South*. Sulphur: Private, 1998 Revised 2002.

Wise, Erbon W. *Tall Pines – II: A History of Vernon Parish, Louisiana and its People.* Sulphur: Privately Printed, 1988.

Wood, Peter H. *Black Majority: Negroes in Colonial South Carolina.* New York: Knopf, 1974.

Wright, Gavin. *The Political Economy of the Cotton South.* New York: Norton, 1978

Unpublished Articles/Internet Articles

Furman, McDonald. "The Redbones" Original longhand copy in the South Caroliniana Library.

Inabinett, E. L. *McDonald Furman: As Seen Through His Papers*, Presented to the Sumter County Historical Society, 2 Oct. 1954.

Marler, Don C. "The Louisiana Redbones", paper presented at First Union, a meeting of Melungeons at the University of Virginia at Wise, Va., 1997.

McFatter, Don, "History of Sugartown", Paper presented to members of the Beauregard Museum on June 16, 1996.

McKeehan, Wallace L. "Alphabetical List of San Jacinto Veterans" Sons of DeWitt Colony Texas – website.

Withrow, Scott, "Red Bones: The Appalachian Connection" Paper presented at the Fourth Union, Kingsport, Tennessee, June 22, 2002.

Thesis – Dissertations - Manuscripts
Webpages - Newsletters

Ferrell, Geoffrey. *The Brotherhood of Timber Workers and the Southern Lumber Trust, 1910-1914.* Dissertation University of Texas at Austin, 1982.

Gildemeister, Enrique Eugene, *Local Complexities of Race in the Rural South: Racially Mixed People in South Carolina,* Thesis, State University of New York, June, 1977.

Bibliography

Gowen Research Foundation Newsletter – Various numbers. Lubbock, Texas.

Hotten, John Camden. *The original lists of persons of quality, emigrants, religious exiles, political rebels, serving men sold for a term of years, apprentices, children stolen, maidens, pressed, and others, who went from Great Britain to the American Plantations, 1600-1700.* New York: Empire State Book, Co. [n.d.]

Log Brands, Unpublished – Ledger, 1879.

McMillon, Hamilton. Letter in long hand to McDonald Furman from Hamilton M. Mellon dated Aug. 8, 1889 – located in the Furman Collection at The South Caroliniana Library.

Prejean, Lana Jean Fagot. *Occupy Til I Come: The Redbones of Louisiana's No Man's Land.* For the MA Degree at University of Southwestern Louisiana, 1999.

~~Price, Edward T., Jr. *Mixed-Blood Populations of Eastern United States as to Origins, Localizations, and Persistence.* PhD Dissertation, University of California, 1937~~. This work has since been proven unreliable.

Prince, Diane Elizabeth. *William Goyens, Free Negro on The Texas Frontier.* Thesis; Stephen F. Austin State College, Nacogdoches, Texas, July, 1967.

Rigmaiden, Thomas. *Thomas Rigmaiden Diary.* Mr. Rigmaiden was born in England and married in Louisiana. He began his diary in 1836 and continued it to 1846. He lived in Old Imperial Calcasieu Parish.

White, Wes D., Jr. *A History of the Turks Who Live in Sumter County, South Carolina, From 1805-1972.* Written for the Smithsonian Institution, Washington, DC, 1975. Located in the Sumter County Genealogical Society Library, Sumter, South Carolina. This is a draft copy of the manuscript.

Wood, Pearlie S. *History of the Clifton School, Rapides Parish, Louisiana.* Unpublished College paper, undated.

EDITOR BIBLIOGRAPHY

Adams, K. J., & Gould, L. L. (Eds.). (1999). *Inside the Natchez Trace Collection.* Baton Rouge: Louisiana State University Press.

Aikman, William, and Daniel Murray Pamphlet Collection. The future of the colored race in America: being an article in the Presbyterian quarterly review, of July. Philadelphia: W. S. Young, Printer, 1862. Pdf. https://www.loc.gov/item/12003258/.

Beale, C. (1957). "American Triracial Isolates". *Eugenics Quarterly, 4*(4), 187-96.

Beam, L. (1967). *He Called Them by the Lightning: A Teacher's Odyssey in the Negro South, 1908-1919.* Indianapolis: Bobbs-Merrill.

Comegna, Anthony (2016). *"The Loco-Focos'"life long War on Monopoly,' resulting in a long series of events which in many ways diffused and democratized power throughout the populace,"* Part 1, Part 2

Green, T. (2005). "Further Considerations on the Sephardim of the Petite Côte". *History in Africa, 32*, 165-83.

Dennis, J. V. (1988). *The Great Cypress Swamps* (First ed.). Baton Rouge, LA: Louisiana State University Press.

Elbl, I. (1996). "Men without Wives: Sexual Arrangements in the Early Portuguese Expansion in West Africa". In J. Murray , & K. Eisenbichler (Eds.), *Desire and Discipline: Sex and Sexuality in the Postmodern West* (pp. 61-87). Toronto: University of Toronto Press.

Fleming, T. J. (2003). The Louisiana Purchase (First ed.). Hoboken, NJ: John Wiley & Sons, Inc.

Gresham D, Morar B, Underhill PA, et al. Origins and divergence of the Roma (gypsies). *Am J Hum Genet.* 2001;69(6):1314-1331. doi:10.1086/324681

Gannon, M. V. (1965). The Cross in the Sand. Gainsville, FL: University of Florida.

Giraud, M. (1974). A History of French Louisiana. In The Reign of Louis XIV, 1698-1715 (J. C. Lambert, Trans., Vol. 1,

Bibliography

pp. 68, 222). Baton Rouge, LA: Louisiana State University Press

Hill, S. P. (2010). *Strangers In Their Own Land: South Carolina's State Indian Tribes* (Second ed.). Palm Coast, FL: Backintyme Publishing.

McAdams, M. H. (1929). *Kentucky Pioneer & Court Records.* Lexington: Genealogical Publishing Company, Inc.

McBee, M. W. (1953). *Natchez Court Records, 1767-1805: Abstracts of Early Records* (Vol. II). Ann Arbor, Michigan: Edward Brothers, Inc.

McBee, M. W. (1967). *Mississippi County Court Records from The May Wilson McBee Papers.* Baltimore: Genealogical Publishing Comapny, Inc.

McBee, M. W. (1994). *The Natchez Court Records, 1767-1805 Abstracts of Early Records.* Baltimore, Maryland: Genealogical Publishing Co., Inc.

Mendes, A. d. (2008). "The Foundations of the System: A Reassessment of the Slave Trade to the Spanish Americas in the Sixteenth and Seventeenth Centuries". In D. Eltis, & D. Richardson (Eds.), *Extending the Frontiers: Essays on the New Transatlantic Slave Trade Database* (pp. 63-94). New Haven and London: Yale University Press.

Mills, D. R. (1992). *Florida's First families: Translated Abstracts of pre-1821 Spanish Censuses.* Tuscaloosa, AL: Mills Historical Press.

Mills, E. S. (1981, October). "François (Guyon) Dion Despres Derbanne: Premier Citoyen, Poste St. Jean Baptiste des Natchitoches". *The Natchitoches Genealogist, 6,* 1-10.

Mills, E. S. (1981). *Family and Social Patterns Of The Colonial Louisiana Frontier: A Quantitative Analysis, 1714-1803.* Gasden, Alabama: University of Alabama.

Mills, E. S., & Mills, G. B. (1978). *Tales of Old Natchitoches* (Vol. 3). Natchitoches: Association for the Preservation of Historic Natchitoches.

Mills, F., & Nugent, R. (2010). *If the Devil Had a Wife: A True Texas Tale.* North Charleston, SC: Booksurge Publishing, LLC.

Mills, G. B. (1977). *The Forgotten People: Cane River's Creoles of Color.* Baton Rouge: Louisiana State University.

Mills, G. B. (1981, June). "Miscegenation and the Free Negro in Antebellum 'Anglo' Alabama: A Reexamination of Southern Race Relations". *Journal of American History, 68*(no. 1), 16-34.

Mira, M. (2001). *The Portuguese Making Of America.* Franklin, NC: The Portuguese-American Historical Research Foundation, Inc.

Marshall, T. B., & Evans, G. (1939). *They Found It In Natchez.* New Orleans, La.: Pelican Press, Inc.

Martínez-Cruz B, Mendizabal I, Harmant C, et al. Origins, admixture and founder lineages in European Roma. *Eur J Hum Genet.* 2016;24(6):937-943. doi:10.1038/ejhg.2015.201

McBee, M. W. (1953). *Natchez Court Records, 1767-1805: Abstracts of Early Records* (Vol. II). Ann Arbor, Michigan: Edward Brothers, Inc.

Shields, J. D. (1930). *Natchez: Its Early History.* (E. D. Murray, Ed.) Louisville, KY: John P. Morton & Company Incorporated.

Sibley, D. J. (1996). *Indian Notes and Monographs, A Report from Natchitoches in 1807.* (A. H. Abel, & F. Hodge, Eds.) Hemphill, Texas: Dogwood Press.

Sweet, F. W. (2005). *Legal History of the Color Line: The Rise and Triumph of the One-Drop Rule.* Paml Coast, Florida: Backintyme Publishing.

Sweet, J. H. (1997, Jan). "The Iberian Roots of American Racist Thought". *The William and Mary Quarterly, 54*(1), 143-66.

Sweet, J. H. (2003). *Recreating Africa: Culture, Kinship, and Religion in the African-Portuguese World, 1441-1770.* Chapel Hill: University of North Carolina Press.

Sweet, J. H. (2009, April). "Mistaken Identities?: Olaudah Equiano, Domingos Álvares, and the Methodological Challenges of Studying the African Diaspora". *The American Historical Review, 114*(2), 278-306.

MacLeod, M. J. (1984). "Spain and America: The Atlantic Trade 1492-1720". In L. Bethell (Ed.), *The Cambridge History of Latin America: Colonial Latin America* (Vol. 1, pp. 341-88). Cambridge, UK: Cambridge University.

Maginnis, J. (1984). *The Last Hayride* (First ed.). Baton Rouge, LA: Darkhorse Press.

Bibliography

Mahon, J. K. (1985). *History of the Second Seminole War 1835-1842* (revised ed.). Gainesville: University of Florida.

Mahon, J. K., & Weisman, B. R. (1996). "Florida's Seminole and Miccosukee Peoples". In M. Gannon (Ed.), *The New History of Florida* (pp. 183-206). Gainesville: University of Florida.

Nardini, L. (1999). *No Man's Land: A History of El Camino Real (Louisiana Parish Histories Series)*. Gretna, LA: Pelican Publishing Company, Inc.

Nash Family Cemetery North Zulch Madison County Texas Est 1881: Descendants of James Nash. (n.d.).

Nash, G. (1990). *Race and Revolution*. Madison, WI: Madison House.

Nash, G. B. (1982). *Red, White, and Black: The Peoples of Early America* (2nd ed.). Englewood Cliffs, NJ: Prentice-Hall.

Nash, G., & Jeffrey, J. R. (Eds.). (2003). *The American People: Creating a Nation and a Society* (4th ed.). New York: Longman.

National Genealogical Society Conference in the States and Family History Fair 2007. (2007). *Richmond 16-19 May 2007*. National Genealogical Society.

Nevin, D. (1975). *The Texans*. (T.-L. Books, Ed.) New York: Time-Life Books.

Newson, L. A., & Minchin, S. (2004, Dec.). "Slave Mortality and African Origins: A View from Cartagena, Colombia, in the Early Seventeenth Century". *Salvery & Abolition, 25*(3), 18-43.

Newson, L. A., & Minchin, S. (2007). *From Capture to Sale: The Portuguese Slave Trade to Spanish South America in the Early Seventeenth Century*. Leiden and Boston: Brill.

Northrup, D. (2000, Dec). "Igbo and Myth Igbo: Culture and Ethnicity in the Atlantic World, 1600-1850". *Slavery & Abolition, 21*(3), 1-20.

Ortiz, F. (1995). *Cuban Counterpoint: Tobacco and Sugar*. (H. de Onis, Trans.) Durham and London: Duke University Press.

How the Irish and Scots Became Indians: Colonial Traders and Agents and the Southeastern Tribes James E. Doan New Hibernia Review / Iris Éireannach Nua
Vol. 3, No. 3 (Autumn, 1999), pp. 9-19 (11 pages)
Published By: University of St. Thomas (Center for Irish Studies) https://www.jstor.org/stable/20557571
1000 Genomes Project Consortium, Abecasis, G. R., Altshuler, D., Auton, A., Brooks, L. D., Durbin, R. M., Gibbs, R. A., Hurles, M. E., & McVean, G. A. (2010). A map of human genome variation from population-scale sequencing. Nature, 467(7319), 1061–1073. https://doi.org/10.1038/nature09534
Fisher, George P. (George Purnell), 1817-1899. The so-called "Moors" of Delaware. By Hon. George P. Fisher. [n.p., n.d.] https://lccn.loc.gov/tmp92006657
6 l. 21 cm. F142.S9 F5
Forensic Science International: Genetics, 13 (2004) 1-2; Science *Direct Mitochondrial DNA control region analysis of three ethnic groups in the Republic of Macedonia.*

Cope, Compiled by Gilbert, 1840-1928, Samuel Lightfoot 1732-1894. *Genealogy of the Smedley Family From George and Sarah Smedley: Settlers in Chester County, Penna.* On Line. Prod. Internet Library of the American Library of Congress. Lancaster: Wickersham Printing Company, 1901.
Gazette, Attakapas. "Vol. XII, No.3 87 ." *Attakapas Gazette* , 1977: p. 137.
Lee, Danya Bowker. *The Talimali Band of Apalachee.* Louisiana Regional Folklife Program, n.d.
Morris, Michael P. *George Galphin and the Transformation of the Georgia-South Carolina Backcountry.* London: Lexington Books, 2014.

Bibliography

Papers, United States Congression. "George Washington Papers." *Virginia State University.* n.d. http://gwpapers.virginia.edu/index/colonial/clist.htm (accessed 2003).

Weaver, Transcribed by Jeffrey C. "New River Notes ." *Historical and Genealogical Resources for the Upper New River Valley of North Carolina and Virginia,* December 8, 1998.

INDEX

A

A.J. Perkins 412
Adams 264, 298, 331, 357, 358, 420, 478, 548, 565, 583, 586
Alfred Mayo 368
Allen 101, 108, 254, 266, 332, 366, 546, 586, 589
Allyon, Lucas Vasquez ... 33
Anderson, ... 68, 333
Anna, Santa 351
Arthur, S.J. 550
Ash 360, 361, 471, 472, 474, 475, 476
Ashworth 11, 158, 261, 266, 285, 286, 354, 361, 362, 363, 387, 392, 410, 414, 585, 616, 619
Ashworth, Abner 286
Ashworth, Amen 414
Ashworth, Andrew 412
Ashworth, Austin 414
Ashworth, Owen 412, 414
Ashworth, Sarah 350

B

Baggett 259, 266, 585
Baggett, Jim 410
Bailey, ... 68, 259, 352, 589
Bales, Carolyn Dyess viii
Ball, Bonnie ... 127, 158, 159
Barker, Ted 134
Barnwell, Colonel 233
Barton 352, 546
Basco 167, 263, 264, 298, 585
Bass 257, 258, 261, 265, 347, 355, 360, 361, 362, 363, 565, 585
Bass, Brenda 452
Batchelor, Charles 261
Bauder, Professor 234
Bell 333, 352, 357, 546, 548, 587
Benegeli, Joseph 142
Benenhaley 142
Bennet 333, 548
Bennett 265, 266, 352, 367, 547, 584, 585, 587, 589
Berry 4, 13, 99, 125, 138, 139, 352, 357, 547, 548, 587, 590, 607
Berry, Brewton 4, 13, 99, 138, 139, 607
Berry, Henry 98, 100, 101, 232, 233
Berwick 333, 585
Berwick, Delphine 351
Big Black 115, 116, 117
Bill Starks 260
Bird. 300, 366, 420, 422, 587
Birdsong, George F. 5
Blanc 231
Blue-Eye, Amos 166
Boddie 422
Boland 354, 607
Bond 258, 352
Boones 13
Bowels 333
Boyd, ... 352, 422
Brandy, King 166

INDEX

Brooks 352, 502, 547, 565, 587, 608
Brown 241, 245, 264, 333, 339, 352, 545, 547, 608
Brues, Alice 22
Bullard 436
Bul-look-chah-sha Creek 117
Bunch 123, 139, 211, 266, 343, 347, 356, 361, 363, 365, 494, 495, 518, 549, 554, 566, 585, 587
Bunch, 139, 266, 356, 361, 554, 566
Burch, ... 352
Butler, Nell 58
Buxston 363
Buxton 11, 258, 261, 357, 362, 363, 364, 386, 388, 422, 585
Byrd 104, 108, 298, 422, 549, 565
Byrd, Lem 104

C

Cain 68, 258, 422, 585
Cambiarie, Celestin Pierre 122
Canarians 538, 539
Canary Islanders .. 538, 539
Carter 68, 298, 355, 420, 547, 549, 557, 585, 587
Charry 17
Chavis, 9, 139, 146, 147, 226, 228, 241, 249, 362
Chavis, Bill 147
Chavis, Fannie 146
Chavis, Lewis 238
Chavis, Nelson ... 9, 228, 247

Chavis, Tom 147
Chism, Robert 93
Choctaw Nation 118, 119
Clark 32, 69, 250, 258, 260, 261, 264, 299, 333, 352, 354, 357, 358, 359, 360, 361, 362, 363, 365, 389, 391, 395, 412, 422, 478, 502, 547, 549, 564, 583, 584, 587
Cloud 298, 357, 585, 587
Coffee 357, 366
Cole 69, 108, 258, 259, 263, 300, 333, 352, 354, 422, 502, 547, 549, 583, 585, 587
Coleman 98, 300, 352, 356, 422, 547, 549, 564, 565, 585, 587
Colins 98, 352
Collins 123, 162, 298, 300, 330, 332, 334, 335, 336, 337, 338, 339, 346, 354, 359, 420, 422, 448, 491, 497, 498, 501, 554, 557, 565, 566, 584, 585, 587
Conder, Abel 140, 141
Cooper 162, 367, 547, 565, 585, 586, 589
Cooper, James Fenimore . 93
Courtney, Joe 412
Cox 17, 264, 357, 548, 571, 576, 584, 587
Craft 98, 352
Crawford 167, 283, 352, 407, 422
Crawford, Webster Talma 167
Crier 352

631

Crowder 117, 120
Cumba, ... 352, 358, 359
Cumbie, Adeline 370
Curry 298, 338, 356, 420, 548, 549
Curtis 261, 300, 352, 587, 613
Curtis, Richard 299, 421
Cynthia Ann Parker 382

D

D'Guin 231
Daubrig, Henry 140
David Paul 268
Davis 32, 69, 71, 241, 242, 258, 298, 299, 352, 359, 548, 549, 585, 587, 618
Dean .70, 157, 298, 420, 587
DeMarce, Virginia 127
DeSoto 440
Dial 11, 100, 231, 258, 266, 346, 347, 354, 361, 362, 363, 365, 385, 390, 393, 422, 432, 471, 502, 546, 547, 585, 609
Dile 231
Doaksville 118
Doil 363
Douglas, Frederick 56
Downs, Solomon W. 48
Doyle 258, 261, 385, 390, 393, 432, 471, 502, 585
Drake 11, 261, 347, 350, 365, 422, 585, 587, 609
Drake, John Aaron 350
Du Bois, W.E.B 609
Dyal 258, 356, 585
Dyes 364

Dyess .... viii, 298, 585
Dyson 266, 299, 410
Dyson, Jesse ... 410, 412, 414
Dysons 409

E

Ebarb xvi, 103, 166, 167, 326
Elder, Pat 123
Elliot, Buck 411
Ellis 247, 332, 335, 587, 590, 591
Ephraim Sweat 347
Epperson, Jean L. ...346, 351
Epps, Adeline 147
Epps, Edward 248
Epps, Pauline 147
Eromdreque, Juan 351
Esclavant 11
Esmitt, Serafina 351
Evans 17, 70, 71, 72, 99, 101, 162, 298, 299, 358, 420, 422, 547, 549, 587, 609
Evans, George 356

F

Faris 352
Farley, Gloria 133
Farris 258, 298, 585
Fields 254, 352, 372, 378, 549, 587
Fitzhugh, George 47
Flowers 299
Forbes, Jack D 610
Fry 118
Fulton, Sam 410
Furman, McDonald 8, 9, 10, 11, 12, 14, 147, 219, 220, 221, 224, 225, 227, 229,

INDEX

230, 234, 235, 239, 240, 249, 610, 611, 614, 618, 619, 620, 621

G

Gallegos, Eloy 128
George Brooks 338
Gibbes, Tom 222, 223
Gibbs226, 242, 247, 248, 298, 585
*Gibson*98, 108, 123, 162, 267, 299, 349, 354, 356, 357, 358, 422, 548, 554, 557, 566, 585
Gibson, Charles 123
Gidion Gibson 299
Gilbert Sweat 347, 354
Gilbert, W.H. 12, 171
Gildemeister, Enrique ... 137
Gill 259, 352, 442, 585
Gillis 260, 611
Goan 363
Goin 354, 360
Going 267, 349, 360, 361
Goings109, 110, 111, 114, 117, 139, 249, 495, 502, 518, 548
Goings (1)109, 110, 117, 495, 502, 518
Goings (1) Clan109, 110, 117, 518
Goinsviii, 11, 117, 118, 119, 123, 127, 139, 146, 147, 162, 223, 224, 226, 231, 242, 248, 249, 264, 365, 547, 548, 566, 585, 611, 618
Goins, Edie 223

Goins, Jack 123
Goins, Jerry 223
Goins, Matilda 224
Goins, W.D. 147
Goins, W.W. 147
Goins, Wade 223, 224
Goodwin 299, 352, 422
Gowens 362
Goyens Clan84, 109, 115, 284, 287, 292, 513, 595
Goyens, William 621
Green17, 68, 69, 121, 258, 298, 299, 333, 352, 357, 359, 421, 422, 444, 585
Griffin68, 98, 299, 478, 587, 590, 612
Groves, James 78
Guanches 538

H

Hall36, 69, 77, 118, 119, 162, 258, 298, 352, 356, 422, 545, 548, 583, 584, 585, 586, 612
Hall, Gwendolyn 76
Hammond, James Henry . 47
Hancock, Ian 149
Handlin, Oscar 41
Hardy 17
Harper258, 298, 352, 420, 422, 585, 608
Harper, William 46
Harvey243, 298, 352, 547, 585
Heinegg, Paul 55, 346
Hellen, Jesse 411
Henry47, 70, 98, 100, 101, 140, 232, 248, 267, 332,

335, 339, 352, 357, 358, 359, 366, 367, 439, 545, 546, 588, 589, 590, 591, 607, 615
Henry, Thomas 5
Hicks 267, 298, 368, 369, 370, 420, 422, 545, 564, 587
Hill 56, 78, 96, 129, 254, 257, 258, 260, 298, 299, 357, 368, 369, 405, 448, 465, 549, 584, 608, 614, 617
Hodes, Martha 56, 57
Hollandsworth, Skip 160
Holmes .. 299, 352, 366, 565
Holt 264, 299, 427, 587
Hoozer 11
Hopkins, Harry 44
Howell ... 108, 258, 359, 565
Hudsen, Judge 236
Hunt 147, 264, 352, 418, 448, 547
Hunter, Robert A. 446

I

Ishmael, Ben 92, 93, 614
Isleños 538
Ivey, William 268
Ivy 299, 587

J

Jackson, Andrew 108
Jackson, Beverly viii
Jacobs, Curtis 261
James 9, 33, 47, 69, 70, 71, 72, 78, 81, 82, 93, 129, 134, 220, 227, 232, 242, 243, 246, 251, 257, 260, 261, 266, 267, 271, 298, 299, 333, 334, 339, 347, 349, 350, 354, 355, 356, 357, 358, 359, 366, 367, 386, 392, 422, 472, 474, 546, 558, 585, 590, 608, 610, 613, 614, 615, 617
James E. Smiling 9
James Mooney 220
Jean Bible 127
Jefferson, Thomas 24
Jeremiah Bass 347
Jesse Ashworth 347
Jesse Ward 410, 411
John McDaniel 347
Johnson 11, 70, 108, 127, 172, 243, 257, 258, 259, 261, 262, 264, 265, 267, 298, 299, 335, 349, 350, 352, 353, 354, 355, 356, 358, 359, 360, 361, 362, 363, 364, 365, 367, 369, 370, 371, 386, 392, 418, 422, 547, 565, 585, 587, 590, 607, 608, 613
Johnson, James A. 260
Johnson, Levi 367
Johnson, Nathaniel 34
Johnson, Neil Harding ... 368
Johnson, Tommy 352, 365
Jolly 422
Jones 70, 96, 98, 130, 131, 176, 178, 243, 259, 264, 298, 299, 335, 352, 357, 358, 384, 418, 420, 422, 545, 547, 549, 585, 587, 590, 591, 608
Jones, Kevin 130
Jordan, Terry 464

INDEX

Josh Perkins 412, 414
Juan Pardo 129, 612

K

Kadlecek, Mabel and Bullard 263, 264, 432, 436, 437, 613
Kelley, Jewel Rougeou .. 371
Kelly, Redbone 6
Kendall, Elaine 40
Kennedy, Brentiv, 8, 124, 125, 353, 582
Kennedy, Robyn 124
Kennon, Governor 416
Kiamishi 118
Killen, Jesse 410
Kimball, Geoffrey 7
Kimbrell, Dan 419
King 25, 36, 140, 152, 166, 175, 179, 266, 299, 333, 336, 546, 565, 587, 613
King, Jim 410, 411
Kniffen 4, 613
Knight 96, 97, 98, 422, 585, 614
Knight, Newton 96, 97

L

Lacaze, Louis 3
LaComb, Dupree 410
Lacomb, Louis 411
Laffite, Jean 77, 78
Laney 151, 152
Lang, E. 412
Larouche, Daniel 140
Lawson 358, 549, 587
Leaming, Hugo P. 92

Lee 98, 162, 241, 243, 264, 352, 412, 414, 546, 566, 587, 612
Legg 259, 352, 586
Lewis 238, 259, 298, 299, 300, 333, 352, 353, 355, 356, 366, 369, 370, 371, 420, 422, 555, 586, 613
Lewis, Allen 366
Lewis, Nancy Riley 366, 370, 371
Linnaeus, Carl 22
Locklear 238
Locofoco party 195
Lowrie, David 232
Lowrie, Henry Berry 232
Lowrie, James 232
Lowrie, Stephen 233
Lowrie, Tom 233
Lowry, Allen 101
LUKE COLLINS 335

M

Madden 263, 299
Madoc 129, 609
Mahemut 140
Manuel ... 126, 299, 352, 615
Marion Men 296
Marion, Francis 296
Marish 355
Marks 182, 190, 328, 504, 506
Marsh 355
Martin 118, 178, 259, 264, 267, 269, 298, 299, 332, 352, 356, 357, 359, 368, 420, 505, 547, 548, 565, 586, 587, 589, 591

Martin, Rob "Redbone"..... 6
Martin, Robert W.......... 268
Martin, Steve 269
Mathis 259, 267, 298, 350, 420, 422, 547, 586, 588
Matte, Jacqueline 107
Mayo, Alfred Franklin . 366, 369, 370, 371
Mayo, Bertha Terrell..... 368
Mayo, Eziekel............... 368
Mayo, George Washington 370
Mayo, Karl 615
Mayo, Samual............... 368
McCann, Gordon 150
McCulloch, Oscar C........ 93
McElveen, W. A., Jr...... 142
McIntyre........................ 333
McLaughlin, Zack 233
McManus 167, 258, 265, 283, 320, 346, 406, 449, 463, 614, 615
Mellon, Hamilton M. 621
Metoyer, Claude Thomas Pierre 170
Miller 70, 108, 144, 259, 332, 352, 418, 588
Miller, Elizabeth 142
Mims, Candey 228
Mira, Manuel................. 128
Mobley, Frank 297
Moon 564
Mooney, James 134, 220
Moore 17, 157, 167, 258, 259, 260, 264, 298, 350, 352, 354, 406, 409, 548, 556, 566, 584, 586, 588
Moore, James... 81, 422, 558

Morris, Hooker 410, 411, 412
Mouton, Alexandre 413
Mouton, Paul and Rufus 413
Munro, Pamela.................. 5
Murcles, Marion 412
Murphy, Laura F. 103
Murrell, John................. 418
Musgrove, Gordon 406
Musslewhite 232

N

Nash 263, 300, 347, 352, 355, 358, 471, 472, 474, 475, 476, 547, 548, 584, 586
Nelson 9, 228, 241, 242, 247, 360, 361, 362, 363, 364, 365, 367, 565, 588
Nettles 224, 422, 423
Nichols 202, 358, 359, 366, 367, 548, 585, 588, 590
Nichols, Brittan, Jr. 367
Nichols, Martin Jasper... 368
Nipihomma....................... 7
Northrup, Solomon........ 295
Nott, Josiah Clark............ 32
Nugent 333, 588

O

O'Guin........................... 231
O'Leary 231
O'Quinn, Ezekiel 421
Ocksenstein................... 231
Orr 127, 131, 352, 355, 359, 422, 548, 585, 616
Orr, Evelyn 616
Orr, George............ 347, 351
Osborne . 131, 352, 548, 616

INDEX

Owens 98, 299, 422, 585, 588, 614
Oxendine 144, 145, 147, 231, 232, 243, 547
Oxendine, Henderson.... 233
Oxendine, Mary Ann Benenhaley 144

P

Page 5, 129, 136, 352, 550, 565, 585
Parker 70, 98, 259, 264, 265, 320, 346, 352, 382, 418, 422, 449, 545, 585, 588, 615
Perkins 11, 257, 258, 259, 266, 267, 279, 298, 299, 347, 349, 354, 355, 356, 358, 360, 361, 362, 363, 364, 366, 387, 396, 398, 409, 411, 412, 413, 414, 422, 444, 472, 474, 502, 585
Perkins, Lee 414
Perry 299, 548, 586, 587
Philip Goin 347, 354
Pinder.... 261, 298, 362, 363
Plecker, W. A. 94, 549, 550, 552, 563, 567
Polly Ashworth 347
Powell 17, 98, 264, 352, 357, 358, 545, 546, 552, 553, 564, 586, 591
Prejean, Lana J............... 274
Priber, Christian.............. 95
Price 4, 76, 81, 103, 108, 163, 352, 359, 360, 364, 586, 588, 616, 621

Price, Edward............ 4, 359
Price, Richard 75, 76, 619
Psellee 7

Q

Quicks 236

R

Rachal, Slave Woman 96
Ray 249, 258, 264, 298, 367, 418, 586, 588
Reaves 352, 549
Redbone, Jennifer.............. 6
Redbone, Leon.................. 5
Redbone, Martha............... 6
Reece 17
Reed 104, 108, 157, 216, 259, 300, 352, 513, 516, 588, 599
Reed, Freed Slave 104
Reeves ... 298, 354, 583, 586
Rigmaiden, A.................. 10
Riley 242, 243, 249, 353, 366, 369, 370, 371, 545, 566, 588, 613
Robert Goins vs. Choctaw Nation 117
Roberts 71, 264, 298, 332, 352, 423, 545, 564, 586
Robinson 232, 267, 352, 354, 357, 418, 549, 565, 588
Roosevelt, Franklin . 44, 415
Rougeou, Mary Jane Lewis 370

S

Sam Fulton,............410, 411

637

Scott 71, 139, 144, 145, 158, 172, 256, 279, 352, 356, 547, 554, 566, 586, 588, 620
Self. 131, 267, 352, 586, 616
Shelby, Senator 107
Shook, Judson 350
Sibley, Mary 289
Simmons 259, 298, 350, 420
Simons 300
Smiley 16, 249, 423
Smiling 9, 146, 148, 224, 226, 227, 243, 244, 245, 247, 248, 249, 298
Smiling, J.E. 224
Smiling, James 227
Smith 71, 108, 162, 166, 259, 263, 300, 333, 352, 355, 356, 357, 358, 394, 395, 423, 545, 547, 586, 591, 608, 618
Smith, Charity 351
Spencer, Rainier 24
St. Denis, Sieur Louis Jauchereau 169
Standly 300
Stanley 162, 298, 358, 367, 546, 548, 585
Stasby, Sam 431
Strong, Andrew 232
Strong, Rhoda 232
Strother 3, 259, 356, 361, 363, 364, 365, 423, 585, 618
Strother, Greene 3
Strother, J. E. 3
Sullivan 98, 108, 330
Swan, T. T. 411

Sweat 11, 139, 241, 245, 246, 248, 259, 264, 265, 298, 346, 347, 358, 360, 361, 362, 364, 471, 548, 585, 588, 619
Swet 362
Swett 139, 363, 365

T

T.T. Swan 414
tabors 508
Talbot 16
Talbots 17
Taylor 108, 264, 298, 300, 347, 352, 354, 355, 547, 548, 588, 591
Teal 352
Tenzer, Lawrence 26
Thérèse, Marie 169
Thomas 5, 17, 24, 68, 123, 166, 169, 239, 242, 246, 264, 266, 267, 286, 299, 300, 330, 332, 335, 347, 355, 356, 359, 422, 545, 547, 566, 589, 590, 591, 618, 621
Thomas Ash 355
Thomas Nash . 267, 300, 356
Thomas, J. A. W. 618
Thompson 17, 71, 246, 248, 249, 259, 267, 285, 298, 335, 352, 360, 361, 363, 420, 585, 587, 616, 619
Trillin, Calvin 143
Troublefield 232
Tubbs 390
Turbeville 232

INDEX

Turner 98, 265, 354, 356, 358, 366, 420, 548, 585
Turner, Jacob 238
Twenty and Odd xxxviii
Tyler 166, 172, 352, 547

V

Vaughn 124, 241, 300, 352, 432, 548, 613, 619
Vianna Mary Ashworth. 288
Voohries 17

W

Wallace 333, 352, 620
Ward 117
Ware 361, 364, 588
Watson 162, 258, 259, 352, 588
Weaver 108, 330, 355, 565, 583
Welch 98, 259, 300, 352, 367
Wells 56, 247, 300, 332, 352, 586, 588, 617
Wells-Barnett, Ida B. 56, 617
Wesley, John 447
West 4, 35, 36, 81, 125, 126, 152, 162, 163, 233, 246, 259, 278, 298, 300, 330, 332, 353, 365, 368, 420, 423, 430, 505, 541, 575, 586, 588, 607, 610, 611, 613, 615, 617
West, John 419
White ix, 1, 4, 7, 15, 22, 23, 24, 25, 26, 28, 29, 30, 32, 35, 39, 40, 41, 42, 43, 45, 49, 50, 55, 56, 57, 58, 60, 67, 72, 76, 81, 97, 99, 101, 108, 138, 139, 141, 142, 143, 157, 166, 171, 220, 230, 231, 264, 281, 282, 287, 300, 357, 360, 374, 378, 379, 380, 381, 384, 389, 407, 541, 543, 546, 547, 548, 571, 583, 586, 588, 590, 607, 612, 619, 621
White, Wes D., Jr. 139
Whitehead 17, 98
Whitted 357
Will, George 30
Williams 17, 42, 44, 108, 139, 172, 242, 264, 298, 356, 357, 358, 420, 548, 554, 583, 586, 588, 619
Williams Taylor 116
Willis 414
Willis, 3, 259, 279, 354, 355, 356, 360, 361, 362, 363, 364, 373, 403, 414, 421, 564, 618
Willis, Joseph 3, 257, 279, 354, 355, 373, 403, 421, 422, 423, 618, 619
Wilson 29, 117, 120, 259, 264, 298, 300, 352, 420, 546, 548, 588, 619
Wilson, Darlene 2, 3, 550, 563
Wily 352
Wisby 261, 361, 363, 407, 586
Wise 130, 160, 167, 259, 298, 346, 350, 423, 566, 586, 589, 619, 620
Wise, Erbon 349

639

Withrow, Scott 145, 158, 256, 279
Wood 34, 352, 356, 357, 423, 448, 547, 564, 588, 591, 620, 621
Wright 166, 247, 352, 359, 502, 547, 548, 586, 588, 590, 620
Wylie 423
Wyndham 423

Y

Ybarbo .... xvi, 318, 326
Y'Barbo, Antonio Gil 166
Yngles, Bele 290
Young 162, 259, 338, 350, 423, 565, 588
Youngblood, Catherine . 370

Other Titles
By Don C. Marler & Dogwood Press

Title: **The Neutral Zone: Backdoor to the United States.** Author: Don C. Marler. This book presents a comprehensive view of the No Man's Land—239 pages. It is a popular book in the region, coming soon!

Title: **General Thomas S. Woodward and Woodward's Reminiscences.** Author: Don C. Marler This is a 335-page book. The letters of General Woodward

Title: **Reflections on Life in the Swamp.** Author: Don C. Marler This 81-page book has been quite popular since it was published in 2004.

Title: **The Cherry Winche Country** Author: William Talma Crawford edited by Don C. Marler and Jane McManus. This 87-page book is a history of the battle between the "Redbones" and "Whites" in Rapides Parish, La. in the former Neutral Zone or No Man's Land. It has been a popular book in the region.

Title: **Historic Hineston** Author: Don C. Marler This 277-page book has been a favorite in the region of which it is the subject. It is in 3rd edition. The origins and status of many small towns and communities in the area are documented.

Title: **Fort Teran on the Neches River** Author: Don C. Marler This is a comprehensive history of Ft. Teran built by the Mexican government to prevent immigration into the territory from the United States after the Neutral Zone question was settled. The book is 145 pages.

Title: **The Marler Family History** Author: Sherry Wilson Manuel, Don C. Marler and Kimble Marler Genealogy. 431 pages.

Title: **Imprisoned In The Brotherhood: A search into the fundamentalists' "web of tradition"** 62 pages, Backintyme Publishing, 2017.

www.ingramcontent.com/pod-product-compliance
Lightning Source LLC
Chambersburg PA
CBHW062000300426
44117CB00010B/1413